McGRAW-HILL's

15 PRACTICE
SAT
SUBJECT TESTS

McGRAW-HILL's

15 PRACTICE

SAT

SUBJECT TESTS

McGRAW-HILL

New York / Chicago / San Francisco / Lisbon / London / Madrid / Mexico City

Milan / New Delhi / San Juan / Seoul / Singapore / Sydney / Toronto

ISBN 0-07-146896-X

SAT is a registered trademark of the College Entrance Examination
Board, which was not involved in the production of, and does not
endorse, this product.

McGraw-Hill books are available at special quantity discounts to use
as premiums and sales promotions, or for use in corporate training
programs. For more information, please write to the Director of Special Sales, Professional Publishing, McGraw-Hill, Two Penn Plaza,
New York, NY 10121-2298. Or contact your local bookstore.

CONTRIBUTORS

U.S. History
Daniel Farabaugh, Editor
Westfield High School, Westfield, NJ

Math Level 1 and Level 2
John J. Diehl, Editor
Mathematics Department
Hinsdale Central High School
Hinsdale, IL

Christine E. Joyce
Mathematics Department
Canton High School, Canton, MA

Chemistry
Thomas A. Evangelist
Assistant Principal Supervision of Science
New York City Department of Education
New York, NY

Biology-E/M
Stephanie M. Zinn, Editor
Columbia Preparatory School, New York, NY

Nick Tarasen

Physics
Christine Caputo

French
Patrick L. Day, Ph.D.
Assistant Professor of French
Department of Foreign Languages
University of Wisconsin–Eau Claire
Eau Claire, WI

Spanish
Paul H. Hoff
Professor, Spanish and Foreign Language Education
Director, University Honors Program
University of Wisconsin–Eau Claire
Eau Claire, WI

Nuria Ibarrechevea Hoff
Senior Lecturer, Spanish
University of Wisconsin–Eau Claire
Eau Claire, WI

World History
Literature
Stephanie Muntone

CONTENTS

All About the SAT Subject Tests

What Are the SAT Subject Tests?

The SAT Subject Tests (formerly called the Achievement Tests) are a series of college entrance tests that cover specific academic subject areas. Like the better-known SAT Reasoning Test, which measures general verbal and math skills, the SAT Subject Tests are given by the College Entrance Examination Board. Colleges and universities often require applicants to take one or more SAT Subject Tests along with the SAT Reasoning Test.

SAT Subject Tests are generally not as difficult as Advanced Placement tests, but they may cover more than is taught in basic high school courses. Students usually take an SAT Subject Test after completing an Advanced Placement course or an Honors course in the subject area.

How Do I Know if I Need to Take SAT Subject Tests?

Review the admissions requirements of the colleges to which you plan to apply. Each college will have its own requirements. Many colleges require that you take a minimum number of SAT Subject Tests—usually one or two. Some require that you take SAT Subject Tests in specific subjects. Some may not require SAT Subject Test scores at all.

When Are SAT Subject Tests Given, and How Do I Register for Them?

SAT Subject Tests are usually given on six weekend dates spread throughout the academic year. These dates are usually the same ones on which the SAT Reasoning Test is given. To find out the test dates, visit the College Board website at www.collegeboard.com. You can also register for a test at the website. Click on the tabs marked "students" and follow the directions you are given. You will need to use a credit card if you register online. As an alternative, you can register for SAT Subject Tests by mail using the registration form in the SAT Registration Bulletin, which should be available from your high school guidance counselor.

How Many SAT Subject Tests Should I Take?

You can take as many SAT Subject Tests as you wish. According to the College Board, more than one-half of all SAT Subject Test takers take three tests, and about one-quarter take four or more tests. Keep in mind, however, that you can take only three tests on a single day. If you want to take more than three tests, you will need to take the others on a different testing date. When deciding how many SAT Subject Tests to take, base your decision on the requirements of the colleges to which you plan to apply. It is probably not a good idea to take many more SAT Subject Tests than you need. You will probably do better by focusing only on those your preferred colleges require.

Which SAT Subject Tests Should I Take?

If a college to which you are applying requires one or more specific SAT Subject Tests, then, of course, you must take those particular tests. If the college simply requires that you take a minimum number of SAT Subject Tests, then choose the test or tests for which you think you are best prepared and likely to get the best score. If you have taken an Advanced Placement course or an Honors course in a particular subject and done well in that course, then you should probably consider taking an SAT Subject Test in that subject.

When Should I Take SAT Subject Tests?

Timing is important. It is a good idea to take an SAT Subject Test as soon as possible after completing a course in the test subject, while the course material is still fresh in your mind. If you plan to take an SAT Subject Test in a subject that you have not studied recently, make sure to leave yourself enough time to review the course material before taking the test.

What Do I Need on the Day of the Test?

To take an SAT Subject Test, you will need an admission ticket to enter the exam room and acceptable forms of photo identification. You will also need two number 2 pencils. Be sure that the erasers work well at erasing without leaving smudge marks. The tests are scored by machine, and scoring can be inaccurate if there are smudges or other stray marks on the answer sheet.

Any devices that make noise, such as cell phones or wristwatch alarms, should be turned off during the test. Such study aids as dictionaries and review books, as well as food and beverages, are barred from the test room.

How Are SAT Subject Tests Scored?

On an SAT Subject Test, your "raw score" is calculated as follows: You receive one point for each question you answer correctly, but you lose one-quarter of a point (one-third of a point on the language tests) for each question you answer incorrectly. You do not gain or lose any points for questions that you do not answer at all. Your raw score is then converted into a scaled score by a statistical method that takes into account how well you did compared to others who took the same test. Scaled scores range from 200 to 800 points. Your scaled score will be reported to you, to your high school, and to the colleges and universities that you designate to receive it.

When Will I Receive My Score?

Scores are mailed to students approximately 3 to 4 weeks after the test. If you want to find out your score a week or so earlier, you can do so for free by accessing the College Board website or for $10 by calling 800-SAT-SCORE.

How Do I Submit My Score to Colleges and Universities?

When you register to take the SAT Reasoning Test or SAT Subject Tests, your fee includes free reporting of your scores to up to four colleges and universities. To have your scores reported to additional schools, visit the College Board website or call 800-SAT-SCORE. You will need to pay an additional fee.

Strategies for Top Scores

When you take any SAT Subject Test, you'll want to do everything you can to make sure you get your best possible score. That means studying right, building good problem-solving skills, and learning proven test-taking strategies. Here are some tips to help you do your best.

Study Strategies

- **Get to know the format of the exam.** Use the practice tests in this book to familiarize yourself with the test format, which does not change from year to year. That way, you will know exactly what to expect when you see the real thing on test day.
- **Get to know the test directions.** If you are familiar with the directions ahead of time, you won't have to waste valuable test time reading them and trying to understand them. The format and directions used in the practice exams in this book are modeled on those you will see on the actual SAT Subject Tests.
- **Get to know what topics are covered.** Get to know what specific topics are covered on the exam. You will find them listed in the introductory material for each of the practice tests in this book.
- **Study hard.** If possible, plan to study for at least an hour a day for 2 weeks before the test. Review the textbook from your course and work through the corresponding practice test or tests in this book. Make study cards from a set of index cards. Those cards can "go where you go" during the weeks and days before the test. If you are pressed for time, focus on taking the practice test or tests, reading the explanations, and reviewing the particular topics that give you the most trouble.

Problem-Solving Strategies for Math and Science Tests

- **Solve math or science problems in whatever way is easiest for you.** There are usually several ways to solve math or science problems and arrive at the correct answer. For example, when converting units some students prefer to use a dimensional analysis, whereas others prefer to set up a proportion. Do what is easiest for you. Remember that the SAT Subject Test is all multiple choice. That means that no one is going to be checking your work and judging you by which solution method you chose. So solve the problem any way you like.
- **Build good problem-solving skills.** When you tackle math or science problems, try following this three-step process.
  1. When you first read a question, make a list of the given values and variables and the units for the variables.
  2. Ask yourself, "What do I have and what do I need to get?" The link between what you have and what you need to get is either an equation that you should be familiar with or certain specific steps to follow to solve particular types of problems.
  3. Solve the problem and see if the answer makes sense. For example, if you know that one variable should be much larger than another, make sure your answer reflects that relationship. You will see how this works with many of the problems in this book.

- **Make sure you know what the question is asking.** The questions on SAT Subject Tests in math or science are not deliberately designed to trick you; however, it is still important that you look closely at each one to make sure you know what it is asking. If a question asks which compound has the lowest hydrogen ion concentration, do not pick the answer choice with the highest concentration. Pay special attention to questions that include the words NOT or EXCEPT. You may want to circle these words to make sure you take them into account as you choose your answer.

Test-Taking Strategies

- **Answer all the easy problems first, then tackle the harder ones.** Keep in mind that the test is only 1 hour long. There isn't much time to spend trying to figure out the answers to harder questions, so skip them and come back to them later. There are three reasons why you should do this. The first is that every question counts the same in the scoring of the exam. That means that you are better off spending time answering the easier questions, where you are sure to pick up points. The second reason to skip past harder questions is that later on in the test you might come to a question or a set of answer choices that jogs your memory and helps you to go back and answer the question you skipped. The third reason is that by answering the easier questions, you will build your confidence and get into a helpful test-taking rhythm. Then, when you go back to a question you skipped, you may find that it is not as hard as you had first thought.
- **Use the process of elimination.** Keep in mind that on any SAT Subject Test, as on any other multiple-choice test, the answer is right in front of you. Try eliminating answer choices that you know are incorrect. Often this can help you select the correct answer.
- **If you must guess, make an educated guess.** The SAT Subject Test has a fractional-point penalty for wrong answers to discourage random guessing. So if you have absolutely no idea how to answer a question, you are better off skipping it entirely. However, you may be able to eliminate one or more answer choices. If you can do that, you can increase your odds of guessing the correct answer. If you can make this kind of educated guess, go ahead. If you guess correctly, you will earn another point.
- **Be wary of answer choices that look familiar but are incorrect.** Sometimes in the set of answer choices there will be one or more wrong answers that include familiar expressions or phrases. You might be tempted to pick one of these choices if you do not work out the problem completely. That is why it is important to work through each problem thoroughly and carefully to make sure that you pick the correct answer choice.
- **You do not have to answer every question.** If you do not know the answer to a question and cannot eliminate any answer choices, skip it and go on. It is better to do that than to risk losing one-quarter of a point for a wrong answer. If you have time at the end of the test, you can return to skipped questions and try to make an educated guess. But you do not have to answer every question to get a good score.

Tips for Test Day

- **Don't panic!** Once test day comes, you are as prepared as you are ever going to be, so there is no point in panicking. Use your energy to make sure that you are extra careful in answering questions and marking the answer sheet.

- **Use your test booklet as scratch paper.** Your test booklet is not going to be reused by anyone when you are finished with it, so feel free to mark it up in whatever way is most helpful to you. Circle important words, underline important points, write your calculations in the margins, and cross out wrong answer choices.

- **Be careful when marking your answer sheet.** Remember that the answer sheet is scored by a machine, so mark it carefully. Fill in answer ovals completely, erase thoroughly if you change your mind, and do not make any stray marks anywhere on the sheet. Also, make sure that the answer space you are marking matches the number of the question you are answering. If you skip a question, make sure that you skip the corresponding space on the answer sheet. Every five or ten questions, check the question numbers and make sure that you are marking in the right spot. You may want to mark your answers in groups of five or ten to make sure that you are marking the answer sheet correctly.

- **Watch the time.** Keep track of the time as you work your way through the test. Try to pace yourself so that you can tackle as many of the questions as possible within the 1-hour time limit. Check yourself at 10- or 15-minute intervals using your watch or a timer.

- **Do not panic if time runs out.** If you have paced yourself carefully, you should have time to tackle all or most of the questions. But if you do run out of time, do not panic. Make sure that you have marked your answer sheet for all the questions that you have answered so far. Then look ahead at the questions you have not yet read. Can you answer any of them quickly, without taking the time to do lengthy calculations? If you can, mark your answers in the time you have left. Every point counts!

- **Use extra time to check your work.** If you have time left over at the end of the test, go back and check your work. Make sure that you have marked the answer sheet correctly. Check any calculations you may have made to make sure that they are correct. Take another look at any questions you may have skipped. Can you eliminate one or more answer choices and make an educated guess? Resist the urge to second guess too many of your answers, however, because this may lead you to change an already correct answer to a wrong one.

McGRAW-HILL's

15 PRACTICE

SAT

SUBJECT TESTS

THE SAT U.S. HISTORY TEST

All About the SAT U.S. History Test

What Is the Format of the SAT U.S. History Test?

The SAT U.S. History test is a 1-hour examination consisting of 90 to 95 multiple-choice questions. The questions deal with historical events, developments, trends, and concepts, as well as with social science concepts and methods as they are used in the study of history. According to the College Board, the test measures the following knowledge and skills:

- Familiarity with historical concepts, cause-and-effect relationships, geography, and other data necessary for understanding major historical developments
- Grasp of concepts essential to historical analysis
- Ability to use historical knowledge in interpreting data in maps, graphs, charts, and cartoons

The test covers U.S. history from pre-Columbian times to the present. It covers not just political history and foreign policy but also economic, social, intellectual, and cultural history. The following chart shows the general test subject areas, as well as the approximate portion of the test devoted to each subject.

SAT U.S. History Questions by Subject Area

Subject Area	Approximate Percentage of Test
Political History	32–36%
Economic History	18–20%
Social History	18–22%
Intellectual and Cultural History	10–12%
Foreign Policy	13–17%

This next chart shows the breakdown of test questions by historical period.

SAT U.S. History Questions by Historical Period

Historical Period	Approximate Percentage of Test
Pre-Columbian Era to 1789	20%
1790 to 1898	40%
1899 to the present	40%

What School Background Do I Need for the SAT U.S. History Test?

The College Board recommends that you have at least the following experience before taking the SAT U.S. History test:

- 1-year comprehensive course in U.S. history at the college preparatory level
- Social studies courses and outside reading
- Familiarity with "periodization," the trends within major historical periods

How Is the SAT U.S. History Test Scored?

On the SAT U.S. History test, your "raw score" is calculated as follows: You receive one point for each question you answer correctly, but you lose one-quarter of a point for each question you answer incorrectly. You do not gain or lose any points for questions you do not answer at all. Your raw score then is converted into a scaled score by a statistical method that takes into account how well you did compared with others who took the same test. Scaled scores range from 200 to 800 points. Your scaled score will be reported to you, to your high school, and to the colleges and universities you designate to receive it.

Scoring scales differ slightly from one version of the test to the next. The scoring scales provided after each practice test in this book are only samples that show you your approximate scaled score.

Test-Taking Strategies for the U.S. History Test

The SAT U.S. History test covers a huge number of topics, and there is no avoiding the fact that the best way to get a high score is to study, study, study. However, because it is a multiple-choice test and because it includes particular types of questions, there are some specific test-taking strategies that you should know to achieve your best score. This chapter explains some of those strategies and provides examples to show you how to use them when test day comes.

STRATEGY: Make sure you know what the question is asking.

1. Watch for key words such as not, except, *and* most often.

It is important to make sure you know exactly what the question is asking. A single word such as *not* or *except* can change the whole meaning, and if you miss it when you read the question, you will never pick the correct answer. Therefore, make sure to read very carefully. If you come to a word such as *not* or *except,* it's a good idea to underline it so that you keep it in mind as you read through the answer choices.

Example:

32. Which of the following was NOT a primary aim of the Progressive movement of the early 1900s?

    (A) Passing laws that would improve slum conditions in large cities
    (B) Teaching immigrants to read, write, and speak English
    (C) Supporting legislation that would make the workplace safer
    (D) Creating public baths, parks, and playgrounds in urban areas
    (E) Making English the official language of the United States

If you do not read this question correctly and miss the word *not,* you could spend your time trying to decide if A, B, C, or D was the best answer. But because of the word *not,* the only choice that could possibly be correct is choice E. You may think that reading questions correctly is a simple matter that you don't have to worry about, but remember how stressed you're likely to be on test day. Make sure you read carefully and accurately. It's better to be safe than sorry!

2. Watch for key words that summarize the question.

In each question there is usually one key word that summarizes what the question is about. That word may be the name of a person, a place, a historical era, or a political doctrine or party. When you find that word, underline or circle it. Then, after choosing the answer you think is correct, go back and look at your underlined or circled word to make sure it agrees with your choice.

Example:

19. Which of the following quotations best explains the concept of Manifest Destiny?

    (A) "Our fathers brought forth on this continent a new nation, conceived in Liberty, and dedicated to the proposition that all men are created equal."

    (B) "We have it in our power to begin the world over again."

    (C) "We hold these truths to be self-evident: that all men are created equal. . . ."

    (D) "The American colonies stand no longer in need of England's protection."

    (E) "The American claim is . . . to overspread and possess the whole of the continent which Providence has given us. . . ."

This question is asking about the concept known as Manifest Destiny, a very important idea in U.S. history. Underline the words "Manifest Destiny" so that your mind focuses on what you know about that particular idea. Now the question looks like this:

19. Which of the following quotations best explains the concept of <u>Manifest Destiny</u>?

Now it is easier to go through the distracters and pick out the correct answer.

    (A) "Our fathers brought forth on this continent a new nation, conceived in Liberty, and dedicated to the proposition that all men are created equal." (*Wrong*)

    (B) "We have it in our power to begin the world over again." (*Wrong*)

    (C) "We hold these truths to be self-evident: that all men are created equal. . . ." (*Wrong*)

    (D) "The American colonies stand no longer in need of England's protection." (*Wrong*)

    (E) "The American claim is . . . to overspread and possess the whole of the continent which Providence has given us. . . ." (*Correct*)

3. Summarize lengthy or confusing distracters.

If you don't know the correct answer and find the distracters lengthy and confusing, try to summarize the idea in each distracter in just a few words. That way, you can compare the different answer choices quickly and easily and try to decide which one is correct. This technique also can be helpful if you decide to skip a question and come back to it later. Study the following example to see how this works.

Example:

60. As the Constitutional Convention ended, Benjamin Franklin commented about a half-sun with its rays painted on George Washington's chair that "now at length I have the happiness to know that it is <u>a rising and not a setting sun</u>." Franklin meant these words as

    (A) a <u>criticism</u> of the delegates in the Convention who did not share his faith in the Constitution

    (B) an indication that he knew the <u>fight</u> for the ratification of the Constitution would be <u>difficult</u>

    (C) a <u>joke</u> about the poor quality of the furniture in Independence Hall

    (D) an <u>expression of hope</u> and optimism for the new government he had helped design

    (E) a <u>criticism</u> of the painter of the chair

Several of the distracters in this question are lengthy and confusing. To make it easier to understand them and compare them with each other, each one has been summarized by having a key word or phrase underlined. The summaries make it clear that you are comparing a few simple alternatives: "a criticism," an indication of a "difficult fight," a "joke," an "expression of hope," and another "criticism." Choice C can be eliminated because it is highly unlikely that a joke would have historical significance. Choices A and E can be eliminated because a "rising sun" is not an image used to express criticism. It is also not an image that evokes the idea of a "difficult fight" (choice B). The only answer choice that makes sense is choice D: a rising sun often is used as an image of hope and optimism.

STRATEGY: Look for clues in the distracters.

1. Look in the distracters for terms that are synonyms for words in the question.

Many important events and ideas in U.S. history can be referred to by several different names. Often a question will use one name in the question stem but use the synonymous term for the same idea in the correct answer. By doing this, the test makers are trying to hide the correct answer, but their words can give you the clue for which you are looking. To see how this works, study the following example.

Example:

28. "The survival of the fittest is simply the survival of the strong, which implies and would better be called the destruction of the weak. If nature progresses through the destruction of the weak, man progresses through the protection of the weak."

The speaker of the above quotation most likely opposed

    (A) Progressivism
    (B) Social Darwinism
    (C) Prohibition
    (D) labor unions
    (E) woman suffrage

The key term in the question is underlined for you. The term *survival of the fittest* derives from Charles Darwin's theory of natural selection. Some thinkers, especially in the late nineteenth century and early twentieth century, believed that the principle of natural selection applies to human society as well and that unfettered economic competition is the best way of organizing human relations because it will produce a society dominated by the "fittest." If you are familiar with Darwin's theory, the name "Social Darwinism" in choice B should be an immediate tip-off that this is the correct answer. You should still read the other distracters and eliminate them, but recognizing that "Darwinism" is a synonym for "survival of the fittest" is the clue you are looking for.

2. When two distracters say the same thing in different words, you can rule out both of them.

In some questions you will find two distracters that say essentially the same or almost the same thing but in different words. Remember: A question cannot have two correct answers! That means that both of these distracters must be incorrect and you can rule them out immediately. Here is an example.

Example:

32. Between 1891 and 1910, millions of immigrants came to the United States for all the following reasons EXCEPT:

    (A) to seek economic opportunity
    (B) to escape poverty at home
    (C) to escape religious or political persecution at home
    (D) to earn enough money to return home and live well there
    (E) to lose their cultural identities as soon as possible

Choices A and B say pretty much the same thing: people who want to "escape poverty" also want to "seek economic opportunity." Both of these choices are essentially the same answer, and so both must be incorrect. Furthermore, choice D is not too different from choices A and B, and so you can rule it out as well. That means that you need to deal only with choices C and E, and if you have studied immigration, you should be able to pick choice E as the correct answer.

3. When two distracters contradict each other, you can rule out one of them.

In some questions you will find distracters that express opposite or nearly opposite ideas. Only one of them can be correct, and so one of the two can be ruled out. Of course, you will need to have some knowledge of the topic or find some other hints in the question before you can choose which one to rule out, but it can be helpful to recognize that one of two contradictory distracters is sure to be wrong.

Example:

15. The Jim Crow laws were

    (A) Southern state laws designed to enforce racial segregation
    (B) laws supported by civil rights activists of the 1960s
    (C) proposals for liquor taxes made by Senator James Crow of Missouri
    (D) regulations that provoked the Whiskey Rebellion
    (E) tariffs imposed on the colonies by Great Britain

Distracters A and B express directly contradictory ideas (segregation laws versus civil rights laws), and so one of the two must be incorrect. If you have studied the history of racial segregation in the South, you should know that choice B is incorrect. The Jim Crow laws were the laws enacted in Southern states in the late nineteenth century and early twentieth century to enforce racial segregation.

STRATEGY: Use the process of elimination to narrow down your choices.

1. Rule out any distracters that you know are wrong.

When you cannot pick the answer to a question immediately, the best strategy is to use the process of elimination to narrow down your choices. Start by reading over the distracters and ruling out any that you know for certain are not the correct answer. Don't be shy about marking up the test booklet! Use your pencil to cross out incorrect distracters. That way you will remove them from your field of vision and be able to concentrate on the remaining choices.

Example:

3. The earliest people to arrive in the Americas probably followed animal herds over a wide land bridge that connected

   (A) Siberia to Greenland
   (B) Siberia to North America
   (C) Europe to Iceland
   (D) North America to Cuba
   (E) Europe to Canada

If you know your geography, you can quickly cross out choices A and C. Choice A must be incorrect because Greenland and Siberia are nowhere near each other and could not possibly be connected by a land bridge. Choice C must be incorrect because people crossing a land bridge from Europe to Iceland still would not yet have arrived in North America. Now the question looks like this:

3. The earliest people to arrive in the Americas probably followed animal herds over a wide land bridge that connected

   (A) ~~Siberia to Greenland~~
   (B) Siberia to North America
   (C) ~~Europe to Iceland~~
   (D) Cuba to North America
   (E) Europe to Canada

This makes the question much easier to deal with, and if you have to guess, your odds of picking the right answer are one in three. Suppose, however, that instead of guessing you decide to move on and come back to this question later. In that case, the fact that you have crossed out two distracters will make the question that much easier to deal with when you return. (The correct answer to this question is choice B.)

   Crossing out distracters is especially important in longer, wordier items. Look at the following example. Try to choose the correct answer without crossing out distracters and see how many times you have to reread the question and the distracters. If you find yourself rereading something that you already know is wrong, you'll understand why crossing out is a useful strategy.

Example:

32. All the following suggest that President Theodore Roosevelt did not support the interests of large corporations EXCEPT:

   (A) He signed laws that broke up monopolies into smaller businesses.
   (B) He ordered an investigation into the practices of the food-processing and food-manufacturing industry.
   (C) He set aside nearly 150 million acres of land for national parks.
   (D) He signed laws that gave the government the authority to regulate the railroads.
   (E) He encouraged arbitration of labor disputes.

It is hard to keep straight what each of these distracters says. To do so, you have to go back and look at each one again and again. Furthermore, the use of the word *except* makes the question even more confusing. Keep in mind that you are looking for an answer choice that does *not* reflect a policy that was against the interests of big business. In other words, you can eliminate any choice that *does* reflect an antibusiness policy. Choice A is clearly a policy that was against big business, and so it can be eliminated. Choice B also can be eliminated; an investigation into industrial practices is definitely not likely to be favored by big business. Now the question looks like this:

32. All the following suggest that President Theodore Roosevelt did not support the interests of large corporations EXCEPT:

    (A) ~~He signed laws that broke up monopolies into smaller businesses.~~
    (B) ~~He ordered an investigation into the practices of the food-processing and food-manufacturing industry.~~
    (C) He set aside nearly 150 million acres of land for national parks.
    (D) He signed laws that gave the government the authority to regulate the railroads.
    (E) He encouraged arbitration of labor disputes.

Now you can focus on figuring out the meaning of distracters C, D, and E. Choice D can be eliminated because the railroads were among the biggest corporations in Roosevelt's day, and laws designed to impose government regulation would not have been in the railroads' interest. Choice E also can be eliminated; the big corporations in Roosevelt's day strongly resisted arbitration of labor disputes. That leaves choice C, which is the correct answer; creating national parks was not necessarily against the interests of large corporations.

2. If you can rule out one or more distracters, make an educated guess.

It's true that on the SAT U.S. History test you will lose a fraction of a point for a wrong answer and that it is a bad idea to guess if you are completely stumped and cannot rule out even one distracter. The reason is that if you cannot rule out any distracters, your chances of guessing the correct answer are very slim. However, if you can rule out one or two or more distracters, the odds start to improve in your favor. If you have to choose among only three distracters, you have a one in three chance of picking the correct answer. If you have to choose between only two distracters, your chances are one in two. Guessing when you can eliminate one or more distracters is called educated guessing. If you can make an educated guess, go ahead and do so. You have more to gain than you have to lose.

STRATEGY: Use what you know about time periods to rule out wrong answers.

One of the most important things to look for in a question is the time period. If you know the time period the question relates to, you can rule out any distracters that do not fall into that period. Ruling out distracters is your key goal. If the question asks about a war, a presidential term, a particular era, or the like, you can exclude anything that is not in the same period.

Example:

11. The Fourteen Points, presented in January 1918, were

    (A) Winston Churchill's plans for dealing with Hitler
    (B) American suffragists' demands for women's rights

  (C) Woodrow Wilson's plan for building peace in the post–World War I world
  (D) sections of the income tax amendment to the Constitution
  (E) the Socialist Party's proposal for economic fairness

Use the time period to exclude distracters that do not belong. Choice A can be eliminated because Hitler did not come to power in Germany until 1933, long after 1918. Choice D can be eliminated because the constitutional amendment authorizing the income tax was ratified in 1913. Now the question looks like this:

11. The Fourteen Points, presented in January 1918, were

  (A) ~~Winston Churchill's plans for dealing with Hitler~~
  (B) American suffragists' demands for women's rights
  (C) Woodrow Wilson's plan for building peace in the post–World War I world
  (D) ~~sections of the income-tax amendment to the Constitution~~
  (E) the Socialist Party's proposal for economic fairness

Now your chance of picking the correct answer is one in three. Look again at the question. What was going on in January 1918? If you have studied the period, you know that that the United States had entered World War I in April 1917 and that the war would come to an end in November 1918. Therefore, it makes sense to infer that in January 1918 leaders such as Woodrow Wilson were concerned with planning the postwar world. That would make choice C the most likely answer, and it is indeed correct.

STRATEGY: Learn how to answer quotation questions.

One special kind of question that appears commonly on the SAT U.S. History test is the quotation question. In this kind of question you are presented with a quotation from some era in U.S. history. You then may be asked to decide who said the quoted words. The choices may be famous people in history, or they may be unnamed persons such as "a former slave" or "a factory worker" who would be likely to have said the words in question. Other variations of this kind of question might ask, "The speaker quoted above would most likely agree with which of the following statements?" or "This statement [or question] was used by [a particular historical figure] to justify which of the following?" or "The sentiments in this quotation are most characteristic of which of the following?"

Quotation questions can be daunting. The first thing to realize is that even though you sometimes are told who is speaking, often you are not given that information, and, in fact, you do not always have to know the name of the individual. Usually it is more important to be able to place the quote within its historical background, that is, what event or historical development it refers to, what historical era it most likely dates from, what ideas or opinions it expresses, and who or what sorts of people might have held those ideas or opinions. To figure this out, start by examining the words in the quote. What clues do you see? What ideas does the speaker emphasize? What references are there, if any, to people, places, and events? Who in history—individuals or groups—might have emphasized those ideas or made those references, and why? Then read through the answer choices. If you can't pick the correct answer immediately, try finding it through the process of elimination.

Example:

1. "Slavery now stands erect, clanking its chains on the territory of Kansas, surrounded by a code of death and trampling upon all cherished liberties."

This statement was most likely made by a(n)

    (A) Whig
    (B) "muckraker"
    (C) plantation owner
    (D) Democrat
    (E) abolitionist

Examine the words of the quote. The speaker is describing slavery in the harshest terms, as "clanking its chains" and "surrounded by a code of death." There is also another clue: Kansas is described as a territory, which means that the quote dates from the pre–Civil War era. Now you can start eliminating choices. Choice B can be eliminated because "muckraker" is a term used to describe crusading journalists in the Progressive Era of the early twentieth century, long after the end of the Civil War. Choice C can be eliminated because plantation owners in the old South probably would have been supporters, not opponents, of slavery. Now the question looks like this:

1. "Slavery now stands erect, clanking its chains on the territory of Kansas, surrounded by a code of death and trampling upon all cherished liberties."

This statement was most likely made by a(n)

    (A) Whig
    (B) ~~"muckraker"~~
    (C) ~~plantation owner~~
    (D) Democrat
    (E) abolitionist

If you have studied this era, you know that "abolitionist" is a term used to describe those who, in the pre–Civil War era, vigorously opposed slavery and called for its abolition. That matches the ideas presented in the quote, and so choice E must be the correct answer.

STRATEGY: Learn how to answer "cartoon" questions.

Political cartoons have a long and lively history in the United States, and the SAT U.S. History test usually includes a question about a political cartoon. The cartoons that appear on the test often are taken from nineteenth-century or early twentieth-century newspapers. They satirize political figures and events of the day, usually expressing strong positive or negative opinions. You may be asked to tell who or what is being satirized in the cartoon, what point of view is being expressed, or even what other persons might agree or disagree with that point of view.

    To interpret political cartoons, keep the following suggestions in mind. First, the people and objects in the cartoons often are labeled to tell readers who or what they are. Look for those labels if you need help understanding what is being represented. Second, the people in cartoons often are shown in situations that parody those that actually took place. The parody is the source of the cartoon humor. Third, many cartoons use symbols to stand for political parties, social groups, political ideas, and the like. These symbols are fairly standard, and so it pays to get to know them. Here is a list of some of the most common symbols used in political cartoons:

Well-dressed portly man = businessman or powerful politician
Skinny beggar = the poor
Donkey = Democrat or Democratic Party
Elephant = Republican or Republican Party
Blindfolded woman or scales = justice
Statue of Liberty = liberty or freedom
Uncle Sam = United States
Young African American man or woman = slave or slavery in general
Eagle = United States
Dove = person who wishes for peace
Hawk = person who wishes for war

Cartoons also frequently deal in stereotypes and caricatures. Although many of them are offensive today, they have been common throughout U.S. history. African Americans, Asians, and other minority groups often have been portrayed negatively in propaganda and cartoons. For the U.S. History test, you need to be able to recognize these various stereotypes.

Cartoons from two particular periods are especially common on the test. The first period is the antebellum period, when cartoons frequently used caricatures and stereotypes to depict Northerners, Southerners, and slaves. The second period is the post–Civil War "Gilded Age," when the artist Thomas Nast drew many cartoons satirizing contemporary political figures, especially the notoriously corrupt "Boss" William Tweed and his associates in New York City's Tammany Hall Democratic political machine. Nast has a very distinctive style that is easily recognized. His cartoons appear very frequently on the SAT U.S. History test. The following are two typical Nast cartoons.

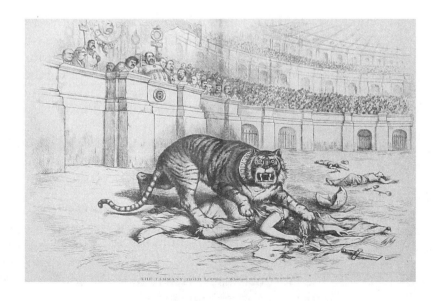

THE TAMMANY TIGER LOOSE—"What are you going to do about it?"

"THAT'S WHAT'S THE MATTER."

Boss Tweed. "As long as I count the Votes, what are you going to do about it? say?"

© 1999 HARPWEEK®

Nast often symbolizes the corruption and venality of Tammany Hall by picturing it as a ferocious-looking tiger. He likewise often portrays Boss Tweed as an overweight, unkempt ruffian with an air of violence about him. He also almost invariably portrays Tweed in the act of destroying the public trust by ravaging symbolic figures of common people or justice or by using intimidation to steal public funds or bully voters. These are quite standard depictions, and they appear over and over in SAT test items.

STRATEGY: Learn how to answer map questions.

First and foremost, map questions on the SAT U.S. History test refer to a significant event in American history. You are not going to get a map question that asks about the establishment of the municipal boundaries of Peoria, Illinois. With all due respect to the residents of that city, that is not a significant national event. The geography you need to know for the test has to do with major national events. You will need to know the states of the Union and the Confederacy, the location of the original 13 colonies, the Northwest Ordinance, the Missouri Compromise, the Compromise of 1850, and the various additions to the Union. Map questions on these topics come up again and again, and there is no trick to help you answer them. You just have to know these subjects by heart.

SAT map questions typically highlight something on a map and ask you to identify the highlighted item. Thus, you should sharpen your map-reading skills. What is being highlighted? Is it a particular state? Is it a specific historical dividing line? If you encounter this kind of question, do not be intimidated just because there is a map. All you have to do is identify what the map represents and nothing more.

Example:

23. Which number on the map marks the Northwest Territory?

    (A) I
    (B) II
    (C) III
    (D) IV
    (E) V

This question is asking you only to identify what the map represents. As is usually the case with map questions, it is no more complex than that. There is no reason to be daunted just because a map is involved.

You are asked to identify the Northwest Territory. Even if you don't know what that term signifies, the name itself is a clue: it must be located either "northwest of something" or "in the Northwest." You can rule out choice D because area IV is neither of those things; it is Texas. You also can rule out choice E because area V is located in the Southeast. It is in fact the state of Florida. You also can rule out choice C because it is in the Southwest.

That leaves choices A and B. Area I is what we now call the Northwest; today it consists of the states of Oregon, Washington, and Idaho. However, that is different from the Northwest Territory, and so choice A is not the correct answer. You should know from your studies that the Northwest Territory included those areas to the northwest of the original 13 states that became part of the United States after the Revolutionary War. Today they make up the states of Ohio, Michigan, Illinois, Indiana, and Wisconsin. Thus, the correct answer is choice B.

STRATEGY: If you don't know the answer and cannot even make an educated guess, skip the question.

Remember: On the SAT tests, you get one point for each question you answer correctly, but if your answer is incorrect, you *lose* a fraction of a point. In other words, wrong answers can hurt you. Therefore, if you really do not know the answer and cannot even rule out any distracters so that you can make an educated guess, skip the question. It's a fact that you do not have to answer every question on the test to get a good score! The following are some examples of questions that you might decide to skip.

1. Either/or questions that you just can't answer

Some questions on the SAT U.S. History test fall into the category of "either you know it or you don't." These questions are usually very simple and straightforward. They ask for a single, precise item of information, and each answer choice is usually just a single word. If you do not know the answer, these questions can be very frustrating because they give you almost nothing to go on. You will not be able to eliminate answer choices because the one-word alternatives do not give you a single hint or clue. If you find yourself stuck on a question of this kind, skip it, get over your frustration, and move on to other questions where you are more likely to pick up points.

Example:

76. Congress passed the War Powers Act in response to the

    (A) Korean War
    (B) Vietnam War
    (C) Persian Gulf War
    (D) War of 1812
    (E) Iraq War

Now, if you happen to know that the War Powers Act was passed in response to the Vietnam War, you are in luck. Mark your answer and get the credit. But if you do not know that vital piece of information, the question gives you absolutely nothing more to go on than the name of the act. If you do not know the answer to a question like this, skip it and go on to other questions where you are more likely to pick up points.

2. Questions about totally unfamiliar people or events

You may be unlucky enough to come across a question that asks about someone or something that is totally unfamiliar to you. The problem here is not that there is nothing in the question stem or the distracters that might give you a hint or a clue; it is simply that you have no information on which to base a decision. Here is an example.

Example:

14. The United States became involved in the affairs of Indochina because of the departure from that area of which colonial power?

    (A) France
    (B) Great Britain
    (C) the Netherlands
    (D) Spain
    (E) Germany

If you do not know the answer to this question, any one of the answer choices might seem plausible. Do you have any idea which areas were included in the British and French empires? Do you know which areas were colonized by the

Netherlands, Spain, or Germany? This information could help you rule out answer choices and at least make an educated guess. But if you recall nothing at all about which European country ruled Indochina, you have nothing to gain by staring at this question. Do not try to spin an answer out of nothing. Skip the question and move on to other questions where you are more likely to pick up points.

3. Questions that leave you confused even after a second reading

Some SAT U.S. History questions are very long and intricate. They take time to read and are filled with extremely detailed information. Some may be so lengthy and complicated that even after you read them over twice, you still have no idea what is being asked. If that happens, do not pause to fret and worry as you try to decipher the meaning. Your time is precious! It is better spent going on to questions that are easy for you to answer and that will add quick points to your score. Skip the very lengthy and complex question for now. Star it or circle it so that you can find it again easily. Then, if you have time at the end of the test, you can come back to the question and try to figure it out. Here is an example of this kind of question.

Example:

41. The Antifederalists opposed the original Constitution for all the following reasons EXCEPT:

    (A) Delegates had conspired under a "veil of mystery" to create a new government beyond what they had been charged to do.
    (B) A strong central government would destroy states' rights.
    (C) The new system of government resembled a monarchy and thus violated the principle of liberty for all citizens.
    (D) The system of the electoral college was undemocratic.
    (E) The Constitution included a bill of rights that specified the privileges of all citizens.

This question requires you to know a lot of information. You need to know about the politics of the early Federal period, the political ideas of the Federalists and the Antifederalists, and the provisions of the original Constitution. The Federalists were proponents of a strong central government. The Antifederalists, in contrast, were proponents of states' rights and were fearful of the power of a strong central government. The Antifederalists opposed the original Constitution because they thought it gave too much power to the federal government and did not reserve enough power to the individual states. This matches choice B, which is the correct answer.

Note that it took a full paragraph just to tell what you have to know to answer this question. If you are not very familiar with this era, you are going to have a hard time figuring out the correct answer. Because there is a lot of information in the question, you may be able to work it out eventually, but is it worth the time that would take? In a case like this, if you cannot spot the correct answer immediately, you might be better off skipping this question and moving on to others that you can answer much more rapidly.

U.S. HISTORY PRACTICE TEST 1

The following Practice Test is designed to be just like the real SAT U.S. History test. It matches the actual test in content coverage and level of difficulty.

When you are finished with the test, determine your score and carefully read the answer explanations for the questions you answered incorrectly. Identify any weak areas by determining the areas in which you made the most errors. Review those chapters of the book first. Then, as time permits, go back and review your stronger areas.

Allow 1 hour to take the test. Time yourself and work uninterrupted. If you run out of time, take note of where you ended when time ran out. Remember that you lose one-quarter of a point for each incorrect answer. Because of this penalty, do not guess on a question unless you can eliminate one or more of the answers. Your score is calculated by using the following formula:

Number of correct answers − 0.25 × Number of incorrect answers

This Practice Test will be an accurate reflection of how you will do on test day if you treat it as the real examination. Here are some hints on how to take the test under conditions similar to those of the actual examination:

- Complete the test in one sitting.
- Time yourself.
- Tear out your Answer Sheet and fill in the ovals just as you would on the actual test day.
- Become familiar with the directions to the test and the reference information provided. You will save time on the actual test day by already being familiar with this information.

U.S. HISTORY PRACTICE TEST 1

ANSWER SHEET

Tear out this answer sheet and use it to mark your answers. Determine the BEST answer for each question. Then fill in the appropriate oval.

1. Ⓐ Ⓑ Ⓒ Ⓓ Ⓔ	26. Ⓐ Ⓑ Ⓒ Ⓓ Ⓔ	51. Ⓐ Ⓑ Ⓒ Ⓓ Ⓔ	76. Ⓐ Ⓑ Ⓒ Ⓓ Ⓔ
2. Ⓐ Ⓑ Ⓒ Ⓓ Ⓔ	27. Ⓐ Ⓑ Ⓒ Ⓓ Ⓔ	52. Ⓐ Ⓑ Ⓒ Ⓓ Ⓔ	77. Ⓐ Ⓑ Ⓒ Ⓓ Ⓔ
3. Ⓐ Ⓑ Ⓒ Ⓓ Ⓔ	28. Ⓐ Ⓑ Ⓒ Ⓓ Ⓔ	53. Ⓐ Ⓑ Ⓒ Ⓓ Ⓔ	78. Ⓐ Ⓑ Ⓒ Ⓓ Ⓔ
4. Ⓐ Ⓑ Ⓒ Ⓓ Ⓔ	29. Ⓐ Ⓑ Ⓒ Ⓓ Ⓔ	54. Ⓐ Ⓑ Ⓒ Ⓓ Ⓔ	79. Ⓐ Ⓑ Ⓒ Ⓓ Ⓔ
5. Ⓐ Ⓑ Ⓒ Ⓓ Ⓔ	30. Ⓐ Ⓑ Ⓒ Ⓓ Ⓔ	55. Ⓐ Ⓑ Ⓒ Ⓓ Ⓔ	80. Ⓐ Ⓑ Ⓒ Ⓓ Ⓔ
6. Ⓐ Ⓑ Ⓒ Ⓓ Ⓔ	31. Ⓐ Ⓑ Ⓒ Ⓓ Ⓔ	56. Ⓐ Ⓑ Ⓒ Ⓓ Ⓔ	81. Ⓐ Ⓑ Ⓒ Ⓓ Ⓔ
7. Ⓐ Ⓑ Ⓒ Ⓓ Ⓔ	32. Ⓐ Ⓑ Ⓒ Ⓓ Ⓔ	57. Ⓐ Ⓑ Ⓒ Ⓓ Ⓔ	82. Ⓐ Ⓑ Ⓒ Ⓓ Ⓔ
8. Ⓐ Ⓑ Ⓒ Ⓓ Ⓔ	33. Ⓐ Ⓑ Ⓒ Ⓓ Ⓔ	58. Ⓐ Ⓑ Ⓒ Ⓓ Ⓔ	83. Ⓐ Ⓑ Ⓒ Ⓓ Ⓔ
9. Ⓐ Ⓑ Ⓒ Ⓓ Ⓔ	34. Ⓐ Ⓑ Ⓒ Ⓓ Ⓔ	59. Ⓐ Ⓑ Ⓒ Ⓓ Ⓔ	84. Ⓐ Ⓑ Ⓒ Ⓓ Ⓔ
10. Ⓐ Ⓑ Ⓒ Ⓓ Ⓔ	35. Ⓐ Ⓑ Ⓒ Ⓓ Ⓔ	60. Ⓐ Ⓑ Ⓒ Ⓓ Ⓔ	85. Ⓐ Ⓑ Ⓒ Ⓓ Ⓔ
11. Ⓐ Ⓑ Ⓒ Ⓓ Ⓔ	36. Ⓐ Ⓑ Ⓒ Ⓓ Ⓔ	61. Ⓐ Ⓑ Ⓒ Ⓓ Ⓔ	86. Ⓐ Ⓑ Ⓒ Ⓓ Ⓔ
12. Ⓐ Ⓑ Ⓒ Ⓓ Ⓔ	37. Ⓐ Ⓑ Ⓒ Ⓓ Ⓔ	62. Ⓐ Ⓑ Ⓒ Ⓓ Ⓔ	87. Ⓐ Ⓑ Ⓒ Ⓓ Ⓔ
13. Ⓐ Ⓑ Ⓒ Ⓓ Ⓔ	38. Ⓐ Ⓑ Ⓒ Ⓓ Ⓔ	63. Ⓐ Ⓑ Ⓒ Ⓓ Ⓔ	88. Ⓐ Ⓑ Ⓒ Ⓓ Ⓔ
14. Ⓐ Ⓑ Ⓒ Ⓓ Ⓔ	39. Ⓐ Ⓑ Ⓒ Ⓓ Ⓔ	64. Ⓐ Ⓑ Ⓒ Ⓓ Ⓔ	89. Ⓐ Ⓑ Ⓒ Ⓓ Ⓔ
15. Ⓐ Ⓑ Ⓒ Ⓓ Ⓔ	40. Ⓐ Ⓑ Ⓒ Ⓓ Ⓔ	65. Ⓐ Ⓑ Ⓒ Ⓓ Ⓔ	90. Ⓐ Ⓑ Ⓒ Ⓓ Ⓔ
16. Ⓐ Ⓑ Ⓒ Ⓓ Ⓔ	41. Ⓐ Ⓑ Ⓒ Ⓓ Ⓔ	66. Ⓐ Ⓑ Ⓒ Ⓓ Ⓔ	
17. Ⓐ Ⓑ Ⓒ Ⓓ Ⓔ	42. Ⓐ Ⓑ Ⓒ Ⓓ Ⓔ	67. Ⓐ Ⓑ Ⓒ Ⓓ Ⓔ	
18. Ⓐ Ⓑ Ⓒ Ⓓ Ⓔ	43. Ⓐ Ⓑ Ⓒ Ⓓ Ⓔ	68. Ⓐ Ⓑ Ⓒ Ⓓ Ⓔ	
19. Ⓐ Ⓑ Ⓒ Ⓓ Ⓔ	44. Ⓐ Ⓑ Ⓒ Ⓓ Ⓔ	69. Ⓐ Ⓑ Ⓒ Ⓓ Ⓔ	
20. Ⓐ Ⓑ Ⓒ Ⓓ Ⓔ	45. Ⓐ Ⓑ Ⓒ Ⓓ Ⓔ	70. Ⓐ Ⓑ Ⓒ Ⓓ Ⓔ	
21. Ⓐ Ⓑ Ⓒ Ⓓ Ⓔ	46. Ⓐ Ⓑ Ⓒ Ⓓ Ⓔ	71. Ⓐ Ⓑ Ⓒ Ⓓ Ⓔ	
22. Ⓐ Ⓑ Ⓒ Ⓓ Ⓔ	47. Ⓐ Ⓑ Ⓒ Ⓓ Ⓔ	72. Ⓐ Ⓑ Ⓒ Ⓓ Ⓔ	
23. Ⓐ Ⓑ Ⓒ Ⓓ Ⓔ	48. Ⓐ Ⓑ Ⓒ Ⓓ Ⓔ	73. Ⓐ Ⓑ Ⓒ Ⓓ Ⓔ	
24. Ⓐ Ⓑ Ⓒ Ⓓ Ⓔ	49. Ⓐ Ⓑ Ⓒ Ⓓ Ⓔ	74. Ⓐ Ⓑ Ⓒ Ⓓ Ⓔ	
25. Ⓐ Ⓑ Ⓒ Ⓓ Ⓔ	50. Ⓐ Ⓑ Ⓒ Ⓓ Ⓔ	75. Ⓐ Ⓑ Ⓒ Ⓓ Ⓔ	

U. S. HISTORY PRACTICE TEST 1
Time: 60 Minutes

Directions: Each of the questions or incomplete statements below is followed by five suggested answers or completions. Select the one that is best in each case and then fill in the corresponding oval on the answer sheet.

1. Women who opposed passage of the Equal Rights Amendment did so primarily because
   (A) they believed that women do not deserve the same rights as men
   (B) they did not want to lose certain privileges, such as exemption from the military draft
   (C) they felt that it would destroy women's role in the home
   (D) they thought it was best to fight for equality on a local level
   (E) they did not want to lose any of the rights for which they had fought for so many decades

2. Which of the following granted all African American men age 21 and over the right to vote?
   (A) The Emancipation Proclamation
   (B) The Reconstruction Acts
   (C) The Freedmen's Bureau
   (D) The Fifteenth Amendment
   (E) The Enforcement Acts

3. Which of the following administrations authorized continued financial aid to the Nicaraguan Contras in defiance of congressional laws against it?
   (A) Gerald Ford
   (B) Jimmy Carter
   (C) Ronald Reagan
   (D) George H. W. Bush
   (E) George W. Bush

4. The Northwest Ordinance of 1787 specified which of the following?
   (A) The federal government would sell land in the Northwest Territory on credit.
   (B) The Northwest Territory was divided into townships and lots that were sold to the public.
   (C) Any precious metals discovered in the Northwest Territory were the property of the federal government.
   (D) Only Native Americans were entitled to live in the Northwest Territory.
   (E) When a section of the Northwest Territory had a large enough population, it could draft a constitution and apply for statehood.

5. Eleanor Roosevelt accomplished all the following EXCEPT:
   (A) writing a daily newspaper column
   (B) holding the post of special ambassador to the United Nations
   (C) visiting soldiers in dangerous combat zones such as Guadalcanal
   (D) taking a public stand in favor of civil rights for African Americans
   (E) founding the National Organization for Women

6. In the aftermath of World War I, President Woodrow Wilson
   (A) urged U.S. neutrality toward European nations
   (B) fought for the establishment of the League of Nations
   (C) signed the Balfour Declaration with Great Britain
   (D) participated in a peace conference in Berlin
   (E) vetoed the Espionage and Sedition Acts

7. Hillary Rodham Clinton is the first first lady to do which of the following?
   (A) hold elected political office
   (B) publish an autobiography
   (C) fight for education and health-care reform
   (D) get a college education
   (E) restore and redecorate public rooms in the White House

8. The Black Codes of the late 1860s had which of the following purposes?
   (A) to restore the status quo of Southern society before the Civil War
   (B) to enforce freedmen's right to vote
   (C) to allow African Americans to hold elected office
   (D) to intimidate Democrats into staying away from the polls
   (E) to nullify the Secession Acts of 1860 and 1861

GO ON TO THE NEXT PAGE ➔

9. During the mid-1800s farmers faced all the following problems EXCEPT:

   (A) The supply of crops exceeded the demand for them.
   (B) They incurred debt from purchases of land or equipment.
   (C) The prices of crops had fallen.
   (D) There were no protective tariffs on imported crops.
   (E) The Grange and Alliance movements prevented them from organizing.

10. Strikes led by members of the International Ladies' Garment Workers' Union had all the following effects EXCEPT:

    (A) Employers agreed to raise wages.
    (B) Employers agreed to shorten the workweek.
    (C) Employers agreed to a closed shop.
    (D) Union membership rose by the tens of thousands.
    (E) Many African American women joined the strikers.

11. Theodore Roosevelt began his presidency with all the following goals EXCEPT:

    (A) fighting rigid class distinctions in U.S. society
    (B) speaking his mind on important issues of the day
    (C) forcing corporations to serve the public good
    (D) overseeing ratification of the Nineteenth Amendment
    (E) fighting unethical and illegal conduct in big businesses

12. Which of the following does NOT characterize the Clinton administrations of the 1990s?

    (A) Economic prosperity
    (B) Federal budget surpluses
    (C) Low unemployment rates
    (D) Passage of important social legislation
    (E) Strained relations with foreign allies

13. American Tories remained loyal to Great Britain during the Revolutionary War for all the following reasons EXCEPT:

    (A) belief that it was immoral to turn against a hereditary monarch
    (B) desire to protect the power and wealth they enjoyed as British subjects
    (C) personal loyalty to King George III
    (D) unwillingness to commit what they believed was treason by taking up arms against Britain
    (E) belief that the various acts of Parliament were neither onerous nor oppressive

14. All the following factors led to the decline and fall of the Industrial Workers of the World EXCEPT:

    (A) the failure of several labor strikes
    (B) people's fear of the IWW's methods and goals
    (C) refusal of employers to accept an open shop
    (D) a government crackdown on union activity
    (E) conflict within the IWW leadership

15. Europeans dared to explore and colonize the New World for all the following motives EXCEPT:

    (A) desire for religious and political freedom
    (B) expansion of European-based empires
    (C) discovery of the Northwest Passage
    (D) greed for gold, treasure, and natural resources
    (E) assimilation into New World cultures

16. Which of the following was NOT a prominent protest group during the civil rights era?

    (A) Southern Christian Leadership Conference
    (B) Fair Employment Practices Committee
    (C) Montgomery Improvement Association
    (D) Student Nonviolent Coordinating Committee
    (E) Congress of Racial Equality

17. American pop music of the 1960s is characterized by all the following EXCEPT:

    (A) song lyrics with political messages
    (B) use of electrically amplified instruments
    (C) a new link between rock and folk music
    (D) a rise in the popularity of big bands
    (E) song lyrics that protested against the establishment

GO ON TO THE NEXT PAGE

18. "We are people of this generation, bred in at least modest comfort, housed now in universities, looking uncomfortably to the world we inherit."

   The author of the above quotation most likely would have supported which of the following movements?

   (A) Counterculture
   (B) Labor
   (C) Temperance
   (D) Religious revival
   (E) Feminist

19. The Seneca Falls Convention of 1848 was called primarily to

   (A) integrate U.S. society along race, gender, and class lines
   (B) declare that women and men should have equal rights
   (C) revise the Declaration of Independence
   (D) force the president of the United States to grant women the right to vote
   (E) do away with the economic system based on owning private property

20. All the following authors were considered members of the nineteenth-century Transcendentalist community EXCEPT:

   (A) Bronson Alcott
   (B) Ralph Waldo Emerson
   (C) Margaret Fuller
   (D) Henry David Thoreau
   (E) Emily Dickinson

21. Henry Clay's American System called for all the following EXCEPT:

   (A) a national bank
   (B) protective tariffs
   (C) a national transportation system
   (D) a sound national currency
   (E) a free-trade agreement with Great Britain

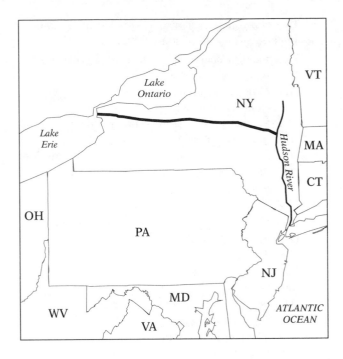

22. The heavy line on the map shows

   (A) the Pony Express
   (B) the Erie Canal
   (C) the Cumberland Road
   (D) the Trail of Tears
   (E) the Appalachian Trail

23. Which one of the following men did NOT play a key role in the U.S. military during the Revolutionary War?

   (A) Benedict Arnold
   (B) Ethan Allen
   (C) Samuel Adams
   (D) George Rogers Clark
   (E) Nathaniel Greene

24. All the following are immigrants who played important roles in U.S. history EXCEPT:

   (A) Madeleine Albright
   (B) Henry Kissinger
   (C) Thomas Paine
   (D) Mary Harris Jones
   (E) Leonard Bernstein

GO ON TO THE NEXT PAGE →

25. Demobilization after World War I had all the follow-
    ing effects on the economy EXCEPT:

    (A) Factories cut back production and dismissed
        workers.
    (B) Crop prices fell to new lows.
    (C) Prices of consumer goods went up.
    (D) Women were pressured into giving up their
        jobs to men.
    (E) Employment rates rose as veterans returned to
        the workforce.

26. During the 1920s African Americans migrated to the
    North primarily to

    (A) join the NAACP
    (B) escape violence and oppression
    (C) organize unions for African American
        laborers
    (D) take jobs on cattle ranches or acquire
        homesteads
    (E) take part in major protests against racial
        discrimination

27. "This bill will destroy our common life and will rob
    us of everything which we hold dear—our lands, our
    customs, our traditions."

    The speaker of the above quotation most
    likely was referring to which of the following?

    (A) The Bursum Bill
    (B) The Taft–Hartley Act
    (C) The Sherman Antitrust Act
    (D) The Immigration Act
    (E) The Equal Rights Amendment

28. All the following were Union generals during the
    Civil War EXCEPT:

    (A) William Tecumseh Sherman
    (B) Ambrose Burnside
    (C) Thomas "Stonewall" Jackson
    (D) Ulysses S. Grant
    (E) George McClellan

29. The GI Bill of Rights gave millions of veterans the
    opportunity to

    (A) get a college education
    (B) join a branch of the armed forces
    (C) refuse combat duty
    (D) move to Canada
    (E) be given a fair trial if court-martialed

30. All the following were parts of the Anaconda Plan in
    the Civil War EXCEPT:

    (A) a Union blockade of Confederate ports
    (B) a siege of Richmond by federal troops
    (C) a campaign to destroy Southern railroads and
        industries
    (D) cutting the South in half by seizing the
        Mississippi
    (E) assaulting coastal ports to seize trading
        vessels

31. Theodore Roosevelt's "Square Deal" called for all
    the following EXCEPT:

    (A) limiting the power of trusts
    (B) enacting cuts in personal income taxes
    (C) promoting public health and safety
    (D) improving working conditions for the laboring
        class
    (E) balancing the interests of big business,
        consumers, and labor

32. Which of the following novels is a literary icon of the
    Jazz Age?

    (A) *Babbitt* by Sinclair Lewis
    (B) *The Great Gatsby* by F. Scott Fitzgerald
    (C) *The House of Mirth* by Edith Wharton
    (D) *Of Mice and Men* by John Steinbeck
    (E) *The Portrait of a Lady* by Henry James

33. In *Powell v. Alabama,* the Supreme Court revoked
    the death sentences of the "Scottsboro boys" on the
    grounds that

    (A) the police had forced the defendants to con-
        fess their guilt
    (B) the defendants had been denied the right to a
        trial by jury
    (C) the defendants had alibis from eyewitnesses
        who had not been allowed to testify
    (D) the defendants had been denied the right to
        due process
    (E) the defendants had been framed for crimes
        committed by other people

GO ON TO THE NEXT PAGE

34. "For what did you throw off the yoke of Britain and call yourselves independent? Was it from a disposition fond of change, or to procure new masters? . . . This new form of national government . . . will be dangerous to your liberty and happiness."

    The speaker of the above quotation was most likely a member of which group?

    (A) Federalists
    (B) Sons of Liberty
    (C) Democrats
    (D) Antifederalists
    (E) Tories

35. All the following were New Deal programs EXCEPT:

    (A) Civil Works Administration
    (B) Reconstruction Finance Corporation
    (C) National Labor Relations Act
    (D) Farm Security Administration
    (E) Federal Housing Administration

36. Which of the following was a leader of Sioux resistance in the 1870s?

    (A) Chief Joseph (Nez Percé)
    (B) Geronimo (Apache)
    (C) Squanto
    (D) Sitting Bull
    (E) Powhatan

37. The eastern half of which present-day state was called "Indian Territory" until 1907?

    (A) Nebraska
    (B) Kansas
    (C) Oklahoma
    (D) Colorado
    (E) Arizona

38. Nativists took all the following steps to protest immigration EXCEPT:

    (A) committing violence against immigrants
    (B) vandalizing Catholic churches because they were centers of immigrant neighborhoods
    (C) forming a political party to support restrictions on immigration
    (D) lynching immigrants and blaming African Americans for the crimes
    (E) electing many state and local officials who discriminated against immigrants

39. Before 1800, most immigrants to the United States were

    (A) Mexican
    (B) British
    (C) Dutch
    (D) African
    (E) Chinese

40. The United States acquired the last of the territory that would make up the contiguous United States during which decade?

    (A) 1770s
    (B) 1800s
    (C) 1840s
    (D) 1860s
    (E) 1950s

41. Between 1830 and 1860, the majority of European immigrants to the United States were from

    (A) France and Hungary
    (B) Belgium and Switzerland
    (C) Italy and Spain
    (D) Ireland and Germany
    (E) Russia and Greece

42. Which section of Article VI of the Constitution states that when federal and state laws come into conflict with each other, ultimate authority is given to federal laws?

    (A) Eminent domain
    (B) Supremacy clause
    (C) Public domain
    (D) Sovereignty clause
    (E) Elastic clause

43. The Indian Removal Act of 1830 stated that

    (A) all East Indian immigrants were to be deported
    (B) burial grounds would be established for Native Americans killed in conflict with federal troops
    (C) all Native American images would be removed from public display
    (D) Native American tribes living east of the Mississippi River would be relocated
    (E) all government officials of Native American ancestry would be dismissed from their posts

GO ON TO THE NEXT PAGE ➤

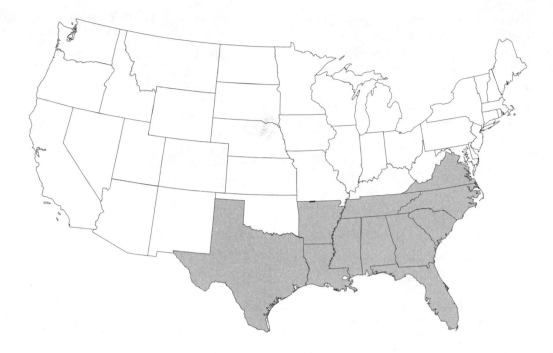

44. The shaded area on the map above represents

(A) the Gadsden Purchase
(B) the Louisiana Purchase
(C) the Confederate States of America
(D) the Mexican Cession
(E) Indian Territory

45. William Jennings Bryan's "Cross of Gold" speech at the Democratic Convention of 1896 proposed which of the following?

(A) that the United States maintain the gold standard
(B) that a cross of gold be erected on the White House lawn
(C) that silver be coined to create more money for the less fortunate
(D) that churches pay income taxes to aid the poor
(E) that the United States sell gold to foreign investors

46. Cesar Chavez became prominent in the 1960s as

(A) the speaker of the house in Texas
(B) a bilingual television host in California
(C) the head of an organization that promoted Hispanic boxers
(D) the leader of the United Farm Workers
(E) the first Hispanic mayor of a U.S. city

47. The first President of the Independent Republic of Texas was

(A) Sam Houston
(B) Walter Dallas
(C) Stephen F. Austin
(D) Jim Bowie
(E) Dallas Green

48. All the following innovations were a direct result of the growth of U.S. cities from 1865 to 1900 EXCEPT:

(A) the elevator
(B) the skyscraper
(C) the automobile
(D) trolley cars
(E) steel frame construction

GO ON TO THE NEXT PAGE

49. "One of the best ways to cope with (fear), is to turn it around and put it out to others . . . if you are afraid of the dark, you put the audience in a dark theater. I had a great fear of the ocean."

   This quotation most likely describes which of the following blockbuster American films?

   (A) *Gone With the Wind*
   (B) *Star Wars*
   (C) *Jaws*
   (D) *The Sound of Music*
   (E) *The Wizard of Oz*

50. Which of the following made New York the first state to grant women the right to own property?

   (A) the Nineteenth Amendment, 1920
   (B) the Married Women's Property Act, 1848
   (C) the Emancipation Proclamation, 1863
   (D) the Seneca Falls Declaration of Sentiments, 1848
   (E) the Fourteenth Amendment, 1868

51. Which of the following helped make the Second Great Awakening a success?

   (A) the growth of Lutheranism
   (B) early German immigration
   (C) the preaching of Jonathan Edwards
   (D) a decline in Protestant denominations
   (E) circuit riders, or itinerant ministers

52. Which of the following is a nickname for the generation born between 1945 and 1965?

   (A) The lost generation
   (B) The beat generation
   (C) The baby boom generation
   (D) The peace generation
   (E) Generation X

53. Which of the following is a broad program created by Martin Luther King, Jr., to protest the misuse of government funding, among other things?

   (A) The Poor People's Campaign
   (B) The March on Washington
   (C) Affirmative action
   (D) Black power
   (E) War on Poverty

54. Which of the 13 British colonies was founded on the southern frontier of British North America to provide a fresh start for debtors?

   (A) South Carolina
   (B) Virginia
   (C) Florida
   (D) Georgia
   (E) North Carolina

55. Pickett's Charge became the turning point for the Union against the Confederacy in which of the following Civil War battles?

   (A) Chancellorsville
   (B) Gettysburg
   (C) Antietam
   (D) Vicksburg
   (E) Second Bull Run

56. During the 1860s and 1870s federal troops repeatedly clashed with Native Americans in which of the following regions?

   (A) Northeast
   (B) Great Lakes
   (C) Southeast
   (D) Mississippi Valley
   (E) Great Plains

57. Which of the following proposed a 1930s relief program in which money would be taken from the wealthy and given to the poor?

   (A) Harold Ickes
   (B) Huey Long
   (C) John Nance Garner
   (D) Alf Landon
   (E) Father Charles Coughlin

58. Mary Boykin Chesnut is best known for which of the following?

   (A) Writing a diary that documents home life on the plantation during the Civil War
   (B) Acting as a spy, passing secret troop placements to the Union
   (C) Writing newspaper editorials opposing the Confederacy
   (D) Running for the Senate in 1864
   (E) Harboring runaway slaves in South Carolina

GO ON TO THE NEXT PAGE

59. Which group opposed ratification of the Constitution because its members feared a powerful national government?

    (A) Whigs
    (B) Continentalists
    (C) Tories
    (D) Democratic-Republicans
    (E) Antifederalists

60. Which of the following leaders did NOT sign the Treaty of Versailles, ending World War I?

    (A) Woodrow Wilson
    (B) Georges Clemenceau
    (C) Vittorio Orlando
    (D) Henry Cabot Lodge
    (E) David Lloyd George

61. The active colonial protest group called Sons of Liberty first organized in which of the following cities?

    (A) Philadelphia
    (B) New York
    (C) Boston
    (D) Williamsburg
    (E) Charleston

62. Powers shared by the federal and state governments are called

    (A) concurrent powers
    (B) sovereign powers
    (C) bicameral powers
    (D) reduced powers
    (E) federal powers

63. The first election in which the Twenty-Sixth Amendment was in effect was held in

    (A) 1948
    (B) 1964
    (C) 1972
    (D) 1976
    (E) 1980

64. The term "planned obsolescence" refers to which of the following?

    (A) The practice of letting a contract expire
    (B) An urban planning strategy designed to rebuild neighborhoods on a timed schedule
    (C) The business practice of manufacturing products specifically designed to go out of style and be replaced by new models
    (D) A temporary construction site
    (E) The government system for maturing savings bonds

65. The skyscraper boom in U.S. cities was facilitated by Elisha Otis's development of

    (A) the revolving door
    (B) the elevator
    (C) the telephone
    (D) refrigeration
    (E) the lightbulb

66. Which of the following Eastern tribes was NOT a member of the Iroquois League?

    (A) Seneca
    (B) Mohawk
    (C) Onondaga
    (D) Delaware
    (E) Cayuga

67. Which prominent U.S. inventor was known as "the Wizard of Menlo Park"?

    (A) Albert Einstein
    (B) Alexander Graham Bell
    (C) Henry Ford
    (D) Tobias Fuller
    (E) Thomas Edison

68. All the following statements support the theory that the West was developed by big business, big government, and technology EXCEPT:

    (A) The government gave away land to anyone who would claim it, live on it, and farm it.
    (B) The railroad companies brought thousands of Chinese immigrants to the West.
    (C) Many African Americans moved west after the Civil War to claim homesteads and work on the railroad.
    (D) The railroad made it possible to transport necessary supplies to pioneer farmers in rural areas.
    (E) Farmers had no national association to which they could apply for help.

GO ON TO THE NEXT PAGE

69. The phrase "Great White Hope" refers to which of the following?

 (A) Babe Ruth, whose home run hitting restored faith in baseball after the Black Sox scandal of 1919
 (B) Boston Celtics basketball star Larry Bird
 (C) The women's gymnastics team at the 1980 Olympic Games
 (D) A white boxer good enough to defeat Jack Johnson, world heavyweight champion in 1908
 (E) Swedish tennis champion Bjorn Borg

70. All the following factors combined to cause the United States to declare war on Great Britain in 1812 EXCEPT:

 (A) U.S. desire to acquire Canada and Florida
 (B) conflict between Democratic-Republicans and Federalists
 (C) impressment of U.S. sailors into the British Navy
 (D) British alliance with and support of Native American tribes
 (E) U.S. purchase of New France, later called the Louisiana Territory

71. In 1837 Horace Mann passed all the following public-school reforms in Massachusetts EXCEPT:

 (A) raising teacher salaries
 (B) pressuring the legislature to increase funding for schools
 (C) opening the nation's first public high schools
 (D) starting teacher training schools
 (E) updating the curriculum

72. The Civil War began in April 1861 when

 (A) John Brown led a raid on the federal arsenal at Harpers Ferry
 (B) South Carolina seceded from the United States
 (C) Confederate forces fired on Fort Sumter, South Carolina
 (D) President Lincoln issued the Emancipation Proclamation
 (E) Union troops laid siege to Richmond, Virginia

73. The primary cause of the market revolution of the early 1800s was

 (A) the creation of a national bank
 (B) the building of national roads and canals
 (C) the abandonment of the gold standard
 (D) the development of refrigeration
 (E) the signing of an international trade agreement

74. The Voting Rights Act of 1975 stated which of the following?

 (A) Young people between the ages of 18 and 21 had the right to vote.
 (B) People must register with a political party in order to vote.
 (C) Resident aliens could vote in local elections.
 (D) People did not have to reveal which candidates they voted for.
 (E) Voting materials must be made available in a variety of languages.

75. "The party reached out mostly to men, to young, black urban men who were on the streets, who knew that there were no options somewhere in their lives."

 The speaker of the above quotation most likely is referring to which of the following?

 (A) the Black Panther Party
 (B) the civil rights movement
 (C) the Reform Party
 (D) the Urban League
 (E) the Socialist Party

76. Which of the following was NOT a U.S. victory in the Pacific in World War II?

 (A) the attack on Guadalcanal
 (B) the Battle of the Coral Sea
 (C) the Battle of the Bulge
 (D) the Battle of Midway
 (E) the Battle of Leyte Gulf

GO ON TO THE NEXT PAGE

77. Congress passed the War Powers Act primarily because

   (A) Presidents Johnson and Nixon had usurped congressional authority in making war on Vietnam
   (B) the United States had not achieved a clear victory in Vietnam
   (C) the Vietnam War had been unpopular with the voters from the beginning
   (D) Congress believed that only the president should have the power to declare war
   (E) the public wanted to end the military draft and replace it with an all-volunteer army

78. The U.S. Department of Agriculture was created primarily to assist which of the following?

   (A) tenant farmers who were forced off their land during the Dust Bowl era
   (B) former slaves who wanted to acquire homesteads in the West
   (C) miners who fought against unsafe working conditions
   (D) struggling farmers on the Great Plains
   (E) ranchers who wanted to import a healthier breed of cattle

79. The Atlantic Charter, signed by the United States and Great Britain in 1941, stated all the following EXCEPT:

   (A) Aggressor nations would be disarmed after the end of the war.
   (B) All nations had the right to choose their own form of government.
   (C) All nations should have equal and free access to international trade.
   (D) The United States and Great Britain would not expand their territory.
   (E) Germany would be split into two nations at the end of the war.

80. "I didn't want to believe it at first—people protesting against us when we were putting our lives on the line for our country."

   The speaker of the above quotation is most likely a veteran of the

   (A) Korean War
   (B) Vietnam War
   (C) Persian Gulf War
   (D) invasion of Afghanistan
   (E) war in Iraq

81. All the following are major photojournalists of the Great Depression EXCEPT:

   (A) Margaret Bourke-White
   (B) Walker Evans
   (C) Althea Gibson
   (D) Dorothea Lange
   (E) Gordon Parks

82. The first U.S. school where women and African Americans, as well as men, could earn a 4-year college degree was

   (A) Oberlin College, Oberlin, Ohio
   (B) Bryn Mawr College, Bryn Mawr, Pennsylvania
   (C) Harvard University, Cambridge, Massachusetts
   (D) Yale University, New Haven, Connecticut
   (E) The University of Pennsylvania, Philadelphia, Pennsylvania

83. Which of the following works of the American theater explicitly compares McCarthyism to the Puritan "witch hunts" of Salem, Massachusetts?

   (A) *A Man for All Seasons* by Robert Bolt
   (B) *The Crucible* by Arthur Miller
   (C) *Strange Interlude* by Eugene O'Neill
   (D) *Angels in America* by Tony Kushner
   (E) *Assassins* by Stephen Sondheim

84. Samuel Colt's revolver, which was patented in the United States in 1836, revolutionized armed combat because of which of the following innovations?

   (A) It did not have to be taken apart during reloading.
   (B) It could be used as either a firing weapon or a bayonet.
   (C) It had sights along the barrel that improved accuracy.
   (D) It could be fired six times before being reloaded.
   (E) It enabled the soldier to shoot from a greater distance.

85. Which of the following machines, invented in 1793, was primarily responsible for an economic boom in the South?

   (A) Eli Whitney's cotton gin
   (B) Robert Fulton's steam engine
   (C) Henry Bessemer's steel converter
   (D) John Deere's tractor
   (E) Edwin L. Drake's oil drill

GO ON TO THE NEXT PAGE

86. The Great Migration took place during which of the following decades?

    (A) 1910s
    (B) 1850s
    (C) 1930s
    (D) 1960s
    (E) 1990s

87. The growth of the railroad industry in the 1870s stimulated all the following EXCEPT:

    (A) settlement of Western states
    (B) growth in the steel industry
    (C) expansion of markets for trade and sales
    (D) high employment rates
    (E) development of the automobile

88. James Madison, Alexander Hamilton, and John Jay were all

    (A) members of President George Washington's cabinet
    (B) signers of the Declaration of Independence
    (C) authors of the *Federalist Papers*
    (D) prominent Antifederalists
    (E) heroes of Revolutionary War battles

89. All the following characterize the Native American literary tradition EXCEPT:

    (A) trickster tales
    (B) creation stories
    (C) fables featuring animal characters
    (D) tales based on the sacred books of Native American religion
    (E) stories passed down orally over generations

90. During the 1770s punitive Acts of Parliament were aimed primarily at Massachusetts because

    (A) Massachusetts's governor was a member of the Sons of Liberty
    (B) Bostonians had provoked the Boston Massacre and had held the Boston Tea Party
    (C) the stamp agent for Massachusetts had been attacked and thrown out of town
    (D) the Massachusetts legislature had abolished slavery throughout the colony
    (E) the people of Massachusetts did not believe in the separation of church and state

S T O P

IF YOU FINISH BEFORE TIME IS CALLED, YOU MAY CHECK YOUR WORK ON THIS TEST ONLY.
DO NOT TURN TO ANY OTHER TEST IN THIS BOOK.

ANSWER KEY

1. B	19. B	37. C	55. B	73. B
2. D	20. E	38. D	56. E	74. E
3. C	21. E	39. B	57. B	75. A
4. E	22. B	40. C	58. A	76. C
5. E	23. C	41. D	59. E	77. A
6. B	24. E	42. B	60. D	78. D
7. A	25. E	43. D	61. C	79. E
8. A	26. B	44. C	62. A	80. B
9. E	27. A	45. C	63. C	81. C
10. C	28. C	46. D	64. C	82. A
11. D	29. A	47. A	65. B	83. B
12. E	30. A	48. C	66. D	84. D
13. E	31. B	49. C	67. E	85. A
14. C	32. B	50. B	68. E	86. A
15. E	33. D	51. E	69. D	87. E
16. B	34. D	52. C	70. E	88. C
17. D	35. B	53. A	71. C	89. D
18. A	36. D	54. D	72. C	90. B

ANSWERS AND EXPLANATIONS

1. **B** Women have certain privileges in U.S. society, such as exemption from the military draft. Women who opposed the ERA preferred to retain those privileges.

2. **D** The Fifteenth Amendment states that no one can be banned from voting because of "race, color, or previous condition of servitude."

3. **C** Reagan was exonerated from any wrongdoing, but it was his administration that aided the Nicaraguan Contras in defiance of congressional laws.

4. **E** The Northwest Ordinance of 1787 set forth the rules for how the sections of the Northwest Territory could become states.

5. **E** Eleanor Roosevelt's daily column was called "My Day"; she was instrumental in passing the UN Declaration of Human Rights; she frequently traveled abroad to visit U.S. servicemen in hospitals; and she is famous for having resigned from an organization that would not allow the African American contralto Marian Anderson to sing in its hall, and then helping to arrange Anderson's concert at the Lincoln Memorial.

6. **B** Wilson fought an uphill battle against the U.S. Congress to establish the League of Nations, which he lost; the League was founded, but the United States did not play any part in it.

7. **A** Clinton was elected to the U.S. Senate from New York after she left the White House.

8. **A** The Black Codes varied from state to state, but they all abridged the rights of African Americans. Southern legislatures could not restore slavery, but they insisted on continuing a system of racial segregation and oppression.

9. **E** The Grange and Alliance movements did the opposite; they were national organizations that helped farmers band together to achieve common goals.

10. **C** Employers continued to fight the idea of a closed shop; they insisted that they would not require any workers to join unions.

11. **D** The Nineteenth Amendment was passed during the presidency of Woodrow Wilson.

12. **E** President Clinton had exceptionally good relations with traditional U.S. allies.

13. **E** Tories did not like the acts of Parliament any better than other colonists, but they did not see independence as a viable solution.

14. **C** An open shop is one in which workers are not required to join a union. The IWW and other labor organizations always fought for a closed shop because they knew that unions were most effective when all the employees belonged.

15. **E** Europeans never even considered assimilating themselves into whatever culture they might find in the Americas.

16. **B** The Fair Employment Practices Committee was established in 1941 to ensure that there would be no discrimination in hiring by the defense industry.

17. **D** Big bands were popular during the late 1930s and through the 1940s.

18. **A** The speaker is clearly ill at ease with being financially and socially secure; this points to someone who would become a supporter of and a participant in the counterculture.

19. **B** The Seneca Falls Convention was convened primarily to raise awareness and to be the springboard to a fight for women's suffrage.

20. **E** Emily Dickinson did not belong to any literary movement or school; she lived as a recluse and wrote highly individual and idiosyncratic poetry.

21. **E** Protective tariffs and a free-trade agreement are mutually exclusive.

22. **B** The Erie Canal stretched from the Great Lakes to the Hudson River.

23. **C** Samuel Adams was a political activist who took no part in armed combat during the Revolution.

24. **E** Albright and Kissinger were both secretaries of state; one was born in Czechoslovakia, the other in Germany. Paine was the Englishman who wrote *Common Sense*. Jones was a labor organizer who was born in Ireland.

25. **E** Veterans were ready to return to the workforce, but there were not always jobs for them. Overall, employment rates fell.

26. **B** When African Americans left the South it was always for the same reason: to escape the all-pervasive discrimination and segregation.

27. **A** The Bursum Bill would have made it possible for non–Native Americans to claim Pueblo land.

28. **C** "Stonewall" Jackson was one of the wiliest generals of the Confederate Army.

29. **A** The GI Bill made it possible for veterans—many of whom were from poor families—to go to college in an era when most people who attended college were children of the wealthy.

30. **A** The Anaconda Plan refers specifically to the blockade, which was meant to crush the life out of the South as an anaconda squeezes the life out of its prey.

31. **B** There were no personal income taxes in the United States until the ratification of the Sixteenth Amendment in 1913, well after Roosevelt left office.

32. **B** F. Scott and Zelda Fitzgerald were considered by many people as the embodiment of the Jazz Age, and *The Great Gatsby* captures the era in which it was written.

33. **D** The Supreme Court found that the defendants were not assigned attorneys until the morning of the trial; thus, they had no opportunity to speak with their counsel or prepare a defense. This violated their Fourteenth Amendment right to due process and a fair trial.

34. **D** The reference to "the yoke of Britain" and the objection to the "new form of national government" make it clear that the speaker must have been an Antifederalist objecting to the Constitution.

35. **B** The Reconstruction Finance Corporation predated Roosevelt's presidency.

36. **D** Chief Joseph was a Nez Percé, Geronimo was an Apache, and Squanto and Powhatan were from East Coast nations. The Sioux were a tribe from the Great Plains.

37. **C** When Oklahoma was granted statehood in 1907, the eastern half, called Indian Territory, was included within the borders of the new state.

38. **D** Nativists did not lynch immigrants. They committed acts of violence against them, but those acts usually were intended to intimidate, not to murder.

39. **B** In the decade after the Revolution the majority of immigrants to the United States were British.

40. **C** The United States acquired the last of its contiguous territory when the Mexican War ended.

41. **D** The huge influx into the United States of Italian, Eastern European, and Chinese immigrants did not begin until after the Civil War.

42. **B** The Constitution states that it is "the supreme law of the land . . . laws of any state to the contrary notwithstanding."

43. **D** The Indian Removal Act, like most laws of the 1800s relating to Native Americans, had to do with their forced relocation.

44. **C** The Confederacy included the group of 11 states shaded on the map.

45. **C** Bryan opposed the gold standard and supported the notion of coining silver.

46. **D** Cesar Chavez was a successful Mexican-American labor leader.

47. **A** Sam Houston, who played a major role in the capture of Santa Anna, became the first president of Texas.

48. **C** The automobile was not the result of the growth of cities; millions of people who lived in cities could not afford a car and had no use for one.

49. **C** Only *Jaws* has a plot that is related to fear of monsters (sharks) lurking under the water.

50. **B** Only the Married Women's Property Act relates to ownership of property.

51. **E** Ministers who traveled and held revival meetings in outlying areas were largely responsible for the widespread success of the Second Great Awakening.

52. **C** The post–World War II generation is called the "baby boom generation" because so many babies were born during those years.

53. **A** King was angry that so much of the money that had been designated for social programs was being diverted to defense.

54. **D** British debtors could win release from debtors' prison if they agreed to go to Georgia and start anew.

55. **B** Gettysburg was the turning point of the Civil War for the Union.

56. **E** The other areas of the nation were already settled, and Native Americans had been driven out or agreements had been made with them. The clashes in the Great Plains occurred while those areas were being settled during the 1860s and 1870s.

57. **B** Huey Long was the author of this Robin Hood–style idea.

58. **A** Mary Chesnut's diary of the Civil War is an important primary source for historians.

59. **E** The Antifederalists got their name from their opposition to a strong federal government.

60. **D** Wilson, Clemenceau, Lloyd George, and Orlando were the chief executives of the Big Four nations that signed the treaty.

61. **C** The first group of Sons of Liberty was organized in Boston in the mid-1760s. Other colonies soon copied that organization.

62. **A** These powers are called concurrent precisely because they are held jointly by two authorities.

63. **C** The Twenty-Sixth Amendment lowered the voting age to 18; this was largely a response to protests against the Vietnam War. Young people felt that if they were old enough to fight and die, they were old enough to vote.

64. **C** "Obsolescence" means that something passes into a state of uselessness. Businesses employ this practice so that consumers will have to spend more money to buy the new model.

65. **B** People would not walk up more than about six flights of steps; skyscrapers would never have been practical without elevators and escalators.

66. **D** The Iroquois lived in New York State; the Delaware are from somewhat farther south, near the Delaware River.

67. **E** Edison's laboratory was in Menlo Park, New Jersey.

68. **E** The first four choices all describe direct action taken by the government, big business, and technology to settle the West.

69. **D** When Jack Johnson became world heavyweight champion, almost every sports journalist in the country expressed the desire for a "great white hope" to come along and defeat him; at that time and for a long time afterward, sports were as discriminatory as the rest of society.

70. **E** The Louisiana Purchase had happened in 1803, well before war was declared; it was not a factor in the war.

71. **C** The first public high schools were already open before Mann began his crusade.

72. **C** The official start of the war was the attack on Fort Sumter.

73. **B** The market revolution refers to the expansion of local markets into regional and national ones. The transportation system was what made this possible.

74. **E** The Voting Rights Act was passed to ensure that any community with a large foreign-born population would make it possible for them to vote by distributing information and sample ballots in a variety of languages.

75. **A** The Black Panther Party urged African Americans to carry guns and take an active role in defending themselves against white oppression. That message spoke powerfully to urban young black men.

76. **C** The Battle of the Bulge took place in Europe.

77. **A** Johnson and Nixon had gone to war without Congress having declared war; that robbed Congress of one of its most important constitutional powers. The War Powers Act stated that the president could commit troops to a conflict for only 60 days without congressional authorization.

78. **D** The Department of Agriculture was created in 1862 to help farmers on the Great Plains who were not used to farming terrain with a small water supply and no trees to use for timber.

79. **E** Germany was split into two nations after the war because of Cold War tensions between the United States and the Soviet Union, not because of anything in the Atlantic Charter.

80. **B** Especially during the later years of the Vietnam War, antiwar protests were common.

81. **C** Althea Gibson was a famous tennis player, not a photojournalist.

82. **A** Oberlin accepted female and black students in the 1830s. Bryn Mawr was not founded until the 1880s; the other three schools are older than Oberlin but did not welcome female students until well into the twentieth century.

83. **B** *The Crucible* is a historical play based on Miller's reading of the Salem witch trial transcripts. Miller drew a deliberate and explicit analogy between those times in U.S. history and the period of McCarthyism during which he was living; both were times when an accusation was enough to ruin a person's reputation and deprive him or her of a livelihood.

84. **D** Before the Colt revolver, a weapon could be fired only once before the soldier had to stop and reload. The Colt was much more efficient. Later models did not have to be taken apart for reloading, but this was not true of the original 1836 Colt.

85. **A** The cotton gin could process more cotton than hundreds of slaves could process by hand in the same amount of time.

86. **A** During the Great Migration, people traveled west to the Northwest Territory and the Mississippi River Valley, which were then the frontier.

87. **E** The growth of the railroad had no effect on the development of the automobile.

88. **C** The Federalists Madison, Hamilton, and Jay strongly supported ratification of the Constitution and wrote the *Federalist Papers* to persuade voters to support it too.

89. **D** The Native American literary tradition is an oral, not a written, one. There are no sacred books of Native American religion; religion is preserved in stories, customs, and artifacts.

90. **B** Conflict with soldiers and the deliberate destruction of valuable property made Boston the target of Parliament's anger.

SCORE SHEET

Number of questions correct: _____

Less: 0.25 × number of questions wrong: _____

(Remember that omitted questions are not counted as wrong.)

Raw score: _____

Raw Score	Scaled Score	Raw Score	Scaled Score	Raw Score	Scaled Score	Raw Score	Scaled Score	Raw Score	Scaled Score
90	800	65	710	40	550	15	420	−10	300
89	800	64	700	39	550	14	420	−11	290
88	800	63	700	38	540	13	410	−12	290
87	800	62	690	37	540	12	410	−13	280
86	800	61	680	36	530	11	400	−14	280
85	800	60	680	35	530	10	400	−15	270
84	800	59	670	34	520	9	390	−16	260
83	800	58	660	33	520	8	390	−17	260
82	800	57	660	32	510	7	380	−18	250
81	800	56	650	31	510	6	380	−19	240
80	790	55	640	30	500	5	370	−20	230
79	780	54	630	29	500	4	370	−21	230
78	780	53	630	28	490	3	360	−22	230
77	770	52	620	27	480	2	360		
76	760	51	620	26	480	1	350		
75	760	50	610	25	470	0	350		
74	750	49	610	24	470	−1	340		
73	750	48	600	23	460	−2	340		
72	740	47	600	22	460	−3	330		
71	740	46	590	21	450	−4	330		
70	730	45	590	20	450	−5	320		
69	730	44	580	19	440	−6	320		
68	720	43	570	18	440	−7	320		
67	720	42	560	17	430	−8	310		
66	710	41	560	16	430	−9	310		

Note: This is only a sample scoring scale. Scoring scales differ from exam to exam.

U.S. HISTORY PRACTICE TEST 2

The following Practice Test is designed to be just like the real SAT U.S. History test. It matches the actual test in content coverage and level of difficulty.

When you are finished with the test, determine your score and carefully read the answer explanations for the questions you answered incorrectly. Identify any weak areas by determining the areas in which you made the most errors. Review those chapters of the book first. Then, as time permits, go back and review your stronger areas.

Allow 1 hour to take the test. Time yourself and work uninterrupted. If you run out of time, take note of where you ended when time ran out. Remember that you lose one-quarter of a point for each incorrect answer. Because of this penalty, do not guess on a question unless you can eliminate one or more of the answers. Your score is calculated by using the following formula:

Number of correct answers − 0.25 × Number of incorrect answers

This Practice Test will be an accurate reflection of how you will do on test day if you treat it as the real examination. Here are some hints on how to take the test under conditions similar to those of the actual examination:

- Complete the test in one sitting.
- Time yourself.
- Tear out your Answer Sheet and fill in the ovals just as you would on the actual test day.
- Become familiar with the directions to the test and the reference information provided. You will save time on the actual test day by already being familiar with this information.

U.S. HISTORY PRACTICE TEST 2

▬▬ ANSWER SHEET

Tear out this answer sheet and use it to mark your answers. Determine the BEST answer for each question. Then fill in the appropriate oval.

1. (A) (B) (C) (D) (E)	26. (A) (B) (C) (D) (E)	51. (A) (B) (C) (D) (E)	76. (A) (B) (C) (D) (E)
2. (A) (B) (C) (D) (E)	27. (A) (B) (C) (D) (E)	52. (A) (B) (C) (D) (E)	77. (A) (B) (C) (D) (E)
3. (A) (B) (C) (D) (E)	28. (A) (B) (C) (D) (E)	53. (A) (B) (C) (D) (E)	78. (A) (B) (C) (D) (E)
4. (A) (B) (C) (D) (E)	29. (A) (B) (C) (D) (E)	54. (A) (B) (C) (D) (E)	79. (A) (B) (C) (D) (E)
5. (A) (B) (C) (D) (E)	30. (A) (B) (C) (D) (E)	55. (A) (B) (C) (D) (E)	80. (A) (B) (C) (D) (E)
6. (A) (B) (C) (D) (E)	31. (A) (B) (C) (D) (E)	56. (A) (B) (C) (D) (E)	81. (A) (B) (C) (D) (E)
7. (A) (B) (C) (D) (E)	32. (A) (B) (C) (D) (E)	57. (A) (B) (C) (D) (E)	82. (A) (B) (C) (D) (E)
8. (A) (B) (C) (D) (E)	33. (A) (B) (C) (D) (E)	58. (A) (B) (C) (D) (E)	83. (A) (B) (C) (D) (E)
9. (A) (B) (C) (D) (E)	34. (A) (B) (C) (D) (E)	59. (A) (B) (C) (D) (E)	84. (A) (B) (C) (D) (E)
10. (A) (B) (C) (D) (E)	35. (A) (B) (C) (D) (E)	60. (A) (B) (C) (D) (E)	85. (A) (B) (C) (D) (E)
11. (A) (B) (C) (D) (E)	36. (A) (B) (C) (D) (E)	61. (A) (B) (C) (D) (E)	86. (A) (B) (C) (D) (E)
12. (A) (B) (C) (D) (E)	37. (A) (B) (C) (D) (E)	62. (A) (B) (C) (D) (E)	87. (A) (B) (C) (D) (E)
13. (A) (B) (C) (D) (E)	38. (A) (B) (C) (D) (E)	63. (A) (B) (C) (D) (E)	88. (A) (B) (C) (D) (E)
14. (A) (B) (C) (D) (E)	39. (A) (B) (C) (D) (E)	64. (A) (B) (C) (D) (E)	89. (A) (B) (C) (D) (E)
15. (A) (B) (C) (D) (E)	40. (A) (B) (C) (D) (E)	65. (A) (B) (C) (D) (E)	90. (A) (B) (C) (D) (E)
16. (A) (B) (C) (D) (E)	41. (A) (B) (C) (D) (E)	66. (A) (B) (C) (D) (E)	
17. (A) (B) (C) (D) (E)	42. (A) (B) (C) (D) (E)	67. (A) (B) (C) (D) (E)	
18. (A) (B) (C) (D) (E)	43. (A) (B) (C) (D) (E)	68. (A) (B) (C) (D) (E)	
19. (A) (B) (C) (D) (E)	44. (A) (B) (C) (D) (E)	69. (A) (B) (C) (D) (E)	
20. (A) (B) (C) (D) (E)	45. (A) (B) (C) (D) (E)	70. (A) (B) (C) (D) (E)	
21. (A) (B) (C) (D) (E)	46. (A) (B) (C) (D) (E)	71. (A) (B) (C) (D) (E)	
22. (A) (B) (C) (D) (E)	47. (A) (B) (C) (D) (E)	72. (A) (B) (C) (D) (E)	
23. (A) (B) (C) (D) (E)	48. (A) (B) (C) (D) (E)	73. (A) (B) (C) (D) (E)	
24. (A) (B) (C) (D) (E)	49. (A) (B) (C) (D) (E)	74. (A) (B) (C) (D) (E)	
25. (A) (B) (C) (D) (E)	50. (A) (B) (C) (D) (E)	75. (A) (B) (C) (D) (E)	

U.S. HISTORY PRACTICE TEST 2
Time: 60 Minutes

Directions: Each of the questions or incomplete statements below is followed by five suggested answers or completions. Select the one that is best in each case and then fill in the corresponding oval on the answer sheet.

1. The main components of Henry Clay's American System were

   (A) a canal, railroads, and lower taxes
   (B) low tariffs, public education, military spending, and agriculture
   (C) a national bank, a protective tariff, and a national transportation system
   (D) trade with Europe, income taxes, and deficit spending
   (E) states' rights, local transportation, and a tax on Southern farmers

2. All the following were possible motives for President Harry S. Truman using the atomic bomb against Japan EXCEPT:

   (A) Japan refused to surrender.
   (B) Truman wanted to dismantle Japan's nuclear facilities.
   (C) The bombing could prevent a costly U.S. land invasion of Japan.
   (D) Truman wished to demonstrate the power of the bomb to the Soviet Union.
   (E) The United States wanted revenge for Japan's attack on Pearl Harbor.

3. As the automobile industry developed, it promoted the growth of all the following EXCEPT:

   (A) the asphalt and road-paving industries
   (B) the advertising business
   (C) the oil-refining industry
   (D) the telephone and telegraph industries
   (E) the importation of rubber

4. The nickname "Star Wars" refers to which of the following?

   (A) public arguments among cabinet members during the Ford administration
   (B) the race to be the first nation to land an astronaut on the moon
   (C) a missile-based defense system conceived by President Ronald Reagan
   (D) the race for the top ratings for the evening network news broadcasts in the 1990s
   (E) special Prosecutor Kenneth Starr's tactics during his investigation of allegations against President Bill Clinton

5. Jazz is a blend of all the following musical influences EXCEPT:

   (A) spirituals
   (B) the blues
   (C) hymns
   (D) work songs
   (E) ragtime

6. "It was a pleasure to live in those good old days, when a Federalist could knock a Republican down in the streets and not be questioned about it."

   The speaker of the above quotation most likely was referring to which decade in history?

   (A) 1800s
   (B) 1850s
   (C) 1870s
   (D) 1920s
   (E) 1960s

7. Which political party was formed during the 1890s to address the concerns of U.S. farmers?

   (A) Democratic Party
   (B) Republican Party
   (C) Progressive Party
   (D) Populist Party
   (E) Socialist Party

8. African Americans and women first served in combat duty in which of the following wars?

   (A) Revolutionary War
   (B) World War I
   (C) Vietnam War
   (D) Persian Gulf War
   (E) War in Iraq

9. Which of the following groups did NOT help form the Free-Soil Party in 1848?

   (A) Abolitionists
   (B) Farmers
   (C) Industrial workers
   (D) Land reformers
   (E) Southern conservatives

GO ON TO THE NEXT PAGE

10. Which of the following works would be most useful to a historian researching the living conditions of immigrants in New York City in the 1890s?

    (A) *The House of Mirth* by Edith Wharton
    (B) *How the Other Half Lives* by Jacob Riis
    (C) *Theory of the Leisure Class* by Thorstein Veblen
    (D) *The Bloodhounds of Broadway* by Damon Runyon
    (E) *The Gangs of New York* by Herbert Asbury

11. Civil rights groups opposed the Vietnam War primarily because

    (A) they supported the North Vietnamese and the communists
    (B) the media had stopped covering the civil rights movement in order to cover the war news
    (C) money that had been earmarked for social programs was diverted to military use
    (D) they objected to the war on religious and pacifist grounds
    (E) they wanted to prevent the reelection of President Lyndon Johnson

12. Accusations of improper conduct in the personal life of a candidate for high office are an example of which of the following?

    (A) muckraking
    (B) mudslinging
    (C) gerrymandering
    (D) grandstanding
    (E) posturing

13. "Whenever I hear anyone arguing for slavery, I feel a strong impulse to see it tried on him personally."

    The speaker of the above quotation is probably which of the following?

    (A) Jefferson Davis
    (B) Abraham Lincoln
    (C) Theodore Roosevelt
    (D) "Stonewall" Jackson
    (E) Robert E. Lee

14. The precedent for a free press in the United States was set by a trial involving which of the following?

    (A) Thomas Paine
    (B) John Peter Zenger
    (C) Samuel Adams
    (D) Phillis Wheatley
    (E) Frederick Douglass

15. In 1837, Democratic Party members of Congress passed a "gag rule" forbidding any discussion or debate of

    (A) corruption
    (B) sedition
    (C) abolition
    (D) expansion
    (E) imperialism

16. Which of the following established a court system in the United States?

    (A) The Constitution
    (B) The Bill of Rights
    (C) The Fifth Amendment
    (D) The Sixth Amendment
    (E) The Judiciary Act of 1789

17. "A man who is good enough to shed his blood for his country is good enough to be given a square deal afterwards. More than that no man is entitled to, and less than that no man shall have."

    Which of the following is most likely true of the speaker of the above quotation?

    (A) He believed in equal opportunities for people of all social classes.
    (B) He approved of U.S. involvement in foreign wars.
    (C) He felt that veterans were entitled to special benefits.
    (D) He was likely to side with owners rather than workers in labor disputes.
    (E) He supported an all-volunteer military rather than a military draft.

18. Which of the following was the greatest influence on Alexander Hamilton's economic theories?

    (A) Thomas Jefferson
    (B) Adam Smith
    (C) Benjamin Franklin
    (D) John Locke
    (E) Samuel Adams

GO ON TO THE NEXT PAGE

19. Which of the following did President Abraham Lincoln quote from in his Gettysburg Address?

    (A) The Constitution
    (B) The Declaration of Independence
    (C) *Common Sense*
    (D) The *Federalist Papers*
    (E) The Emancipation Proclamation

20. The American Federation of Labor was founded in 1886 as a result of

    (A) the Haymarket Riot
    (B) the election of President Grover Cleveland
    (C) a severe financial panic
    (D) federal legislation
    (E) negotiations between owners and workers

21. Which of the following spurred young people in the United States to push for the ratification of the Twenty-Sixth Amendment?

    (A) opposition to the Vietnam War
    (B) support for a Republican administration
    (C) concern for veterans' rights
    (D) commitment to civil rights for all Americans
    (E) determination to ensure equal rights for men and women

22. Which of the following was designed to enforce the provisions of the Eighteenth Amendment?

    (A) Kansas-Nebraska Act
    (B) War Powers Act
    (C) Voting Rights Act
    (D) Volstead Act
    (E) Pure Food and Drug Act

23. A supporter of the Niagara Movement of 1905 probably would applaud all the following EXCEPT:

    (A) civil rights
    (B) federal antilynching legislation
    (C) integration of the public schools
    (D) the African Colonization Society
    (E) the founding of the NAACP

24. To show their opposition to the Stamp Act, colonists took all the following actions EXCEPT:

    (A) holding a meeting of colonial leaders in New York City
    (B) calling up the members of the various colonial militias to active duty
    (C) passing local legislation that declared the Stamp Act illegal
    (D) refusing to purchase any products imported from Great Britain
    (E) tarring and feathering the stamp agents

25. All the following are major African American literary figures EXCEPT:

    (A) Frederick Douglass
    (B) Richard Wright
    (C) Ralph Ellison
    (D) James Weldon Johnson
    (E) Harriet Beecher Stowe

26. The Erie Canal connected the Great Lakes with which of the following?

    (A) the Pacific Ocean
    (B) the Mississippi River
    (C) the Hudson River
    (D) the Cumberland Road
    (E) the Chesapeake Bay

27. All the following contributed to President Franklin D. Roosevelt's election to an unprecedented third term EXCEPT:

    (A) his skill at conducting the war in Europe
    (B) his outstanding skill as a political campaigner
    (C) his success in creating jobs
    (D) his opponent's failure to offer attractive alternatives to Roosevelt's policies
    (E) his enormous personal popularity and ability to inspire people with his courage and optimism

28. W. E. B. DuBois disagreed with Booker T. Washington's argument against African American political activism primarily because

    (A) DuBois felt that African Americans' political activism would force the white majority to correct racial injustice
    (B) DuBois felt that only African Americans had any right to speak about racial issues
    (C) DuBois felt that Washington was a tool of the white majority
    (D) DuBois had no faith in African Americans' ability to help themselves
    (E) DuBois supported the African Colonization Society

GO ON TO THE NEXT PAGE

29. President Harry S Truman ordered the dropping of atomic bombs on Japanese cities primarily because

    (A) he wanted to save U.S. lives by forcing the Japanese to surrender
    (B) he wanted to intimidate the German Army into surrendering
    (C) he wanted the United States to be in the strongest possible position during peace negotiations with the other Allied Powers
    (D) he wanted Japan to shut down its own nuclear facilities
    (E) he wanted to destroy the capital city of Japan

30. The resignations of which two men made Gerald R. Ford president of the United States?

    (A) Bob Haldeman and John Erlichman
    (B) Spiro Agnew and Richard Nixon
    (C) Jimmy Carter and Ronald Reagan
    (D) Robert Kennedy and Lyndon Johnson
    (E) Henry Morgenthau and Harold Ickes

31. Which of the following most accurately defines Transcendentalism?

    (A) the belief that people can rise above material things in life to reach a higher understanding
    (B) the belief that one religion could transcend denominationalism
    (C) the belief that the Puritan faith could be combined with Unitarianism
    (D) the belief that Native Americans could never attain heaven
    (E) the belief in predestination and God's assignment at birth of people to their fate

32. The Sixteenth Amendment, passed in 1913, did which of the following?

    (A) made the sale of alcoholic beverages illegal
    (B) gave women the right to vote
    (C) allowed for direct election of U.S. senators
    (D) enabled Congress to levy taxes on income
    (E) raised the voting age to 21

33. The Lincoln–Douglas debates took place during

    (A) the presidential election of 1860
    (B) the presidential election of 1864
    (C) the congressional debate over secession
    (D) the House of Representatives elections of 1854
    (E) the Senate elections of 1858

34. The Wright Brothers developed an airplane using experience gained from

    (A) working with locomotives and large engines
    (B) operating a bicycle shop and experimenting with small engines
    (C) repairing tractors and farm equipment
    (D) designing steam engines
    (E) manufacturing sewing machines

35. Which of the following describes one major effect of President Warren G. Harding's economic policies?

    (A) the elimination of tariffs on imported goods
    (B) a rise in union membership
    (C) increased profits for business owners
    (D) increased profits for farmers
    (E) strict enforcement of antitrust legislation

36. Which of the following took its name from a British political party that opposed the power of the monarch?

    (A) the Know-Nothings
    (B) the Mugwumps
    (C) the Republicans
    (D) the Bull Moose Party
    (E) the Whigs

37. Native American literature is best described as which of the following?

    (A) classical poetry
    (B) folk songs
    (C) sermons
    (D) creation myths and legends
    (E) oral history

38. Which of the following commanded the United States Expeditionary Forces during World War I?

    (A) John J. Pershing
    (B) George S. Patton
    (C) Douglas MacArthur
    (D) Nathanael Greene
    (E) Dwight D. Eisenhower

39. The hunter/gatherer/farmer cultures of the Eastern Woodlands often are called

    (A) the Toltec
    (B) the Choctaw
    (C) the Mound Builders
    (D) the Creek Nation
    (E) the Anasazi

GO ON TO THE NEXT PAGE

40. ". . . government of the people, by the people, for the people, shall not perish from the earth."

    This statement was first made in which of the following?

    (A) the Preamble to the Constitution
    (B) the Declaration of Independence
    (C) the Magna Carta
    (D) the Fifteenth Amendment
    (E) the Gettysburg Address

41. The total value of all goods and services produced in a nation during a given year is referred to as

    (A) the federal deficit
    (B) the import-export ratio
    (C) the federal budget
    (D) the gross national product
    (E) the distribution of wealth

42. The Iran hostage crisis had an impact on which presidential election?

    (A) 1972
    (B) 1976
    (C) 1980
    (D) 1984
    (E) 1988

43. Spirituals were of great importance to which of the following?

    (A) the Methodist Church
    (B) occult groups in New Orleans
    (C) the religious practices of the slaves on plantations
    (D) Catholic missions in the Southwest
    (E) immigrant funerals

44. Which of the following best describes Andrew Carnegie's practice of acquiring companies that provided raw materials and services for his steel business?

    (A) vertical integration
    (B) lateral growth
    (C) cross-disciplinary exploitation
    (D) venture capitalism
    (E) horizontal integration

45. "The ability to get to the verge without getting into war is the necessary art."

    The speaker is describing which of the following?

    (A) Brinksmanship
    (B) Appeasement
    (C) Imperialism
    (D) Dollar diplomacy
    (E) Containment

46. Which of the following was NOT an action authorized by the Federal Trade Commission (FTC) in 1914?

    (A) the investigation of corporations
    (B) a ban on fraudulent or unfair business practices
    (C) the use of the courts to enforce FTC rulings
    (D) the levying of taxes on interstate commerce
    (E) the targeting of abuses such as mislabeling and false claims

47. Which of the following constituted the most significant international impact of the War of 1812?

    (A) It caused diplomatic tensions between the United States and Spain.
    (B) It forced France to nullify the Louisiana Purchase.
    (C) It lessened shipping commerce on the Great Lakes.
    (D) It forced the United States to police the Atlantic Ocean.
    (E) It removed the British from the Northwest Territories.

48. George Washington's first cabinet consisted of

    (A) secretaries of war, state, commerce, and treasury
    (B) attorney and postmaster generals and secretaries of state, treasury, and war
    (C) secretaries of war, state, labor, and commerce
    (D) secretaries of war, state, treasury, commerce, and Indian affairs
    (E) chief justice, attorney general, and secretaries of state, war, and treasury

49. Congressional Republicans challenged President Clinton's domestic agenda in 1996 with their own proposals, popularly known as

    (A) the Reform Act
    (B) the Economic Initiative
    (C) the Contract with America
    (D) the McCain–Feingold Bill
    (E) Operation Restore Hope

50. The Zapruder film, which was shot with a hand-held camera in 1963, depicts which of the following?

    (A) the invention of the hula hoop
    (B) the construction of the *Pioneer 6* spacecraft
    (C) the development of the measles vaccine
    (D) the assassination of President John F. Kennedy
    (E) the Watergate hearings

GO ON TO THE NEXT PAGE

51. All or parts of the following present-day states were part of the Mexican Cession EXCEPT:

    (A) California
    (B) Nevada
    (C) Utah
    (D) Colorado
    (E) Oklahoma

52. The first 10 constitutional amendments are known as

    (A) the Bill of Rights
    (B) Article VIII of the Constitution
    (C) the Civil Rights amendments
    (D) the elastic clause
    (E) the Federalist amendments

53. "There never has yet existed a wealthy and a civilized society in which one portion of the community did not . . . live on the labor of another."

    The speaker of the above quotation was defending which of the following?

    (A) the establishment of the Confederacy
    (B) South Carolina's right to secede from the United States
    (C) the creation of the National Bank
    (D) the institution of slavery
    (E) the doctrine of nullification

54. The two-party political system emerged in part because of which of the following?

    (A) Progressivism
    (B) Civil unrest
    (C) Sectionalism
    (D) Republicanism
    (E) Nationalism

55. Which one of the following people became the first pilot after Charles Lindbergh to complete a solo transatlantic flight?

    (A) Wiley Post
    (B) Wilbur Wright
    (C) Jim Thorpe
    (D) Gertrude Ederle
    (E) Amelia Earhart

56. The government's policy of allowing cattle ranchers to let their herds graze on public land was called

    (A) the roundup
    (B) range riding
    (C) the long drive
    (D) rustling
    (E) open range

57. Which of the following best describes the purpose of the Seneca Falls Convention of 1848?

    (A) to unite the Native American tribes of New York State
    (B) to discuss agricultural problems for farmers in the Eastern states
    (C) to form a society to advance the rights of women
    (D) to discuss antislavery strategies
    (E) to select a leader for a group of evangelist congregations

58. The turning point of the Revolutionary War was a battle fought at

    (A) Bunker Hill, Massachusetts
    (B) Saratoga, New York
    (C) Brandywine, Pennsylvania
    (D) Cowpens, South Carolina
    (E) Ticonderoga, Vermont

59. Which of the following was a marketing innovation of General Motors in the 1920s to help consumers buy more expensive cars?

    (A) subliminal advertising
    (B) rebates
    (C) discounts for trading in an old car
    (D) bargaining
    (E) the installment plan

60. Which of the following was most likely NOT a goal of George W. Bush in creating the Department of Homeland Security?

    (A) improving airport security
    (B) protecting transportation systems from attack
    (C) expanding law-enforcement powers to combat terrorism
    (D) building impenetrable walls along the Mexican and Canadian borders
    (E) protecting vital power networks from attack

61. The political party formed in opposition to President Rutherford B. Hayes's support of civil service reform was which of the following?

    (A) Progressives
    (B) National Grangers
    (C) Populists
    (D) Half-Breeds
    (E) Stalwarts

GO ON TO THE NEXT PAGE ▶

62. *Uncle Tom's Cabin* provoked strong reactions in the South because

    (A) it justified Southerners' view that slavery was morally permissible
    (B) it depicted slavery as wrong and slaveholders as corrupt
    (C) it depicted romantic relations between African Americans and whites
    (D) it predicted that the South would lose the Civil War
    (E) it had no white characters

63. Who of the following helped the Pilgrims survive their first year in Plymouth by showing them how to grow crops?

    (A) Pocahontas
    (B) Sacagawea
    (C) Squanto
    (D) Powhatan
    (E) Sequoya

64. Which of the following geographical markings established the boundary between the United States and Spanish Florida in 1795?

    (A) the 38th parallel
    (B) fifty-four/forty
    (C) seventy-six degrees longitude, forty degrees latitude
    (D) the 31st parallel
    (E) the Tropic of Cancer

65. Which of the following most aptly describes Booker T. Washington's belief about the key to social and political equality for African Americans?

    (A) economic independence through training and education
    (B) protesting against discrimination
    (C) overthrowing the U.S. government
    (D) militant opposition to U.S. policies
    (E) activist religious organizations

66. During Prohibition people drank alcohol at places called

    (A) back-room pubs
    (B) bathtub gin mills
    (C) stills
    (D) speakeasies
    (E) fraternity clubs

67. Which of the following congressional actions gave the president authority to take "all necessary measures to repel any attack against forces of the United States"?

    (A) the Bursum Bill
    (B) the Dawes Act
    (C) the Tonkin Gulf Resolution
    (D) the Smoot-Hawley Tariff
    (E) the War Powers Act

68. Sitting Bull was an important spiritual leader of the

    (A) Apache
    (B) Comanche
    (C) Navajo
    (D) Sioux
    (E) Creek

69. Shays' Rebellion in 1786 is significant because it

    (A) gave the U.S. militia a chance to demonstrate its efficiency
    (B) raised doubts about the ability of a decentralized government to deal with civil unrest
    (C) opened the door to westward expansion
    (D) united farmers against Native Americans
    (E) allowed former Revolutionary War officers to take up arms again

70. All the following were major crops in the antebellum South EXCEPT:

    (A) cotton
    (B) tobacco
    (C) maple syrup
    (D) rice
    (E) sugarcane

71. Nearly 600,000 U.S. lives were claimed in 1918 by

    (A) an epidemic of influenza
    (B) World War I
    (C) an outbreak of polio
    (D) violent labor strikes
    (E) border violence with Mexico

GO ON TO THE NEXT PAGE

72. President Richard Nixon and Secretary of State Henry Kissinger shared a belief in "realpolitik," which is best described as

    (A) a realistic belief in the ideal of democracy over any other interests
    (B) a foreign policy that puts human rights first
    (C) a foreign policy patterned after that of Germany
    (D) diplomacy guided by the writings of Immanuel Kant
    (E) a foreign policy guided by national interests rather than ideals

73. Which of the following was the first major farmers' organization, founded in 1867?

    (A) the 4-H Club
    (B) the National Grange
    (C) the Alliance
    (D) the American Federation of Labor
    (E) FarmAid

74. Which of the following was a severe low point for the Continental Army in the Revolutionary War?

    (A) the siege of Boston
    (B) the Battle of Brandywine
    (C) the Battle of Trenton
    (D) the winter at Valley Forge
    (E) the surrender at Yorktown

75. Balboa's sighting of the Pacific Ocean and Magellan's voyage around the tip of South America motivated other European explorers to seek which of the following?

    (A) a land route to India
    (B) Spanish permission to sail the Pacific
    (C) a caravan route to the Indies
    (D) a Northwest Passage to the Pacific and Asia
    (E) the Middle Passage to the Americas

76. Which of the following five Republicans who ran for president in 1824 won the election?

    (A) William Crawford of Georgia
    (B) John C. Calhoun of South Carolina
    (C) John Quincy Adams of Massachusetts
    (D) Henry Clay of Kentucky
    (E) Andrew Jackson of Tennessee

77. During President Theodore Roosevelt's administration, the federal government first began making damaged land productive again in a process called

    (A) reclamation
    (B) rejuvenation
    (C) progressivism
    (D) conservation
    (E) preservation

78. Which of the following generals did President Harry S. Truman fire for interfering with peace negotiations with Korea?

    (A) Dwight D. Eisenhower
    (B) Omar Bradley
    (C) Douglas MacArthur
    (D) James Stewart
    (E) Mark Clark

79. A second Industrial Revolution in the late 1800s was generated by innovations in which industries?

    (A) automobile and railroad
    (B) steel and oil refining
    (C) telephone and telegraph
    (D) advertising and radio
    (E) agriculture and livestock

80. The Twenty-Third Amendment gave residents of the District of Columbia

    (A) exemption from the income tax
    (B) the right to sue the federal government
    (C) the right to vote in presidential elections
    (D) exemption from property taxes
    (E) the right to elect their own Congress

81. The Fundamental Orders of Connecticut of 1639 can be described as which of the following?

    (A) a set of strict religious guidelines
    (B) precepts of the Puritans
    (C) a royal charter that established a hierarchy of authority
    (D) a peace treaty with the local Native Americans
    (E) the first written constitution in the colonies

82. Which of the following names the typical shelters built by the first white settlers on the Great Plains?

    (A) Adobe houses
    (B) Tepees
    (C) Sod houses
    (D) Log cabins
    (E) Prairie schooners

GO ON TO THE NEXT PAGE ➡

83. Which of the following explains the original purpose of the Federal Deposit Insurance Corporation (FDIC)?

    (A) to force poor people to deposit their income tax returns
    (B) to force employers to insure workers against injury
    (C) to insure corporations exploring for mineral deposits
    (D) to insure bank deposits up to $5,000
    (E) to protect banks against securities fraud

84. The attack launched by North Vietnamese troops on January 30, 1968, is called the Tet Offensive because

    (A) January 30 is Tet, the Vietnamese New Year
    (B) Tet is the province where fighting was launched
    (C) General Tet and his staff advisors planned the attack
    (D) the fighting began with the troops crossing the Tet River
    (E) Tet was a Vietnamese code name for the operation

85. Which of the following describes the most popular form of stage entertainment during the late 1800s?

    (A) opera
    (B) ballet
    (C) vaudeville
    (D) musical comedy
    (E) tableaux

86. Which of the following describes General William T. Sherman's strategy of total war against the Confederacy?

    (A) using both navy and army troops
    (B) employing all the troops all the time
    (C) destroying everything that would allow the Confederacy to keep fighting
    (D) killing all enemies rather than taking them prisoner
    (E) enlisting civilians to fight

87. The power of the courts to declare an act of Congress unconstitutional was established in the landmark Supreme Court case

    (A) *Roe v. Wade*
    (B) *Marbury v. Madison*
    (C) *McCulloch v. Maryland*
    (D) *Plessy v. Ferguson*
    (E) *Dred Scott v. Sandford*

88. The Americans with Disabilities Act of 1990 provides all the following EXCEPT:

    (A) prohibits discrimination in employment
    (B) requires access for the physically disabled to all public buildings
    (C) prohibits discrimination against the mentally handicapped in transportation
    (D) guarantees fair and easy access to telephone services
    (E) guarantees scholarship opportunities for people with learning disabilities

89. Madame C. J. Walker became a millionaire in the early 1900s by marketing

    (A) canned peas and greens
    (B) Walker's sweet potato pies
    (C) a bottled tonic for digestion
    (D) a hair-conditioning treatment for African American women
    (E) the Walker bicycle for girls

90. The Pilgrims were called Separatists because they had broken with

    (A) the king of England
    (B) the Catholics
    (C) the Anglican Church
    (D) the New England Way
    (E) the Jamestown Colony

S T O P

IF YOU FINISH BEFORE TIME IS CALLED, YOU MAY CHECK YOUR WORK ON THIS TEST ONLY.
DO NOT TURN TO ANY OTHER TEST IN THIS BOOK.

ANSWER KEY

1. C	19. B	37. D	55. E	73. B
2. B	20. A	38. A	56. E	74. D
3. D	21. A	39. C	57. C	75. D
4. C	22. D	40. E	58. B	76. C
5. C	23. D	41. D	59. E	77. A
6. A	24. B	42. C	60. D	78. C
7. D	25. E	43. C	61. E	79. B
8. A	26. C	44. A	62. B	80. C
9. E	27. A	45. A	63. C	81. E
10. B	28. A	46. D	64. D	82. C
11. C	29. A	47. E	65. A	83. D
12. B	30. B	48. B	66. D	84. A
13. B	31. A	49. C	67. C	85. C
14. B	32. D	50. D	68. D	86. C
15. C	33. E	51. E	69. B	87. B
16. E	34. B	52. A	70. C	88. E
17. A	35. C	53. D	71. A	89. D
18. B	36. E	54. C	72. E	90. C

ANSWERS AND EXPLANATIONS

1. **C** The American System advocated a national bank with a sound national currency, protective tariffs that would encourage people to buy U.S.-made goods, and a national transportation system that would open new markets and make trade easier within the United States.

2. **B** Japan had no nuclear facilities of its own in 1945.

3. **D** The rise in auto ownership meant a rise in paved roads on which to drive; auto makers increased advertising so that people would buy their cars and not those of their rivals; oil refining was necessary for fuel for cars; and more rubber had to be imported to meet the need for tires.

4. **C** The missile defense system was nicknamed for a popular fantasy movie of the era.

5. **C** Jazz music was developed from African American religious and popular music, which did not include hymns.

6. **A** The Federalist Party had disappeared by 1810, and so choice A is the only possible answer.

7. **D** The Populist Party was created specifically to address the concerns of rural dwellers.

8. **A** African Americans have served with distinction in combat in every war the United States has ever fought, although the armed forces were segregated from 1812 until after World War II. Women fought in combat in the Revolutionary War, some in disguise, such as Deborah Sampson, and others openly in an emergency, such as Mary Ludwig Hayes.

9. **E** The Free-Soil Party was made up of those who wanted Kansas to become a free state; this did not include Southern conservatives.

10. **B** *How the Other Half Lives* specifically addresses the living conditions of poor immigrants in New York City tenements. *The Gangs of New York* also deals with this subject, but in an earlier era.

11. **C** Civil rights groups did not approve of spending money to fight a dubious foreign war when that money could be better spent fighting a war on poverty and discrimination at home.

12. **B** Mudslinging is the process of trying to turn voters against a candidate by spreading ugly personal rumors, whether true or untrue, about him or her.

13. **B** The speaker of the quotation is clearly against the institution of slavery, and among the choices, only Abraham Lincoln falls into this category. It is not likely that Theodore Roosevelt (choice C) is the speaker because slavery had been abolished by the time he became an adult.

14. **B** Zenger was put on trial and was found innocent of slander because his paper had printed the truth.

15. **C** The Democratic Party was the proslavery party; therefore, Democrats did not want to discuss the issue of abolition.

16. **E** The Constitution gave Congress the authority to set up a court system; Congress fulfilled that obligation by passing the Judiciary Act of 1789.

17. **A** Theodore Roosevelt makes it clear in this statement that he believes that all men of all social classes should have the same opportunities and benefits.

18. **B** The Scottish economist Adam Smith's belief in a capitalist system was the greatest influence on Hamilton's thinking.

19. **B** Lincoln began his Gettysburg Address with a direct allusion to and quotation from the Declaration of Independence. "Fourscore and seven years ago" refers to 1776, and "all men are created equal" is a quotation from the document.

20. **A** The Haymarket Riot led skilled workers to break away from unskilled workers and join the AFL, which was founded by Samuel Gompers in 1886.

21. **A** The Twenty-Sixth Amendment lowered the voting age from 21 to 18, largely in response to protests by young people that if they were old enough to fight in a war and die for their country, they were old enough to vote for or against leaders who might send them to war.

22. **D** The Volstead Act enforced the Eighteenth Amendment's ban on the sale, production, and transport of liquor.

23. **D** The Niagara Movement protested discrimination against African Americans. The Colonization Society was an example of discrimination, although many people associated with it claimed it was well intentioned.

24. **B** The colonial militias were not called up for duty until long after the repeal of the Stamp Act.

25. **E** Harriet Beecher Stowe's novel *Uncle Tom's Cabin* certainly supported the cause of African Americans, but Stowe was not African American.

26. **C** The Erie Canal connected Lake Erie and the Hudson River.

27. **A** The United States was not yet involved in World War II, except to provide financial and material support to the Allies, when Roosevelt ran for reelection in 1940.

28. **A** DuBois believed that African Americans must be politically active and force the white majority to correct racial injustice. He felt that Washington's attitude would never achieve that goal.

29. **A** The Germans already had surrendered; Japan had no nuclear facilities; Japan's capital city, Tokyo, was not attacked with an atomic bomb; and peace negotiations with the other Allies already had taken place, although more were to follow. Truman simply wanted to end the fighting as soon as possible.

30. **B** Spiro Agnew resigned as vice president and was replaced by Gerald Ford. Ford became president when Richard Nixon resigned in order to avoid impeachment.

31. **A** Transcendentalists were influenced by Kant and by Romantic poets. They believed that the way to perfection was through the acquisition of knowledge.

32. **D** Progressives believed that a graduated income tax based on the amount of money a person earned was a fair means of funding necessary government programs and services.

33. **E** Abraham Lincoln and Stephen Douglas held their famous series of debates when both were candidates for the Illinois Senate seat that Douglas already held. Douglas won the election; two years later, Lincoln became president.

34. **B** In their home town of Dayton the Wright brothers ran a bicycle shop together. They and their sister Kate had been fascinated by the idea of flight since they were small children.

35. **C** Harding was unapologetically probusiness, and his policies meant increased profits for owners but not for workers.

36. **E** Whigs and Tories were the two major British political parties during the late 1700s.

37. **D** The Native American literary tradition is an oral tradition of stories, legends, and myths, many of which account for the creation of the world.

38. **A** Pershing was a veteran of the Spanish–American War who was appointed commander of the American Expeditionary Force in 1917. Patton and Eisenhower became famous during World War II; MacArthur is best known for his role in helping Japan recover after World War II; Greene fought during the Revolutionary War.

39. **C** The Mound Builders' culture developed in the Mississippi Valley of the American Southeast.

40. **E** Abraham Lincoln made this statement in the final sentence of the Gettysburg Address.

41. **D** The gross national product includes all the goods and services a nation produces.

42. **C** Many people held President Jimmy Carter responsible for failing to resolve the Iran hostage crisis; Ronald Reagan made this a centerpiece of his victorious campaign against Carter.

43. **C** Slaves sang spirituals because of the comfort they brought. Slaves likened their situation to that of the Jews in the Bible who were led to the Promised Land by Moses.

44. **A** Carnegie integrated his business vertically by owning all aspects of production and service related to it, from bottom to top.

45. **A** John Foster Dulles was speaking of getting to the brink, or edge, of war without actually having to fight.

46. **D** There have never been any taxes imposed on interstate commerce in the United States.

47. **E** Driving the British away from the Northwest Territories for good was an important step toward the United States gaining control of the central portion of the North American continent.

48. **B** Washington's first cabinet had only five officers, as specified in choice B.

49. **C** The Contract with America pledged that Congress would reform itself by implementing a series of new rules.

50. **D** Abraham Zapruder's home movie of the Dallas motorcade and the assassination was used by members of the Warren Commission who investigated the crime. It has appeared repeatedly ever since on television and in documentaries on the president's assassination.

51. **E** The Mexican Cession included all or part of the following states: California, Nevada, Utah, Arizona, Colorado, New Mexico, and Wyoming.

52. **A** The Bill of Rights was added to the Constitution soon after it was ratified and was a condition of ratification.

53. **D** The speaker clearly is defending slavery by stating that there are historical precedents for it.

54. **C** Sectionalism divided the nation in half along regional lines, and each region came to be identified with a political party.

55. **E** Amelia Earhart completed her flight across the Atlantic only one year after Lindbergh.

56. **E** The open range was called "open" because it was land free to all, with none of it closed off by fences.

57. **C** The Seneca Falls Convention was called to bring the issue of women's rights to public notice.

58. **B** Saratoga was a turning point because it was after that victory that the French agreed to support the American colonists in their fight against Britain.

59. **E** General Motors allowed customers to make a down payment on a car and then pay a certain mount each month, including interest, until the full price was paid.

60. **D** No official of the Bush administration ever suggested building walls along the Mexican or Canadian border.

61. **E** The Half-Breeds supported civil service reform. The other three parties were not primarily concerned with the issue of civil service reform.

62. **B** Choices A, C, D, and E are inaccurate descriptions of the novel. Southerners did not like it because it portrayed slavery in a bad light.

63. **C** Squanto is the name of the Indian who befriended the Pilgrims and without whose help they probably would not have survived.

64. **D** The 31st Parallel marks the border of Spanish Florida.

65. **A** Washington believed that African Americans eventually would win full civil rights and independence once they achieved education and economic independence.

66. **D** "Speakeasy" was coined in the 1920s to describe a club that served alcoholic beverages.

67. **C** With the Tonkin Gulf Resolution, Congress ceded to the president its constitutional power to declare war.

68. **D** Sitting Bull was a leader of the Sioux.

69. **B** Shays' Rebellion made it clear that the Articles of Confederation did not give the central government enough authority to hold the nation together.

70. **C** Maple syrup is harvested in the United States in northern locations such as Wisconsin, Vermont, New York, and Pennsylvania.

71. **A** The worldwide epidemic of influenza killed millions; the world war that was going on at the time helped the virus spread. Far more Americans died of the flu than of bullet wounds.

72. **E** Realpolitik first was practiced by Otto von Bismarck in Germany in the nineteenth century. It involves dealing with realities rather than ideals.

73. **B** The National Grange was the first major farmers' movement.

74. **D** The Army of the United States made camp at Valley Forge in what one soldier described as "a truly forlorn condition," with almost no food, dressed in rags, and with little hope of victory. The soldiers had only their determination to hold them together.

75. **D** The famous "Northwest Passage" never existed; until the Panama Canal was completed, there was no water route from the Atlantic to the Pacific without going all the way around South America or somehow negotiating the frigid waters of the chain of islands north of mainland Canada.

76. **C** Adams became president in 1824; in 1828 Jackson defeated him to become president.

77. **A** The conversion of damaged land to productive land is called reclamation.

78. **C** MacArthur had defied orders from his superior, which is the worst sin a soldier can commit; other generals agreed that he should be fired for that offense.

79. **B** Steel and oil refining made possible the rest of the innovations of the second Industrial Revolution.

80. **C** Until the Twenty-Third Amendment was ratified in 1961, residents of Washington, D.C., could not vote for president.

81. **E** The Fundamental Orders set out how the colony would be governed.

82. **C** People built sod houses because there was almost no timber on the Great Plains; there also were no large rocks or any factories that made bricks.

83. **D** The original purpose of the FDIC was to make sure that if there was another widespread bank failure, people would not lose everything they had saved. The federal government would guarantee that up to $5,000 of their money would be safe.

84. **A** "Tet" is the Vietnamese name for the New Year's holiday.

85. **C** Vaudeville, with its variety of acts—juggling, dramatic scenes, tumbling, child performers, song-and-dance numbers, knockabout comedy acts, and trained animal acts—offered something for everybody.

86. **C** Sherman wanted to defeat the South as quickly as possible; therefore, his troops were ordered to destroy anything they came across that might conceivably help the South. The Union troops set fire to cotton fields, burned down houses, stole livestock, and so on.

87. **B** This principle is known as judicial review.

88. **E** The Americans with Disabilities Act forbids any school to discriminate against a disabled student but does not offer disabled students any financial aid.

89. **D** Walker made a fortune on her line of hair-care products.

90. **C** The Puritans had broken with the Anglican Church, and the Pilgrims were a radical sect of Puritans.

SCORE SHEET

Number of questions correct: _____

Less: 0.25 × number of questions wrong: _____

(Remember that omitted questions are not counted as wrong.)

Raw score: _____

Raw Score	Scaled Score	Raw Score	Scaled Score	Raw Score	Scaled Score	Raw Score	Scaled Score	Raw Score	Scaled Score
90	800	65	710	40	550	15	420	−10	300
89	800	64	700	39	550	14	420	−11	290
88	800	63	700	38	540	13	410	−12	290
87	800	62	690	37	540	12	410	−13	280
86	800	61	680	36	530	11	400	−14	280
85	800	60	680	35	530	10	400	−15	270
84	800	59	670	34	520	9	390	−16	260
83	800	58	660	33	520	8	390	−17	260
82	800	57	660	32	510	7	380	−18	250
81	800	56	650	31	510	6	380	−19	240
80	790	55	640	30	500	5	370	−20	230
79	780	54	630	29	500	4	370	−21	230
78	780	53	630	28	490	3	360	−22	230
77	770	52	620	27	480	2	360		
76	760	51	620	26	480	1	350		
75	760	50	610	25	470	0	350		
74	750	49	610	24	470	−1	340		
73	750	48	600	23	460	−2	340		
72	740	47	600	22	460	−3	330		
71	740	46	590	21	450	−4	330		
70	730	45	590	20	450	−5	320		
69	730	44	580	19	440	−6	320		
68	720	43	570	18	440	−7	320		
67	720	42	560	17	430	−8	310		
66	710	41	560	16	430	−9	310		

Note: This is only a sample scoring scale. Scoring scales differ from exam to exam.

THE SAT WORLD HISTORY TEST

All About the SAT World History Test

What Is the Format of the SAT World History Test?

The SAT World History test is a 1-hour exam consisting of 95 multiple-choice questions. It covers the whole history of the world, spanning events and historical developments in every geographical area except the United States. The questions refer not just to political events such as wars and revolutions, but also to the major intellectual, cultural, social, and economic trends that have shaped our world.

According to the College Board, the questions are distributed by geographical area in approximately the following percentages:

SAT World History Questions by Geographical Area

Area	Approximate Percentage of Test
Europe	25%
Africa	10%
Middle East (Southwest Asia)	10%
South and Southeast Asia	10%
East Asia	10%
The Americas (excluding the United States)	10%
World (comparative)	25%

The questions are also distributed by historical time period in approximately the following percentages:

SAT World History Questions by Time Period

Time Period	Approximate Percentage of Test
Pre-History up to the year 500 C.E. (Common Era)	25%
500 to 1500 C.E.	20%
1500–1900 C.E.	25%
1900 C.E.–Present	20%
Cross-chronological	10%

The test questions measure not only how well you understand important events and developments in global history, but also how well you are able to interpret and analyze materials from history such as quotations, maps, charts and graphs, political cartoons, works of art, and the like. You will need to know terms such as the names of historical periods, and you will also need to be familiar with basic world geography. Finally, you will need to be aware of the important cause-and-effect relationships that have determined major historical trends.

What School Background Do I Need for the SAT World History Test?

For the SAT World History test, the College Board simply recommends that you take world history courses that focus on cultural or area studies. You are also advised simply to do as much reading as possible on world history, including works of cultural, social, and economic history.

How Is the SAT World History Test Scored?

On the SAT World History test, your "raw score" is calculated as follows. You receive one point for each question you answer correctly, but you lose one-quarter of a point for each question you answer incorrectly. You do not gain or lose any points for questions that you do not answer at all. Your raw score is then converted into a scaled score by a statistical method that takes into account how well you did compared to others who took the same test. Scaled scores range from 200 to 800 points. Your scaled score will be reported to you, your high school, and to the colleges and universities you designate to receive it.

Scoring scales differ slightly from one version of the test to the next. The scoring scale provided after the World History test in this book is only a sample that will show you your approximate scaled score.

SUCCEEDING ON THE SAT WORLD HISTORY TEST

The SAT World History test covers the history of the world from the development of human beings to the present day. The best way to guarantee a high score on the test is to take a high school course in world history. (Note that this test EXCLUDES the history of the United States; however, because nations have always traded, fought, and negotiated with one another, facts about the United States may come up occasionally.)

The World History test is a multiple-choice test that includes certain specific types of questions. Therefore, there are specific strategies that can help you to improve your score. This chapter explains some of these strategies and provide examples to show you how to use them when test day comes.

STRATEGY: Skip difficult questions the first time through the test and return to them later.

The best way to get a good score on the World History test is to choose as many correct answers as possible, and as few wrong answers. You are not required to answer the questions in numerical order; you are free to skip around as much as you like. Therefore, work straight through the test once, answering only the questions you are certain about. Skip any question that makes you hesitate. When you reach the end of the test, turn back to the first page and work on the more challenging questions. Answering the easy questions first will give you more confidence and help you accumulate a stock of correct answers to build on.

STRATEGY: Use the process of elimination to narrow down the answer choices.

Once you have answered all the questions you are sure of, go back to the beginning of the test and look at the questions that remain. If you can narrow down the answer choices to two or three, you have good odds of choosing the correct answer. Because more correct answers will raise your score, it's a good idea to make educated guesses. It is NOT a good idea to make wild guesses. If there are questions where you truly have no idea of the answer, and there are not enough hints in the question to help you narrow the choices down from five to two or three, you should not guess blindly.

There are many ways to eliminate answers. First, look for clues in the questions. Look for people's names, time periods, and the name of a nation, empire, or region. All these clues can help you eliminate choices.

Example:

1. The *Book of the Thousand and One Nights* is a collection of comic and erotic tales from

   (A) tenth-century Iraq
   (B) twelfth-century Japan
   (C) fourteenth-century Italy
   (D) sixteenth-century China
   (E) nineteenth-century Spain

You can probably identify the *Thousand and One Nights* by another title—many people refer to it as the *Arabian Nights*. This is an important clue to the culture that collected and wrote down these stories. The only Arab culture listed among the choices is Iraq. Therefore, by the process of elimination, this must be the correct answer. The question gives you a choice of five different time periods, and you may well have absolutely no idea which of those is correct, but the process of elimination assures you that the tales must have come from Iraq. So you can fill in the oval for choice A with confidence.

STRATEGY: Watch for key words such as *NOT* and *EXCEPT.*

Make sure you don't misread a question because you are anxious or in too much of a hurry. Some questions on the SAT World History test contain the capitalized words NOT or EXCEPT. If you don't notice one of these words, you will misinterpret the question and choose the wrong answer. It's a good strategy to circle this word in your booklet when you see it in a question. That way you won't forget it.

Example:

2. All of the following beliefs characterized the *philosophes* of the Enlightenment EXCEPT:

   (A) All people were born free and equal.
   (B) People had the right to design their own governments and to choose their representatives.

    (C) All religious creeds were equal and all should be tolerated.
    (D) Journalists must be free to publish facts and opinions without fear of official punishment.
    (E) Science, not God, had created the universe and human beings.

If you miss the word EXCEPT in the question, you will be sorely puzzled trying to choose among the first four answers. Even though the test tries to make it easy for you by printing this word in capital letters, you can miss things like this if you are nervous or if you skim rather than reading carefully. When you see the word NOT or EXCEPT in a question, circle it.

Read the question again. Four of the answer choices describe commonly held beliefs of the *philosophes*—French thinkers who were at the spearhead of the eighteenth-century Enlightenment. You are looking for the one choice that does NOT fit. If you have studied the Enlightenment, you know that its ideas included social and political equality, personal and political freedom, and religious tolerance. You also know that most of the *philosophes* believed in God; many of them took the position that God had indeed created the universe and set it going, just as a watchmaker creates and winds a watch. Therefore you know choice E is correct.

STRATEGY: Use what you know about time periods to rule out wrong answers.

Some questions in the SAT World History test will mention a specific time period. This information can help you rule out wrong answers.

Example:

3. The Scientific Revolution of the 1600s led naturally to

    (A) the Manchurian invasion of China
    (B) the secularization of education
    (C) the development of the Stoic philosophy
    (D) the Enlightenment
    (E) the spread of hereditary monarchies through the West

The question tells you that the correct answer must be an event or phenomenon that arose just after the 1600s. With this information, you can rule out choice C; Stoicism is an ancient philosophy. You can rule out choice E; at this period of history monarchy was on the wane. You have now used the information in the question to narrow down the choices. If you have studied the Enlightenment, you know that it (a) followed just on the heels of the Scientific Revolution and (b) was the same kind of intellectual movement. Therefore it seems to be the best answer, and, in fact, it is correct.

STRATEGY: Learn how to answer quotation questions.

Several questions on the SAT World History test will present you with a short passage or quotation and ask you a question about it. You will rarely be asked to identify the speaker of the quotation. Instead, the question is more likely to ask you to draw a reasonable conclusion—the event or historical development the quotation refers to, the historical era it probably dates from, the ideas or opinions it expresses, and who might have held those ideas or opinions.

Example:

"I do not feel obliged to believe that the same God who has endowed us with senses, reason, and intellect has intended us to forgo their use and by some other means to give us knowledge which we can attain by them."

4. The writer of the above statement would have supported which of the following?

   (A) Humanism
   (B) Socialism
   (C) Fundamentalism
   (D) Communism
   (E) Deism

Chances are that you have never seen this quotation before. The test gives you no information about the time period in which it might have been written, nor the place. Therefore, you have to think carefully about the implications of the writer's words, and to know the meaning of the five terms in the answer choices.

The writer states that God has endowed human beings with the ability to reason, and that therefore people who reason are obeying the laws of God. You can immediately eliminate Communism and Socialism from consideration because those are political philosophies, and the quotation does not seem to have any relationship to politics. You can eliminate Fundamentalism, because Fundamentalists do not believe in reliance on reason. Humanism is a belief in man's ability to achieve by using his own talents and abilities. Choice A is the correct answer. (In fact, the quotation was written by Galileo in the seventeenth century.)

STRATEGY: Learn how to answer questions that ask you to interpret a work of fine art.

The SAT World History test will feature pictures of a certain number of works of fine art or architecture and ask you questions about them. You may be shown a building and be asked to identify its architectural style, or the culture that most influenced the architect. You may be shown a painting and asked to identify the historical event it depicts or the school or artistic movement to which it belongs.

Pay attention to details in the visual image. Ask yourself questions such as: *Have I seen this image, or something very similar to it, before? What can I recall about it? What architectural features can I see in this building? When was technology discovered that could have created such a building? Are the people in the painting presented realistically as they would be in a modern photograph? What style of clothing are they wearing? In which historical culture and era did people dress that way?*

Example:

5. The wall painting shown above is from which of the following ancient civilizations?

(A) Egypt
(B) Greece
(C) Rome
(D) China
(E) India

Even if you have not seen this specific painting before, you have probably seen others like it. Note that the person is shown in profile and that the image appears to be a flat cutout; there is no attempt to convey the illusion of three dimensions. Note the symbols painted above and around the person. These are hieroglyphs. Look at the style of clothing and the long, narrow dark eyes of the person in the painting. All these clues should help you identify it as Egyptian, choice A.

STRATEGY: Learn how to answer map questions.

Some SAT World History questions will ask you about a map pictured in the test booklet. It may be a political map, showing national or provincial borders. It may be a topographical map, showing natural features such as mountains and rivers. Don't worry that a map question may ask you about a trivial detail; map questions will ask about the locations of major civilizations and nations, or show you outlines and ask you to identify a nation.

The best way to prepare yourself for these questions is to become familiar with the material. Make sure you can identify outline maps of the continents and that you know where the major nations lie on those continents. Make sure you can roughly locate the extent of major ancient civilizations such as Mesopotamia and the Roman Empire.

Example:

Europe in the Thirteenth Century

6. The shaded area on this map of medieval Europe represents which of the following?

(A) the Papal States
(B) Castile
(C) Germany
(D) the Holy Roman Empire
(E) the Austro-Hungarian Empire

This question is simple: it presents you with the map and asks you to identify the political entity that is shaded.

The question itself gives you some important information. It tells you that you are looking at a map of Europe. It also gives you a time period: the thirteenth century. Armed with that knowledge, you can begin to eliminate wrong answer choices.

Even if you don't remember the map of Europe very well, common sense should tell you that the Papal States were part of modern Italy and never extended all the way north to the Baltic Sea. You can eliminate choice A. If you can correctly recall that the kingdoms of Castile and Aragon were united to form modern-day Spain, you can eliminate choice B: Spain is on the peninsula at the southwestern tip of the continent. You may hesitate over the last three choices. You should be able to eliminate choice E because the shaded part of the map is considerably north and west of Hungary. The clue "thirteenth century" should help you choose the correct answer, D. There was no unified German nation until the early nineteenth century.

WORLD HISTORY PRACTICE TEST

Treat this practice test as the actual test and complete it in one 60-minute sitting. Use the following answer sheet to fill in your multiple-choice answers. Once you have completed the practice test:

1. Check your answers using the Answer Key.
2. Review the Answers and Explanations.
3. Complete the Score Sheet to see how well you did.

ANSWER SHEET

Tear out this answer sheet and use it to complete the practice test. Determine the BEST answer for each question. Then fill in the appropriate oval.

1. Ⓐ Ⓑ Ⓒ Ⓓ Ⓔ	26. Ⓐ Ⓑ Ⓒ Ⓓ Ⓔ	51. Ⓐ Ⓑ Ⓒ Ⓓ Ⓔ	76. Ⓐ Ⓑ Ⓒ Ⓓ Ⓔ
2. Ⓐ Ⓑ Ⓒ Ⓓ Ⓔ	27. Ⓐ Ⓑ Ⓒ Ⓓ Ⓔ	52. Ⓐ Ⓑ Ⓒ Ⓓ Ⓔ	77. Ⓐ Ⓑ Ⓒ Ⓓ Ⓔ
3. Ⓐ Ⓑ Ⓒ Ⓓ Ⓔ	28. Ⓐ Ⓑ Ⓒ Ⓓ Ⓔ	53. Ⓐ Ⓑ Ⓒ Ⓓ Ⓔ	78. Ⓐ Ⓑ Ⓒ Ⓓ Ⓔ
4. Ⓐ Ⓑ Ⓒ Ⓓ Ⓔ	29. Ⓐ Ⓑ Ⓒ Ⓓ Ⓔ	54. Ⓐ Ⓑ Ⓒ Ⓓ Ⓔ	79. Ⓐ Ⓑ Ⓒ Ⓓ Ⓔ
5. Ⓐ Ⓑ Ⓒ Ⓓ Ⓔ	30. Ⓐ Ⓑ Ⓒ Ⓓ Ⓔ	55. Ⓐ Ⓑ Ⓒ Ⓓ Ⓔ	80. Ⓐ Ⓑ Ⓒ Ⓓ Ⓔ
6. Ⓐ Ⓑ Ⓒ Ⓓ Ⓔ	31. Ⓐ Ⓑ Ⓒ Ⓓ Ⓔ	56. Ⓐ Ⓑ Ⓒ Ⓓ Ⓔ	81. Ⓐ Ⓑ Ⓒ Ⓓ Ⓔ
7. Ⓐ Ⓑ Ⓒ Ⓓ Ⓔ	32. Ⓐ Ⓑ Ⓒ Ⓓ Ⓔ	57. Ⓐ Ⓑ Ⓒ Ⓓ Ⓔ	82. Ⓐ Ⓑ Ⓒ Ⓓ Ⓔ
8. Ⓐ Ⓑ Ⓒ Ⓓ Ⓔ	33. Ⓐ Ⓑ Ⓒ Ⓓ Ⓔ	58. Ⓐ Ⓑ Ⓒ Ⓓ Ⓔ	83. Ⓐ Ⓑ Ⓒ Ⓓ Ⓔ
9. Ⓐ Ⓑ Ⓒ Ⓓ Ⓔ	34. Ⓐ Ⓑ Ⓒ Ⓓ Ⓔ	59. Ⓐ Ⓑ Ⓒ Ⓓ Ⓔ	84. Ⓐ Ⓑ Ⓒ Ⓓ Ⓔ
10. Ⓐ Ⓑ Ⓒ Ⓓ Ⓔ	35. Ⓐ Ⓑ Ⓒ Ⓓ Ⓔ	60. Ⓐ Ⓑ Ⓒ Ⓓ Ⓔ	85. Ⓐ Ⓑ Ⓒ Ⓓ Ⓔ
11. Ⓐ Ⓑ Ⓒ Ⓓ Ⓔ	36. Ⓐ Ⓑ Ⓒ Ⓓ Ⓔ	61. Ⓐ Ⓑ Ⓒ Ⓓ Ⓔ	86. Ⓐ Ⓑ Ⓒ Ⓓ Ⓔ
12. Ⓐ Ⓑ Ⓒ Ⓓ Ⓔ	37. Ⓐ Ⓑ Ⓒ Ⓓ Ⓔ	62. Ⓐ Ⓑ Ⓒ Ⓓ Ⓔ	87. Ⓐ Ⓑ Ⓒ Ⓓ Ⓔ
13. Ⓐ Ⓑ Ⓒ Ⓓ Ⓔ	38. Ⓐ Ⓑ Ⓒ Ⓓ Ⓔ	63. Ⓐ Ⓑ Ⓒ Ⓓ Ⓔ	88. Ⓐ Ⓑ Ⓒ Ⓓ Ⓔ
14. Ⓐ Ⓑ Ⓒ Ⓓ Ⓔ	39. Ⓐ Ⓑ Ⓒ Ⓓ Ⓔ	64. Ⓐ Ⓑ Ⓒ Ⓓ Ⓔ	89. Ⓐ Ⓑ Ⓒ Ⓓ Ⓔ
15. Ⓐ Ⓑ Ⓒ Ⓓ Ⓔ	40. Ⓐ Ⓑ Ⓒ Ⓓ Ⓔ	65. Ⓐ Ⓑ Ⓒ Ⓓ Ⓔ	90. Ⓐ Ⓑ Ⓒ Ⓓ Ⓔ
16. Ⓐ Ⓑ Ⓒ Ⓓ Ⓔ	41. Ⓐ Ⓑ Ⓒ Ⓓ Ⓔ	66. Ⓐ Ⓑ Ⓒ Ⓓ Ⓔ	91. Ⓐ Ⓑ Ⓒ Ⓓ Ⓔ
17. Ⓐ Ⓑ Ⓒ Ⓓ Ⓔ	42. Ⓐ Ⓑ Ⓒ Ⓓ Ⓔ	67. Ⓐ Ⓑ Ⓒ Ⓓ Ⓔ	92. Ⓐ Ⓑ Ⓒ Ⓓ Ⓔ
18. Ⓐ Ⓑ Ⓒ Ⓓ Ⓔ	43. Ⓐ Ⓑ Ⓒ Ⓓ Ⓔ	68. Ⓐ Ⓑ Ⓒ Ⓓ Ⓔ	93. Ⓐ Ⓑ Ⓒ Ⓓ Ⓔ
19. Ⓐ Ⓑ Ⓒ Ⓓ Ⓔ	44. Ⓐ Ⓑ Ⓒ Ⓓ Ⓔ	69. Ⓐ Ⓑ Ⓒ Ⓓ Ⓔ	94. Ⓐ Ⓑ Ⓒ Ⓓ Ⓔ
20. Ⓐ Ⓑ Ⓒ Ⓓ Ⓔ	45. Ⓐ Ⓑ Ⓒ Ⓓ Ⓔ	70. Ⓐ Ⓑ Ⓒ Ⓓ Ⓔ	95. Ⓐ Ⓑ Ⓒ Ⓓ Ⓔ
21. Ⓐ Ⓑ Ⓒ Ⓓ Ⓔ	46. Ⓐ Ⓑ Ⓒ Ⓓ Ⓔ	71. Ⓐ Ⓑ Ⓒ Ⓓ Ⓔ	
22. Ⓐ Ⓑ Ⓒ Ⓓ Ⓔ	47. Ⓐ Ⓑ Ⓒ Ⓓ Ⓔ	72. Ⓐ Ⓑ Ⓒ Ⓓ Ⓔ	
23. Ⓐ Ⓑ Ⓒ Ⓓ Ⓔ	48. Ⓐ Ⓑ Ⓒ Ⓓ Ⓔ	73. Ⓐ Ⓑ Ⓒ Ⓓ Ⓔ	
24. Ⓐ Ⓑ Ⓒ Ⓓ Ⓔ	49. Ⓐ Ⓑ Ⓒ Ⓓ Ⓔ	74. Ⓐ Ⓑ Ⓒ Ⓓ Ⓔ	
25. Ⓐ Ⓑ Ⓒ Ⓓ Ⓔ	50. Ⓐ Ⓑ Ⓒ Ⓓ Ⓔ	75. Ⓐ Ⓑ Ⓒ Ⓓ Ⓔ	

WORLD HISTORY PRACTICE TEST

Directions: Each of the questions or incomplete statements below is followed by five suggested answers or completions. Select the one that is best in each case and then fill in the corresponding oval on the answer sheet.

1. The leaders who met at Congress of Vienna (1814–1815) had all of the following goals EXCEPT:
   (A) to bring about a lasting peace in Europe
   (B) to create a balance of military and political power among nations
   (C) to draw permanent national boundaries
   (D) to ensure the perpetuation of monarchy as a system of government
   (E) to establish a permanent international organization of nations

2. The bas-relief above is probably from
   (A) an Egyptian pyramid
   (B) an Indian palace
   (C) a Roman home
   (D) a Greek temple
   (E) a Celtic church

   "With coarse rice to eat, with water to drink, and my bended arm for a pillow—I have still joy in the midst of these things. Riches and honors acquired by unrighteousness are to me as a floating cloud."

3. The statement above was most likely written by which of the following?
   (A) Hammurabi
   (B) Confucius
   (C) Plato
   (D) Mohammed
   (E) Quetzalcoatl

4. England's industrial revolution was slow to spread to continental Europe for all the following reasons EXCEPT:
   (A) the Napoleonic wars had hurt European economies
   (B) European nations lacked skilled scientists and thinkers
   (C) European nations maintained an active economic rivalry
   (D) entrepreneurship was less imaginative and versatile
   (E) banking and credit institutions were not as well developed

5. This painting is a product of which of the following cultures?
   (A) Ancient Greece
   (B) Ancient Rome
   (C) Medieval France
   (D) Renaissance Italy
   (E) 19th-century Britain

6. The Roman empire was spectacularly successful at conquest primarily because of the
   (A) excellence of the Roman military system
   (B) superiority of Roman culture
   (C) mildness of the Mediterranean climate
   (D) leadership skills of Alexander the Great
   (E) lack of representative government in Rome

GO ON TO THE NEXT PAGE

7. The power of the city-state of Athens in the 500s derived from

   (A) silver mines and maritime empire
   (B) militaristic culture
   (C) republican form of government
   (D) universal suffrage for adults
   (E) lack of any strong enemy in the region

8. Byzantines contributed all of the following to eastern European civilization EXCEPT:

   (A) conversion to Christianity
   (B) development of the Cyrillic alphabet
   (C) imperial form of government
   (D) art, architecture, and literature
   (E) scientific and technological innovations

9. Which of the following was most responsible for the European policy of appeasement toward Germany during the 1930s?

   (A) ignorance of Nazi rearmament of Germany
   (B) knowledge that the United States was allied with Germany
   (C) failure to defeat Germany during World War I
   (D) overwhelming popular opposition to war
   (E) belief that Germany had the right to annex Austria and Poland

10. Which of the following is the correct chronological order, from earliest to latest, of the pre-Columbian civilizations listed below?

    (A) Olmec, Maya, Aztec
    (B) Aztec, Maya, Olmec
    (C) Aztec, Olmec, Maya
    (D) Maya, Olmec, Aztec
    (E) Olmec, Aztec, Maya

11. Archaeologists believe that the first human beings developed on the continent of

    (A) Africa
    (B) Asia
    (C) Europe
    (D) North America
    (E) South America

"This war is an end and, also, a beginning. Never again will darker people of the world occupy just the place they had before. Out of this war will rise, soon or late, an independent China, a self-governing India, an Egypt with representative institutions, an Africa for the Africans. . . ."

12. The writer of the above statement was most likely referring to which of the following?

    (A) the Cuban Revolution
    (B) the Spanish–American War
    (C) World War I
    (D) the War of 1812
    (E) the Sepoy Rebellion

13. Which of the following divided the Roman Empire into the two halves which later became the Roman and Byzantine empires?

    (A) Justinian
    (B) Julian
    (C) Eusebius
    (D) Constantine
    (E) Diocletian

14. Henry VIII of England founded the Anglican Church for which of the following reasons?

    (A) He felt that reform was needed in the Catholic Church.
    (B) He was determined to divorce Catherine of Aragon.
    (C) He felt that the English clergy had too much power.
    (D) He was tolerant of all religious creeds.
    (E) He wanted to ensure that his daughter Mary would succeed to the English throne.

15. Which of the following was the major turning point in the war between the ancient Persians and Greeks?

    (A) the sack of Athens
    (B) the battle of Marathon
    (C) the battle of Thermopylae
    (D) the battle of Salamis
    (E) the conquest of Thrace

GO ON TO THE NEXT PAGE ▶

"If there were only one religion in England there would be danger of despotism, if there were two they would cut each other's throats, but there are thirty, and they live in peace and happiness."

16. Which of the following principles would the writer of the above most likely support?

    (A) Secularism
    (B) Deism
    (C) Ecumenism
    (D) Atheism
    (E) Paganism

17. Which of the following best describes the ultimate goal of the Indian National Congress?

    (A) to achieve Indian self-government through peaceful means
    (B) to raise an army that would drive the British from India
    (C) to eliminate British and Islamic culture from an independent India
    (D) to achieve equal representation throughout India for Hindus and Muslims
    (E) to establish a common official Indian language

18. Otto von Bismarck achieved his goal of uniting Germany by means of a war against

    (A) Britain
    (B) France
    (C) Austria
    (D) Russia
    (E) Spain

19. Which of the following was the most important factor in linking sub-Saharan and West Africa to the rest of the world?

    (A) the annual flooding of the Nile River
    (B) the spread of Islam
    (C) the introduction of the camel
    (D) the introduction of the horse
    (E) the beginning of the slave trade

20. Which of the following was the most important factor in the development of Mesopotamian civilization?

    (A) technological advances
    (B) food surpluses
    (C) the Tigris and Euphrates rivers
    (D) the development of writing
    (E) the discovery of bronze

21. All of the following are characteristic of the rise of a communist state EXCEPT:

    (A) the use of propaganda that promotes Party ideology
    (B) the crushing of any opposition party
    (C) the support of the middle class
    (D) Party control of all news media
    (E) a violent overthrow of the previous government

"If the tiger ever stands still, the elephant will crush him. . . . But [the tiger] will leap on the back of the elephant, tearing huge chunks from his hide. . . . And slowly the elephant will bleed to death."

22. Which of the following best explains the meaning of this statement made by the Vietnamese communist leader Ho Chi Minh in 1946?

    (A) Outsiders would never conquer Vietnam in spite of superior size or strength.
    (B) The French would never become expert tiger hunters.
    (C) The North Vietnamese government would soon crush and control South Vietnam.
    (D) European invaders had stripped Vietnam of its most valuable natural resources.
    (E) Someday Vietnam would control France as France now controlled Vietnam.

23. As a result of the Seven Years' War, control of Canada passed from

    (A) Britain to France
    (B) Spain to Britain
    (C) Britain to Spain
    (D) France to Britain
    (E) Spain to France

"What a piece of work is man! How noble in reason! how infinite in faculty! in form, in moving, how express and admirable! in action how like an angel! in apprehension how like a god!"

24. The writer of this speech would probably have espoused

    (A) humanism
    (B) existentialism
    (C) deconstructionism
    (D) nihilism
    (E) social Darwinism

GO ON TO THE NEXT PAGE

25. Spanish *conquistadores* called the Anasazi Indians of North America "Pueblos" because

    (A) Anasazi women were powerful and respected, unlike Spanish women
    (B) Anasazi architecture strongly resembled the buildings and design of Spanish towns
    (C) the Anasazi were clearly a peaceful and hospitable people
    (D) the Anasazi helped Spanish missionaries to build Catholic churches
    (E) the Anasazi were enemies of the Apache and Navajo

26. The Great Wall of China was built to protect the Qin empire from

    (A) the Vietnamese
    (B) the Huns
    (C) the Persians
    (D) the peasants
    (E) the Aryans

27. Which of the following invaded Ghana and forced its collapse in AD 1076?

    (A) the Egyptian army
    (B) Muslim Berbers
    (C) Sundiata of Mali
    (D) the sultan of Morocco
    (E) the tribes of Benin

28. The primary reason for the partition of India into the states of India and Pakistan was which of the following?

    (A) fall in popularity of Mohandas Gandhi
    (B) British desire to make India into two weak states rather than one strong state
    (C) British refusal to understand that Muslim and Hindu Indians wanted one state
    (D) widespread Muslim refusal to continue living in a Hindu-dominated state
    (E) agreement between India and Pakistan that Kashmir would be an independent republic

29. Which of the following best describes the impact of the writing system developed in ancient China?

    (A) It unified all Chinese regions by providing a common form of communication.
    (B) It enabled China to maintain sway over Japan and Korea.
    (C) It allowed people in outlying regions to pass messages swiftly to the interior.
    (D) It permitted Chinese to communicate with neighboring nations.
    (E) It was the catalyst for scientific advances such as the development of gunpowder.

30. The image above depicts events from which of the following?

    (A) the defeat of the Spanish Armada
    (B) the Norman conquest of Britain
    (C) the Wars of the Roses
    (D) the Peloponnesian War
    (E) the life of King Arthur

31. Which of the following geographical factors protected ancient Egypt from its hostile neighbors?

    (A) the Nile River
    (B) the rainy season
    (C) the annual floods
    (D) the surrounding mountains and deserts
    (E) the hot, dry climate

32. Which numbered area on the map on page 73 represents an Asian country that was never colonized by a European power?

    (A) 1
    (B) 2
    (C) 3
    (D) 4
    (E) 5

"It is said that the Toltecs were very wealthy, and that they had all they needed for eating and drinking. The squash were huge, two meters in circumference. And the ears of maize were so big that a single pair of arms could not stretch around them."

33. The above passage describes a people who flourished from about 950 to 1200 AD on which of the following continents?

    (A) Africa
    (B) Asia
    (C) Australia
    (D) Europe
    (E) South America

GO ON TO THE NEXT PAGE

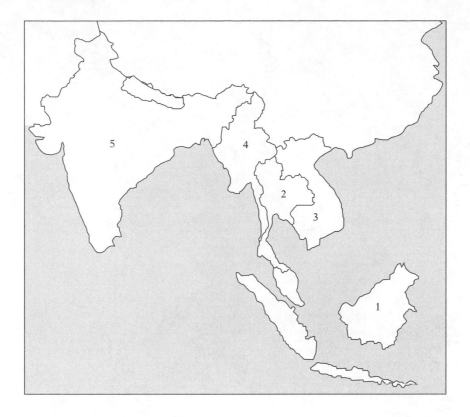

34. Murasaki Shikibu is an important figure in Japanese history because she

    (A) wrote Japan's oldest surviving novel
    (B) served as the power behind the Japanese emperor
    (C) was the first Japanese woman to travel to the West in the nineteenth century
    (D) revolutionized the form of poetry known as *haiku*
    (E) led the samurai to victory against an invading Korean army

35. The ancient Persians were unable to conquer Constantinople for which of the following reasons?

    (A) Khosrow was determined to avenge the death of Maurice.
    (B) The Egyptians fought on the Byzantine side.
    (C) The Byzantines controlled the sea.
    (D) The Persian army was poorly trained and disciplined.
    (E) The Persians had ended the supremacy of the Huns.

36. Which of the following African nations was founded as a homeland for freed slaves?

    (A) Ghana
    (B) Benin
    (C) Zulu
    (D) Zimbabwe
    (E) Sierra Leone

37. Which of the following scientists proved conclusively that Earth orbits the Sun?

    (A) Nicolaus Copernicus
    (B) Tyco Brahe
    (C) Johannes Kepler
    (D) Galileo Galilei
    (E) Isaac Newton

38. Which of the following was the most important obstacle to the growth of the African independence movement?

    (A) the importance of tribal as opposed to national identity
    (B) the lack of modern transportation systems such as a railroad
    (C) the low literacy rate throughout sub-Saharan Africa
    (D) the spread of Christianity throughout the continent
    (E) the pervasive system of racial segregation imposed by the colonizers

GO ON TO THE NEXT PAGE

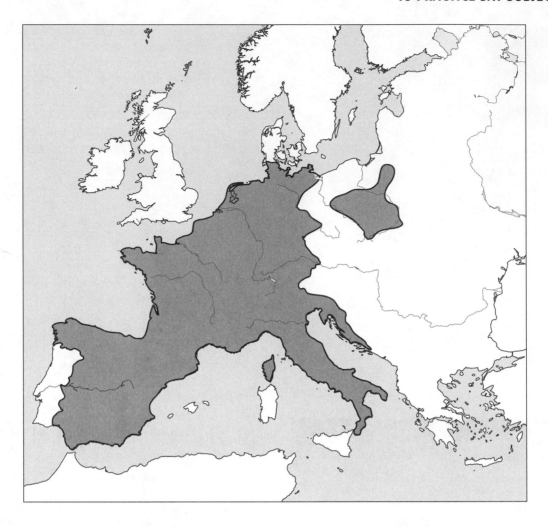

39. The shaded area of the map above shows the extent of which of the following at its height?

    (A) the Byzantine Empire
    (B) the Third Reich
    (C) the Napoleonic Empire
    (D) the Roman Empire
    (E) the British Empire

40. Which of the following actions of the emperor Asoka hastened the collapse of the Mauryan Empire?

    (A) his policy of war and expansion
    (B) his promotion of manufacture and trade in the private sector
    (C) the frequency of the royal tours he took through the kingdom
    (D) his decision to divide the empire between two heirs
    (E) his tolerance of all religious creeds

41. Portuguese imperialism in the Pacific was made possible by

    (A) the discovery of sea routes by Vasco da Gama
    (B) the transatlantic voyages of Christopher Columbus
    (C) the opening of the Suez Canal
    (D) the distance between Australia and Asia
    (E) the self-imposed isolation of Japan

GO ON TO THE NEXT PAGE

42. This painting of a nineteenth-century Englishwoman was made possible by which of the following historical events?

(A) the discovery of the treasures in the pharaoh's tombs in Egypt
(B) the elimination of the African slave trade
(C) the relaxation of social conventions after the revolutions of 1848
(D) the emancipation of women in Great Britain
(E) the opening of Japan to international trade

"If we deny our constitution, a democratic one which was given to us by the Allies after the war . . . then I would not understand the world. . . . I must be allowed to help a person who wants to get away from there and come over here, who has the right under our constitution."

43. The speaker of the above statement is most likely describing his opposition to

(A) the building of the Berlin Wall
(B) the Israeli occupation of Palestinian territories
(C) the division of Germany into four occupied zones
(D) the partition of India and Pakistan
(E) the German invasion of Poland

44. An era of military expansion began in Western Europe in the eleventh century for all of the following reasons EXCEPT:

(A) feudal lords knew no other occupation except to wage war
(B) major enemies from the East had lost power or been defeated
(C) Europe's growing population and wealth could support large-scale military endeavors
(D) the Catholic Church supported war because of its missionary aims
(E) European powers were eager to colonize the Western hemisphere

45. All of the following nations signed the 1921 Four-Power Treaty EXCEPT:

(A) France
(B) Great Britain
(C) Japan
(D) the Netherlands
(E) the United States

46. Amenhotep IV created a formal state religion in place of traditional religious cults in order to

(A) check the power of the priests
(B) indulge his personal interest in theology
(C) subjugate the Egyptian masses
(D) encourage laborers to build more pyramids
(E) combat several seasons of severe drought

GO ON TO THE NEXT PAGE

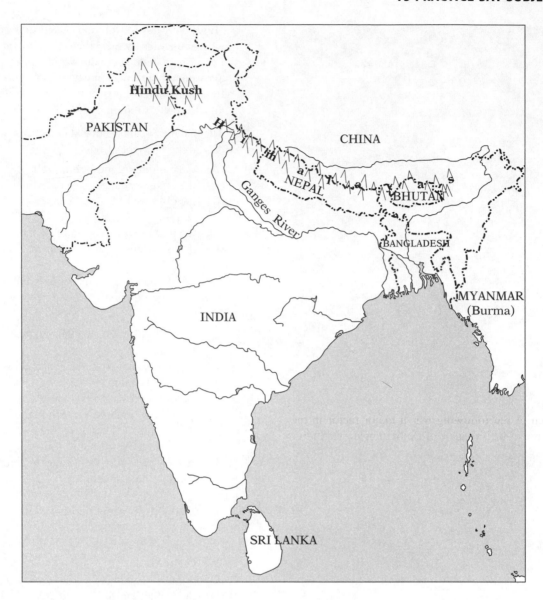

47. The Tokugawa shogunate closed Japan to almost all contact with the outside world primarily in order to

    (A) maintain a favorable balance of trade with China
    (B) avoid involvement in foreign wars
    (C) supervise the nobility closely
    (D) save the expense of maintaining an army and navy
    (E) prevent the spread of Christianity

48. José de San Martín's primary motive for leading a military attack on Chile in 1816 was

    (A) his belief that to secure independence, all Latin American colonies must rebel against Spain
    (B) his desire to become Chile's first democratically elected president
    (C) his private agreement to help Ferdinand VII restore the monarchy in Chile
    (D) his determination to achieve political and social equality for all races and classes
    (E) his ambition to lead the first successful socialist revolution

GO ON TO THE NEXT PAGE

49. Which of the following statements is best supported by the map on page 76?

    (A) The Himalayas have protected India from overland invasion.
    (B) Eastern India is home to more farmers than western India.
    (C) India is subject to annual monsoons.
    (D) The majority of Indians speak Hindi.
    (E) People in India and Bangladesh eat many of the same foods.

50. During the 1950s, friendly relations between China and the Soviet Union were severely strained for all of the following reasons EXCEPT:

    (A) disagreement over the pace of the Communist takeover of China
    (B) disputes over borders
    (C) different views of the ultimate goal of the Chinese revolution
    (D) fundamental ideological differences between leaders
    (E) China's economic dominance over the Soviet Union

51. Which of the following was a major factor in the collapse of the sultanate of Delhi in medieval India?

    (A) the founding of the Sikh religion
    (B) the invasion of Tamerlane
    (C) growing discontent with the caste system
    (D) lack of Hindu military resistance to the enemy
    (E) a series of severe annual floods and famine

    "The waders are of course indispensable. In 2 ½ miles of trench which I waded yesterday there was not one inch of dry ground. There is a mean depth of two feet of water."

    "Water knee deep and up to the waist in places. Rumors of being relieved by the Grand Fleet."

52. The soldiers quoted above are describing infantry combat conditions during

    (A) the War of 1812
    (B) the revolution of 1848
    (C) the Franco-Prussian War
    (D) World War I
    (E) World War II

53. Buddhism originated in which of the following civilizations?

    (A) China
    (B) Korea
    (C) Japan
    (D) Tibet
    (E) India

54. China's "Great Leap Forward" was designed to

    (A) improve the national economy by increasing agricultural and industrial output
    (B) ensure that every child attend school through age 16
    (C) force small farmers to turn their land over to local communes
    (D) guarantee each person employment in a field of his or her choice
    (E) stabilize the population by instituting a one-child-per-family rule

55. Which of the following correctly describes the spreading of the Black Death of 1347?

    (A) from Southwest Asia to Europe
    (B) from the Americas to Europe
    (C) from Spain to South America
    (D) from China to Southwest Asia
    (E) from Europe to Africa

56. At its greatest extent, the Mongol Empire ruled all of the following modern-day nations EXCEPT:

    (A) Turkey
    (B) Russia
    (C) Iran
    (D) China
    (E) India

57. Which of the following was NOT a factor in the political and economic instability that characterized nineteenth-century Mexico?

    (A) a poor transportation system
    (B) a lack of capital to invest in improvements
    (C) constant struggles for power between various factions
    (D) vulnerability to the interference of foreign nations
    (E) lack of experience with a republican form of government

58. The Hittite Empire collapsed in 1200 BC because

    (A) the Hittites had decimated the mine-rich resources of the region
    (B) enemies of the Hittites had joined together to attack the empire
    (C) farmers suffered several years of poor harvests
    (D) the lower classes rose up in a revolution against the emperor
    (E) a devastating earthquake destroyed much of the region

GO ON TO THE NEXT PAGE

59. St. Paul's Cathedral, pictured above, represents which of the following architectural styles?

    (A) Gothic
    (B) Avant-garde
    (C) Neoclassical
    (D) Romanesque
    (E) Baroque

60. The Lateran Treaty of 1929 resulted in which of the following?

    (A) the abdication of the hereditary monarch of Italy
    (B) the outlawing of all political parties that opposed the Fascist Party
    (C) a military alliance between Italy and Germany
    (D) the establishment of Vatican City as a sovereign nation ruled by the Catholic Church
    (E) the founding of the Fascist party in Italy

61. Sale of which of the following enabled Britain to overcome its negative trade balance with China in the 1800s?

    (A) cotton
    (B) silver
    (C) tea
    (D) porcelain
    (E) opium

62. Ethiopia survived as the only Christian state in Africa by means of

    (A) its strong military
    (B) its refusal to trade with its neighbors
    (C) its hereditary monarchy
    (D) its democratic government
    (E) its natural resources

63. The Fujiwara clan lost power over Japan in 1156 as a result of

    (A) civil wars among rival military factions
    (B) frequent abdications by hereditary emperors
    (C) the isolation of the aristocratic clique at the court
    (D) the rise of the samurai class
    (E) the spread of Buddhism through the islands

64. The *Vedas* of ancient India are best described as collections of

    (A) prayers to the gods and goddesses
    (B) biographies of holy men
    (C) comic and erotic tales
    (D) hymns and rituals
    (E) epic poetry

65. All of the following are permanent members of the United Nations Security Council EXCEPT:

    (A) China
    (B) France
    (C) India
    (D) Russia
    (E) United Kingdom

"A prince, and especially a new prince, cannot observe all those things which give men a reputation for virtue, because in order to maintain his state he is often forced to act in defiance of good faith, of charity, of kindness, of religion. And so he should have a flexible disposition, varying as fortune and circumstance dictate. . . . He should not deviate from what is good, if that is possible, but he should know how to do evil, if that is necessary."

66. The political philosophy expressed by the writer of the above paragraph is best characterized as

    (A) Utopian
    (B) Darwinian
    (C) Machiavellian
    (D) Marxist
    (E) Napoleonic

GO ON TO THE NEXT PAGE

67. Which of the following did NOT control Jerusalem at any point in the city's history?

    (A) the British
    (B) the Romans
    (C) the Israelis
    (D) the Persians
    (E) the Greeks

68. This late nineteenth-century print by Mary Cassatt shows the artistic influence of which of the following cultures?

    (A) Japanese
    (B) Indian
    (C) Persian
    (D) Greek
    (E) Egyptian

69. Paper was invented in the first century AD in which of the following civilizations?

    (A) Egyptian
    (B) Sumerian
    (C) Chinese
    (D) Indian
    (E) Aztec

70. The modern Western alphabet is a product of which of the following ancient cultures?

    (A) Phoenician and Greek
    (B) Assyrian and Hebrew
    (C) Byzantine and Roman
    (D) Egyptian and Sumerian
    (E) Minoan and Hittite

71. During the 1600s, the Ching or Manchu dynasty achieved early success in ruling China by

    (A) taking over the government of Korea
    (B) permitting intermarriage between Manchus and Chinese
    (C) continuing the successful policies of the Ming dynasty
    (D) replacing Chinese culture with Manchurian culture
    (E) establishing an absolute ruler on the throne of China for the first time

72. The Egyptian *Book of the Dead* consists of

    (A) lists of the Egyptian gods and goddesses
    (B) writings of the divine pharaohs
    (C) myths and legends
    (D) omens and spells
    (E) biographies of important Egyptians from the past

73. Which of the following was the dominant social class in the Latin American colonies of Spain and Portugal?

    (A) *Creoles*
    (B) *Peninsulares*
    (C) people of mixed native and European ancestry
    (D) people of native ancestry
    (E) people of African descent

GO ON TO THE NEXT PAGE

74. After its defeat in World War II, Japan wrote which of the following unusual provisions into its new constitution?

    (A) The emperor had the divine right to rule Japan.
    (B) Japan would never again send troops into war.
    (C) Only female citizens would have the right to vote in national elections.
    (D) Japan would close its islands to trade from the outside world.
    (E) Cities destroyed by Allied bombing would be not be rebuilt because they were considered cemeteries.

75. Acceptance by everyone of the caste system in ancient India had which of the following effects?

    (A) It protected India against invasion by foreign nations.
    (B) It maintained a stable society on the subcontinent.
    (C) It distributed political power evenly across all the castes.
    (D) It laid the foundations for a social revolution.
    (E) It ensured that everyone in society would be able to read and write.

76. A sharp drop worldwide in the price of which of the following destroyed Brazil's economy during the 1930s?

    (A) coffee
    (B) tin
    (C) diamonds
    (D) stocks
    (E) wheat

77. Which of the following explains how Tilglath Pileser III transformed Assyria into the greatest power in southwest Asia?

    (A) He curbed the power of the nobility.
    (B) He created a permanent imperial army.
    (C) He established Aramaic as a common language.
    (D) He ordered the construction of new roads.
    (E) He ruled the distant provinces through territorial governors.

"An air-raid alert sounded on the first night of the war, the night of June 22–23. It terrified me. I was shaken by the very strangeness of an attack from the air, of murder out of the skies."

78. The diary entry above most likely refers to which of the following?

    (A) the German bombing of Leningrad, 1941
    (B) the Allied bombing of Dresden, 1945
    (C) the American bombing of Hiroshima, 1945
    (D) the German invasion of Austria, 1939
    (E) the Allied invasion of Normandy, 1944

"[He] accomplished great things in a short space of time, and by his acumen and courage surpassed in the magnitude of his achievements all kings whose memory is recorded from the beginning of time. In twelve years he conquered no small part of Europe and practically all of Asia, and so acquired a fabulous reputation like that of the heroes and demi-gods of old."

79. This biographical excerpt describes the deeds of who of the following?

    (A) Cleopatra
    (B) Julius Caesar
    (C) Alexander the Great
    (D) William the Conqueror
    (E) King Arthur of Britain

80. Parthian power declined during the second century AD for all of the following reasons EXCEPT:

    (A) partial Roman takeover of the Red Sea trade route to Eurasia
    (B) fighting in Eurasia making trade along the Silk Road more problematic
    (C) establishment of the Kushan empire on the eastern border
    (D) internal political strife among various factions
    (E) inability to combat the Roman archer and cavalry on the battlefield

GO ON TO THE NEXT PAGE

81. Which of the following best supports the theory that before 500 AD, the ancient Iranian military system was the finest in the world?

    (A) The Iranians conquered Egypt, Syria, Anatolia, and Jerusalem between 612 and 615.
    (B) The king could maintain his position of power only with the consent of the priests and nobles.
    (C) The Arab nations were united by near-universal belief in the religion of Islam.
    (D) The Iranians made a lasting peace with the Byzantine empire.
    (E) The Roman army adopted many aspects of the Iranian military, such as armor, weapons, and techniques.

82. Which of the following invaded Spain in AD 711?

    (A) Muslims
    (B) Egyptians
    (C) French
    (D) British
    (E) Italians

83. This painting is an example of which of the following?

    (A) Post-Impressionism
    (B) Fauvism
    (C) Realism
    (D) Cubism
    (E) Pre-Raphaelitism

84. Which of the following best describes the chief political goal of the Holy Roman Emperor Frederick II?

    (A) to rule the holy city of Jerusalem
    (B) to unite German and Italian lands into one empire
    (C) to persuade the Pope to readmit him into the Church
    (D) to form an alliance with the Plantagenets of Britain
    (E) to defeat the French armies commanded by Joan of Arc

85. Which of the following best describes the major goal of westward expansion under Peter the Great and Catherine the Great of Russia?

    (A) the conversion of millions of eastern Europeans to Orthodox Christianity
    (B) the acquisition of warm-water ports to facilitate international trade
    (C) the dissemination of Russian language and culture throughout the world
    (D) the desire to acquire colonies rich in important natural resources
    (E) the elimination of China as a major rival power in the region

"As a philosophy [socialism] is far superior to capitalism, but as an economic system it does not work. And there is no compromise between the two systems, no middle way. Forty years of experimentation with a planned economy have ended in failure. Socialism is dead."

86. The speaker of the above quotation is most probably referring to which of the following?

    (A) the failure of the Cuban revolution
    (B) the establishment of the People's Republic of China
    (C) the fall of the Berlin Wall
    (D) the Allied victory in World War I
    (E) the rise of Islamic terrorism

GO ON TO THE NEXT PAGE ➡

87. The Opium War exemplifies which of the following effects of the Industrial Revolution?

    (A) Republican governments took every opportunity to spread democracy.
    (B) Large nations were invariably able to over-power and colonize smaller ones.
    (C) Modern weapons enabled industrial nations to subjugate traditional civilizations.
    (D) Social revolutions began to depose absolute monarchs.
    (E) Nations began to rely on diplomatic negotia-tions rather than immediately resorting to force of arms.

88. Muslim settlers in West Africa introduced all of the following Islamic elements to the culture EXCEPT:

    (A) the alphabet
    (B) government
    (C) law
    (D) architecture
    (E) the slave trade

89. Which of the following did NOT participate in the Congress of Vienna (1814–1815)?

    (A) Austria
    (B) Britain
    (C) France
    (D) Prussia
    (E) Russia

90. The primary goal of the reforms undertaken by Peter the Great was

    (A) to make Russia a modern world power
    (B) to defeat his sister Sofia and take control of the throne
    (C) to expand Russian boundaries by taking over eastern European territory
    (D) to form new alliances with nations such as France and Prussia
    (E) to make French the official language of Russia

91. Which of the following cultures had the greatest influence on Mughal Indian culture?

    (A) Turkish and Byzantine
    (B) British and French
    (C) Chinese and Tibetan
    (D) Greek and Roman
    (E) Persian and Hindu

92. Which of the following Italians is NOT correctly paired with his principal field of intellectual/artistic activity?

    (A) Dante . . literature
    (B) Puccini . . music
    (C) Galileo . . physics
    (D) Fellini . . cinema
    (E) Bramante . . sculpture

93. Which of the following best describes the process by which Cuba became a Communist nation?

    (A) The Soviet Union promised support to Castro if he would convert Cuba to Communism.
    (B) Guerrillas led by Castro defeated the Bautista regime, seized power, and quickly established Communist policies.
    (C) The Soviet Union occupied Cuba, finding it an ideal Western military base.
    (D) The last of the Cuban royal family died, leaving an ideal opening for Castro and his Communist followers to seize power.
    (E) Popular free elections held in 1960 brought the Communist Party to power.

94. Which of the following enabled the Ottomans to conquer Constantinople in 1453?

    (A) the military genius of Sulemain the Magnificent
    (B) the chaotic state of politics in the Byzantine empire
    (C) the strength of Islam over Orthodoxy Christianity
    (D) the development of artillery
    (E) the alliance with Syria and Egypt

"In my person alone lies the sovereign power whose very nature is the spirit of counsel, justice and reason. . . . The fullness of [the courts'] authority, which they exercise in my name only, remains permanently vested in me, and its use can never be turned against me. Legislative power is mine alone. . . . My people are one with me, and the rights and interests of the nation . . . are of necessity united with my own and rest entirely in my hands."

95. The speaker of the above describes his role as

    (A) a military dictator
    (B) a revolutionary leader
    (C) an absolute monarch
    (D) an Egyptian pharaoh
    (E) an elected representative

STOP

IF YOU FINISH BEFORE TIME IS CALLED, YOU MAY CHECK YOUR WORK ON THIS TEST ONLY.
DO NOT TURN TO ANY OTHER TEST IN THIS BOOK.

ANSWER KEY

1. E	21. C	41. A	61. E	81. E
2. D	22. A	42. E	62. A	82. A
3. B	23. D	43. A	63. A	83. D
4. B	24. A	44. E	64. D	84. B
5. D	25. B	45. D	65. C	85. B
6. A	26. B	46. A	66. C	86. C
7. A	27. B	47. E	67. E	87. C
8. E	28. D	48. A	68. A	88. E
9. D	29. A	49. A	69. C	89. C
10. A	30. B	50. E	70. A	90. A
11. A	31. D	51. B	71. C	91. E
12. C	32. B	52. D	72. D	92. E
13. E	33. E	53. E	73. B	93. B
14. B	34. A	54. A	74. B	94. D
15. D	35. C	55. A	75. B	95. C
16. C	36. E	56. E	76. A	
17. A	37. D	57. D	77. B	
18. B	38. A	58. B	78. A	
19. C	39. C	59. C	79. C	
20. C	40. D	60. D	80. E	

ANSWERS AND EXPLANATIONS

1. **E** The idea of a League of Nations, or United Nations, would not be seriously discussed for another hundred years.

2. **D** The subject matter, style, and level of deterioration show that the sculpture in question is from the Classical era. It is far more likely that such images would be carved on the walls of a ceremonial temple, not a private house. In fact, these sculptures once decorated the Parthenon in Athens.

3. **B** The reference to rice and the simple image from nature "as a floating cloud" suggest that the writer was from East Asia.

4. **B** It is common sense and common knowledge that some of the greatest scientists and thinkers were born in continental Europe.

5. **D** The subject matter alludes to the Classical world. However, a viewer looking closely would recognize Renaissance Italian garments on some of the figures, and would recall that the celebration of Classical subjects was common during the Renaissance. In addition, the massing of the figures and the use of vanishing-point perspective mark this painting as very definitely from the high Renaissance in Italy. It is in fact by Raphael.

6. **A** The strong military was what allowed Rome to succeed in conquering so many nations and territories. The other factors made the empire able to hold onto its possessions, but it would have gotten nowhere at all without the army.

7. **A** Athens was famous for the silver mines that brought it prosperity and the maritime empire that made it secure.

8. **E** The Byzantine empire was not notable for scientific achievement or the dissemination of technology. Its achievements were notable in religion, government, politics, architecture, artistic styles, and law. The Byzantine empire was also the birthplace of the Cyrillic alphabet that is still used today throughout the Russian Federation.

9. **D** The British and French people had suffered greatly in World War I and resisted any suggestion that any other such war should ever take place.

10. **A** The Olmec civilization lasted from 1500 to 400 BCE; the Maya from AD 200 to 850, and the Aztec from 1325 to 1521.

11. **A** The oldest human remains have been found in Africa, which suggests that the origin of humans lies there.

12. **C** The quotation clearly refers to an event with global implications, and only World War I qualifies among the choices.

13. **E** Diocletian, who reigned from AD 284 to 305, divided the empire into two halves for better administrative control. The eastern half eventually became the Byzantine Empire.

14. **B** Henry had petitioned the Pope for an annulment of his marriage, largely because he lacked a male heir. The Pope refused the petition. Henry thereupon made himself Supreme Head of the Church in England and granted himself his divorce. The Anglican and Catholic religions remain very similar in ritual to this day; Henry's main concern was to get his divorce and remarry so that he might father sons.

15. **D** The Battle of Salamis proved that the Persians could not defeat the Greeks in a naval battle.

16. **C** "Ecumenism" refers to the treatment of all religions as equal.

17. **A** The Indian National Congress was founded in 1885 with the purpose of gradually achieving independence from the British. The Congress was dominated by Hindus, and Muslims did not feel it fairly represented their interests.

18. **B** Bismarck manipulated France into declaring war on Prussia, the strongest German state. The South German princes joined the war as allies of Prussia. Combined, the German states defeated France and were declared a united German nation in 1871.

19. **C** The camel is the only animal that can easily cross vast deserts like the Sahara. It was the camel that made anything like frequent travel, and trade, possible between civilizations on opposite sides of the Sahara.

20. **C** Without the presence of plentiful sources of fresh water, there can be no human civilization. All four of the other choices characterize the civilization, but none was the cause of it.

21. **C** To succeed, a Communist revolution relies on the support of the laboring class, not the middle class; communism means the destruction of the middle class.

22. **A** Ho imagines Vietnam as the tiger and the colonizer France as the elephant. Ho states that Vietnam is smaller, poorer, and weaker than France, but that it has resources that will enable it to hold out against France and eventually defeat her.

23. **D** British and colonial troops defeated the French in Canada. As a result of the war, French gave up all of its claims to colonies on the North American continent.

24. **A** This Shakespearean quotation espouses the principles of Humanism; that man is God's highest creation and should rejoice in his own talents and abilities, using them to their limit.

25. **B** Spain and southwestern North America have similar hot, dry climates. The Anasazi build plain buildings with thick adobe walls, laid out around open plazas; to the Spaniards, Anasazi towns looked just like their *pueblos* back home.

26. **B** The Huns came from the northwest, and their advance was blocked by the placement of the Wall.

27. **B** Muslim Berbers sacked the capital city of Kumbi, which quickly led to Ghana's collapse.

28. **D** The Muslims, concentrated in northwestern India, led the fight for an independent Muslim state of their own.

29. **A** Chinese regions shared the same written language, although pronunciation differed from one region to the next. Thus, the written language served as a unifying force.

30. **B** The style of the art and the clothing and weapons clearly mark this tapestry as medieval. The text is in Latin. The Bayeux Tapestry is world-famous for depicting the Norman conquest of Britain.

31. **D** The Egyptian civilization grew up on the banks of the Nile because that was the only water in the area. The surrounding desert and mountains made it nearly impossible for an invader to approach.

32. **B** Siam, present-day Thailand, was never colonized by a European power.

33. **E** The reference to maize in the time period specified means the Toltecs had to be from the Americas. Maize is native to the Americas and was not cultivated elsewhere until after 1492.

34. **A** Murasaki's *The Tale of Genji*, completed in the early years of the eleventh century, is considered Japan's oldest surviving novel.

35. **C** Constantinople was the Byzantine capital. The Byzantines had the better navy and were able to protect their city.

36. **E** Sierra Leone was founded in 1787. It represented one aspect of the British movement toward abolition.

37. **D** Copernicus first suggested the theory of a solar system, and Brahe and Kepler agreed with this theory, but Galileo was the first to look through a telescope and prove it.

38. **A** Africans traditionally thought of loyalty to a small local tribe, not to a nation with political borders as understood by Westerners.

39. **C** Napoleon conquered virtually all of continental Europe.

40. **D** Once the empire was divided, the two heirs and their followers each wanted to seize the other's half. This division weakened both sides and led to the downfall of the empire.

41. **A** In 1498, Vasco da Gama discovered that by sailing around Africa, he could reach India. Beginning in 1505, Portugal exploited that knowledge to conquer Pacific ports in order to gain control of major trade routes.

42. **E** The woman is English, but she is dressed in a Japanese kimono, holding a Japanese fan, and posed against a Japanese screen. None of these items could have been brought to England before the opening of Japan to foreign trade in the mid-1800s.

43. **A** The most important clue is the comment "given to us by the Allies after the war." "Allies" means the comment must refer to one of the two world wars. The surrounding context of being forbidden to cross a border makes it clear the speaker is referring to the Berlin Wall.

44. **E** In the eleventh century, Europeans did not know of the existence of a Western hemisphere.

45. **D** The Netherlands had colonized in the Pacific, but did not participate in the Four-Power Treaty.

46. **A** The clergy were enormously powerful at this period of Egyptian history. By establishing a state religion, Amenhotep transferred people's feelings of religious loyalty to the state, and thus to himself.

47. **E** The Tokugawa saw the spread of Christianity as a serious threat to traditional Japanese society, and boldly eliminated the threat by closing the borders and by persecuting Japanese Christians.

48. **A** He believed that for one Latin American nation to achieve lasting independence, all had to claim and fight for the same thing.

49. **A** The Himalayas, the world's highest mountain range, were impassable.

50. **E** Communist China had too many domestic economic problems to dominate over any nation on this score.

51. **B** Tamerlane invaded India and sacked Delhi in 1398, delivering the final blow to the collapse of the sultanate. Muslims would go on to dominate Indian culture for some time afterward.

52. **D** World War I is famous for the horrific conditions of trench warfare.

53. **E** Buddhism originated in India and eventually spread throughout the eastern world.

54. **A** The ultimate goal of the "Great Leap Forward" was to improve the economy.

55. **A** Medieval trading ships sailing west carried rats who carried infected fleas. The disease spread rapidly through Europe and within a few years had killed one-third of the population.

56. **E** The Mongols raided northern India on a number of occasions, but India never became part of the Mongol Empire.

57. **D** Vulnerability to invasion was not a factor in creating Mexican instability; it was a result of that instability.

58. **B** Hostility toward the Hittites united their enemies into a force powerful enough to defeat their empire.

59. **C** The dome, the columns, the triangular pediment, and the symmetry of the building are all hallmarks of the Neoclassical style that was fashionable in the early 1800s.

60. **D** By giving the Pope sovereignty over his own tiny nation, Mussolini restored power and dignity to the Church and made it, in effect, the state religion of Italy.

61. **E** The British imported vast amounts of tea from China, but the Chinese did not have an equal interest in importing British products until the British began shipping Indian-grown opium to China.

62. **A** Ethiopia was the strongest military power in east Africa.

63. **A** The Fujiwara had encouraged the growth of the provincial aristocracy. In the short term this had gained them financial support, but in the long term, it gave these landed aristocrats their own resources so that they could build up their own military factions.

64. **D** The *Vedas* are a prominent work of ancient Indian religious literature.

65. **C** The UN was designed in the wake of World War II, and the five most powerful nations on the Security Council are those that were the major Allies in that war: the United States in addition to choices A, B, D, and E.

66. **C** This is, in fact, a quotation from *The Prince* by Machiavelli, a Renaissance Florentine statesman who gave his name to a school of thought advocating pragmatism. The Germans later called this philosophy *Realpolitik*.

67. **E** Jerusalem has been a bone of contention for many centuries, but was never an object of Greek conquest.

68. **A** The subject matter is not Japanese, but the techniques are very strongly influenced by Japanese printmakers. The stylization, the colors, the outlines of the figures, the delicacy of touch, all show Japanese influence.

69. **C** The Chinese had written on silk and bamboo before they invented paper. The invention spread in use to Southwest Asia (the Middle East) in the eighth century, and thence to Europe.

70. **A** The Phoenicians invented a 21-letter alphabet of consonants. The Greeks improved it by adding 5 letters for vowel sounds.

71. **C** The Manchurians had little experience of national politics and decided the safest course was to continue the policies that had worked well for the preceding dynasty.

72. **D** The *Book of the Dead* describes omens and spells.

73. **B** As in all colonial societies, the colonizers established themselves as the ruling class. *Peninsulares* were those born in Europe. *Creoles* were those born in the colonies of exclusively European descent, and because of their birthplace they were considered one rung lower on the social ladder.

74. **B** In the wake of enormous suffering and death after the atomic bombs dropped by the United States, Article 9 of the Japanese constitution states that Japan "will forever renounce war as a sovereign right" and that Japan will not maintain an army, a navy, or an air force, except forces necessary to defend itself. Only since 1991 has Japan sent out a small number of military personnel to play noncombat roles in international peacekeeping missions.

75. **B** The fact that all Indians accepted the caste system meant that they knew their place in society and were content not to start revolutions for the sake of equality. The caste system offered the incentive that a proper person in this life would be raised to a higher form in the next. This contentment with the system meant social stability.

76. **A** The wealth of Brazil came from its agricultural exports, most notably coffee.

77. **B** In order to be a great power, every nation first needs to achieve military superiority.

78. **A** The clue "on the first night of the war" eliminates choices B, C, and E. The German invasion of Austria did not involve bombing.

79. **C** The important clues in the passage are the reference to "twelve years" and the conquest of Europe and Asia. Cleopatra can be eliminated immediately on the basis of the pronoun "he." The excerpt is from a first-century BC biography of Alexander.

80. **E** The opposite of this choice is true; Parthian archers and cavalry were generally superior to their Roman counterparts. The Romans were better at building forts and conducting a siege.

81. **E** The Roman military is justly famed through world history as one of the most successful of all military systems. The fact that they borrowed so heavily from the Iranians indicates that the Iranian system had a great deal to recommend it.

82. **A** Moroccan Muslims invaded Spain, progressing as far as southern France by the year 732. They remained in Spain for centuries, making it an important center of Islamic culture and dominating it politically.

83. **D** This painting by Pablo Picasso shows all the hallmarks of Cubism, which include the geometric forms, the near-monochrome palette, and the attempt to convey the same figure from different points of view simultaneously.

84. **B** Frederick wanted to unite the Holy Roman Empire and the Italian city-states, together with the Holy Land invaded by the Crusades, into one empire. He was unable to do this because, among other reasons, the pope did not support his ambitions.

85. **B** With warm-water ports, Russia could greatly expand her trade with European nations.

86. **C** The clue "forty years" suggests that the person is speaking in the late 1980s, 40 years after the establishment of the Iron Curtain and the major spread of Socialist/Communist states throughout the world. This date shows that he must be referring to the fall of the Berlin Wall as a failure of socialism and a planned economy.

87. **C** The British won the Opium War because the Chinese had no weapons that could compare to British guns. This war showed that a tiny nation like Britain could easily dictate terms to a huge, proud, ancient nation like China simply because it was more technologically advanced.

88. **E** All aspects of Islamic culture pervaded West Africa from the ninth century onward, but Muslims did not introduce the slave trade.

89. **C** The Congress of Vienna was convened in part to decide on the best means of checking the spread of French power under Napoleon.

90. **A** Peter's primary goal was to make Russia a modern European nation, culturally, politically, and socially.

91. **E** Mughal Indian culture combines Hindu, the dominant culture of its own people, and Persian Muslim, the dominant culture of its near neighbor.

92. **E** Bramante was an architect, not a sculptor. He is best known for the renovations to St. Peter's Basilica, completed by Michelangelo.

93. **B** The Cuban Revolution was led by Castro who retuned from exile in Mexico, toppled the Bautista government, and took dictatorial powers for himself. Soon after taking power, he openly embraced Marxism.

94. **D** The fortified walls of Constantinople were no match for Turkish artillery.

95. **C** Although a military dictator also insists on absolute power, he normally phrases it in terms that emphasize the state as the object of highest loyalty. To an absolute monarch, the monarch and the state were the same thing. These words were in fact written by Louis XV of France.

SCORE SHEET

Number of questions correct: _____

Less: 0.25 × number of questions wrong: _____

(Remember that omitted questions are not counted as wrong.)

Raw score: _____

Raw Score	Scaled Score	Raw Score	Scaled Score	Raw Score	Scaled Score	Raw Score	Scaled Score	Raw Score	Scaled Score
95	800	70	710	45	580	20	440	−5	300
94	800	69	710	44	580	19	440	−6	290
93	800	68	700	43	570	18	430	−7	290
92	800	67	700	42	570	17	430	−8	280
91	800	66	690	41	560	16	420	−9	280
80	800	65	690	40	560	15	420	−10	270
89	800	64	680	39	550	14	410	−11	260
88	800	63	680	38	550	13	410	−12	260
87	800	62	670	37	540	12	400	−13	250
86	800	61	670	36	530	11	390	−14	240
85	800	60	660	35	530	10	390	−15	230
84	800	59	660	34	520	9	380	−16	230
83	800	58	650	33	510	8	380	−17	220
82	800	57	650	32	510	7	370	−18	220
81	800	56	640	31	500	6	370	−19	210
80	800	55	630	30	490	5	360	−20	210
79	770	54	630	29	490	4	360	−21	200
78	760	53	620	28	480	3	350	−22	200
77	750	52	620	27	480	2	340	−23	200
76	740	51	610	26	470	1	340	−24	200
75	730	50	610	25	470	0	330		
74	720	49	600	24	460	−1	320		
73	720	48	600	23	460	−2	320		
72	720	47	590	22	450	−3	310		
71	710	46	590	21	450	−4	310		

Note: This is only a sample scoring scale. Scoring scales differ from exam to exam.

THE SAT LITERATURE TEST

All About the SAT Literature Test

What Is the Format of the SAT Literature Test?

The SAT Literature test is a 1-hour exam consisting of 60 multiple-choice questions. It is designed to measure how well you have learned to read and interpret literature.

The test usually includes six to eight literary texts. Each text is followed by a set of six to eight questions based on that text.

According to the College Board, the questions on the test are distributed by genre in approximately the following percentages:

SAT Literature Questions by Genre

Genre	Approximate Percentage of Test
Prose (primarily fiction and essays)	50%
Poetry	50%
Drama	Up to 20%

Usually about half of the literary texts on the test are by authors from the United States, and about half are by authors from Great Britain. However, many tests include at least one text written by an author from another country where English is spoken, such as Ireland, Canada, India, or one of the Caribbean islands.

Also, usually about 60% of the texts on the test are from works written before 1900. Several of these may be from works written before 1700, such as plays by Shakespeare. Only about 40% of the texts on the test are from modern works written since 1900.

The SAT Literature test measures not only how well you understand the subject matter of each text, but also how well you understand specific literary concepts such as theme, genre, tone, and characterization. You may be asked about the structure and organization of a text, or you may be asked about the author's use of narrative voice. You may also be asked about syntax, diction, vocabulary, and the author's use of figurative language, including imagery. You should be familiar with these concepts from your English and Language Arts classes.

What School Background Do I Need for the SAT Literature Test?

For the SAT Literature test, the College Board simply recommends that you have as much experience as possible in reading and carefully analyzing a wide variety of American and English literary works from different historical periods and in different genres. The more texts you have read and closely studied, the better prepared you will be. Note, however, that there is no particular reading list for the test, so you cannot know beforehand which literary works you will encounter on the exam you take.

How Is the SAT Literature Test Scored?

On the SAT Literature test, your "raw score" is calculated as follows: you receive one point for each question you answer correctly, but you lose one-quarter of a point for each question you answer incorrectly. You do not gain or lose any points for questions that you do not answer at all. Your raw score is then converted into a scaled score by a statistical method that takes into account how well you did compared to others who took the same test. Scaled scores range from 200 to 800 points. Your scaled score will be reported to you, your high school, and to the colleges and universities you designate to receive it.

Scoring scales differ slightly from one version of the test to the next. The scoring scale provided after the Literature test in this book is only a sample that will show you your approximate scaled score.

SUCCEEDING ON THE SAT LITERATURE TEST

The best way to get a high score on the SAT Literature test is to be an avid and active reader. You won't be required to have read any specific literary works. Nor will you have to memorize author's names or lists of the books and poems they wrote. Prior familiarity with the passages that appear on the test probably won't affect your score. It will help to be generally familiar with literature of different periods: for example, the style and vocabulary used by writers of the Renaissance and seventeenth and eighteenth centuries is quite different from the style used by modern writers.

It is also best to get into the habit of thinking about what you read. That is what the test will ask you to do. You will have to analyze passages, to identify specific details, and to draw conclusions. You can practice this skill just as you would practice any other. Every time you read a book or a story, ask yourself questions about it as you go. Use homework assignments from English class to help yourself prepare for the test. The more accustomed you are to thinking about what you read, to picking up clues and implications in a text, the stronger position you will be in to do well on the Literature test.

The SAT Literature test will present you with several poems and prose passages to read. They were all originally written in the English language: there are no translations from other languages. In many cases, the poems and passages will be excerpted from longer works; in some cases they will be complete. Each passage will have the date of original publication at the end. You are not expected to identify the authors, or to have read these works before.

Each poem or passage will be followed by a set of approximately six to twelve questions. Sometimes two poems or two passages will be presented as a pair, and questions in the set that follows will refer to both poems or passages. You will have to read the passage or poem and then answer the questions.

The SAT Literature test includes certain types of questions. Below, you will find sample questions and instructions for working through them to arrive at the correct answer. You can try these strategies out on practice tests, and use them on the day when you take the real test.

STRATEGY: Skip difficult poems or passages and return to them later.

The literary works and excerpts that appear on the SAT Literature test were chosen with college-bound high school students in mind. The works were selected on the assumption that they were appropriate for your current reading level. However, everyone brings different knowledge and experience to literature, and everyone has different areas of difficulty. For example, some students who can easily read the most challenging prose selections have trouble understanding poetry, and those who enjoy reading modern literature can not decipher the archaic language and word order of pieces from earlier centuries.

The best way to get a good score on the test is to choose as many correct answers as possible and as few wrong answers. Therefore, it is a smart strategy to read through, or at least glance at, all the passages before you look at any of the questions. Begin with the selection that seems the easiest to understand, and then go back and work on the more challenging selections. You are not required to answer the questions in numerical order; you are free to skip around as much as you like. It's best to concentrate on the easy sections first. This will give you more confidence and help you accumulate a stock of correct answers to build on.

Questions 1–3 refer to the passage below.

The grill-room clock struck eleven with the respectful unobtrusiveness of one whose mission in life is to be ignored. When the flight of time should really have rendered abstinence and migration imperative the lighting apparatus would signal the fact in the usual way.

Clovis approached the supper-table, in the blessed expectancy of one who has dined sketchily and long ago.

"I'm starving," he announced, making an effort to sit down gracefully and read the menu at the same time.

"So I gathered," said his host, "from the fact that you were nearly punctual. I ought to have told you that I'm a Food Reformer. I've ordered two bowls of bread-and-milk and some health biscuits. I hope you don't mind."

Clovis pretended afterwards that he didn't go white above the collar-line for the fraction of a second.

"All the same," he said, "you ought not to joke about such things. There really are such people. I've known people who've met them. To think of all the adorable things there are to eat in the world and then to go through life munching sawdust and being proud of it."

"They're like the Flagellants of the Middle Ages, who went about mortifying themselves."

"They had some excuse," said Clovis. "They did it to save their immortal souls, didn't they? You needn't tell me that a man who doesn't love oysters and asparagus and good wines has got a soul, or a stomach either. He's simply got the instinct for being unhappy highly developed."

(1911)

STRATEGY: Weigh three given options to decide if one, two, or all three are correct.

The SAT Literature test uses a question format you may not have encountered before. Some of the questions will ask you which of three options is correct, then give you five lettered choices that show different combinations of those three options. The important thing to keep in mind is that any one, any two, or all three of the options may be correct.

First, read the three options and decide which is/are correct. Circle those numbers in your test booklet. Then look among the five answer choices to see if there is one that agrees with your answer. If there isn't, then go back and check the numbered options against the original passage.

Example:

1. The author most likely wrote the work from which this passage is taken in order to

> I.   persuade readers to eat health food
> II. entertain readers with an amusing story
> III. inform readers what it's like to be a Food Reformer

  (A) I only
  (B) I and II only
  (C) II only
  (D) II and III only
  (E) III only

Read the question and the three choices. Cross out the choice or choices that do not answer the question correctly. Then look under the lettered choices to see if your answer is among them. That will be the correct answer.

Remember that any one, any two, or all three of the choices may be correct. Do not hesitate to choose any of the lettered answers simply because they contain one, two, or all of the three options.

In this case, choice I is clearly wrong. The writer does not mention any benefits that would accrue to the reader from eating health food. Choice II is correct, because the story is entertaining and amusing. Choice III is wrong because the writer does not dwell on what it's like to be a Food Reformer. He mentions the idea of health food simply in order to create an amusing moment between the host and Clovis.

You have decided that of the three options, only choice II is correct. Therefore, the right answer to the question is C.

STRATEGY: Learn how to answer questions about grammar.

Some of the questions on the SAT Literature test will ask about the part of speech of a specific word in a passage or poem. One type of question will ask you to identify a certain part of speech, such as the main verb, in a specific sentence. In this case, go back to the passage and underline each of the five words given in the answer choices. Then look at the whole sentence to see which word matches the part of speech mentioned in the question.

Example:

2. The main verb in the second sentence in the passage beginning "When the flight of time" (line 2) is

  (A) flight
  (B) should
  (C) would
  (D) rendered
  (E) signal

Go back to the passage and underline the five words. Which one is the main action of the sentence? When you are asked to find a verb, the first thing to do is identify the subject that goes with that verb. This sentence opens with a long independent clause beginning with the word *when* and ending with the word *imperative.* You can, therefore, eliminate choices A and B, which are part of that clause. Examining the rest of the sentence, you can see that the subject is *lighting apparatus.* You know that in most English sentences, the verb follows immediately after the subject. The verb, the action taken by the apparatus, is *would signal. Would* is a helping verb; *signal* is the main verb. Therefore, the correct answer is E.

STRATEGY: Learn how to answer questions about vocabulary.

The SAT Literature test will ask you to choose the correct definition of a word from a passage or poem. The best way to answer such a question is to go back to the passage to find the word, then mentally replace it with each of the five answer choices. The correct answer will be the one that best fits the context of the sentence in the original.

The question may ask about a word you have never seen before. Don't panic. Often, the context in which a word is used will make the meaning clear, or at least will enable you to eliminate two or three obviously wrong answers. You will then have good odds of guessing the correct answer.

Use your knowledge of word parts—prefixes, suffixes, and roots—when asked about unfamiliar vocabulary words. For example, you know that the prefix *uni-* means "one." This would help you define the word *unicycle* if you had never seen it before.

Remember, don't answer a vocabulary question without looking back at the word in the original passage! English has many words that can be used to mean different things depending on the context. *Cleave,* for example, can mean "to cling together" or "to split apart." If you don't look back at the passage, you won't know which is the correct answer.

Example:

3. The word "unobtrusiveness" in the first sentence (line 1) means

     (A) anger
     (B) inconspicuousness
     (C) heartiness
     (D) sullenness
     (E) invisibility

If you know the meaning of *unobtrusiveness,* good, you can answer the question without taking any further time. If not, go back to the passage and circle the word. Try each of the five answer choices in its place. Which one makes the most sense? The context clues are "respectful" and "mission in life is to be ignored." *Anger* and *heartiness* clearly do not fit with the notion of being ignored; you are looking for something that conveys a meaning of quietness, modesty, and keeping a low profile. *Invisibility* is too extreme and does not fit the idea of a clock striking, which is a sound rather than a sight. *Sullenness* goes with the idea of being ignored, but not with being respectful. Choice B, *inconspicuousness,* is a perfect synonym for *unobtrusiveness. Inconspicuous* means "not obvious, apparent, or noticeable." It makes perfect sense in the context and is the correct answer.

Questions 4–5 refer to the poems below.

Strange Meeting

It seemed that out of battle I escaped
Down some profound dull tunnel, long since scooped
Through granites which titanic wars had groined.
Yet also there encumbered sleepers groaned,
Too fast in thought or death to be bestirred.
Then, as I probed them, one sprang up, and stared
With piteous recognition in fixed eyes,
Lifting distressful hands, as if to bless.
And by his smile, I knew that sullen hall—
By his dead smile I knew we stood in Hell.
With a thousand pains that vision's face was grained;
Yet no blood reached there from the upper ground,
And no guns thumped, or down the flues made moan.
"Strange friend," I said, "here is no cause to mourn."
"None," said that other, "save the undone years,
The hopelessness. Whatever hope is yours,
Was my life also; I went hunting wild
After the wildest beauty in the world,
Which lies not calm in eyes, or braided hair,
But mocks the steady running of the hour,
And if it grieves, grieves richlier than here.
For by my glee might many men have laughed,
And of my weeping something had been left,
Which must die now. I mean the truth untold,
The pity of war, the pity war distilled.
Now men will go content with what we spoiled,
Or, discontent, boil bloody, and be spilled.
They will be swift with swiftness of the tigress.
None will break ranks, though nations trek from progress.
Courage was mine, and I had mystery,
Wisdom was mine, and I had mastery:
To miss the march of this retreating world
Into vain citadels that are not walled.
Then, when much blood had clogged their chariot-wheels,
I would go up and wash them from sweet wells
Even with truths that lie too deep for taint.
I would have poured my spirit without stint
But not through wounds; not on the cess of war.
Foreheads of men have bled where no wounds were.
I am the enemy you killed, my friend.
I knew you in this dark: for so you frowned
Yesterday through me as you jabbed and killed.
I parried; but my hands were loath and cold.
Let us sleep now . . ."
(1917)

The Man He Killed

"Had he and I but met
By some old ancient inn,
We should have sat us down to wet
Right many a nipperkin!

"But ranged as infantry,
And staring face to face,
I shot at him as he at me,
And killed him in his place.

"I shot him dead because—
Because he was my foe,
Just so: my foe of course he was;
That's clear enough; although

"He thought he'd 'list, perhaps,
Off-hand like—just as I—
Was out of work—had sold his traps—
No other reason why.

"Yes; quaint and curious war is!
You shoot a fellow down
You'd treat, if met where any bar is,
Or help to half-a-crown."
(1917)

STRATEGY: Learn how to answer a question that refers to two selections that are presented as a pair.

The SAT Literature test will feature one or two paired selections. Normally, they will be of the same type: two poems, or two prose passages. Some of the questions will refer to both selections. Therefore, you will have to check both as you eliminate options in arriving at the correct answer.

Example:

4. Which of the following themes do both poems share?

   (A) the stupidity of having to kill people you have nothing against
   (B) the fear of taking part in a battle
   (C) the pleasure of meeting friends in unexpected places
   (D) the nobility of desertion when war is morally wrong
   (E) the unpredictability of the future

The first thing is to note that the question contains the phrase *both poems*. Therefore, you know you need to find an answer that applies equally well not to just one or the other, but both. Choice B is wrong because neither poem mentions a soldier's fear of battle. Choice C is wrong because neither poem dwells on pleasure in meeting friends; they describe meeting potential friends who are enemies because of circumstances. Choice D is wrong because neither poem suggests that desertion is noble. Choice E is more or less true; both poems suggest that the future brings things one cannot foresee—but it is a vague answer. Choice A is the best answer because both poems deal specifically with this theme.

STRATEGY: If you don't know the answer, make an educated guess.

Most questions on the SAT Literature test will refer you right back to the passage, asking you to draw a conclusion or correctly identify a detail. However, some questions will ask about literary terms, and if you don't know the definitions of those terms, you may have trouble with the question. It is a good idea to study the meaning of literary terms such as *enjambment, sonnet,* and *metaphor* before you take the test.

However, if you come across unfamiliar literary terms on the test, you should still be able to make an educated guess. If five terms are listed as answer choices, you will probably recognize at least one or two of them. You may be able to figure out the meaning of others just by looking at them. For example, the word *simile* looks enough like the word *similar* that you might be able to approximate its meaning for the purposes of answering a multiple-choice question.

Example:

5. The structure of "Strange Meeting" relies on which of the following literary devices?

   (A) exact rhyme
   (B) free verse
   (C) hyperbole
   (D) colloquialisms
   (E) heroic couplets

The first thing to notice is that the question refers to only one of the two poems: in this case, "Strange Meeting." Make sure you look only at that poem as you work out the answer to the question.

This question requires you to know the literary terms used. If you know what four or five of them mean, then this is a gift question for you. If not, then see if you can use the process of elimination to make an educated guess at the correct answer.

It's pretty easy to figure out that "exact rhyme" is a self-explanatory term that refers to words that rhyme precisely, such as *know* and *snow.* A glance at *Strange Meeting* shows you that you can eliminate this term. This poem uses slant rhymes such as *mystery/mastery.* So choice A is wrong. "Free verse" contains a clue to its definition in its name: it means "free of structure," not relying on regular rhyme scheme or meter. Therefore, choice B is wrong: *Strange Meeting* does have a regular rhyme scheme and meter. *Hyperbole* and *colloquialisms* you may have to skip if you don't know their meanings. You can look at the last choice and figure out that a *couplet* is "two rhyming lines," and *heroic* is a certain type of couplet. If you look at *Strange Meeting,* you can see that it is entirely written in rhymed couplets. Therefore, choice E seems to be a very likely answer, and is, in fact, the right answer. Heroic couplets are rhymed couplets in iambic pentameter; you may be familiar with them from Shakespearean plays.

Questions 6–7 refer to the poem below.

That time of year thou may'st in me behold   1
When yellow leaves, or none, or few, do hang
Upon those boughs which shake against the cold,

Bare ruined choirs, where late the sweet birds sang.
In me thou see'st the twilight of such day   5
As after sunset fadeth in the west;
Which by and by black night doth take away,
Death's second self, that seals up all in rest.
In me thou see'st the glowing of such fire,
That on the ashes of his youth doth lie,   10
As the deathbed whereon it must expire,
Consumed with that which it was nourished by.
This thou perceiv'st, which makes thy love more strong.
To love that well which thou must leave ere long.
(1609)

STRATEGY: Learn how to answer quotation questions.

One special kind of question that appears commonly on the SAT Literature test is a question that quotes a specific sentence, line, or phrase in the passage or poem. The best strategy in this case is to read the question, go back to the passage and read the phrase or line in its context, and then look at the answer choices to see which one is best.

Example:

6. "Death's second self" (line 8) refers to

    (A) sleep
    (B) twilight
    (C) night
    (D) old age
    (E) sunset

Look back at line 8 of the poem to find the reference to "Death's second self." Read back a few lines to find the beginning of the sentence. Remember that in poems, sentences can begin at any point; each line is not a sentence. In this case, the sentence begins at line 5, "In me thou see'st." In line 7 you find the phrase "black night," which is what the speaker describes as "Death's second self." The correct answer is choice C.

STRATEGY: Understand archaic word order and usage.

The SAT Literature test will feature one or more selections from the premodern era. For example, this sonnet comes from the English Renaissance of the late 16th–early 17th centuries. At that time, English usage was somewhat different from the modern usage to which you are accustomed. For example, this poem uses a verb tense that we no longer use: the familiar second-person *thou* and the verbs that go with it, ending in -*st*. When questions ask you abut the meaning of words and phrases, you need to consider carefully how they are being used in a selection that dates back to a time before 1800. This is especially true of poetry.

Example:

7. Which of the following best paraphrases the final two lines of the sonnet (lines 13–14)?

 (A) Your love for me is stronger than my love for you.
 (B) Because you can see how old I am, there is no sense in you loving me so much.
 (C) Your love is strong because I am too old for you.
 (D) You are brave to love me when you know that you are bound to lose me to death before long.
 (E) I love you, so I regret that I will die long before you will.

This question asks you to rephrase two lines of a poem in modern language. The best way to do that is to go over those two lines to be sure you understand exactly what they say. You may want to rewrite the lines yourself, then see which answer comes closest to your version. Remember that a paraphrase must include all the same ideas as the original.

This thou perceiv'st, which makes thy love more strong.
To love that well which thou must leave ere long.

You need to know that *ere* means *before* and that *thou perceiv'st* means *you perceive.* You also need to know that *thy* is the possessive form of *thou.* Your version might say:

Your ability to see my old age makes your love more admirable.
It takes great strength to love someone who will soon leave you because he will soon die of old age.

This paraphrase includes all the ideas expressed in the original. Note that you have to read back a little further than line 13 of the sonnet in order to figure out exactly what the speaker means. You can see right away that the speaker does not refer at all to his own feelings toward the person he is addressing; therefore, you can eliminate choices A and E. You can eliminate choice B because the speaker says nothing about the love being unwise. Choice D encompasses the important ideas expressed in the two lines and is the correct answer.

Question 8 refers to the passage below.

When Jane and Elizabeth were alone, the former, who had been cautious in her praise of Mr. Bingley before, expressed to her sister how very much she admired him.

"He is just what a young man ought to be," said she, "sensible, good-humored, lively; and I never saw such happy manners!—so much ease, with such perfect good-breeding!"

"He is also handsome," replied Elizabeth; "which a young man ought likewise to be, if he possibly can. His character is thereby complete."

"I was very much flattered by his asking me to dance a second time. I did not expect such a compliment."

"Did not you? *I* did for you. But that is one great difference between us. Compliments always take *you* by surprise, and *me* never. What could be more natural than his asking you again? He could not help seeing that you were about five times as pretty as every other woman in the room. No thanks to his gallantry for that. Well, he certainly is very agreeable, and I give you leave to like him. You have liked many a stupider person."

"Dear Lizzy!"

"Oh! you are a great deal too apt, you know, to like people in general. You never see a fault in anybody. All the world are good and agreeable in your eyes. I never heard you speak ill of a human being in my life."

"I would not wish to be hasty in censuring anyone; but I always speak what I think."

"I know you do; and it is *that* which makes the wonder. With *your* good sense, to be so honestly blind to the follies and nonsense of others! Affectation of candor is common enough—one meets it everywhere. But to be candid without ostentation or design—to take the good of everybody's character and make it still better, and say nothing of the bad—belongs to you alone."

(1813)

STRATEGY: Pay attention to capitalized words in the questions, such as NOT and EXCEPT.

Make sure you don't carelessly misread a question. Some questions on the SAT Literature test contain the capitalized words NOT, EXCEPT, or LEAST. If you don't notice this word, you will misinterpret the question and choose the wrong answer. The best strategy is to circle this word when you see it in a question. That will help you concentrate on what the question is really asking you to find.

Example:

8. Which of the following does NOT characterize Jane?

   (A) friendliness
   (B) perceptiveness
   (C) pleasantness
   (D) popularity
   (E) modesty

The word NOT tells you that four of the choices should describe Jane accurately, while the other one does not. The one that does not describe her accurately is the correct answer.

Look over the four choices. Anyone who sees the good in others and never comments on the bad is bound to be friendly, popular, and pleasant. Moreover, because *friendly* and *pleasant* mean more or less the same thing, they must both be either wrong or right. Because there is only one right answer to every test question, both must be wrong. Therefore, you can eliminate choices A, C, and D. Elizabeth's statements "Compliments always take you by surprise" and "you were about five times as pretty as any other woman" make it clear that Jane is modest; a pretty woman should not be surprised at a compliment, unless she is unusually modest about her own good looks. This leaves choice B, *perceptiveness*. You know from Elizabeth's comment "so honestly blind to the follies and nonsense of others" that Jane sees the good but not the bad in people. This makes her kind, but not truly perceptive. choice B is the correct answer.

LITERATURE PRACTICE TEST

Treat this practice test as the actual test and complete it in one 60-minute sitting. Use the following answer sheet to fill in your multiple-choice answers. Once you have completed the practice test:

1. Check your answers using the Answer Key.
2. Review the Answers and Explanations.
3. Complete the Score Sheet to see how well you did.

ANSWER SHEET

Tear out this answer sheet and use it to complete the practice test. Determine the BEST answer for each question. Then fill in the appropriate oval.

1. Ⓐ Ⓑ Ⓒ Ⓓ Ⓔ	21. Ⓐ Ⓑ Ⓒ Ⓓ Ⓔ	41. Ⓐ Ⓑ Ⓒ Ⓓ Ⓔ
2. Ⓐ Ⓑ Ⓒ Ⓓ Ⓔ	22. Ⓐ Ⓑ Ⓒ Ⓓ Ⓔ	42. Ⓐ Ⓑ Ⓒ Ⓓ Ⓔ
3. Ⓐ Ⓑ Ⓒ Ⓓ Ⓔ	23. Ⓐ Ⓑ Ⓒ Ⓓ Ⓔ	43. Ⓐ Ⓑ Ⓒ Ⓓ Ⓔ
4. Ⓐ Ⓑ Ⓒ Ⓓ Ⓔ	24. Ⓐ Ⓑ Ⓒ Ⓓ Ⓔ	44. Ⓐ Ⓑ Ⓒ Ⓓ Ⓔ
5. Ⓐ Ⓑ Ⓒ Ⓓ Ⓔ	25. Ⓐ Ⓑ Ⓒ Ⓓ Ⓔ	45. Ⓐ Ⓑ Ⓒ Ⓓ Ⓔ
6. Ⓐ Ⓑ Ⓒ Ⓓ Ⓔ	26. Ⓐ Ⓑ Ⓒ Ⓓ Ⓔ	46. Ⓐ Ⓑ Ⓒ Ⓓ Ⓔ
7. Ⓐ Ⓑ Ⓒ Ⓓ Ⓔ	27. Ⓐ Ⓑ Ⓒ Ⓓ Ⓔ	47. Ⓐ Ⓑ Ⓒ Ⓓ Ⓔ
8. Ⓐ Ⓑ Ⓒ Ⓓ Ⓔ	28. Ⓐ Ⓑ Ⓒ Ⓓ Ⓔ	48. Ⓐ Ⓑ Ⓒ Ⓓ Ⓔ
9. Ⓐ Ⓑ Ⓒ Ⓓ Ⓔ	29. Ⓐ Ⓑ Ⓒ Ⓓ Ⓔ	49. Ⓐ Ⓑ Ⓒ Ⓓ Ⓔ
10. Ⓐ Ⓑ Ⓒ Ⓓ Ⓔ	30. Ⓐ Ⓑ Ⓒ Ⓓ Ⓔ	50. Ⓐ Ⓑ Ⓒ Ⓓ Ⓔ
11. Ⓐ Ⓑ Ⓒ Ⓓ Ⓔ	31. Ⓐ Ⓑ Ⓒ Ⓓ Ⓔ	51. Ⓐ Ⓑ Ⓒ Ⓓ Ⓔ
12. Ⓐ Ⓑ Ⓒ Ⓓ Ⓔ	32. Ⓐ Ⓑ Ⓒ Ⓓ Ⓔ	52. Ⓐ Ⓑ Ⓒ Ⓓ Ⓔ
13. Ⓐ Ⓑ Ⓒ Ⓓ Ⓔ	33. Ⓐ Ⓑ Ⓒ Ⓓ Ⓔ	53. Ⓐ Ⓑ Ⓒ Ⓓ Ⓔ
14. Ⓐ Ⓑ Ⓒ Ⓓ Ⓔ	34. Ⓐ Ⓑ Ⓒ Ⓓ Ⓔ	54. Ⓐ Ⓑ Ⓒ Ⓓ Ⓔ
15. Ⓐ Ⓑ Ⓒ Ⓓ Ⓔ	35. Ⓐ Ⓑ Ⓒ Ⓓ Ⓔ	55. Ⓐ Ⓑ Ⓒ Ⓓ Ⓔ
16. Ⓐ Ⓑ Ⓒ Ⓓ Ⓔ	36. Ⓐ Ⓑ Ⓒ Ⓓ Ⓔ	56. Ⓐ Ⓑ Ⓒ Ⓓ Ⓔ
17. Ⓐ Ⓑ Ⓒ Ⓓ Ⓔ	37. Ⓐ Ⓑ Ⓒ Ⓓ Ⓔ	57. Ⓐ Ⓑ Ⓒ Ⓓ Ⓔ
18. Ⓐ Ⓑ Ⓒ Ⓓ Ⓔ	38. Ⓐ Ⓑ Ⓒ Ⓓ Ⓔ	58. Ⓐ Ⓑ Ⓒ Ⓓ Ⓔ
19. Ⓐ Ⓑ Ⓒ Ⓓ Ⓔ	39. Ⓐ Ⓑ Ⓒ Ⓓ Ⓔ	59. Ⓐ Ⓑ Ⓒ Ⓓ Ⓔ
20. Ⓐ Ⓑ Ⓒ Ⓓ Ⓔ	40. Ⓐ Ⓑ Ⓒ Ⓓ Ⓔ	60. Ⓐ Ⓑ Ⓒ Ⓓ Ⓔ

LITERATURE PRACTICE TEST

Directions: This test consists of selections from literary works and questions on their content, form, and style. After reading each passage or poem, choose the best answer to each question and then fill in the corresponding oval on the answer sheet.

Note: Pay particular attention to the requirements of questions that contain the words NOT, LEAST, or EXCEPT.

Questions 1–9. Read the following poem carefully before you choose your answers.

Loving in truth, and fain in verse my love to show,   1
That she (dear She) might take some pleasure of my pain:
Pleasure might cause her read, reading might make her know,
Knowledge might pity win, and pity grace obtain;
I sought fit words to paint the blackest face of woe,   5
Studying inventions fine, her wits to entertain:
Oft turning others' leaves, to see if thence would flow
Some fresh and fruitful showers upon my sun-burn'd brain.
But words came halting forth, wanting Invention's stay,
Invention, Nature's child, fled step-dame Study's blows,   10
And others' feet still seem'd but strangers in my way.
Thus, great with child to speak, and helpless in my throes,
Biting my truant pen, beating myself for spite—
"Fool," said my Muse to me, "look in thy heart and write."
(circa 1581)

1. "Turning others' leaves . . . fruitful showers" in lines 7–8 refers to

   (A) looking to the beauties of nature for inspiration
   (B) sitting in the shade because the sunlight was too strong
   (C) calling to his muse to help him write about his love
   (D) searching for ideas in the work of other poets
   (E) praying for help when he is unable to think of anything to write

2. Which of the following best describes the speaker's reasoning in lines 1–4?

   (A) If she reads what I write, she may fall in love with me.
   (B) If she feels sorry for me, she will turn away from me in disgust.
   (C) If she reads my poems, she will admire me as a writer.
   (D) As long as I love her, I will be unable to write anything good.
   (E) As long as she loves me, I cannot concentrate on my work.

3. Which of the following does the Muse's response in line 14 imply?

   I.   that the speaker is trying too hard
   II. that if the speaker writes what he feels, he will achieve his goal
   III. that appealing to a Muse will not help a writer out of difficulties

   (A) I only
   (B) I and II only
   (C) I, II, and III
   (D) II only
   (E) II and III only

4. Which of the following best describes the speaker's mood throughout the poem?

   (A) optimistic and energetic
   (B) frustrated and anxious
   (C) discouraged and melancholy
   (D) bitter and jealous
   (E) introspective and pensive

5. The sonnet makes extensive use of which of the following types of figurative language?

   (A) poetry
   (B) metaphor
   (C) simile
   (D) hyperbole
   (E) contrast

GO ON TO THE NEXT PAGE

6. Which of the following does the speaker imply that "She" feels toward him?
   (A) indifference
   (B) love
   (C) anger
   (D) friendship
   (E) warmth

7. Which of the following best describes the relationship between the speaker and the poem's author?
   I.   The speaker and the author are the same person.
   II. The speaker and the author are both poets.
   III. The speaker and the author may or may not be the same person.

   (A) I and II only
   (B) I and III only

(C) II and III only
(D) II only
(E) III only

8. The speaker describes his pen as "truant" (line 13) in order to
   (A) suggest that his muse has abandoned him
   (B) explain that his pen is missing
   (C) blame his faulty tools for his bad writing
   (D) point out that his pen is not nourishing food
   (E) emphasize his inability to write

9. Which of the following elements of this poem does NOT conform to the normal standards for a sonnet?
   (A) the number of lines
   (B) the rhyme scheme
   (C) the subject matter
   (D) the first-person point of view
   (E) the meter

Questions 10–17. Read the following passage carefully before you choose your answers.

The afternoon sun was pouring in at the back windows of Mrs. Farmer's long, uneven parlour, making   1
the dusky room look like a cavern with a fire at one end of it. The furniture was all in its cool, figured
summer cretonnes. The glass flower vases that stood about on little tables caught the sunlight and
twinkled like tiny lamps. Claude had been sitting there for a long while, and he knew he ought to go.
Through the window at his elbow he could see rows of double hollyhocks, the flat leaves of the sprawling   5
catalpa, and the spires of the tangled mint bed, all transparent in the gold-powdered light. They had
talked about everything but the thing he had come to say. As he looked out into the garden he felt that he
would never get it out. There was something in the way the mint bed burned and floated that made one a
fatalist,—afraid to meddle. But after he was far away, he would regret; uncertainty would tease him like a
splinter in his thumb.   10

He rose suddenly and said without apology: "Gladys, I wish I could feel sure you'd never
marry my brother."

She did not reply, but sat in her easy chair, looking up at him with a strange kind of calmness.

"I know all the advantages," he went on hastily, "but they wouldn't make it up to you. That sort of
a—compromise would make you awfully unhappy. I know."   15

"I don't think I shall ever marry Bayliss," Gladys spoke in her usual low, round voice, but her quick
breathing showed he had touched something that hurt. "I suppose I have used him. It gives a school-
teacher a certain prestige if people think she can marry the rich bachelor of the town whenever she
wants to. But I am afraid I won't marry him,—because you are the member of the family I have
always admired."   20

Claude turned away to the window. "A fine lot I've been to admire," he muttered.

"Well, it's true, anyway. It was like that when we went to High School, and it's kept up. Everything
you do always seems exciting to me."

Claude felt a cold perspiration on his forehead. He wished now that he had never come. "But that's it,
Gladys. What *have* I ever done, except make one blunder after another?"   25

She came over to the window and stood beside him. "I don't know; perhaps it's by their blunders that
one gets to know people,—by what they can't do. If you'd been like all the rest, you could have got on
in their way. That was the one thing I couldn't have stood."

GO ON TO THE NEXT PAGE

Claude was frowning out into the flaming garden. He had not heard a word of her reply. "Why didn't you keep me from making a fool of myself?" he asked in a low voice.   30

"I think I tried—once. Anyhow, it's all turning out better than I thought. You didn't get stuck here. You've found your place. You're sailing away. You've just begun."

"And what about you?"

She laughed softly. "Oh, I shall teach in the High School!"

Claude took her hands and they stood looking searchingly at each other in the swimming golden   35
light that made everything transparent. He never knew exactly how he found his hat and made his way out of the house. He was only sure that Gladys did not accompany him to the door. He glanced back once, and saw her head against the bright window.
(1922)

10. Which of the following best explains why Gladys is hurt by Claude's reference to Bayliss?

   (A) She feels guilty for having made use of Bayliss.
   (B) She has already agreed to marry Bayliss.
   (C) She has always wanted to marry Claude.
   (D) She knows that Bayliss doesn't want to marry her.
   (E) She doesn't want to lose face in the town by rejecting Bayliss.

11. Which of the following best describes the tone of the passage?

   (A) rueful
   (B) nostalgic
   (C) matter-of-fact
   (D) gentle
   (E) unhappy

12. Which of the following best describes the relationship between Gladys and Claude?

   (A) They are lovers.
   (B) They are husband and wife.
   (C) They are old friends.
   (D) They are acquaintances.
   (E) They are cousins.

13. Which of the following best explains why Claude turns away from Gladys and wishes "that he had never come" (line 24)?

   (A) Claude regrets having spoken to Gladys about his brother.
   (B) Claude is confused because Gladys has paid him a compliment.
   (C) Claude is embarrassed at Gladys' implication that she would like to marry him.
   (D) Claude is upset because he has made Gladys angry.
   (E) Claude realizes that he loves Gladys, but he does not have the courage to say so.

14. The society in which Claude and Gladys live is best characterized as

   (A) conventional
   (B) wealthy

   (C) dishonest
   (D) artistic
   (E) decadent

15. Which of the following best describes Claude's reason for visiting Gladys?

   (A) to say goodbye before he leaves town
   (B) to urge her not to marry his brother
   (C) to tell her that he loves her
   (D) to ask why she has always admired him
   (E) to ask what she will do after he leaves

16. Claude's hesitation to say "the thing he had come to say" (line 7) adds to the portrayal of his character by

   (A) revealing that he does not concern himself with other people
   (B) proving that he has always been blunt and outspoken
   (C) suggesting that speaking out is against his better judgment
   (D) implying that he is not on comfortable terms with Gladys
   (E) showing that he is sensitive to other people's feelings

17. Which of the following does Gladys imply by saying "If you'd been like all the rest, you could have got on in their way. That was the one thing I couldn't have stood" (lines 27–28)?

   I.   Claude has blundered because he was trying to achieve something extraordinary.

   II.   Gladys has always been in love with Claude.

   III. Gladys admires Claude because he is different from their friends and neighbors.

   (A) I only
   (B) I and II only
   (C) I and III only
   (D) II and III only
   (E) III only

GO ON TO THE NEXT PAGE

Questions 18–23. Read the following excerpt carefully before you choose your answers.

(It is the night before the Battle of Agincourt, which will be fought between the British, led by King Henry V, and the French, led by the Dauphin (crown prince) of France. The British are outnumbered five to one.)

(Enter Erpingham)

Erpingham
My lord, your nobles, jealous of your absence,   1
Seek through your camp to find you.

King Henry V
                        Good old knight,
Collect them all together at my tent:
I'll be before thee.   5

Erpingham
                        I shall do't, my lord.

(Exit)

King Henry V
O God of battles! steel my soldiers' hearts;
Possess them not with fear; take from them now
The sense of reckoning, if the opposed numbers
Pluck their hearts from them. Not to-day, O Lord,   10
O, not to-day, think not upon the fault
My father made in compassing the crown!
I Richard's body have interred anew;
And on it have bestow'd more contrite tears
Than from it issued forced drops of blood: 15
Five hundred poor I have in yearly pay,
Who twice a-day their wither'd hands hold up
Toward heaven, to pardon blood; and I have built
Two chantries, where the sad and solemn priests
Sing still for Richard's soul. More will I do;   20
Though all that I can do is nothing worth,
Since that my penitence comes after all,
Imploring pardon.

(Enter Gloucester)

Gloucester
My liege!

King Henry V
My brother Gloucester's voice? Ay;   25
I know thy errand, I will go with thee:
The day, my friends and all things stay for me.
(1599)

18. Which of the following best paraphrases King Henry's prayer "take from them now. . . . their hearts from them" (lines 8–10)?

   (A) Help my soldiers to be brave even though we are outnumbered.
   (B) Remind my soldiers that there is safety in numbers.

   (C) Reassure my soldiers that you, God of battles, are on our side.
   (D) If my soldiers fear being outnumbered, make them forget how to count.
   (E) Don't let my soldiers desert just because we are outnumbered.

GO ON TO THE NEXT PAGE

19. All of the following support the implication that King Henry's father "compassed" the crown unjustly or illegally (line 12) EXCEPT:

    (A) "think not upon the fault" (line 9)
    (B) "my penitence comes after all" (line 20)
    (C) "forced drops of blood" (line 13)
    (D) "I know thy errand" (line 24)
    (E) "I have built / Two chantries" (lines 16–17)

20. Which of the following explains why King Henry believes that his prayer for his soldiers will not be answered?

    (A) He has a premonition that he will be killed in the battle.
    (B) He has no real hope that his soldiers can win the battle the next day.
    (C) He thinks God will not forgive him for the crimes his father committed.
    (D) He does not believe God has the power to affect the battle's outcome.
    (E) He knows that his attempts to atone for his father's crime are not sincere.

21. In line 7, the verb "steel" means

    (A) take without payment
    (B) fill with courage
    (C) harden against compassion
    (D) remove surgically
    (E) melt in a furnace

22. King Henry speaks at length of his attempts to atone for his father's actions in order to

    (A) explain that his father was not guilty of any crime
    (B) express the distaste and disgust he feels at his father's deeds
    (C) assert his divine right to the crown of England
    (D) insist that Richard was a greater criminal than Henry's own father
    (E) persuade the Lord to help his army win the battle

23. Which of the following best conveys the meaning of the phrase "jealous of your absence" (line 1)?

    (A) worried about your state of mind
    (B) urgently in need of your presence
    (C) angry that you are not present
    (D) bitter over your neglect of them
    (E) wondering where you are

Questions 24–31. Read the following speech carefully before you choose your answers.

Fourscore and seven years ago our fathers brought forth on this continent a new nation, conceived in Liberty, and dedicated to the proposition that all men are created equal.   1

Now we are engaged in a great civil war, testing whether that nation, or any nation so conceived and so dedicated, can long endure. We are met on a great battlefield of that war. We have come to dedicate a portion of that field as a final resting-place for those who here gave their lives that that nation might live. It is   5
altogether fitting and proper that we should do this.

But, in a larger sense, we cannot dedicate—we cannot consecrate—we cannot hallow—this ground. The brave men, living and dead, who struggled here, have consecrated it, far above our poor power to add or detract. The world will little note, nor long remember, what we say here, but it can never forget what they did here.

It is for us the living, rather, to be dedicated here to the unfinished work which they who fought here have   10
thus far so nobly advanced. It is rather for us here to be dedicated to the great task remaining before us—that from these honored dead we take increased devotion to that cause for which they gave the last full measure of devotion—that we here highly resolve that these dead shall not have died in vain—that this nation, under God, shall have a new birth of freedom—and that government of the people, by the people, for the people, shall not perish from the earth.   15
(1863)

24. Which of the following contains the main idea of the speech?

    (A) "all men are created equal" (line 2)
    (B) "we are engaged in a great civil war" (line 3)
    (C) "it can never forget what they did here" (line 9)
    (D) "we cannot hallow this ground" (line 7)
    (E) "these dead shall not have died in vain" (line 13)

25. In the first sentence, the speaker compares the founding of the United States to

    (A) independence
    (B) equality
    (C) war
    (D) childbirth
    (E) slavery

GO ON TO THE NEXT PAGE ▶

26. The final sentence of the speech is characterized mainly by

     (A) parallel structure
     (B) metaphor
     (C) personification
     (D) realism
     (E) allusion

27. Which of the following best describes the tone of the speech?

     (A) triumphant
     (B) solemn
     (C) angry
     (D) vengeful
     (E) victorious

28. In the opening sentence of the third paragraph, the speaker uses the words "consecrate" and "hallow" (line 7) to convey which of the following?

     I.   the sense that the battlefield is a cemetery for the dead soldiers
     II.   the belief that the soldiers' sacrifice of their lives was a holy thing
     III. the belief that he cannot give a speech honoring the dead as they deserve

     (A) I only
     (B) I and II only
     (C) I and III only
     (D) II and III only
     (E) III only

29. The main verb in the first sentence is

     (A) brought forth
     (B) conceived
     (C) dedicated
     (D) proposition
     (E) created

30. Which of the following best paraphrases the sentence "The world will little note . . . what they did here" (line 9)?

     (A) The soldiers' sacrifice of their lives is far more meaningful than a speech in their honor.
     (B) No one will ever forget what the soldiers did on this battleground.
     (C) The world will not pay any attention to the speeches we make today.
     (D) Speeches made during a war are rarely remembered; people remember battles and those who fought.
     (E) Our speeches are forgettable, but their actions are unforgettable.

31. The speaker repeats the word "cannot" (line 7) in order to

     (A) emphasize the failure of the armies to end the war
     (B) emphasize that a speech is an empty gesture compared to the sacrifice of a life
     (C) ensure that his audience will always remember his words
     (D) give himself time to remember what he was going to say next
     (E) remind the audience that the battle is over, but the war continues to be fought

Questions 32–40. Read the following passage carefully before you choose your answers.

Reaching the ground floor they naively avoided the hotel candy counter, descended the wide front staircase, and walking through several corridors found a drugstore in the Grand Central Station. After an intense examination of the perfume counter she made her purchase. Then on some mutual unmentioned impulse they strolled, arm in arm, not in the direction from which they had come, but out into Forty-third Street.   5

The night was alive with thaw; it was so nearly warm that a breeze drifting low along the sidewalk brought to Anthony a vision of an unhoped-for hyacynthine spring. Above in the blue oblong of sky, around them in the caress of the drifting air, the illusion of a new season carried relief from the stiff and breathed-over atmosphere they had left, and for a hushed moment the traffic sounds and the murmur of water flowing in the gutters seemed an illusive and rarefied prolongation of that music to which they   10 had lately danced. When Anthony spoke it was with surety that his words came from something breathless and desirous that the night had conceived in their two hearts.

"Let's take a taxi and ride around a bit!" he suggested, without looking at her.

Oh, Gloria, Gloria!

GO ON TO THE NEXT PAGE

A cab yawned at the curb. As it moved off like a boat on a labyrinthine ocean and lost itself among the inchoate   15
night masses of the great buildings, among the now stilled, now strident, cries and clangings, Anthony put
his arm around the girl, drew her over to him and kissed her damp, childish mouth.

She was silent. She turned her face up to him, pale under the wisps and patches of light that trailed
in like moonshine through a foliage. Her eyes were gleaming ripples in the white lake of her face; the
shadows of her hair bordered the brow with a persuasive unintimate dusk. No love was there, surely;   20
nor the imprint of any love. Her beauty was cool as this damp breeze, as the moist softness of her own lips.
(1920)

32. Which of the following best describes the setting of
    this passage?

    (A) a slum neighborhood
    (B) a large city
    (C) a drugstore in a train station
    (D) a small town
    (E) a hotel bedroom

33. The subject of the last sentence in the fifth para-
    graph is

    (A) it
    (B) buildings
    (C) Anthony
    (D) the girl
    (E) mouth

34. Anthony and Gloria's stroll in the night most likely
    takes place in

    (A) March
    (B) May
    (C) July
    (D) October
    (E) December

35. This passage represents the perspective of which of
    the following characters?

    (A) Anthony
    (B) Gloria
    (C) the cab driver
    (D) the author
    (E) an omniscient narrator

36. Which of the following best describes Gloria's atti-
    tude toward Anthony?

    (A) She loves him.
    (B) She does not understand him.
    (C) She is indifferent to him.
    (D) She is fond of him.
    (E) She is afraid of him.

37. Which of the following best describes the theme of
    the passage?

    (A) the cruelty of indifference toward a lover
    (B) the romance of being alone with one's
        beloved
    (C) the anonymity of public places in a large city
    (D) the miracle of the change in seasons
    (E) the foolishness of young men in love

38. The word "inchoate" (line 15) is most probably

    (A) a noun
    (B) a verb
    (C) an adjective
    (D) an adverb
    (E) a conjunction

39. The writer compares the taxi to "a boat on a
    labyrinthine ocean" (line 15) in order to

    I.   emphasize the isolation and privacy of
          being in the taxi together

    II.   heighten the sense of romance and
          adventure Anthony feels at being alone
          with Gloria

    III. convey to the reader a sense of the vast-
          ness of the city

    (A) I only
    (B) I and II only
    (C) III only
    (D) II and III only
    (E) I, II, and III

40. Anthony probably looks away from Gloria when he
    suggests a taxi ride (line 13) in order to

    (A) conceal from her how much he wants to be
        alone with her
    (B) look up and down the street for an empty taxi
    (C) irritate her with his lack of good manners
    (D) persuade her to return with him to the train
        station
    (E) manipulate her into suggesting some other
        way to pass the time

GO ON TO THE NEXT PAGE

Questions 41–49. **Read the following poems carefully before you choose your answers.**

Ode on a Grecian Urn

Thou still unravish'd bride of quietness,   1
    Thou foster-child of Silence and slow Time,
Sylvan historian, who canst thus express
    A flowery tale more sweetly than our rhyme.
What leaf-fringed legend haunts about thy shape   5
    Of deities or mortals, or of both,
        In Tempe or the dales of Arcady?
    What men or gods are these? What maidens loth?
What mad pursuit? What struggle to escape?
    What pipes and timbrels? What wild ecstasy?   10

Heard melodies are sweet, but those unheard
    Are sweeter; therefore, ye soft pipes, play on;
Not to the sensual ear, but, more endear'd,
    Pipe to the spirit ditties of no tone:
Fair youth, beneath the trees, thou canst not leave   15
    Thy song, nor ever can those trees be bare;
        Bold Lover, never, never canst thou kiss,
Though winning near the goal—yet, do not grieve;
        She cannot fade, though thou hast not thy bliss,
    For ever wilt thou love, and she be fair!   20

Ah, happy, happy boughs! that cannot shed
    Your leaves, nor ever bid the Spring adieu;
And, happy melodist, unwearièd,
    For ever piping songs for ever new;
More happy love! more happy, happy love!   25
    For ever warm and still to be enjoy'd,
        For ever panting, and for ever young;
All breathing human passion far above,
    That leaves a heart high-sorrowful and cloy'd,
        A burning forehead, and a parching tongue.   30

Who are these coming to the sacrifice?
    To what green altar, O mysterious priest,
Lead'st thou that heifer lowing at the skies,
    And all her silken flanks with garlands drest?
What little town by river or sea-shore   35
    Or mountain-built with peaceful citadel,
        Is emptied of its folk, this pious morn?
And, little town, thy streets for evermore
    Will silent be; and not a soul, to tell
        Why thou art desolate, can e'er return.   40

O Attic shape! fair attitude! with brede
    Of marble men and maidens overwrought,
With forest branches and the trodden weed
    Thou, silent form! dost tease us out of thought
As doth eternity: Cold Pastoral!   45
    When old age shall this generation waste,
        Thou shalt remain, in midst of other woe
    Than ours, a friend to man, to whom thou say'st,
'Beauty is truth, truth beauty,—that is all
        Ye know on earth, and all ye need to know.'   50
(1819)

GO ON TO THE NEXT PAGE

I Died for Beauty

I died for Beauty—but was scarce   1
Adjusted in the Tomb
When One who died for Truth, was lain
In an adjoining Room—

He questioned softly "Why I failed"?   5
"For Beauty," I replied—
"And I—for truth—Themself are One—
We Brethren, are," He said—

And so, as Kinsmen, met a Night—
We talked between the Rooms—   10
Until the Moss had reached our lips—
And covered up—our names—
(1862)

41. In "Ode," the word "timbrels" (line 10) most probably means

(A) carts
(B) drums
(C) shepherds
(D) poems
(E) trees

42. The speaker of "Ode" implies that the Grecian urn is "a friend to man" (line 48) in what way?

(A) The decorations on the urn present valuable information about the past.
(B) The characters pictured on the urn tell a universal story of love.
(C) The urn is a useful article to people in all periods of history.
(D) The urn's beauty thrills the beholder and reminds him of what is truly important in life.
(E) The urn will continue to inspire poets as long as it remains whole and unbroken.

43. Which of the following can be used to support this statement in lines 11–12 of "Ode": "Heard melodies are sweet, but those unheard/Are sweeter"?

(A) "Thou still unravish'd bride of quietness" (line 1)
(B) "She cannot fade, though thou hast not thy bliss" (line 19)
(C) "Thy streets forevermore/Will silent be" (lines 38–39)
(D) "When old age shall this generation waste,/Thou shall remain" (lines 46–47)
(E) "Beauty is truth, truth beauty" (line 49)

44. Which of the following is the best paraphrase of lines 3–4 of "Ode"?

(A) A poet can tell a love story better than anyone else.
(B) The decorations on the urn tell a love story better than a poet can tell it.

(C) The urn depicts a love story that takes place in the woods.
(D) A writer of history can tell as wonderful love stories as a poet.
(E) The urn depicts a story that the poet finds flowery and sweet.

45. Lines 11 and 12 of "I Died for Beauty" suggest that the speaker and the "One" in the adjoining room

(A) continued talking for many years
(B) talked throughout the night
(C) talked together until they died
(D) could not talk because they were dead
(E) had nothing to say to one another

46. The "One who died for Truth" in line 3 of "I Died for Beauty" might be which of the following?

    I.   the author of "Ode on a Grecian Urn"
    II. Jesus Christ
    III. the speaker's brother

(A) I only
(B) II only
(C) III only
(D) I and II only
(E) I and III only

47. In "I Died for Beauty," what does the statement "We brethren are" (line 8) suggest?

(A) that lonely people should turn to one another for companionship
(B) that the two characters in the poem loved the same person
(C) that the two characters in the poem died at the same time
(D) that the speaker and the "One" are brothers
(E) that people who believe the same things are kindred spirits

GO ON TO THE NEXT PAGE

48. Lines 11–14 and 31–34 of "Ode" share which of the following literary elements with stanzas 2 and 3 of "I Died for Beauty"?

    (A) meter
    (B) slant rhyme
    (C) rhythm
    (D) hyperbole
    (E) personification

49. The two poems share which of the following themes?

    I. Death is a merciful ending to a disappointing life.
    II. Dying for truth or beauty is worthwhile and noble.
    III. Truth and beauty are stronger than death.

    (A) I only
    (B) II only
    (C) III only
    (D) I and II only
    (E) I and III only

Questions 50–60. Read the following passage carefully before you choose your answers.

She was fast asleep.   1

Gabriel, leaning on his elbow, looked for a few moments unresentfully on her tangled hair and half-open mouth, listening to her deep-drawn breath. So she had had that romance in her life: a man had died for her sake. It hardly pained him now to think how poor a part he, her husband, had played in her life. He watched her while she slept as though he and she had never lived together as man and wife. His curious eyes rested long   5 upon her face and on her hair: and, as he thought of what she must have been then, in that time of her first girlish beauty, a strange friendly pity for her entered his soul. He did not like to say even to himself that her face was no longer beautiful but he knew that it was no longer the face for which Michael Furey had braved death.

Perhaps she had not told him all the story. His eyes moved to the chair over which she had thrown some of her clothes. A petticoat string dangled to the floor. One boot stood upright, its limp upper fallen down: 10 the fellow of it lay upon its side. He wondered at his riot of emotions of an hour before. From what had it proceeded? From his aunt's supper, from his own foolish speech, from the wine and dancing, the merry-making when saying good-night in the hall, the pleasure of the walk along the river in the snow. Poor Aunt Julia! She, too, would soon be a shade with the shade of Patrick Morkan and his horse. He had caught that haggard look upon her face for a moment when she was singing *Arrayed for the Bridal.*   15 Soon, perhaps, he would be sitting in that same drawing-room, dressed in black, his silk hat on his knees. The blinds would be drawn down and Aunt Kate would be sitting beside him, crying and blowing her nose and telling him how Julia had died. He would cast about in his mind for some words that might console her, and would find only lame and useless ones. Yes, yes: that would happen very soon.

The air of the room chilled his shoulders. He stretched himself cautiously along under the sheets and lay   20 down beside his wife. One by one they were all becoming shades. Better pass boldly into that other world, in the full glory of some passion, than fade and wither dismally with age. He thought of how she who lay beside him had locked in her heart for so many years that image of her lover's eyes when he had told her that he did not wish to live.

Generous tears filled Gabriel's eyes. He had never felt like that himself towards any woman but he knew   25 that such a feeling must be love. The tears gathered more thickly in his eyes and in the partial darkness he imagined he saw the form of a young man standing under a dripping tree. Other forms were near. His soul had approached that region where dwell the vast hosts of the dead. He was conscious of, but could not apprehend, their wayward and flickering existence. His own identity was fading out into a grey impalpable world: the solid world itself which these dead had one time reared and lived in was dissolving and dwindling.   30

A few light taps upon the pane made him turn to the window. It had begun to snow again. He watched sleepily the flakes, silver and dark, falling obliquely against the lamplight. The time had come for him to set out on his journey westward. Yes, the newspapers were right: snow was general all over Ireland. It was falling on every part of the dark central plain, on the treeless hills, falling softly upon the Bog of Allen and, farther westward, softly falling into the dark mutinous Shannon waves. It was falling, too, upon every part of the lonely churchyard   35 on the hill where Michael Furey lay buried. It lay thickly drifted on the crooked crosses and headstones, on the spears of the little gate, on the barren thorns. His soul swooned slowly as he heard the snow falling faintly through the universe and faintly falling, like the descent of their last end, upon all the living and the dead.
(1916)

GO ON TO THE NEXT PAGE

50. The word "shade" in line 14 means

    (A) shadow
    (B) ghost
    (C) snowfall
    (D) death
    (E) curtain

51. Which of the following best describes Gabriel's feeling toward his wife in these paragraphs?

    (A) sympathetic
    (B) romantic
    (C) jealous
    (D) angry
    (E) amused

52. Which of the following best describes the tone of the passage?

    (A) merry
    (B) hopeless
    (C) ominous
    (D) resigned
    (E) elegiac

53. What happens to Gabriel in the final paragraph?

    (A) He dies of a broken heart.
    (B) He ponders the meaning of his existence.
    (C) He decides to ask his wife for a divorce.
    (D) He falls asleep while watching the snow fall.
    (E) He resolves to be a better person hereafter.

54. Which of the following literary elements appears in the final sentence?

    (A) rhyme
    (B) alliteration
    (C) hyperbole
    (D) comedy
    (E) allusion

55. The author uses snow throughout the passage to symbolize

    (A) death
    (B) winter
    (C) passion
    (D) sleep
    (E) cold

56. The writer describes Gabriel's tears as "generous" (line 25) in order to

    (A) show that Gabriel's wife has never loved him
    (B) reveal Gabriel's sorrow at the death of his friend Michael Furey
    (C) foreshadow Gabriel's grief over the death of Aunt Julia
    (D) emphasize Gabriel's sympathy with his wife's grief over her loss
    (E) underline Gabriel's bitterness over his wife's deception

57. Gabriel's thoughts and emotions in this passage enable the reader to characterize him as

    (A) intellectual and detached
    (B) credulous and naive
    (C) petty and jealous
    (D) kind and unselfish
    (E) stodgy and dull

58. The sentence beginning "It lay thickly drifted" in the final paragraph (lines 36–37) contains three images that allude to

    (A) the death of Michael Furey
    (B) the poetry of Shakespeare
    (C) the history of Ireland
    (D) the cycle of seasons
    (E) the crucifixion of Jesus

59. Which of the following is the main verb in the second sentence of the passage (line 2)?

    (A) leaning
    (B) looked
    (C) tangled
    (D) open
    (E) drawn

60. Which of the following does the author achieve with the repetition of the word "falling" in the final paragraph?

    I.   lulls the reader to sleep with the repetition
    II. helps the reader visualize the gently-falling snow
    III. emphasizes the warmth of the hotel room

    (A) I only
    (B) I and II only
    (C) II only
    (D) II and III only
    (E) III only

STOP

IF YOU FINISH BEFORE TIME IS CALLED, YOU MAY CHECK YOUR WORK ON THIS TEST ONLY.
DO NOT TURN TO ANY OTHER TEST IN THIS BOOK.

ANSWER KEY

1. D	21. B	41. B
2. A	22. E	42. D
3. B	23. B	43. B
4. B	24. E	44. B
5. B	25. D	45. A
6. A	26. A	46. D
7. C	27. B	47. E
8. E	28. C	48. B
9. E	29. A	49. C
10. A	30. E	50. B
11. D	31. B	51. A
12. C	32. B	52. E
13. C	33. C	53. D
14. A	34. E	54. B
15. B	35. A	55. A
16. E	36. C	56. D
17. C	37. B	57. D
18. D	38. C	58. E
19. D	39. E	59. B
20. C	40. A	60. B

ANSWERS AND EXPLANATIONS

1. **D** The "leaves" in the phrase are pages of books, not leaves on trees. The speaker has been "turning others' leaves," or looking in books of verse by other poets, for inspiration.

2. **A** In effect, the speaker reasons that "She" may read his verses, understand that he loves her, take pity on his suffering, and be kind to him.

3. **B** The speaker has spent the entire sonnet describing how hard he has been trying to write his poem, so I must be correct. II must also be correct because it paraphrases what the Muse actually says in line 14. III cannot be among the answers because the Muse gives the speaker very good advice.

4. **B** The speaker is frustrated by his inability to get his feelings down on paper. He does not mention being jealous of any other man, and his tone cannot be described as bitter, because he keeps trying throughout and because the poem ends on a note of hope.

5. **B** A metaphor is a direct comparison between two unlike things, stating in effect that A is B. The poet uses a great number of metaphors in this sonnet.

6. **A** "She" evidently knows him, but does not know of his love for her. This suggests that they are not friends. They are certainly not lovers. He does not suggest that she is angry at him. It is her indifference that has determined him to try to win her love.

7. **C** I cannot be correct because, with rare exceptions such as Walt Whitman's *Song of Myself*, there is never any proof that a speaker and the poet who created that speaker are one and the same. A speaker in a poem is like a first-person narrator in a novel; he or she is a character like any other character. II is obviously correct. III is obviously correct.

8. **E** By "truant pen," the speaker implies that his pen has metaphorically left him; in other words, that he cannot write. The other four choices either misconstrue his meaning altogether or take it too literally.

9. **E** This sonnet is written in iambic hexameter, which has 6 metric feet per line instead of the usual 5. The other four elements meet the usual standards for a sonnet.

10. **A** Gladys says, "I suppose I have used him." The impression of her character as shown in this passage suggests that she has a conscience and, thus, would feel badly about having used him.

11. **D** The author shows a quiet, gentle regard for her two characters and their situation.

12. **C** They went to high school together, Claude feels free to bring up the very personal topic of Gladys' marriage, and Gladys also speaks very personally to Claude. This makes it clear that they are old friends, not mere acquaintances. Nothing in the passage suggests that they are cousins. Because they talk about Gladys' marriage to someone else, they are neither lovers nor married to each other.

13. **C** In effect, Gladys has said she will not marry Claude's brother because she likes Claude better. This is a strong hint that she would like to marry Claude. Given the date of 1922 and the obviously conventional environment, this is naturally embarrassing for a sensitive person like Claude. (Some students may recognize the passage and know that in fact Claude is already—very unhappily—married, which is further reason for his embarrassment. It is the reason he says a bad marriage "would make you awfully unhappy. I know" and that he once "made a fool of himself.")

14. **A** Claude's hesitation to speak out on a personal matter shows that he respects convention. The phrase "without apology" shows that normally a person would apologize for saying something personal. Gladys' comments about acquiring prestige by being able to "marry the rich bachelor of the town" and "if you'd been like the rest, you could have got on in their way" show that they are surrounded by people who stick to certain social conventions.

15. **B** Claude hesitates to say "the thing he had come to say": this makes it clear that although he does also want to say goodbye before leaving, the real, crucial motive for the visit is to reassure himself that Gladys will not throw her life away by marrying the wrong man.

16. **E** Claude's hesitation indicates that he is a sensitive person. He wants to speak about a very intimate, personal concern that is not really his business, but because he cares deeply for Gladys he nerves himself to be "insensitive" and to speak out.

17. **C** "If you'd been like all the rest" makes it clear Claude is different from them, and Gladys clearly likes this quality about him. Claude himself says that he has always made mistakes; Gladys suggests that a lack of mistakes means a person has not reached after anything difficult to achieve, and therefore has nothing particular to be proud of.

18. **D** "Take from them now their sense of reckoning" means "take away their ability to count." If they can't count, they won't know that they are outnumbered, and they won't be afraid.

19. **D** It is the only one that does not refer to the past crimes or to repentance for them.

20. **C** Henry says "my penitence comes after all," meaning that it is too late to be sorry for the sins of his father. He is afraid his sincere repentance will count for nothing with God, and that, therefore, God will not help the English army in the battle.

21. **B** "Steel my soldier's hearts" means "fill my soldier's hearts with courage." The following line "possess them not with fear" suggests that the presence of courage, not the absence of compassion, is most important to Henry.

22. **E** Henry prays to God to help his side win the battle. To make his case more persuasive, he points out in his prayer that he has tried his best to atone for his father's sins, therefore, those sins should not be counted against him when he and his army are badly outnumbered and need divine assistance.

23. **B** The following line, "seek through the camp to find you" makes it clear that they are not "jealous" in the modern, everyday sense of the word. They simply need him to join them as soon as possible.

24. **E** The most important point of the speech is that those who hear it should do everything they can to ensure that the soldiers did not die in vain. They should take up the soldiers' cause and help to end the war and reunite the nation.

25. **D** The speaker uses the language of childbirth in the phrase our *fathers brought forth a new nation, conceived in liberty.*

26. **A** Parallel structure means using the same grammatical pattern in each clause of a sentence. In this case, parallel elements include: "that we take; that we resolve; that this nation shall have, that government shall not perish" and "of the people, by the people, for the people."

27. **B** The event where this speech takes place is the dedication of a battleground as a cemetery for fallen soldiers. Clearly, a solemn tone is most appropriate for such an occasion.

28. **C** This sentence does not talk about the soldiers having already consecrated the battlefield. That idea appears in the next sentence. Therefore, Choice II is incorrect. The ideas described in Choices I and III are present in this sentence.

29. **A** The subject is *fathers* and the main verb is *brought forth. Conceived* and *dedicated* refer to the nation, which is a direct object; *created* refers to *all men* and appears in a dependent clause. *Proposition* is a noun, not a verb.

30. **E** This paraphrase includes all the information in the sentence itself and echoes its grammatical structure. The other choices convey only parts of the sentence's ideas and information, or change its meaning by their choice of words.

31. **B** The repetition of *we cannot dedicate—we cannot consecrate—we cannot hallow* hammers home the idea that speeches in honor of the dead, although appropriate, are not at all meaningful in comparison to the soldiers' sacrifice of their lives for a cause in which they believed.

32. **B** Even if the reader did not identify New York City from the references to Grand Central Station and Forty-third Street, any city with that many numbered streets must be large. Choice C is wrong because the characters do not remain inside the drugstore. Choice A is wrong because it would not be easy to find a taxi or a major train station in a slum.

33. **C** The sentence begins with a very long adverbial clause that describes when the main actions take place, then it arrives at the main clause. The subject who takes the main actions—*put, drew,* and *kissed*—is Anthony.

34. **E** Because the night's improbably moderate temperature makes Anthony look forward to spring, it must be winter now.

35. **A** "Perspective" refers to the point of view represented in the passage. In this passage, the reader experiences the night and the taxi ride through Anthony's eyes and Anthony's emotions.

36. **C** Anthony describes Gloria as "cool," which she would not be if she were afraid, loving, or affectionate. There is no evidence in the passage that she does not understand Anthony.

37. **B** The passage is all about the romance of being alone with Gloria in the night. Anthony is not foolish in his own eyes; the themes of anonymity and the change of season are only alluded to briefly; and Anthony does not seem to feel that Gloria is cruel to him.

38. **C** The placement of the word in the phrase "the inchoate night masses" clearly indicates that it is an adjective modifying "masses."

39. **E** A boat on an ocean conveys a tremendous sense of privacy, isolation, and adventure. An ocean is huge; to compare the city to an ocean suggests that it, too, is huge.

40. **A** The passage emphasizes that Gloria is indifferent to Anthony, whereas Anthony passionately desires Gloria. Anthony does not want to alienate Gloria, so he tries to "play it cool" by not looking at her, making the suggestion in an offhand manner as if he doesn't really care whether they take a taxi ride or not.

41. **B** The context of "pipes and timbrels" and "melodies" makes it clear that timbrels are, like pipes, musical instruments. In fact, a timbrel is a type of drum.

42. **D** The speaker's main point about the urn throughout the poem is that it is a thing of beauty that far surpasses any beauty in real life and that it is more beautiful that his own poems. Because of its beauty, it inspires everyone who looks at it. Its beauty, shared with the world, makes the world a better place. To the speaker, this is the real importance of being alive; being able to appreciate beauty and recognize its great importance.

43. **B** The speaker believes that the pleasure of the imagination is greater than the pleasure of actual possession, because living things change, whereas works of art endure. Therefore, it is sweeter to imagine a song than to hear one, and sweeter to dream about a lover than to kiss her. A real maiden would "fade"—grow old—but the one pictured on the urn will always be beautiful and young.

44. **B** The "sylvan historian" is the urn itself. The speaker is not asking it a question, but making a statement about it: that it can "express a flowery tale more sweetly than our rhyme."

45. **A** They talk until the moss reaches their lips. This would take a great many years; bodies in tombs normally lie on slabs several feet from the ground and moss grows and spreads slowly.

46. **D** Lines 6–7 of "I Died for Beauty" allude specifically to line 49 of "Ode on a Grecian Urn." (The test notes that the second poem was written many years after the first, thus the allusion may be deliberate rather than coincidental.) Emily Dickinson may very well have intended "I Died for Beauty" as an imaginative meeting between herself and Keats, two poets and thus "brethren" meeting after death. Therefore, Choice I is possible. Choice II is possible because writers often capitalize personal pronouns that refer to God or to Jesus Christ, and it could certainly be argued that Jesus "died for Truth." Choice III is not possible because the line "We Brethren are" is clearly metaphorical, meaning kindred spirits, not literal siblings.

47. **E** The character is making a universal statement that applies to everyone, not just himself and the other character in the poem. He is saying that these two are metaphorically brothers because they died for the same ideal; in the same way, any two people who share an intense emotion or believe passionately in the same cause are spiritually "brethren" or "kinsmen."

48. **B** Slant rhyme (or off rhyme) occurs when poets use approximate rather than exact rhymes. Both poems use this technique in the lines specified. *Unheard/endeared, on/tone, (sacri)fice/skies, priest/drest, replied/said,* and *rooms/names* are all examples of slant rhyme.

49. **C** Both poets stress that beauty and truth endure beyond death. In the first poem, the speaker suggests more than once that although people will age and wither, beautiful works of art and imagination like the urn will endure. In the second poem, the speakers continue to converse about Beauty and Truth long after their bodies have died. Neither poem suggests that death was merciful or noble.

50. **B** This definition of "shade" is no longer common usage, but the context of the passage makes it clear that Gabriel is referring to ghosts.

51. **A** The phrase "a strange friendly pity for her entered his soul" makes it clear that he feels sympathetic rather than any of the other choices.

52. **E** An elegy is a speech made over the dead. Gabriel is pondering the subject of death, of those who have died and those who will soon die, and he thinks of his marriage and his life and being "dead" because they both lack intense emotion. The tenderness Gabriel expresses throughout the passage make "hopeless" and "resigned" inappropriate answers.

53. **D** "His soul swooned slowly" is a poetical, metaphorical way of saying he has fallen asleep. Although writers commonly compare sleep metaphorically to death, it is only a metaphor; Gabriel has not actually died; and although he is moved by his wife's story and shares her grief he is not heartbroken.

54. **B** ". . . soul swooned slowly," "faintly falling," and "falling faintly" are examples of alliteration, series of words beginning with the same sound.

55. **A** Throughout the passage, Gabriel is preoccupied with thoughts of death, of people who have died and people who will die soon, and of the living death of people who feel no intense emotions. Snow and winter are common symbols for death because they represent the "death" or sleep of many plants and animals in the cycle of the seasons.

56. **D** Sympathy and generosity go together better than any of the other choices. Gabriel is described as feeling a strange friendly "pity" for his wife.

57. **D** The writer applies the words "generous" and "friendly" to Gabriel, and makes it clear that he thinks only of his wife's grief as she shares her memories of the boy who died for love of her. Many people would be jealous, petty, or bitter in this situation, but Gabriel is sympathetic.

58. **E** The crooked cross, the spears, and the thorns all allude to the Crucifixion. Jesus was crowned with thorns and nailed to a crooked cross; soldiers poked spears in his side to see if he was dead.

59. **B** The subject is "Gabriel," and the main action he takes is to look at his sleeping wife.

60. **B** Repetition always helps to lull a reader. Gabriel is falling asleep during the last paragraph, and the repetition helps the reader "become" Gabriel as he or she too is lulled. So I is correct. II is also correct because the word repeatedly draws attention to the falling snow, reminding the reader of it and helping the reader to picture it. Choice III is incorrect: to emphasize the warmth of the room, the writer should have repeated some word that referred to the cold of the outdoors, such as the word "snow." The repetition of "falling" does not suggest cold.

SCORE SHEET

Number of questions correct: _____

Less: 0.25 × number of questions wrong: _____

(Remember that omitted questions are not counted as wrong.)

Raw score: _____

Raw Score	Scaled Score	Raw Score	Scaled Score	Raw Score	Scaled Score	Raw Score	Scaled Score	Raw Score	Scaled Score
60	800	44	710	28	560	12	420	−4	260
59	800	43	700	27	550	11	410	−5	250
58	800	42	690	26	540	10	400	−6	240
57	800	41	690	25	530	9	390	−7	230
56	800	40	680	24	520	8	380	−8	220
55	800	39	670	23	510	7	370	−9	210
54	790	38	660	22	500	6	360	−10	200
53	790	37	650	21	500	5	350	−11	200
52	780	36	640	20	490	4	340	−12	200
51	770	35	630	19	490	3	330	−13	200
50	760	34	620	18	480	2	320	−14	200
49	750	33	610	17	470	1	310	−15	200
48	740	32	600	16	460	0	300		
47	740	31	590	15	450	−1	290		
46	730	30	580	14	440	−2	280		
45	720	29	570	13	430	−3	270		

Note: This is only a sample scoring scale. Scoring scales differ from exam to exam.

THE SAT MATH LEVEL 1 TEST

All About the SAT Math Level 1 Test

The Math Level 1 test covers the following topics:

Approximate Breakdown of Topics on the Level 1 Test

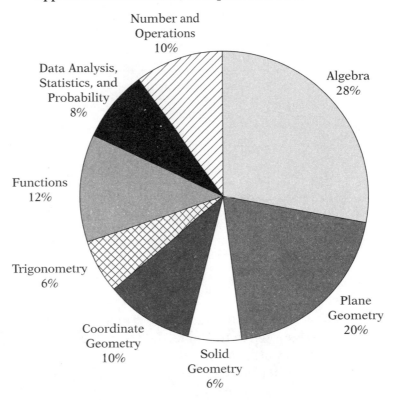

The Math Level 1 test is designed to test a student's math knowledge, ability to apply concepts, and higher-order thinking. Students are not expected to know every topic covered on the test.

When to Take the Test

The Math Level 1 test is recommended for students who have completed 3 years of college-preparatory mathematics. Most students taking the Level 1 test have studied 2 years of algebra and 1 year of geometry. Many students take the math subject tests at the end of their junior year or at the beginning of their senior year.

The Level 1 vs. Level 2 Test

As mentioned, the Math Level 1 test is recommended for students who have completed 3 years of college-preparatory mathematics. The Math Level 2 test is recommended for students who have completed *more than* 3 years of college-preparatory mathematics. Most students taking the Level 2 test have studied 2 years of algebra, 1 year of geometry, and 1 year of precalculus (elementary functions) and/or trigonometry.

Typically, students who have received A or B grades in precalculus and trigonometry elect to take the Level 2 test. If you have taken more than 3 years of high school math and are enrolled in a precalculus or calculus program, don't think that taking the Level 1 test guarantees a higher score. Many of the topics on the Level 1 test will be concepts studied years ago.

Although the topics covered on the two tests overlap somewhat, they differ as shown in the table below. The College Board gives an approximate outline of the mathematics covered on each test as follows:

Topic	Level 1 Test	Level 2 Test
Algebra and Functions	38–42%	48–52%
Plane Euclidean Geometry	18–22%	—
Three-Dimensional Geometry	4–6%	4–6%
Coordinate Geometry	8–12%	10–14%
Trigonometry	6–8%	12–16%
Data Analysis, Statistics, and Probability	6–10%	6–10%
Number and Operations	10–14%	10–14%

Overall, the Level 2 test focuses on more advanced content in each area. As shown in the table, the Level 2 test does not directly cover Plane Euclidean Geometry, although Plane Euclidean Geometry concepts may be applied in other types of questions. Number and Operations was formerly known as Miscellaneous topics.

Scoring

The scoring of the Math Level 1 test is based on a 200- to 800-point scale, similar to that of the math and verbal sections of the SAT I. You receive one point for each correct answer and lose one-quarter of a point for each incorrect answer. You do not lose any points for omitting a question. In addition to your scaled score, your score report shows a percentile ranking indicating the percentage of students scoring below your score. Because there are considerable differences between the Math Level 1 and Level 2 tests, your score on one is not an accurate indicator of your score on the other.

CALCULATOR TIPS

The SAT Math Level 1 test requires the use of a scientific or graphing calculator. The Math Level 1 and Level 2 tests are actually the only Subject Tests for which calculators are allowed. It is not necessary to use a calculator to solve every problem on the test. In fact, there is no advantage to using a calculator for 50–60% of the Level 1 test questions. That means a calculator is helpful for solving approximately 40–50% of the Level 1 test questions.

It is critical to know how and when to use your calculator effectively . . . and how and when NOT to use your calculator. For some problems, using a calculator may actually take longer than solving the problem by hand. Knowing how to operate your calculator properly will affect your test score, so practice using your calculator when completing the practice tests in this book.

The Level 1 test is created with the understanding that most students know how to use a graphing calculator. Although you have a choice of using either a scientific or a graphing calculator, *choose a graphing calculator*. A graphing calculator provides much more functionality (as long as you know how to use it properly!). A graphing calculator is an advantage when solving many problems related to coordinate geometry and functions.

Remember to make sure your calculator is working properly before your test day. Become comfortable with using it and familiar with the common operations. Because calculator policies are ever-changing, refer to www.collegeboard.com for the latest information. According to the College Board, the following types of calculators are NOT allowed on the SAT test:

- Calculators with QWERTY (typewriter-like) keypads
- Calculators that contain electronic dictionaries
- Calculators with paper tape or printers
- Calculators that "talk" or make noise
- Calculators that require an electrical outlet
- Cell-phone calculators
- Pocket organizers or personal digital assistants
- Hand-held minicomputers or laptop computers
- Electronic writing pads or pen-input/stylus-driven devices (such as a Palm Pilot).

There are a few rules to calculator usage on the SAT test. Of course, you may not share your calculator with another student during the test. Doing so may result in dismissal from the test. If your calculator has a large or raised display that can be seen by other test takers, the test supervisor has the right to assign you to an appropriate seat, presumably not in the line of sight of other students. Calculators may not be on your desk during other SAT tests, aside from the Math Level 1 and Level 2 tests. If your calculator malfunctions during the test and you don't have a backup or extra batteries, you can either choose to continue the test without a calculator or choose to cancel your test score.

When choosing what calculator to use for the test, make sure your calculator performs the following functions:

- Squaring a number
- Raising a number to a power other than 2 (usually the {^} button)
- Taking the square root of a number
- Taking the cube root of a number (or, in other words, raising a number to the $\frac{1}{3}$ power)
- Sine, cosine, and tangent
- Sin^{-1}, $\cos^{-1}$, $\tan^{-1}$
- Can be set to degree mode

Also know where the π button and the parentheses buttons are, and understand the difference between the subtraction symbol and the negative sign.

Because programmable calculators are allowed on the SAT II test, some students may frantically program their calculator with commonly used math formulas and facts, such as distance, the quadratic formula, midpoint, slope, circumference, area, volume, surface area, lateral surface area, the trigonometric ratios, trigonometric identities, the Pythagorean Theorem, combinations, permutations, and nth terms of geometric/arithmetic sequences. Of course, if you do not truly understand these math facts and when to use them, you end up wasting significant time scrolling through your calculator searching for them.

On the Day of the Test

- Make sure your calculator works! (Putting new batteries in your calculator will provide you with peace of mind.)
- Bring a backup calculator and extra batteries to the test center.
- Set your calculator to degree mode because all of the angles on the Level 1 test are given in degrees.

MATH LEVEL 1 PRACTICE TEST 1

Treat this practice test as the actual test, and complete it in one 60-minute sitting. Use the following answer sheet to fill in your multiple-choice answers. Once you have completed the practice test:

1. Check your answers using the Answer Key.
2. Review the Answers and Solutions.
3. Fill in the "Diagnose Your Strengths and Weaknesses" sheet and determine areas that require further preparation.

ANSWER SHEET

Tear out this answer sheet and use it to complete the practice test. Determine the BEST answer for each question. Then fill in the appropriate oval.

1. (A) (B) (C) (D) (E)	21. (A) (B) (C) (D) (E)	41. (A) (B) (C) (D) (E)
2. (A) (B) (C) (D) (E)	22. (A) (B) (C) (D) (E)	42. (A) (B) (C) (D) (E)
3. (A) (B) (C) (D) (E)	23. (A) (B) (C) (D) (E)	43. (A) (B) (C) (D) (E)
4. (A) (B) (C) (D) (E)	24. (A) (B) (C) (D) (E)	44. (A) (B) (C) (D) (E)
5. (A) (B) (C) (D) (E)	25. (A) (B) (C) (D) (E)	45. (A) (B) (C) (D) (E)
6. (A) (B) (C) (D) (E)	26. (A) (B) (C) (D) (E)	46. (A) (B) (C) (D) (E)
7. (A) (B) (C) (D) (E)	27. (A) (B) (C) (D) (E)	47. (A) (B) (C) (D) (E)
8. (A) (B) (C) (D) (E)	28. (A) (B) (C) (D) (E)	48. (A) (B) (C) (D) (E)
9. (A) (B) (C) (D) (E)	29. (A) (B) (C) (D) (E)	49. (A) (B) (C) (D) (E)
10. (A) (B) (C) (D) (E)	30. (A) (B) (C) (D) (E)	50. (A) (B) (C) (D) (E)
11. (A) (B) (C) (D) (E)	31. (A) (B) (C) (D) (E)	
12. (A) (B) (C) (D) (E)	32. (A) (B) (C) (D) (E)	
13. (A) (B) (C) (D) (E)	33. (A) (B) (C) (D) (E)	
14. (A) (B) (C) (D) (E)	34. (A) (B) (C) (D) (E)	
15. (A) (B) (C) (D) (E)	35. (A) (B) (C) (D) (E)	
16. (A) (B) (C) (D) (E)	36. (A) (B) (C) (D) (E)	
17. (A) (B) (C) (D) (E)	37. (A) (B) (C) (D) (E)	
18. (A) (B) (C) (D) (E)	38. (A) (B) (C) (D) (E)	
19. (A) (B) (C) (D) (E)	39. (A) (B) (C) (D) (E)	
20. (A) (B) (C) (D) (E)	40. (A) (B) (C) (D) (E)	

MATH LEVEL 1 PRACTICE TEST 1

Directions: Select the BEST answer for each of the 50 multiple-choice questions. If the exact solution is not one of the five choices, select the answer that is the best approximation. Then fill in the appropriate oval on the answer sheet.

1. A calculator will be needed to answer some of the questions on the test. Scientific, programmable, and graphing calculators are permitted. It is up to you to determine when and when not to use your calculator.
2. All angles on the Level 1 test are measured in degrees, not radians. Make sure your calculator is set to degree mode.
3. Figures are drawn as accurately as possible and are intended to help solve some of the test problems. If a figure is not drawn to scale, this will be stated in the problem. All figures lie in a plane unless the problem indicates otherwise.
4. Unless otherwise stated, the domain of a function f is assumed to be the set of real numbers x for which the value of the function, $f(x)$, is a real number.
5. Reference information that may be useful in answering some of the test questions can be found below.

Reference Information	
Right circular cone with radius r and height h:	Volume $= \dfrac{1}{3}\pi r^2 h$
Right circular cone with circumference of base c and slant height ℓ:	Lateral Area $= \dfrac{1}{2}c\ell$
Sphere with radius r:	Volume $= \dfrac{4}{3}\pi r^3$ Surface Area $= 4\pi r^2$
Pyramid with base area B and height h:	Volume $= \dfrac{1}{3}Bh$

GO ON TO THE NEXT PAGE

1. If $a = b^3$ and $b = 4k$, then what is the value of a when $k = -\dfrac{1}{2}$?

   (A) 8
   (B) −8
   (C) 4
   (D) 2
   (E) −2

2. If $\dfrac{3}{8} = \dfrac{1}{4x - 1}$, then $x =$

   (A) $\dfrac{3}{4}$

   (B) $\dfrac{9}{4}$

   (C) 11

   (D) $\dfrac{11}{12}$

   (E) $\dfrac{5}{12}$

3. If $4 - 3(5 - x) = 2(x + 5) - 1$, then $x =$

   (A) −2
   (B) 20
   (C) −15
   (D) 4
   (E) 21

4. $\dfrac{1}{2}$ percent of 50 percent of 1,000 is

   (A) $\dfrac{5}{2}$

   (B) 5
   (C) 0.25
   (D) 25
   (E) 250

5. What is the least positive integer divisible by 2, 6, and 27?

   (A) 108
   (B) 54
   (C) 18
   (D) 324
   (E) 162

USE THIS SPACE AS SCRATCH PAPER

GO ON TO THE NEXT PAGE

6. If the area of a square is 100 cm², then its perimeter is

    (A) 10 cm
    (B) 20 cm
    (C) 40 cm
    (D) 200 cm
    (E) 100 cm

7. The sides of pentagon *ABCDE* in Figure 1 are extended. What is the sum of the measures of the five marked angles?

    (A) 180°
    (B) 270°
    (C) 360°
    (D) 540°
    (E) 720°

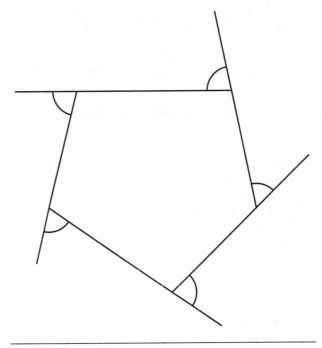

Figure 1

8. What is the *y*-intercept of the line $y - 1 = -\frac{1}{2}(x + 8)$?

    (A) 8
    (B) −4
    (C) −5
    (D) −3
    (E) $-\frac{1}{2}$

9. If $4x - y = 6z + w$, then what does the expression $12 - 4x + y$ equal in terms of z and w?

    (A) $12 - w$
    (B) $12 - 6z$
    (C) $12 + 6z + w$
    (D) $12 - 6z + w$
    (E) $12 - 6z - w$

10. For all x except $x = 9$, $\dfrac{3x^2 - 28x + 9}{9 - x} =$

    (A) $-2x + 28$
    (B) $3x - 1$
    (C) $-3x + 1$
    (D) $3x + 3$
    (E) $3x^2 - 28$

GO ON TO THE NEXT PAGE

11. In Figure 2, if the length of $\overline{DF} = 4x + 2$ and the length of $\overline{EF}$ is $\frac{3}{4}x + 1$, what is the length of $\overline{DE}$?

   (A) $\frac{13}{4}x + 3$

   (B) $\frac{13}{4}x + 1$

   (C) $x + 1$

   (D) $\frac{19}{4}x + 3$

   (E) $3x + 1$

USE THIS SPACE AS SCRATCH PAPER

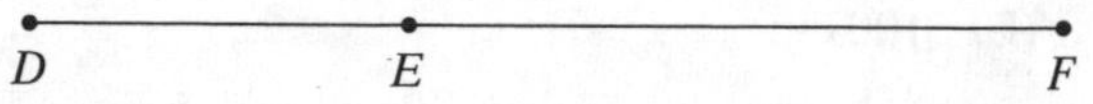

Figure 2

12. What are three consecutive even integers whose sum is 48?

   (A) 12, 14, 16
   (B) 16, 18, 20
   (C) 13, 15, 17
   (D) 15, 16, 17
   (E) 14, 16, 18

13. $\left| |-4| - \left| (-2)^3 \right| \right| =$

   (A) 4
   (B) −4
   (C) 8
   (D) 0
   (E) 2

14. If $x + y = -1$ and $x - y = 6$, then $\frac{x}{y} =$

   (A) $\frac{5}{2}$

   (B) $-\frac{7}{2}$

   (C) $-\frac{5}{7}$

   (D) $-\frac{7}{9}$

   (E) $-\frac{7}{5}$

15. If $f(x) = \frac{16}{x^5}$ and $x \neq 0$, then $f(-2) =$

   (A) $-\frac{1}{2}$

   (B) $\frac{1}{2}$

   (C) $\frac{1}{4}$

   (D) 1
   (E) −1

GO ON TO THE NEXT PAGE

16. How many diagonals can be drawn from one vertex of a 20-gon?
    - (A) 15
    - (B) 16
    - (C) 17
    - (D) 18
    - (E) 170

17. Which of the following lines is perpendicular to the line $y = -3x + 1$?
    - (A) $y = -3x + 4$
    - (B) $y = 3x$
    - (C) $y = \dfrac{1}{3}x + 1$
    - (D) $y = -\dfrac{1}{3}x - 1$
    - (E) $y = -3x - 1$

18. If the point $(-1, 2)$ is on a graph that is symmetric with respect to the y-axis, then which of the following points must also be on the graph?
    - (A) $(1, 2)$
    - (B) $(-1, -2)$
    - (C) $(1, -2)$
    - (D) $(-2, 1)$
    - (E) $(2, -1)$

19. $-9\cos^2 \theta - 9\sin^2 \theta =$
    - (A) 0
    - (B) 1
    - (C) -1
    - (D) 9
    - (E) -9

20. The midpoint of $\overline{AB}$ is $(5, -6)$ and the coordinates of endpoint A are $(-1, 2)$. What are the coordinates of B?
    - (A) $(-7, 10)$
    - (B) $(11, -14)$
    - (C) $(2, -2)$
    - (D) $(-2, 2)$
    - (E) $(-1, 4)$

21. What is the volume of the rectangular pyramid in Figure 3?
    - (A) $\dfrac{3n^2}{2}$
    - (B) $\dfrac{3n^3}{4}$
    - (C) $\dfrac{3n^3}{2}$
    - (D) $\dfrac{n^3}{2}$
    - (E) n^3

USE THIS SPACE AS SCRATCH PAPER

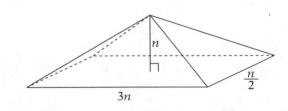

Figure 3

GO ON TO THE NEXT PAGE

22. $2x^3 + 9x^2 + 3x - 4$ divided by $(x + 1) =$

(A) $2x^2 + 11x + 14$
(B) $(2x - 1)(x - 4)$
(C) $2x^2 + 7x + 10$
(D) $2x^2 + 7x - 4$
(E) $2x^3 + 7x^2 - 4x$

23. In the triangle shown in Figure 4, what is the value of c?

(A) $\sqrt{3}$

(B) $3\sqrt{3}$

(C) $6\sqrt{3}$

(D) $9\sqrt{3}$

(E) $9\sqrt{2}$

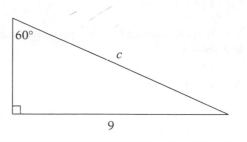

Figure 4

24. Which one of the following is a counterexample to the statement "If two angles are supplementary, then they are right angles?"

(A) If two angles are complementary, then they are not right angles.
(B) If two angles are right angles, then they are supplementary.
(C) If two angles are not supplementary, then they are not right angles.
(D) If two angles are supplementary, then one could measure 100° and one could measure 80°.
(E) If two angles are not right angles, then they are not supplementary.

25. What is the domain of the function $f(x) = \sqrt{36 - x^2}$?

(A) $x \le -6$ or $x \ge 6$
(B) $x \ge \pm 6$
(C) $x \ne \pm 6$
(D) $x \le 6$
(E) $-6 \le x \le 6$

26. What is the maximum value of the function $f(x) = \dfrac{1}{x}$

over the interval $\dfrac{1}{2} \le x \le \dfrac{3}{2}$?

(A) $\dfrac{1}{2}$

(B) $\dfrac{3}{2}$

(C) 2

(D) $\dfrac{2}{3}$

(E) Infinity

GO ON TO THE NEXT PAGE

27. If $a = \dfrac{n+1}{n^4}$ and $b = \dfrac{1-n}{n^4}$, then, for $n \neq 0$, $a - b =$

   (A) $\dfrac{2}{n^4}$

   (B) $\dfrac{2}{n^3}$

   (C) 0

   (D) $2n$

   (E) $\dfrac{2n-2}{n^4}$

28. What is the volume of a sphere whose surface area is 100π square units?

   (A) $\dfrac{100}{3}\pi$ cubic units or units^3

   (B) $\dfrac{500}{3}\pi$ units^3

   (C) 160π units^3

   (D) $\dfrac{375}{4}\pi$ units^3

   (E) 520 units^3

29. What is the circumference of a circle whose area is 64π cm^2?

   (A) 16
   (B) 8π
   (C) 8
   (D) 128π
   (E) 16π

30. Which of the following is the solution of $|2x - 4| < 1$?

   (A) $\dfrac{3}{2} < x < \dfrac{5}{2}$

   (B) $x < \dfrac{5}{2}$

   (C) $x < \dfrac{3}{2}$ or $x > \dfrac{5}{2}$

   (D) $x > 0$

   (E) $x \leq \dfrac{3}{2}$ or $x \geq \dfrac{5}{2}$

31. Which of the following is the equation of a circle with center $(-1, 7)$ and a radius of length 3?

   (A) $(x + 1)^2 - (y + 7)^2 = 9$
   (B) $(x + 1)^2 + (y - 7)^2 = 3$
   (C) $(x - 1)^2 + (y + 7)^2 = 3$
   (D) $(x + 1)^2 + (y - 7)^2 = 9$
   (E) $(x - 1)^2 + (y + 7)^2 = 9$

GO ON TO THE NEXT PAGE

32. An equation of the line parallel to $8x - 2y = 5$ and containing the point $(-2, 2)$ is

    (A) $y - 2 = 4(x - 2)$

    (B) $y = 4x + \dfrac{5}{2}$

    (C) $\bar{y} = 4x - \dfrac{5}{2}$

    (D) $y + 2 = 4(x - 2)$

    (E) $y = 4x + 10$

33. If the letters of the word PROBLEMS are written on cards and put in a hat, what is the probability of randomly drawing either "E" or "S"?

    (A) $\dfrac{1}{8}$

    (B) $\dfrac{1}{56}$

    (C) $\dfrac{1}{4}$

    (D) $\dfrac{1}{64}$

    (E) $\dfrac{1}{16}$

34. If $\tan 10° = \cot \theta$, then $\theta =$

    (A) $10°$

    (B) $80°$

    (C) $70°$

    (D) $-10°$

    (E) $90°$

35. In circle O in Figure 5, $\overline{OE} = 3$, $\overline{OF} = 2$, and $\overline{OG} = 4$. Which of the following lists the three chords in order from longest to shortest?

    (A) OG, OE, OF

    (B) DF, CG, BE

    (C) BC, AB, DC

    (D) DC, AB, BC

    (E) DC, BC, AB

36. If $\cos (45 + 2x)° = \sin (3x)°$, then $x =$

    (A) $18°$

    (B) $27°$

    (C) $45°$

    (D) $22.5°$

    (E) $9°$

USE THIS SPACE AS SCRATCH PAPER

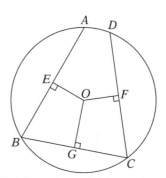

Figure 5

GO ON TO THE NEXT PAGE

37. If $2^3 (2^{3n})(2) = \dfrac{1}{4}$, then $n =$

    (A) $-\dfrac{5}{3}$

    (B) -2

    (C) $-\dfrac{2}{9}$

    (D) $-\dfrac{2}{3}$

    (E) $-\dfrac{1}{3}$

USE THIS SPACE AS SCRATCH PAPER

38. If $f(x) = \dfrac{3}{2}x + \sqrt{x}$, then $f[f(4)] =$

    (A) $12 + 2\sqrt{2}$

    (B) 20

    (C) $14\sqrt{2}$

    (D) 8

    (E) 16

39. The operation ♠ is defined for all real numbers a and b as $a ♠ b = b^{2a}$. If $n ♠ 5 = 125$, then $n =$

    (A) 1

    (B) 2

    (C) 3

    (D) $\dfrac{3}{2}$

    (E) $\dfrac{1}{2}$

40. How many common tangents can be drawn to the two circles in Figure 6?

    (A) 0

    (B) 1

    (C) 2

    (D) 3

    (E) 4

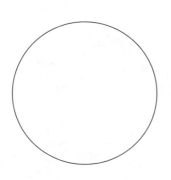
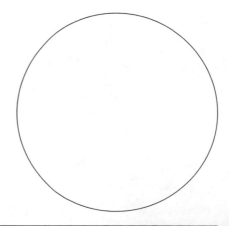

Figure 6

GO ON TO THE NEXT PAGE

41. The boys' basketball team scored an average of 54 points per game in their first 5 games of the season. The girls' basketball team scored an average of 59 points per game in their first 6 games. What was the average of points scored in all 11 games?

    (A) 56.5
    (B) 56.7
    (C) 56.0
    (D) 57.1
    (E) 62.4

42. The rectangle in Figure 7 is rotated about side $\overline{WZ}$. What is the volume of the resulting solid?

    (A) 432
    (B) 108π
    (C) 432π
    (D) 72π
    (E) 330

43. If $i = \sqrt{-1}$, then all of the following expressions are equivalent EXCEPT

    (A) i^4
    (B) $(i^4)^4$
    (C) i^8
    (D) i^{20}
    (E) $i^4 + i^4$

44. For $x \neq -1$ and $x \neq \dfrac{1}{3}$, if $f(x) = 1 - 3x$ and $g(x) = 3x^2 + 2x - 1$, then $\left(\dfrac{f}{g}\right)(x) =$

    (A) $\dfrac{1}{3}x^2 - \dfrac{3}{2}x$
    (B) $\dfrac{-1}{x+1}$
    (C) $\dfrac{1}{x+1}$
    (D) $\dfrac{-1}{x-1}$
    (E) $3x^2 + 5x - 2$

45. If $\sin x = \dfrac{7}{25}$, then $\tan x =$

    (A) $\dfrac{7}{20}$
    (B) $\dfrac{24}{25}$
    (C) $\dfrac{7}{24}$
    (D) $\dfrac{24}{7}$
    (E) $\dfrac{8}{24}$

USE THIS SPACE AS SCRATCH PAPER

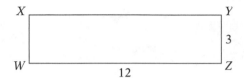

Figure 7

GO ON TO THE NEXT PAGE

46. Kate needs to complete 5 more courses—calculus, English, French, computer science, and history—to graduate from high school. She plans to schedule the courses during the first 5 periods of the school day, and all 5 courses are offered during each of the 5 periods. How many different schedules are possible?

    (A) 25
    (B) 24
    (C) 240
    (D) 120
    (E) 60

47. If the pattern of the terms $3\sqrt{3}$, 27, $81\sqrt{3}$, ... continues, which of the following would be the sixth term of the sequence?

    (A) $\left(3\sqrt{3}\right)^6$

    (B) $\left(\sqrt{3}\right)^6$

    (C) 3^6

    (D) $\left(3\sqrt{3}\right)^5$

    (E) 3^7

48. The quotient from dividing the sum of the measures of the interior angles of a regular polygon by the number of its sides is 157.5°. How many sides does the polygon have?

    (A) 14
    (B) 15
    (C) 16
    (D) 17
    (E) 18

49. What is the value of k if
$$\frac{1}{(x-2)(x+4)} = \frac{h}{(x-2)} + \frac{k}{(x+4)}?$$

    (A) 2
    (B) –4
    (C) $-\dfrac{1}{6}$
    (D) $\dfrac{1}{6}$
    (E) –2

50. What is the perimeter of the regular hexagon shown in Figure 8 if the apothem, XO, measures $2\sqrt{3}$ units?

    (A) 12
    (B) $12\sqrt{3}$
    (C) 24
    (D) $24\sqrt{3}$
    (E) 36

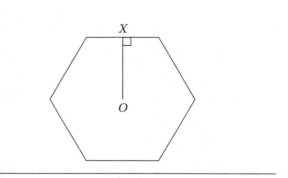

Figure 8

S T O P

IF YOU FINISH BEFORE TIME IS CALLED, YOU MAY CHECK YOUR WORK ON THIS TEST ONLY.
DO NOT TURN TO ANY OTHER TEST IN THIS BOOK.

ANSWER KEY

1. B	11. B	21. D	31. D	41. B
2. D	12. E	22. D	32. E	42. B
3. B	13. A	23. C	33. C	43. E
4. A	14. C	24. D	34. B	44. B
5. B	15. A	25. E	35. D	45. C
6. C	16. C	26. C	36. E	46. D
7. C	17. C	27. B	37. B	47. A
8. D	18. A	28. B	38. A	48. C
9. E	19. E	29. E	39. D	49. C
10. C	20. B	30. A	40. E	50. C

ANSWERS AND SOLUTIONS

1. **B** When $k = -\dfrac{1}{2}$, $b = 4\left(-\dfrac{1}{2}\right) = -2$.

   $a = (-2)^3 = -8$

2. **D**

   $\dfrac{3}{8} = \dfrac{1}{4x - 1}$

   $3(4x - 1) = 8$

   $12x - 3 = 8$

   $12x = 11$

   $x = \dfrac{11}{12}$

3. **B**

   $4 - 3(5 - x) = 2(x + 5) - 1$

   $4 - 15 + 3x = 2x + 10 - 1$

   $3x - 11 = 2x + 9$

   $x = 9 + 11 = 20$

4. **A**

   $\dfrac{1}{2}\%$ of 50% of $1{,}000 = \dfrac{\frac{1}{2}}{100}\left(\dfrac{50}{100}\right)(1{,}000)$

   $= \dfrac{\frac{1}{2}}{100}(500)$

   $= \dfrac{1}{2}(5)$

   $= \dfrac{5}{2}$

5. **B** Take the prime factorization of each of the three numbers.

   2 is prime.

   $6 = 2(3)$

   $27 = 3^3$

   The least integer divisible by all three numbers equals $2(3^3) = 2(27) = 54$.

6. **C** The area of a square is given by the formula $A = s^2$ where s = the length of its side.

$$100 = s^2$$
$$s = 10$$

The square's perimeter is $4(10) = 40$ cm.

7. **C** The five marked angles are the five exterior angles of pentagon *ABCDE*. The sum of the exterior angles of any polygon is $360°$, so C is the correct answer.

8. **D** Rewrite the equation of the line in slope-intercept form, $y = mx + b$ where b is the y-intercept.

$$y - 1 = -\frac{1}{2}(x + 8)$$
$$y - 1 = -\frac{1}{2}x - 4$$
$$y = -\frac{1}{2}x - 3$$

The y-intercept is -3.

9. **E**

$$12 - 4x + y = 12 - (4x - y)$$
$$= 12 - (6z + w)$$
$$= 12 - 6z - w$$

10. **C**

$$\frac{3x^2 - 28x + 9}{9 - x}$$
$$= \frac{(3x - 1)(x - 9)}{-(x - 9)}$$
$$= -(3x - 1) = -3x + 1$$

11. **B**

$$DE = DF - EF$$
$$DE = 4x + 2 - \left(\frac{3}{4}x + 1\right)$$
$$DE = \frac{13}{4}x + 1$$

12. **E** Let x = the first even integer, $x + 2$ = the second even integer, and $x + 4$ = the third.

$$x + x + 2 + x + 4 = 48$$
$$3x + 6 = 48$$
$$3x = 42$$
$$x = 14$$

If 14 is the first even integer, 16 and 18 are the other two.

13. **A**

$|-4| = 4$ and $|(-2)^3| = |-8| = 8$, so the given expression becomes

$$\left| |-4| - |(-2)^3| \right| = |4 - 8| = |-4| = 4$$

14. **C** Set up a system and use the linear combination method to solve for x.

$$\begin{array}{r} x + y = -1 \\ + \; x - y = 6 \\ \hline 2x \quad\;\; = 5 \end{array}$$

$$x = \frac{5}{2}$$

Since $x + y = -1$, $\frac{5}{2} + y = -1$, so $y = -\frac{7}{2}$.

$$\frac{x}{y} = \frac{\frac{5}{2}}{-\frac{7}{2}} = -\frac{5}{7}$$

15. **A**

Since $f(x) = \frac{16}{x^5}$,

$$f(-2) = \frac{16}{(-2)^5} = \frac{16}{(-32)} = -\frac{1}{2}$$

16. **C** $n - 3$ diagonals can be drawn from *one* vertex of any polygon, assuming n = the number of sides of the polygon. $20 - 3 = 17$ diagonals.

17. **C** Perpendicular lines have slopes that are negative reciprocals. The slope of the given lines is $m = -3$. The opposite reciprocal of -3 is $\frac{1}{3}$, and answer C is the only answer in which $m = \frac{1}{3}$.

18. **A** If (a, b) is a point on a graph symmetric with respect to the y-axis, then $(-a, b)$ is also on the graph. $(1, 2)$ is the reflection of the point $(-1, 2)$ over the y-axis.

19. **E**

$$-9\cos^2\theta - 9\sin^2\theta$$
$$= -9(\cos^2\theta + \sin^2\theta)$$
$$= -9(1) = -9$$

20. **B** Let point B have coordinates (x, y). Since you know the coordinates of the midpoint, use the midpoint formula to solve for x and y.

$$\frac{-1+x}{2} = 5 \qquad \frac{2+y}{2} = -6$$
$$-1+x = 10 \qquad 2+y = -12$$
$$x = 11 \qquad y = -14$$

21. **D**

$V = \frac{1}{3}Bh$, where B is the area of the base and h is the height.

$$V = \frac{1}{3}(3n)\left(\frac{n}{2}\right)(n)$$
$$= \frac{n^3}{2}$$

22. **D** $2x^3 + 9x^2 + 3x - 4$ divided by $(x + 1)$ can be simplified using either long division or synthetic division.

$$-1\,\underline{|\,2\quad 9\quad 3\quad -4}$$
$$\,2\quad 7\quad -4\quad 0$$

The remainder is zero. -4 is the constant term. 7 is the coefficient of the first-degree term, and 2 is the coefficient of the second-degree term. The quotient is

$$2x^2 + 7x - 4$$

23. **C** The triangle is a 30°-60°-90° special right triangle. Since the side opposite the 60° angle measures 9, the side opposite the 30° angle measures:

$$\frac{9}{\sqrt{3}} = \frac{9\sqrt{3}}{3} = 3\sqrt{3}$$

The side opposite the 90° angle, c, is, therefore, $2\left(3\sqrt{3}\right)$ or $6\sqrt{3}$ units.

24. **D** A counterexample is an example that proves a statement to be false. Answer D shows one example where angles are supplementary but are not right angles, since one measures 100°, and the other measures 80°.

25. **E** The radicand must be greater than or equal to zero, so

$$36 - x^2 \geq 0$$
$$-x^2 \geq -36$$
$$x^2 \leq 36$$
$$-6 \leq x \leq 6$$

26. **C** The graph of the function $f(x) = \frac{1}{x}$ has asymptotes of the y- and x-axes. As x approaches zero, the value of the function approaches infinity. Since the domain is restricted to the interval $\frac{1}{2} \leq x \leq \frac{3}{2}$, the maximum value of the function occurs when $x = \frac{1}{2}$.

$$f(x) = \frac{1}{\frac{1}{2}} = 2$$

27. **B**

$$a - b = \frac{n+1}{n^4} - \frac{1-n}{n^4}$$
$$= \frac{(n+1-1+n)}{n^4}$$
$$= \frac{2n}{n^4}$$
$$= \frac{2}{n^3}$$

28. **B** The formula for the surface area of a sphere is $SA = 4\pi r^2$.

$$100\pi = 4\pi r^2$$
$$25 = r^2$$
$$5 = r$$

The volume is, therefore, $\frac{4}{3}\pi r^3 = \frac{4}{3}\pi(5)^3 = \frac{4}{3}\pi(125)$
$$= \frac{500}{3}\pi.$$

29. **E**

$$A = \pi r^2$$

$$64\pi = \pi r^2$$

$$r = 8$$

The circumference of a circle is given by the formula $C = 2\pi r$, so $C = 2\pi(8) = 16\pi$.

30. **A**

$$|2x - 4| < 1$$

$$= -1 < 2x - 4 < 1$$

$$= 3 < 2x < 5$$

$$= \frac{3}{2} < x < \frac{5}{2}$$

31. **D** The general equation of a circle is

$(x - h)^2 + (y - k)^2 = r^2$ where (h, k) is the center and r is the length of the radius. The equation of a circle with center $(-1, 7)$ and a radius of length 3 is

$$(x - -1)^2 + (y - 7)^2 = 3^2$$

$$(x + 1)^2 + (y - 7)^2 = 9$$

32. **E** Write the equation of the line $8x - 2y = 5$ in slope-intercept form to determine its slope.

$$-2y = -8x + 5$$

$$y = 4x - \frac{5}{2}$$

$$m = 4$$

The equation of the line parallel to it and passing through the point $(-2, 2)$ is

$$y - 2 = 4(x - -2)$$

$$y - 2 = 4x + 8$$

$$y = 4x + 10$$

33. **C** Drawing either "E" or "S" are mutually exclusive events. The probability of drawing an "E" is $\frac{1}{8}$ and the probability of drawing "S" is $\frac{1}{8}$. The probability of drawing either "E" or "S" is

$$\frac{1}{8} + \frac{1}{8} = \frac{2}{8} = \frac{1}{4}$$

34. **B**

$$\tan 10° = \cot (90 - 10)°$$

$$\tan 10° = \cot 80°$$

$$\theta = 80°$$

35. **D** Recall that a chord is a segment that connects two points on a circle. The longer the chord, the closer it is to the center of the circle. The lengths of $\overline{OE}$, $\overline{OF}$, and $\overline{OG}$ are the distance the three chords are from the center O since the segments are the perpendiculars from point O to each chord. $\overline{OF}$ is the smallest length, so $\overline{DC}$ is the longest chord. $\overline{OE}$ is the middle length, so $\overline{AB}$ is the next to longest chord. $\overline{OG}$ is the largest length, so $\overline{BC}$ is the shortest chord.

36. **E** Since $\cos x = \sin (90 - x)$, you know

$$\cos (45 + 2x) = \sin [90 - (45 + 2x)]$$

$$90 - (45 + 2x) = 3x$$

$$45 - 2x = 3x$$

$$45 = 5x$$

$$x = 9°$$

37. **B**

$$2^3(2^{3n})(2) = \frac{1}{4}$$

$$2^{3 + 3n + 1} = 2^{-2}$$

$$3n + 4 = -2$$

$$3n = -6$$

$$n = -2$$

38. **A**

Since $f(x) = \frac{3}{2}x + \sqrt{x}$,

$$f(4) = \frac{3}{2}(4) + \sqrt{4} = 6 + 2 = 8$$

$$f(f(4)) = f(8) = \frac{3}{2}(8) + \sqrt{8} = 12 + 2\sqrt{2}$$

39. **D** Since $n \spadesuit 5 = 125$, $5^{2n} = 125$.

$5^3 = 125$, so $2n$ must equal 3.

$$2n = 3$$

$$n = \frac{3}{2}$$

40. **E** Four common tangents can be drawn as shown:

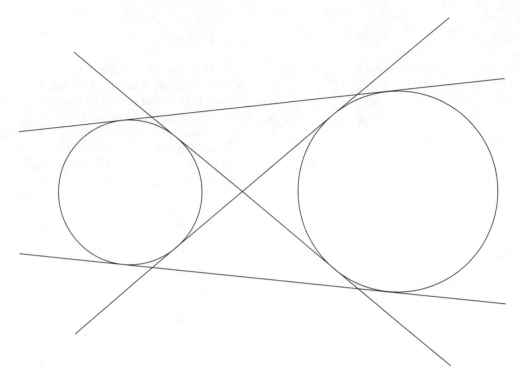

41. **B** Since the boys' team scored a total of 5(54) or 270 points in their first 5 games and the girls' team scored a total of 6(59) or 354 points in their first 6 games, the average for all 11 games is

$$\frac{270 + 354}{11} = 56.7 \text{ points}$$

42. **B** Rotating the rectangle creates a cylinder of radius 3 and height 12. The volume of the cylinder is

$$V = \pi r^2 h = \pi(3^2)(12) = 108\pi$$

43. **E** $i = \sqrt{-1}$, $i^2 = -1$, $i^3 = -i$, and $i^4 = 1$. If i is raised to an exponent that is a multiple of 4, the expression simplifies to 1. All of the expressions simplify to 1, except answer E.

$i^4 = 1$

$(i^4)^4 = i^{16} = 1$

$i^8 = 1$

$i^{20} = 1$

$i^4 + i^4 = 1 + 1 = 2$

44. **B**

$$\left(\frac{f}{g}\right)(x) = \frac{f(g)}{g(x)}$$

$$= \frac{1 - 3x}{3x^2 + 2x - 1}$$

$$= \frac{-(3x - 1)}{(x + 1)(3x - 1)}$$

$$= \frac{-1}{x + 1}$$

45. **C** Think of a right triangle with a hypotenuse of length 25 and a leg of length 7. The sine of one of the acute angles of the triangle would, therefore, be $\frac{7}{25}$.

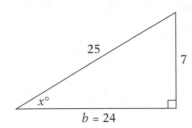

Use the Pythagorean Theorem to find the length of the other leg.

$7^2 + b^2 = 25^2$

$b = 24$

$\tan x = \dfrac{\text{opposite}}{\text{adjacent}} = \dfrac{7}{24}$

46. **D** Kate chooses one course out of the five for her first-period class. She chooses one course out of the remaining four for her second period class. Then, she chooses one out of the remaining three for her third period class and one out of the remaining two for her fourth period class.

$5 \times 4 \times 3 \times 2 \times 1 = 120$

47. **A** The given sequence is a geometric sequence whose nth term is $\left(3\sqrt{3}\right)^n$.

$\left(3\sqrt{3}\right)^1 = 3\sqrt{3}$

$\left(3\sqrt{3}\right)^2 = 9(3) = 27$

$\left(3\sqrt{3}\right)^3 = 3^3\left(\sqrt{3}\right)^3 = 27\left(3\sqrt{3}\right) = 81\sqrt{3}$

The sixth term is, therefore, $\left(3\sqrt{3}\right)^6$.

48. **C** The sum of the interior angles of a polygon is given by the expression $180(n - 2)$ where n = the number of sides of the polygon.

$\dfrac{180(n - 2)}{n} = 157.5$

$180n - 360 = 157.5n$

$22.5n = 360$

$n = 16$ sides

49. **C** Start by multiplying both sides by the LCD:

$\dfrac{1}{(x - 2)(x + 4)} = \dfrac{h}{x - 2} + \dfrac{k}{x + 4}$

$1 = h(x + 4) + k(x - 2)$

How to solve for k may not be immediately obvious. One way to solve for k is to substitute -4 for x, so the h term cancels out.

$1 = h(-4 + 4) + k(-4 - 2)$

$1 = k(-6)$

$k = -\dfrac{1}{6}$

50. **C** Each angle of a regular hexagon measures 120°. Using XO as one leg, sketch a 30°-60°-90° right triangle as shown:

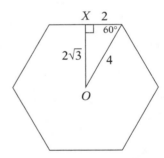

The side opposite the 30° angle measures 2 units. The regular hexagon can be broken into 12 right triangles that are congruent to the one shown in the diagram. The perimeter of the hexagon is, therefore, 12(2) or 24 units.

Diagnose Your Strengths and Weaknesses

Check the number of each question answered correctly and "X" the number of each question answered incorrectly.

Algebra	1	2	3	4	5	10	12	13	14	22	27	30	37	49	Total Number Correct
14 questions															

Plane Geometry	6	7	11	16	23	24	29	35	40	48	50	Total Number Correct
11 questions												

Solid Geometry	18	30	39	Total Number Correct
3 questions				

Coordinate Geometry	8	17	18	20	31	32	Total Number Correct
6 questions							

Trigonometry	19	34	36	45	Total Number Correct
4 questions					

Functions	15	25	26	38	44	Total Number Correct
5 questions						

Data Analysis, Statistics, and Probability	33	41	46	Total Number Correct
3 questions				

Number and Operations	9	39	43	47	Total Number Correct
4 questions					

Number of correct answers $- \dfrac{1}{4}$ **(Number of incorrect answers) = Your raw score**

$$\underline{\hspace{5cm}} - \frac{1}{4} (\underline{\hspace{5cm}}) = \underline{\hspace{3cm}}$$

Compare your raw score with the approximate SAT test score below:

	Raw Score	SAT Approximate Score
Excellent	46–50	750–800
Very Good	41–45	700–750
Good	36–40	640–700
Above Average	29–35	590–640
Average	22–28	510–590
Below Average	< 22	< 510

MATH LEVEL 1 PRACTICE TEST 2

Treat this practice test as the actual test and complete it in one 60-minute sitting. Use the following answer sheet to fill in your multiple-choice answers. Once you have completed the practice test:

1. Check your answers using the Answer Key.
2. Review the Answers and Solutions.
3. Fill in the "Diagnose Your Strengths and Weaknesses" sheet and determine areas that require further preparation.

ANSWER SHEET

Tear out this answer sheet and use it to complete the practice test. Determine the BEST answer for each question. Then fill in the appropriate oval.

1. (A) (B) (C) (D) (E)	21. (A) (B) (C) (D) (E)	41. (A) (B) (C) (D) (E)
2. (A) (B) (C) (D) (E)	22. (A) (B) (C) (D) (E)	42. (A) (B) (C) (D) (E)
3. (A) (B) (C) (D) (E)	23. (A) (B) (C) (D) (E)	43. (A) (B) (C) (D) (E)
4. (A) (B) (C) (D) (E)	24. (A) (B) (C) (D) (E)	44. (A) (B) (C) (D) (E)
5. (A) (B) (C) (D) (E)	25. (A) (B) (C) (D) (E)	45. (A) (B) (C) (D) (E)
6. (A) (B) (C) (D) (E)	26. (A) (B) (C) (D) (E)	46. (A) (B) (C) (D) (E)
7. (A) (B) (C) (D) (E)	27. (A) (B) (C) (D) (E)	47. (A) (B) (C) (D) (E)
8. (A) (B) (C) (D) (E)	28. (A) (B) (C) (D) (E)	48. (A) (B) (C) (D) (E)
9. (A) (B) (C) (D) (E)	29. (A) (B) (C) (D) (E)	49. (A) (B) (C) (D) (E)
10. (A) (B) (C) (D) (E)	30. (A) (B) (C) (D) (E)	50. (A) (B) (C) (D) (E)
11. (A) (B) (C) (D) (E)	31. (A) (B) (C) (D) (E)	
12. (A) (B) (C) (D) (E)	32. (A) (B) (C) (D) (E)	
13. (A) (B) (C) (D) (E)	33. (A) (B) (C) (D) (E)	
14. (A) (B) (C) (D) (E)	34. (A) (B) (C) (D) (E)	
15. (A) (B) (C) (D) (E)	35. (A) (B) (C) (D) (E)	
16. (A) (B) (C) (D) (E)	36. (A) (B) (C) (D) (E)	
17. (A) (B) (C) (D) (E)	37. (A) (B) (C) (D) (E)	
18. (A) (B) (C) (D) (E)	38. (A) (B) (C) (D) (E)	
19. (A) (B) (C) (D) (E)	39. (A) (B) (C) (D) (E)	
20. (A) (B) (C) (D) (E)	40. (A) (B) (C) (D) (E)	

MATH LEVEL 1 PRACTICE TEST 2

Directions: Select the BEST answer for each of the 50 multiple-choice questions. If the exact solution is not one of the five choices, select the answer that is the best approximation. Then fill in the appropriate oval on the answer sheet.

1. A calculator will be needed to answer some of the questions on the test. Scientific, programmable, and graphing calculators are permitted. It is up to you to determine when and when not to use your calculator.

2. All angles on the Level 1 test are measured in degrees, not radians. Make sure your calculator is set to degree mode.

3. Figures are drawn as accurately as possible and are intended to help solve some of the test problems. If a figure is not drawn to scale, this will be stated in the problem. All figures lie in a plane unless the problem indicates otherwise.

4. Unless otherwise stated, the domain of a function f is assumed to be the set of real numbers x for which the value of the function, $f(x)$, is a real number.

5. Reference information that may be useful in answering some of the test questions can be found below.

Reference Information	
Right circular cone with radius r and height h:	Volume $= \dfrac{1}{3}\pi r^2 h$
Right circular cone with circumference of base c and slant height ℓ:	Lateral Area $= \dfrac{1}{2}c\ell$
Sphere with radius r:	Volume $= \dfrac{4}{3}\pi r^3$ Surface Area $= 4\pi r^2$
Pyramid with base area B and height h:	Volume $= \dfrac{1}{3}Bh$

GO ON TO THE NEXT PAGE

1. If $\dfrac{7^2 - x}{7 + x} = 6$, then $x =$

    (A) $\dfrac{6}{7}$

    (B) 1

    (C) $\dfrac{7}{5}$

    (D) -1

    (E) $\dfrac{7}{6}$

2. If $\dfrac{2}{4x^2 + 1} = \dfrac{2}{5}$, then $x =$

    (A) 4

    (B) 1

    (C) ± 1

    (D) $\pm\sqrt{\dfrac{6}{4}}$

    (E) $\pm\sqrt{\dfrac{6}{2}}$

3. Which of the following equations has the same solution(s) as $|x - 5| = 2$?

    (A) $\dfrac{x}{2} = \dfrac{3}{2}$

    (B) $3x = 21$

    (C) $x^2 - 10x + 21 = 0$

    (D) $x^2 - 4x - 21 = 0$

    (E) $x^2 = 49$

4. $x^3 + 8x^2 - 1$ subtracted from $5x^3 - x^2 + 2x + 1$ equals which of the following?

    (A) $4x^3 - 8x^2 + 2x - 2$

    (B) $-4x^3 + 9x^2 - 2x - 2$

    (C) $4x^3 + 7x^2 + 2x$

    (D) $4x^3 - 9x^2 + 2x$

    (E) $4x^3 - 9x^2 + 2x + 2$

5. A cell phone company charges \$30 a month for a phone plan plus an additional 40 cents for each minute over the allotted 300 minutes that come with the plan. Assuming the phone is used for m minutes and $m > 300$, which of the following is an expression for the monthly cost?

    (A) $30 + 0.40m$

    (B) $30 + 0.40(m - 300)$

    (C) $30 + 0.40(m + 300)$

    (D) $30 + 40(m - 300)$

    (E) $30.40m$

USE THIS SPACE AS SCRATCH PAPER

GO ON TO THE NEXT PAGE

6. If $\sqrt[3]{8 - 7x} = -3$, then $x =$

(A) $-\dfrac{19}{7}$

(B) 5

(C) $\dfrac{19}{7}$

(D) -5

(E) $-\dfrac{1}{7}$

7. If two similar octagons have a scale factor of 3:5, then the ratio of their areas is

(A) 3:5

(B) $\sqrt{3} : \sqrt{5}$

(C) 9:25

(D) 27:125

(E) 6:10

8. What is the ratio of the circumference of a circle to its area?

(A) $2{:}r$

(B) $r{:}2$

(C) $1{:}r$

(D) $2r{:}1$

(E) $2{:}r^2$

9. Kelli has taken a job with a starting salary of \$35,000. If she receives annual raises of \$2,800, what will her salary be during her fourth year on the job?

(A) \$11,900

(B) \$37,800

(C) \$40,600

(D) \$43,400

(E) \$46,200

10. If $x = \sqrt[3]{y}$ and $y = 2n$, then what is the value of x when $n = -4$?

(A) 2

(B) -2

(C) 8

(D) -8

(E) $2\sqrt{2}$

GO ON TO THE NEXT PAGE

11. In $\triangle ABC$, $AB = 4$, and $BC = 7$. If the length of the third side is an integer, then what is the greatest possible value for AC?

   (A) 8
   (B) 14
   (C) 11
   (D) 10
   (E) 12

12. If the measure of each exterior angle of a regular polygon is 20°, how many sides does the polygon have?

   (A) 18
   (B) 9
   (C) 27
   (D) 22
   (E) 36

13. The ratio of the measures of the angles of a quadrilateral is 1:2:4:5. What is the measure of the largest angle?

   (A) 30°
   (B) 150°
   (C) 154°
   (D) 120°
   (E) 144°

14. If $-2x + y = -17$ and $x + y = 16$, then $x - y =$

   (A) 5
   (B) 11
   (C) 6
   (D) 4
   (E) 10

15. Which of the following is the graph of $2x - y \geq -1$?

   (A)

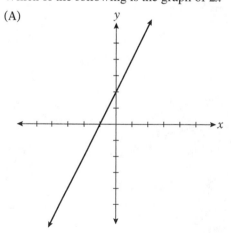

GO ON TO THE NEXT PAGE

(B)

(C)

(D)

(E)

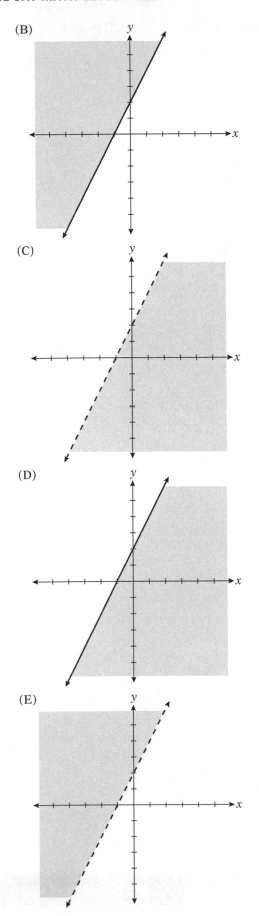

GO ON TO THE NEXT PAGE

16. If the point $(-2, a)$ is on the graph of the equation $y = x^2 - 7$, then $a =$

    (A) 4
    (B) 3
    (C) $\pm\sqrt{5}$
    (D) -11
    (E) -3

17. $(x + y + 5)(x + y - 5) =$

    (A) $(x + y)^2 - 25$
    (B) $(x + y)^2 + 10(x + y) + 25$
    (C) $(x + y)^2 + 10(x + y)$
    (D) $x^2 + y^2 - 5^2$
    (E) $x^2 + 2xy + y^2 + 5^2$

USE THIS SPACE AS SCRATCH PAPER

18. In Figure 1, $\dfrac{ST}{TR} = \dfrac{11}{14}$. $\sin \theta =$

    (A) $\dfrac{11}{317}$
    (B) 0.618
    (C) 0.786
    (D) 0.222
    (E) 0.733

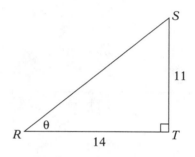

Figure 1

19. If points $(0, 0)$, $(3, 7)$, and $(11, 0)$ are the vertices of an isosceles trapezoid, then which of the following points is the remaining vertex?

    (A) $(8, -7)$
    (B) $(14, 7)$
    (C) $(7, 8)$
    (D) $(3, -7)$
    (E) $(8, 7)$

20. A point Q is in the second quadrant at a distance of $\sqrt{41}$ from the origin. Which of the following could be the coordinates of Q?

    (A) $(-1, 41)$
    (B) $(-4, 5)$
    (C) $\left(-8, \sqrt{23}\right)$
    (D) $(5, -4)$
    (E) $(-6, 5)$

21. If $\sqrt[5]{\sqrt{x}} = 2$, then $x =$

    (A) 20
    (B) 1,024
    (C) 64
    (D) 128
    (E) 512

GO ON TO THE NEXT PAGE

22. What is the area of the triangle in Figure 2?

    (A) $64\sqrt{3}$

    (B) $64\sqrt{2}$

    (C) $32\sqrt{3}$

    (D) 64

    (E) 32

23. If $4^x = 36^3 \div 9^3$, then $x =$

    (A) 2

    (B) 3

    (C) 4

    (D) 5

    (E) 16

24. For $x \neq 0$, if $3^{-2} - 6^{-2} = x^{-2}$, then $x =$

    (A) $3\sqrt{3}$

    (B) $2\sqrt{3}$

    (C) ± 12

    (D) $\pm 2\sqrt{3}$

    (E) ± 6

25. Which of the following is the equation of a line that will never intersect the line $5x - 9y = -1$?

    (A) $-5x - 9y = -1$

    (B) $y = x + \dfrac{1}{9}$

    (C) $y = \dfrac{5}{9}x - 2$

    (D) $5x + 9y = 0$

    (E) $y = \dfrac{9}{5}x + 1$

26. If 2 percent of a 12-gallon solution is sodium, how many gallons of pure sodium must be added to make a new solution that is 6 percent sodium?

    (A) 1.79

    (B) 1.02

    (C) 8

    (D) 5

    (E) 0.51

27. The product of the roots of a quadratic equation is −5 and their sum is −4. Which of the following could be the quadratic equation?

    (A) $x^2 - 4x + 5 = 0$

    (B) $x^2 - 4x - 5 = 0$

    (C) $x^2 + 4x - 5 = 0$

    (D) $x^2 + 5x - 4 = 0$

    (E) $x^2 - 5x - 4 = 0$

USE THIS SPACE AS SCRATCH PAPER

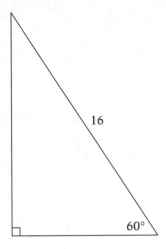

16

60°

Figure 2

GO ON TO THE NEXT PAGE

28. If $f(x) = x^2 + 4$ and $g(x) = 1 - x^3$, then $f[g(-1)] =$

    (A) 6
    (B) 5
    (C) 16
    (D) 4
    (E) 8

USE THIS SPACE AS SCRATCH PAPER

29. $(1 + \sin \theta)(1 - \sin \theta) =$

    (A) $1 - \sin \theta$
    (B) $\cos^2 \theta$
    (C) $1 - 2\sin \theta + \sin^2 \theta$
    (D) $\cos \theta$
    (E) 1

30. If $25x^2 - 20x + k = 0$ has $\dfrac{2}{5}$ as a double root, $k =$

    (A) 4
    (B) $\dfrac{4}{25}$
    (C) 5
    (D) -5
    (E) 1

31. If a is an even integer and b is an odd integer, then which of the following must be odd?

    (A) ab
    (B) a^b
    (C) $a + b + 1$
    (D) $2b + 1$
    (E) $a - 2b$

32. Which of the following equations has roots of 4 and $-\dfrac{1}{2}$?

    (A) $2x^3 + x^2 - 32x - 16 = 0$
    (B) $2x^2 + 7x - 4 = 0$
    (C) $2x^2 - 9x - 4 = 0$
    (D) $2x^2 - 7x - 4 = 0$
    (E) $4(2x + 1) = 0$

33. What is the area of the quadrilateral in Figure 3?

    (A) $2\sqrt{2}$ units^2
    (B) $8\sqrt{2}$ units^2
    (C) $\dfrac{16}{2}$ units^2
    (D) 16 units^2
    (E) 8 units^2

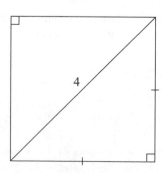

Figure 3

GO ON TO THE NEXT PAGE

34. The volume of a cube is *V*. If the sides of the cube are cut if half, the volume of the resulting solid is

    (A) 2*V*

    (B) $\frac{1}{2}V$

    (C) $\frac{1}{4}V$

    (D) $\frac{1}{8}V$

    (E) $\frac{1}{16}V$

35. $y = f(x)$ is graphed in Figure 4. Which of the following is the graph of $y = |f(x)|$?

    (A)

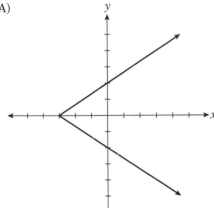

    (B)

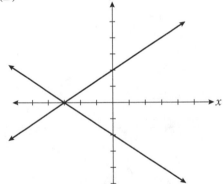

    (C)

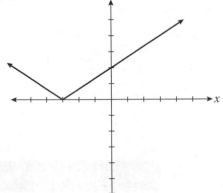

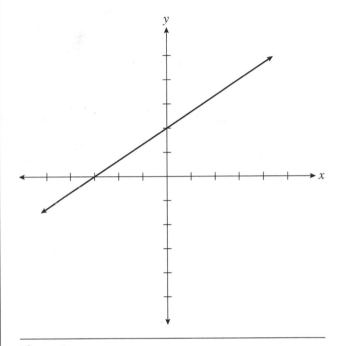

Figure 4

GO ON TO THE NEXT PAGE

(D)

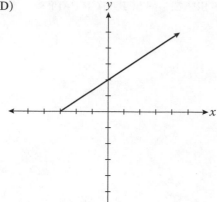

(E)

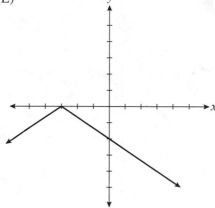

36. In Figure 5, which of the following must be true?

    I. $\cot x = \dfrac{3}{4}$

    II. $\cos x = \sin y$

    III. $\tan x = \tan y$

    (A) I only
    (B) II only
    (C) II and III only
    (D) I and II only
    (E) I, II, and III

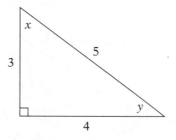

Figure 5

37. What is the lateral area of the right circular cone shown in Figure 6?

    (A) 50π
    (B) 75π
    (C) $\dfrac{125\sqrt{3}}{3}\pi$
    (D) $25\sqrt{3}\pi$
    (E) 100π

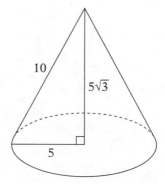

Figure 6

GO ON TO THE NEXT PAGE

USE THIS SPACE AS SCRATCH PAPER

38. If $f(x) = -4(x + 2)^2 - 1$ for $-4 \leq x \leq 0$, then which of the following is the range of f?

    (A) $y \leq -1$
    (B) $-4 \leq y \leq 0$
    (C) $y \leq 0$
    (D) $-17 \leq y \leq -1$
    (E) $y \leq -17$

39. If $f(x) = \sqrt{x}$ and $f[g(x)] = 2\sqrt{x}$, then $g(x) =$

    (A) $4x$
    (B) $2x$
    (C) $2x^2$
    (D) $\dfrac{x}{2}$
    (E) x^3

40. If $i = \sqrt{-1}$, then $(6 - i)(6 + i) =$

    (A) 35
    (B) $36 - i$
    (C) 37
    (D) $35 + 12i$
    (E) 36

41. What is the volume of the right triangular prism in Figure 7?

    (A) 200 cm³
    (B) $100\sqrt{2}$ cm³
    (C) 100 cm³
    (D) $\dfrac{100}{3}$ cm³
    (E) $\dfrac{100\sqrt{2}}{3}$ cm³

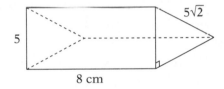

Figure 7

42. $\tan \theta (\sin \theta) + \cos \theta =$

    (A) $2\cos \theta$
    (B) $\cos \theta + \sec \theta$
    (C) $\csc \theta$
    (D) $\sec \theta$
    (E) 1

43. The French Club consists of 10 members and is holding officer elections to select a president, secretary, and treasurer for the club. A member can only be selected for one position. How many possibilities are there for selecting the three officers?

    (A) 30
    (B) 27
    (C) 72
    (D) 720
    (E) 90

GO ON TO THE NEXT PAGE

44. Which of the following is symmetric with respect to the origin?
    (A) $y = x^2 - 1$
    (B) $y = x^3 - 2x$
    (C) $y^2 = x + 8$
    (D) $y = -|x + 1|$
    (E) $y = (x + 3)^2$

45. In parallelogram *JKLM* shown in Figure 8, $\overline{JK} = 18$, $\overline{KL} = 12$, and $m\angle JKL = 120°$. What is the area of *JKLM*?

    (A) $108\sqrt{3}$

    (B) $72\sqrt{3}$

    (C) $54\sqrt{3}$

    (D) $36\sqrt{3}$

    (E) $90\sqrt{3}$

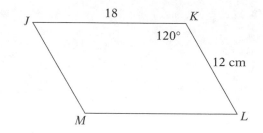

Figure 8

46. Thirteen students receive the following grades on a math test:

    60, 78, 90, 67, 88, 92, 81, 100, 95, 83, 83, 86, 74

    What is the interquartile range of the test scores?
    (A) 14
    (B) 83
    (C) 15
    (D) 16
    (E) 40

47. $p \square q$ is defined as $\dfrac{p^q}{pq}$ for all positive real numbers.

    Which of the following is equivalent to $\dfrac{p}{2}$?
    (A) $p \square 1$
    (B) $p \square p$
    (C) $p \square \dfrac{1}{2}$
    (D) $1 \square q$
    (E) $p \square 2$

GO ON TO THE NEXT PAGE

48. Matt and Alysia are going to get their driver's licenses. The probability that Matt passes his driving test is $\frac{9}{10}$. The probability that Alysia passes her driving test is $\frac{7}{9}$. Assuming that their result is not dependent on how the other does, what is the probability that Matt passes and Alysia fails?

    (A) $\frac{101}{90}$

    (B) $\frac{1}{5}$

    (C) $\frac{7}{10}$

    (D) $\frac{11}{90}$

    (E) $\frac{27}{100}$

49. The circle shown in Figure 9 has an area of 36π cm^2. What is the area of the shaded segment?

    (A) 9π cm^2
    (B) $9\pi - 36$ cm^2
    (C) 18 cm^2
    (D) $9\pi - 18$ cm^2
    (E) $18\pi - 18$ cm^2

50. If $f(n) = 9^{-n}$, then $f\left(-\frac{1}{4}\right) =$

    (A) $9^{-\frac{1}{4}}$
    (B) 3
    (C) $\sqrt{3}$
    (D) $\frac{1}{9}$
    (E) 9

USE THIS SPACE AS SCRATCH PAPER

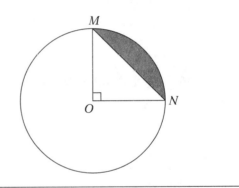

Figure 9

S T O P

IF YOU FINISH BEFORE TIME IS CALLED, YOU MAY CHECK YOUR WORK ON THIS TEST ONLY.
DO NOT TURN TO ANY OTHER TEST IN THIS BOOK.

ANSWER KEY

1. B	11. D	21. B	31. D	41. C
2. C	12. A	22. C	32. D	42. D
3. C	13. B	23. B	33. E	43. D
4. E	14. C	24. D	34. D	44. B
5. B	15. D	25. C	35. C	45. A
6. B	16. E	26. E	36. D	46. C
7. C	17. A	27. C	37. A	47. E
8. A	18. B	28. E	38. D	48. B
9. D	19. E	29. B	39. A	49. D
10. B	20. B	30. A	40. C	50. C

ANSWERS AND SOLUTIONS

1. **B**

$$\frac{7^2 - x}{7 + x} = 6$$

$$7^2 - x = 6(7 + x)$$

$$49 - x = 42 + 6x$$

$$7 = 7x$$

$$x = 1$$

2. **C**

$$\frac{2}{4x^2 + 1} = \frac{2}{5}$$

$$2(4x^2 + 1) = 5(2)$$

$$4x^2 + 1 = 5$$

$$4x^2 = 4$$

$$x^2 = 1$$

$$x = \pm 1$$

3. **C**

$$|x - 5| = 2$$

$$x - 5 = 2 \quad \text{or} \quad x - 5 = -2$$

$$x = 7 \qquad\qquad x = 3$$

The equation in answer C, $x^2 - 10x + 21 = 0$, can be factored as:

$$(x - 7)(x - 3) = 0$$

Its solutions are also $x = 3$ or $x = 7$.

4. **E**

$$5x^3 - x^2 + 2x + 1 - (x^3 + 8x^2 - 1)$$

$$= 5x^3 - x^2 + 2x + 1 - x^3 - 8x^2 + 1$$

$$= 4x^3 - 9x^2 + 2x + 2$$

5. **B** Since $30 is the initial cost and $0.40 is charged for $(m - 300)$ additional minutes, the correct expression is:

$$30 + 0.40(m - 300)$$

6. **B**

$$\sqrt[3]{(8 - 7x)} = -3$$

$$\left[\sqrt[3]{(8 - 7x)}\right]^3 = (-3)^3$$

$$8 - 7x = -27$$

$$-7x = -35$$

$$x = 5$$

7. **C** The scale factor of the similar octagons is 3:5, so their areas must be in the ratio of $3^2:5^2$.

$3^2:5^2$ equals 9:25

8. **A** $C = 2\pi r$ and $A = \pi r^2$, so the ratio of the circumference to area is

$$\frac{2\pi r}{2\pi r^2} = \frac{2}{r} \text{ or } 2:r$$

9. **D** Kelli receives the following salaries during the indicated years:

Year 1: 35,000

Year 2: 35,000 + 2,800 = $37,800

Year 3: 35,000 + 2(2,800) = $40,600

Year 4: 35,000 + 3(2,800) = $43,400

10. **B**

When $n = -4$, $y = 2(-4) = -8$.

$x = \sqrt[3]{-8} = -2$

11. **D** The Triangle Inequality Theorem states that the sum of any two sides of a triangle must be greater than the third side.

$4 + 7 > AC$

$11 > AC$

10 is the greatest integer less than 11.

12. **A** The sum of the exterior angles of any polygon is 360°. If each exterior angle measures 20°, the polygon has

$$\frac{360}{20} = 18 \text{ sides}$$

13. **B** Since the angles are in the ratio 1:2:4:5, let x, $2x$, $4x$, and $5x$ represent the four angle measures.

$x + 2x + 4x + 5x = 360$

$12x = 360$

$x = 30$

The largest angle measures 5(30) or 150°.

14. **C** Multiply the second equation by 2 to get a coefficient of 2 for the x term: $2x + 2y = 32$. Then, solve the system using the linear combination method.

$$\begin{array}{r} -2x + y = -7 \\ +\ 2x + 2y = 32 \\ \hline 3y = 15 \end{array}$$

$y = 5$

If $y = 5$, $x + 5 = 16$, so $x = 11$.

$x - y = 11 - 5 = 6$

15. **D** Graph the line first. The line is solid, not dashed, since the inequality has a "greater than or equal to" sign.

$2x - y \geq -1$

$2x + 1 \geq y$

Test a point, (0, 0) for example, to determine whether to shade above or below the line. The origin satisfies the inequality since $2(0) + 1 \geq 0$, so shade below the line. Answer D is the appropriate graph.

16. **E** Substitute $x = -2$ into the equation, and solve for the corresponding y value.

$y = x^2 - 7$

$y = (-2)^2 - 7$

$y = 4 - 7 = -3$

17. **A**

$(x + y + 5)(x + y - 5)$

$= [(x + y) + 5][(x + y) - 5]$

$= (x + y)^2 - 25$

18. **B**

$$\tan\theta - \frac{ST}{TR} = \frac{11}{14}$$

$$\tan^{-1}\left(\frac{11}{14}\right) = 38.157$$

$\theta = 38.157°$

$\sin 38.157° = 0.618$

You can also solve this problem by using the Pythagorean Theorem to determine the length of the hypotenuse of $\triangle STR$. $SR = \sqrt{317}$, so sin

$$\theta = \frac{11}{\sqrt{317}} = 0.618.$$

19. **E** The vertex (8, 7) results in an isosceles trapezoid as shown:

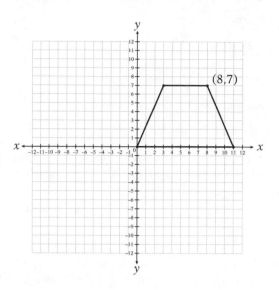

20. **B** (–4, 5) is the only given point that is both in the second quadrant and at a distance of $\sqrt{41}$ from the origin.

$$\sqrt{(-4 - 0)^2 + (5 - 0)^2}$$
$$= \sqrt{4^2 + 5^2}$$
$$= \sqrt{16 + 25}$$
$$= \sqrt{41}$$

21. **B**

$$\sqrt[5]{\sqrt{x}} = 2$$
$$\sqrt{x} = 2^5$$
$$x = \left(2^5\right)^2$$
$$x = 2^{10} = 1{,}024$$

22. **C** Since the triangle is a 30°-60°-90° right triangle, its legs measure 8 and $8\sqrt{3}$ units. Its area is

$$A = \frac{1}{2}bh = \frac{1}{2}(8)\left(8\sqrt{3}\right)$$
$$= \frac{1}{2}\left(64\sqrt{3}\right) = 32\sqrt{3}$$

23. **B**

$$4^x = 36^3 \div 9^3$$
$$4^x = (36 \div 9)^3$$
$$4^x = 4^3$$
$$x = 3$$

24. **D**

$$3^{-2} - 6^{-2} = x^{-2}$$
$$\frac{1}{3^2} - \frac{1}{6^2} = \frac{1}{x^2}$$
$$\frac{1}{9} - \frac{1}{36} = \frac{1}{x^2}$$

Multiply both sides of the equation by the LCD, $36x^2$.

$$4x^2 - x^2 = 36$$
$$3x^2 = 36$$
$$x^2 = 12$$
$$x = \pm\sqrt{12} = \pm 2\sqrt{3}$$

25. **C** In order for two lines to never intersect, they must be parallel. Parallel lines have the same slope, so determine which of the given lines has the same slope as $5x - 9y = -1$.

$$5x - 9y = -1$$
$$-9y = -5x - 1$$
$$y = \frac{5}{9}x + \frac{1}{9}$$

The given line has a slope of $\frac{5}{9}$. Since the equation in answer C is in slope-intercept form, you can quickly determine that its slope is also $\frac{5}{9}$. The line $y = \frac{5}{9}x - 2$ will, therefore, never intersect the line $5x - 9y = -1$.

26. **E** Let x = the number of gallons of sodium added.

$$2\%(12) + 100\%(x) = 6\%(12 + x)$$
$$2(12) + 100(x) = 6(12 + x)$$
$$24 + 100x = 72 + 6x$$
$$94x = 48$$
$$x = \frac{48}{94} = 0.51 \text{ gallons}$$

27. **C** Recall that a quadratic equation can be thought of as:

$a[x^2 - (\text{sum of the roots})x + (\text{product of the roots})] = 0$. Substitute the sum $= -4$ and the product $= -5$ to get:

$a(x^2 - -4x + -5) = 0$

$a(x^2 + 4x - 5) = 0$

When $a = 1$, the result is the equation given in answer C: $x^2 + 4x - 5 = 0$.

28. **E**

$g(-1) = 1 - (-1)^3 = 1 - -1 = 2$

$f(g(-1)) = f(2) = (2)^2 + 4 = 8$

29. **B** Recall that $\sin^2 \theta + \cos^2 \theta = 1$, so $\cos^2 \theta = 1 - \sin^2 \theta$.

$(1 + \sin \theta)(1 - \sin \theta)$

$= 1 - \sin \theta + \sin \theta - \sin^2 \theta$

$= 1 - \sin^2 \theta$

$= \cos^2 \theta$

30. **A** Since $\frac{2}{5}$ is a double root, $\left(x - \frac{2}{5}\right)$ is a factor of the quadratic equation two times.

$\left(x - \frac{2}{5}\right)\left(x - \frac{2}{5}\right) = 0$

$(5x - 2)(5x - 2) = 0$

$25x^2 - 10x + 4 = 0$

$k = 4$

31. **D** Since b is odd, multiplying b by 2 will always result in an even number. Adding 1 to an even product will always result in an odd number, so answer D is the correct choice. If you're not sure about number theory, try substituting values for a and b. Let $a = 4$ and $b = 3$.

$ab = 4(3) = 12$

$a^b = 4^3 = 64$

$a + b + 1 = 4 + 3 + 1 = 8$

$2b + 1 = 2(3) + 1 = 7$

$a - 2b = 4 - 2(3) = 4 - 6 = -2$

7 is the only odd result.

32. **D** An equation with roots of 4 and $-\frac{1}{2}$ has factors $x - 4$ and $x + \frac{1}{2}$.

$(x - 4)\left(x + \frac{1}{2}\right) = 0$

$(x - 4)(2x + 1) = 0$

$2x^2 + x - 8x - 4 = 0$

$2x^2 - 7x - 4 = 0$

33. **E** The diagonal divides the square into 2 congruent right triangles. Since the triangles are isosceles right triangles and the hypotenuse measures 4 units, each leg measures

$\frac{4}{\sqrt{2}} = 4\sqrt{\frac{2}{2}} = 2\sqrt{2}$ units

The area of the square units

$A = bh = 2\sqrt{2}\left(2\sqrt{2}\right) = 4(2) = 8$ square units.

34. **D** The scale factor of the cubes is 2:1, so their volumes are in the ratio $2^3:1^3$. The new volume is $\frac{1}{2^3}$ or $\frac{1}{8} V$ the volume of the original cube.

35. **C** Absolute value results in a number greater than or equal to zero. Since $y = |f(x)|$, y must be positive. The portion of the graph of $f(x)$ below the x-axis should be reflected over the x-axis, resulting in the graph given in answer C.

36. **D**

The first statement is true because

$\cot x = \frac{\text{adjacent}}{\text{opposite}} = \frac{3}{4}$

The second statement is also true, since

$\cos x = \frac{3}{5}$ and $\sin y = \frac{3}{5}$

The third statement is not true, since

$\tan x = \frac{4}{3}$ and $\tan y = \frac{3}{4}$

Answer D is the correct choice.

37. **A** The lateral area of a cone equals $\frac{1}{2}c\ell$, where c = the circumference of the base and ℓ = the slant height.

For the given cone:

$$L = \frac{1}{2}c\ell = \frac{1}{2}(2\pi)(5)(10)$$

$$= \frac{1}{2}(100\pi) = 50\pi$$

38. **D** The graph of $f(x) = -4(x + 2)^2 - 1$ is a parabola concave down with vertex at $(-2, -1)$.

When $x = -4$, $f(-4) = -4(-4 + 2)^2 - 1 = -17$.

When $x = 0$, $f(0) = -4(0 + 2)^2 - 1 = -17$.

The range spans from the least value of y, -17, to the greatest, -1, which occurs at the vertex.

An alternate way to determine the range is to graph the function on your graphing calculator and check the Table values for y when $-4 \leq x \leq 0$.

39. **A** Since you know the composition of f and g results in $2\sqrt{x}$, you need to determine what input value of f will result in $2\sqrt{x}$.

$$\sqrt{4x} = 2\sqrt{x}$$

Therefore, $g(x) = 4x$. Test your answer by checking the composition.

$$g(x) = 4x, \text{ so } f(g(x)) = f(4x) = \sqrt{4x} = 2\sqrt{x}$$

40. **C**

Since $i = \sqrt{-1}$, $i^2 = \sqrt{-1}(\sqrt{-1}) = -1$.

$(6 - i)(6 + i)$

$= 36 + 6i - 6i - i^2$

$= 36 - i^2$

$= 36 - (-1) = 37$

41. **C** $V = BH$ where B = the area of the base. In this case, the base is a right triangle. Since one leg measures 5 cm and the hypotenuse measures $5\sqrt{2}$ cm, the triangle is an isosceles right triangle. The other leg must also measure 5 cm.

The area of the triangle is

$$A = \frac{1}{2}bh = \frac{1}{2}(5)(5) = \frac{25}{2}.$$

The volume of the solid is, therefore,

$$V = BH = \frac{25}{2}(8) = 100 \text{ cm}^3$$

42. **D**

$$\tan\theta(\sin\theta) + \cos\theta$$

$$= \frac{\sin\theta}{\cos\theta}(\sin\theta) + \cos\theta$$

$$= \frac{\sin^2\theta}{\cos\theta} + \frac{\cos^2\theta}{\cos\theta}$$

$$= \frac{\sin^2\theta + \cos^2\theta}{\cos\theta}$$

$$= \frac{1}{\cos\theta} = \sec\theta$$

43. **D** There are 10 possible people that could serve as president. Once the president is chosen, there are 9 possible people that could serve as secretary, and once that person is chosen, there are 8 remaining people that could serve as treasurer. The total number of ways of selecting the three officers is

$$10 \times 9 \times 8 = 720$$

44. **B** If the graph is symmetric with respect to the origin, the points (x, y) and $(-x, -y)$ satisfy the equation. Replace x with $-x$ and y with $-y$ to determine if the resulting equation is equivalent to the given one.

For the equation in answer B:

$-y = (-x)^3 - 2(-x)$

$-y = -x^3 + 2x$

$y = x^3 - 2x$

The resulting equation is equivalent to the original, $y = x^3 - 2x$, so the graph is symmetric with respect to the origin.

45. **A** Consecutive angles in a parallelogram are supplementary so $m\angle KLM = 180 - 120 = 60°$. Sketch a $30°-60°-90°$ right triangle to determine the height of the parallelogram.

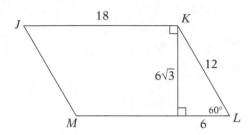

Since the parallelogram's altitude is opposite the 60° angle, the height of the parallelogram is $6\sqrt{3}$. Its area is

$$A = bh = 18\left(6\sqrt{3}\right) = 108\sqrt{3}$$

46. **C** Start by arranging the test scores in order of lowest to highest:

60, 67, 74, 78, 81, 83, 83, 86, 88, 90, 92, 95, 100

The median of the data is 83. To find the interquartile range, find the lower quartile by determining the median of the data to the left of the median, 83. Then find the upper quartile by determining the median of the data to the right of the median, 83.

$$\text{Lower quartile} = \frac{74 + 78}{2} = 76$$

$$\text{Upper quartile} = \frac{90 + 92}{2} = 91$$

The interquartile range is $91 - 76 = 15$.

47. **E**

$$p \,\square\, 2 = \frac{p^2}{p(2)}$$

$$= \frac{p}{2}$$

48. **B** The two events are independent. The probability that Alysia *fails* the test is $1 - \frac{7}{9} = \frac{2}{9}$. The probability that Matt passes and Alysia fails is

$$\frac{9}{10}\left(\frac{2}{9}\right) = \frac{2}{10} = \frac{1}{5}$$

49. **D** Since the area of the circle is 36π, its radius is 6.

$$A = 36\pi = \pi r^2$$

$$r^2 = 36$$

$$r = 6$$

The area of sector $MNO = \frac{1}{4}(36\pi) = 9\pi$.

The area of $\triangle MNO = \frac{1}{2}(6)(6) = 18$.

The area of the shaded segment is, therefore, $9\pi - 18$ cm².

50. **C**

$$f\left(-\frac{1}{4}\right) = 9^{-\left(\frac{1}{4}\right)} = 9^{\frac{1}{4}}$$

$$= \left(3^2\right)^{\frac{1}{4}} = 3^{\frac{2}{4}} = 3^{\frac{1}{2}}$$

$$= \sqrt{3}$$

Diagnose Your Strengths and Weaknesses

Check the number of each question answered correctly and "X" the number of each question answered incorrectly.

Algebra	1	2	3	4	5	6	9	10	14	17	21	23	24	26	30	Total Number Correct
15 questions																

Plane Geometry	7	8	11	12	22	33	37	45	49	Total Number Correct
9 questions										

Solid Geometry	34	37	41	Total Number Correct
3 questions				

Coordinate Geometry	15	16	19	20	25	44	Total Number Correct
6 questions							

Trigonometry	18	29	36	42	Total Number Correct
4 questions					

Functions	27	28	32	35	38	39	50	Total Number Correct
7 questions								

Data Analysis, Statistics, and Probability	43	46	48	Total Number Correct
3 questions				

Number and Operations	31	40	47	Total Number Correct
3 questions				

Number of correct answers $- \frac{1}{4}$ **(Number of incorrect answers) = Your raw score**

_____ $- \frac{1}{4}$ (_____) = _____

Compare your raw score with the approximate SAT test score below:

	Raw Score	**SAT Approximate Score**
Excellent	46–50	750–800
Very Good	41–45	700–750
Good	36–40	640–700
Above Average	29–35	590–640
Average	22–28	510–590
Below Average	< 22	<510

THE SAT MATH LEVEL 2 TEST

All About the SAT Math Level 2 Test

The Math Level 2 test covers the topics shown in the pie chart below.

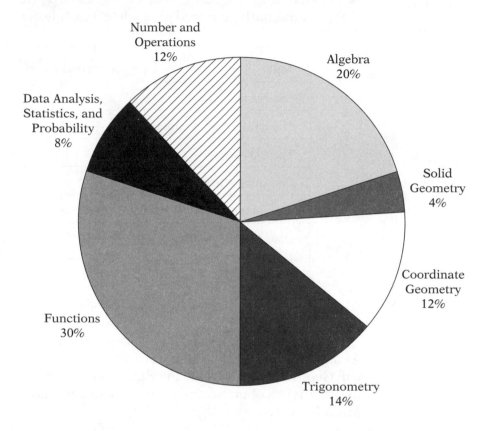

The Math Level 2 test is designed to test a student's math knowledge, ability to apply concepts, and higher-order thinking. Students are not expected to know every topic covered on the test.

When to Take the Test

The Math Level 2 test is recommended for students who have completed *more than* 3 years of college-preparatory mathematics. Most students taking the Level 2 test have studied 2 years of algebra, 1 year of geometry, and 1 year of precalculus (elementary functions) and/or trigonometry. Many students take the math Subject Tests at the end of their junior year or at the beginning of their senior year.

The Level 1 vs. Level 2 Test

As mentioned, the Math Level 2 test is recommended for students who have completed *more than* 3 years of college-preparatory mathematics. The Math Level 1 test is recommended for students who have completed 3 years of college-preparatory mathematics. Most students taking the Level 1 test have studied 2 years of algebra and 1 year of geometry.

Typically, students who have received A or B grades in precalculus and trigonometry elect to take the Level 2 test. If you have taken more than 3 years of high school math and are enrolled in a precalculus or calculus program, don't assume that taking the Level 1 test guarantees a higher score. Many of the topics on the Level 1 test will be concepts studied years ago.

Although the topics covered on the two tests overlap somewhat, they differ as shown in the table below. The College Board gives an approximate outline of the mathematics covered on each test as follows:

Topic	Level 1 Test	Level 2 Test
Algebra and Functions	38–42%	48–52%
Plane Euclidean Geometry	18–22%	—
Three-dimensional Geometry	4–6%	4–6%
Coordinate Geometry	8–12%	10–14%
Trigonometry	6–8%	12–16%
Data Analysis, Statistics, and Probability	6–10%	6–10%
Number and Operations	10–14%	10–14%

Overall, the Level 2 test focuses on more advanced content in each area. As shown in the table, the Level 2 test does not directly cover Plane Euclidean Geometry, although Plane Euclidean Geometry concepts may be applied in other types of questions. Number and Operations was formerly known as Miscellaneous.

Scoring

The scoring of the Math Level 2 test is based on a 200–800-point scale. You receive one point for each correct answer and lose one-quarter of a point for each incorrect answer. You do not lose any points for omitting a question. In addition to your scaled score, your score report shows a percentile ranking indicating the percentage of students scoring below your score. Because there are considerable differences between the Math Level 1 and Level 2 tests, your score on one is not an accurate indicator of your score on the other.

CALCULATOR TIPS

The SAT Math Level 2 test requires the use of a scientific or graphing calculator. The Math Level 1 and Level 2 tests are actually the only Subject Tests for which calculators are allowed. It is not necessary to use a calculator to solve every problem on the test. In fact, there is no advantage to using a calculator for 35–45% of the Level 2 test questions. That means a calculator is helpful for solving approximately 55–65% of the Level 2 test questions.

It is critical to know how and when to use your calculator effectively . . . and how and when NOT to use your calculator. For some problems, using a calculator may actually take longer than solving the problem by hand. Knowing how to operate your calculator properly will affect your test score, so practice using your calculator when completing the practice tests in this book.

The Level 2 test is created with the understanding that most students know how to use a graphing calculator. Although you have a choice of using either a scientific or a graphing calculator, *choose a graphing calculator.* A graphing calculator provides much more functionality (as long as you know how to use it properly!). A graphing calculator is an advantage when solving many problems related to coordinate geometry and functions.

Remember to make sure your calculator is working properly before your test day. Become comfortable with using it and familiar with the common operations. Because calculator policies are ever changing, refer to www.collegeboard.com for the latest information. According to the College Board, the following types of calculators are NOT allowed on the SAT test:

- calculators with QWERTY (typewriter-like) keypads
- calculators that contain electronic dictionaries
- calculators with paper tape or printers
- calculators that "talk" or make noise
- calculators that require an electrical outlet
- cell-phone calculators
- pocket organizers or personal digital assistants
- hand-held minicomputers, powerbooks, or laptop computers
- electronic writing pads or pen-input/stylus-driven devices (such as a Palm Pilot).

There are a few rules to calculator usage on the SAT test. Of course, you may not share your calculator with another student during the test. Doing so may result in dismissal from the test. If your calculator has a large or raised display that can be seen by other test takers, the test supervisor has the right to assign you to an appropriate seat, presumably not in the line of sight of other students. Calculators may not be on your desk during other SAT tests, aside from the Math Level 1 and Level 2 tests. If your calculator malfunctions during the test, and you don't have a backup or extra batteries, you can either choose to continue the test without a calculator or choose to cancel your test score.

When choosing what calculator to use for the test make sure your calculator performs the following functions:

- squaring a number
- raising a number to a power other than 2 (usually the {^} button.)
- taking the square root of a number.
- taking the cube root of a number (or, in other words, raising a number to the $\frac{1}{3}$ power)
- sine, cosine, and tangent
- $\sin^{-1}$, $\cos^{-1}$, $\tan^{-1}$
- can be set to both degree mode and radian mode

Also know where the π button and the parentheses buttons are and understand the difference between the subtraction symbol and the negative sign.

Because programmable calculators are allowed on the SAT II test, some students may frantically program their calculator with commonly used math formulas and facts, such as: distance, the quadratic formula, midpoint, slope, circumference, area, volume, surface area, lateral surface area, the trigonometric ratios, trigonometric identities, the Pythagorean Theorem, combinations, permutations, and *n*th terms of geometric/arithmetic sequences. Of course, if you do not truly understand these math facts and when to use them, you end up wasting significant time scrolling through your calculator searching for them.

On the Day of the Test

- Make sure your calculator works! (Putting new batteries in your calculator will provide you with peace of mind.)
- Bring a backup calculator and extra batteries to the test center.

MATH LEVEL 2 PRACTICE TEST 1

Treat this practice test as the actual test, and complete it in one 60-minute sitting. Use the following answer sheet to fill in your multiple-choice answers. Once you have completed the practice test:

1. Check your answers using the Answer Key.
2. Review the Answers and Solutions.
3. Fill in the "Diagnose Your Strengths and Weaknesses" sheet and determine areas that require further preparation.

ANSWER SHEET

Tear out this answer sheet and use it to complete the practice test. Determine the BEST answer for each question. Then, fill in the appropriate oval.

1. Ⓐ Ⓑ Ⓒ Ⓓ Ⓔ	21. Ⓐ Ⓑ Ⓒ Ⓓ Ⓔ	41. Ⓐ Ⓑ Ⓒ Ⓓ Ⓔ
2. Ⓐ Ⓑ Ⓒ Ⓓ Ⓔ	22. Ⓐ Ⓑ Ⓒ Ⓓ Ⓔ	42. Ⓐ Ⓑ Ⓒ Ⓓ Ⓔ
3. Ⓐ Ⓑ Ⓒ Ⓓ Ⓔ	23. Ⓐ Ⓑ Ⓒ Ⓓ Ⓔ	43. Ⓐ Ⓑ Ⓒ Ⓓ Ⓔ
4. Ⓐ Ⓑ Ⓒ Ⓓ Ⓔ	24. Ⓐ Ⓑ Ⓒ Ⓓ Ⓔ	44. Ⓐ Ⓑ Ⓒ Ⓓ Ⓔ
5. Ⓐ Ⓑ Ⓒ Ⓓ Ⓔ	25. Ⓐ Ⓑ Ⓒ Ⓓ Ⓔ	45. Ⓐ Ⓑ Ⓒ Ⓓ Ⓔ
6. Ⓐ Ⓑ Ⓒ Ⓓ Ⓔ	26. Ⓐ Ⓑ Ⓒ Ⓓ Ⓔ	46. Ⓐ Ⓑ Ⓒ Ⓓ Ⓔ
7. Ⓐ Ⓑ Ⓒ Ⓓ Ⓔ	27. Ⓐ Ⓑ Ⓒ Ⓓ Ⓔ	47. Ⓐ Ⓑ Ⓒ Ⓓ Ⓔ
8. Ⓐ Ⓑ Ⓒ Ⓓ Ⓔ	28. Ⓐ Ⓑ Ⓒ Ⓓ Ⓔ	48. Ⓐ Ⓑ Ⓒ Ⓓ Ⓔ
9. Ⓐ Ⓑ Ⓒ Ⓓ Ⓔ	29. Ⓐ Ⓑ Ⓒ Ⓓ Ⓔ	49. Ⓐ Ⓑ Ⓒ Ⓓ Ⓔ
10. Ⓐ Ⓑ Ⓒ Ⓓ Ⓔ	30. Ⓐ Ⓑ Ⓒ Ⓓ Ⓔ	50. Ⓐ Ⓑ Ⓒ Ⓓ Ⓔ
11. Ⓐ Ⓑ Ⓒ Ⓓ Ⓔ	31. Ⓐ Ⓑ Ⓒ Ⓓ Ⓔ	
12. Ⓐ Ⓑ Ⓒ Ⓓ Ⓔ	32. Ⓐ Ⓑ Ⓒ Ⓓ Ⓔ	
13. Ⓐ Ⓑ Ⓒ Ⓓ Ⓔ	33. Ⓐ Ⓑ Ⓒ Ⓓ Ⓔ	
14. Ⓐ Ⓑ Ⓒ Ⓓ Ⓔ	34. Ⓐ Ⓑ Ⓒ Ⓓ Ⓔ	
15. Ⓐ Ⓑ Ⓒ Ⓓ Ⓔ	35. Ⓐ Ⓑ Ⓒ Ⓓ Ⓔ	
16. Ⓐ Ⓑ Ⓒ Ⓓ Ⓔ	36. Ⓐ Ⓑ Ⓒ Ⓓ Ⓔ	
17. Ⓐ Ⓑ Ⓒ Ⓓ Ⓔ	37. Ⓐ Ⓑ Ⓒ Ⓓ Ⓔ	
18. Ⓐ Ⓑ Ⓒ Ⓓ Ⓔ	38. Ⓐ Ⓑ Ⓒ Ⓓ Ⓔ	
19. Ⓐ Ⓑ Ⓒ Ⓓ Ⓔ	39. Ⓐ Ⓑ Ⓒ Ⓓ Ⓔ	
20. Ⓐ Ⓑ Ⓒ Ⓓ Ⓔ	40. Ⓐ Ⓑ Ⓒ Ⓓ Ⓔ	

MATH LEVEL 2 PRACTICE TEST 1

Directions: Select the BEST answer for each of the 50 multiple-choice questions. If the exact solution is not one of the five choices, select the answer that is the best approximation. Then, fill in the appropriate oval on the answer sheet.

1. A calculator will be needed to answer some of the questions on the test. Scientific, programmable, and graphing calculators are permitted. It is up to you to determine when and when not to use your calculator.

2. Angles on the Level 2 test are measured in degrees and radians. You need to decide whether your calculator should be set to degree mode or radian mode for a particular question.

3. Figures are drawn as accurately as possible and are intended to help solve some of the test problems. If a figure is not drawn to scale, this will be stated in the problem. All figures lie in a plane unless the problem indicates otherwise.

4. Unless otherwise stated, the domain of a function f is assumed to be the set of real numbers x for which the value of the function, $f(x)$, is a real number.

5. Reference information that may be useful in answer some of the test questions can be found below.

Reference Information	
Right circular cone with radius r and height h:	Volume $= \dfrac{1}{3}\pi r^2 h$
Right circular cone with circumference of base c and slant height ℓ:	Lateral Area $= \dfrac{1}{2}c\ell$
Sphere with radius r:	Volume $= \dfrac{4}{3}\pi r^3$ Surface Area $= 4\pi r^2$
Pyramid with base area B and height h:	Volume $= \dfrac{1}{3}Bh$

1. If $3^x = 18$, $18^x =$

   (A) 2.6
   (B) 3
   (C) 108
   (D) 2,007
   (E) 34,012,224

2. A number k is increased by 12. If the cube root of that result equals -3, $k =$

   (A) -39
   (B) -27
   (C) -15
   (D) 15
   (E) 39

3. $\dfrac{(n!)^2}{(n-1)!^2} =$

   (A) n
   (B) $2n$
   (C) n^2
   (D) $(n-1)^2$
   (E) n^4

4. A point Q is in the second quadrant at a distance of $\sqrt{41}$ from the origin. Which of the following could be the coordinates of Q?

   (A) $(-1, 41)$
   (B) $(-4, 5)$
   (C) $\left(-8, \sqrt{23}\right)$
   (D) $(5, -4)$
   (E) $(-6, 5)$

5. $\tan \theta(\sin \theta) + \cos \theta =$

   (A) $2\cos \theta$
   (B) $\cos \theta + \sec \theta$
   (C) $\csc \theta$
   (D) $\sec \theta$
   (E) 1

GO ON TO THE NEXT PAGE

6. What is the domain of $f(x) = \sqrt{2 - x^2}$?

   (A) $x \leq \sqrt{2}$

   (B) $x \geq -\sqrt{2}$

   (C) $-\sqrt{2} \leq x \leq \sqrt{2}$

   (D) $x \leq -\sqrt{2}$ or $x \geq \sqrt{2}$

   (E) All real numbers

7. If $6n^3 = 48n^2$, then which of the following is the solution set for n?

   (A) $\{0\}$
   (B) $\{8\}$
   (C) $\{-8, 0, 8\}$
   (D) $\{0, 8\}$
   (E) $\{-8, 8\}$

8. If $f(x) = \sqrt{x}$ and $f[g(x)] = 2\sqrt{x}$, then $g(x) =$

   (A) $4x$
   (B) $2x$
   (C) $2x^2$

   (D) $\dfrac{x}{2}$

   (E) x^3

9. How many 3-person committees can be formed from a group of 10?

   (A) 6
   (B) 60
   (C) 120
   (D) 240
   (E) 720

10. What is the magnitude of vector v with initial point $(4, -1)$ and terminal point $(0, 2)$?

   (A) 3
   (B) 4
   (C) 5
   (D) $\sqrt{7}$
   (E) 25

GO ON TO THE NEXT PAGE

11. $p \square q$ is defined as $\dfrac{p^q}{pq}$ for all positive real numbers. Which of the following is equivalent to $\dfrac{p}{2}$?

(A) $p \square 1$
(B) $p \square p$
(C) $p \square \dfrac{1}{2}$
(D) $1 \square q$
(E) $p \square 2$

12. If the graph of the equation $y = mx + 5$ has points in the 3rd quadrant, then which of the following must be true for m?

(A) $m = 0$
(B) $m < 0$
(C) $0 < m < 1$
(D) $m > 0$
(E) $m = 5$

13. If a is an even integer, and b is an odd integer, then which of the following must be odd?

(A) ab
(B) a^b
(C) $a + b + 1$
(D) $2b + 1$
(E) $a - 2b$

14. What is the sum of the coefficients in the expansion of $(1 - 2x)^3$?

(A) -7
(B) -1
(C) 9
(D) 18
(E) 27

15. If $25x^2 - 20x + k = 0$ has $\dfrac{2}{5}$ as a double root, $k =$

(A) 4
(B) $\dfrac{4}{25}$
(C) 5
(D) -5
(E) 1

16. A triangle has sides measuring 3, 5, and 7 inches. What is the measure of its largest angle?

    (A) 135°
    (B) 60°
    (C) 120°
    (D) 150°
    (E) 153°

17. Which of the following is the equation of the circle with x-intercept (−3, 0) and y-intercept (0, 3) whose center is in the 2nd quadrant?

    (A) $(x-3)^2 + (y-3)^2 = 9$
    (B) $(x-3)^2 + (y+3)^2 = 9$
    (C) $(x+3)^2 + (y-3)^2 = 3$
    (D) $(x-3)^2 + (y+3)^2 = 3$
    (E) $(x+3)^2 + (y-3)^2 = 9$

18. Cost is a function of the number of units produced as given by: $C(n) = 0.02n^2 - 42n + 5,000$. How many units, n, produce a minimum cost C?

    (A) 525
    (B) 1,050
    (C) 2,100
    (D) 17,050
    (E) 125,000

19. Some number n is added to the three numbers −2, 10, and 94 to create the first three terms of a geometric sequence. What is the value of n?

    (A) 1
    (B) 2
    (C) 3
    (D) 4
    (E) 5

20. A right circular cylinder has a height of 15 and a radius of 4. If A and B are two points on the surface of the cylinder, what is the maximum possible length of AB?

    (A) 15.1
    (B) 15.5
    (C) 17
    (D) 21.2
    (E) 26

USE THIS SPACE AS SCRATCH PAPER

GO ON TO THE NEXT PAGE

21. Five integers are arranged from least to greatest. If the median is 12 and the only mode is 5, what is the least possible range for the 5 numbers?

    (A) 5
    (B) 7
    (C) 8
    (D) 9
    (E) 14

22. Which of the following equations has roots of 4 and $-\dfrac{1}{2}$?

    (A) $2x^3 + x^2 - 32x - 16 = 0$
    (B) $2x^2 + 7x - 4 = 0$
    (C) $2x^2 - 9x - 4 = 0$
    (D) $2x^2 - 7x - 4 = 0$
    (E) $4(2x + 1) = 0$

23. What is the maximum value of $f(x) = 7 - (x - 6)^2$?

    (A) −7
    (B) −6
    (C) 1
    (D) 6
    (E) 7

24. If $\sec\theta < 0$ and $\cot\theta > 0$, then in which quadrant does θ lie?

    (A) I
    (B) II
    (C) III
    (D) IV
    (E) II or III

25. What is the sum of the integers from 1 to 100?

    (A) 4,950
    (B) 5,000
    (C) 5,050
    (D) 9,900
    (E) 10,100

USE THIS SPACE AS SCRATCH PAPER

GO ON TO THE NEXT PAGE

26. The ellipse given by the equation $9x^2 + 4y^2 - 36x - 12y + 18 = 0$ is centered at

 (A) $\left(2, \dfrac{3}{2}\right)$

 (B) $\left(4, \dfrac{9}{4}\right)$

 (C) $\left(\dfrac{3}{2}, 2\right)$

 (D) $\left(-2, -\dfrac{3}{2}\right)$

 (E) $(-2, -3)$

27. Which of the following lines are asymptotes of the graph of $f(x) = \dfrac{2(x-4)}{x^2-1}$?

 I. $x = 4$
 II. $x = \pm 1$
 III. $y = 0$

 (A) I only
 (B) II only
 (C) I and II only
 (D) II and III only
 (E) I, II, and III

28. On a construction job, there is a 0.08 probability a certain tool is in error of 2% or more. If 4 tools are used, what is the probability that all of them are in error of 2% or more?

 (A) 0.00004
 (B) 0.0005
 (C) 0.02
 (D) 0.40
 (E) 0.32

29. If $\cos 2\theta = \dfrac{2}{7}$, then $\dfrac{1}{\cos^2\theta - \sin^2\theta} =$

 (A) -1

 (B) $\dfrac{7}{2}$

 (C) $\dfrac{2}{7}$

 (D) $\dfrac{49}{4}$

 (E) $\dfrac{1}{7}$

GO ON TO THE NEXT PAGE

30. If $8\sin^2\theta + 2\sin\theta - 1 = 0$, then what is the smallest positive value of θ?

    (A) 7.3°
    (B) 14.5°
    (C) 30°
    (D) 60°
    (E) 75.5°

31. What value does $f(x) = \dfrac{3x - 16}{x + 7}$ approach as x gets infinitely large?

    (A) $\dfrac{1}{3}$

    (B) $\dfrac{1}{2}$

    (C) 1
    (D) 2
    (E) 3

32. If $8.1^a = 3.6^b$, then $\dfrac{a}{b} =$

    (A) −0.35
    (B) 0.61
    (C) 0.67
    (D) 1.63
    (E) 1.5

33. A point has rectangular coordinates (2, 5). If the polar coordinates are (r, θ), then $\theta =$

    (A) 21.8°
    (B) 23.6°
    (C) 66.4°
    (D) 68.2°
    (E) 80.2°

34. The graph of $f(x) = x^2$ is translated 2 units down and 4 units left. If the resulting graph represents $g(x)$, then $g(-5) =$

    (A) −1
    (B) 3
    (C) 45
    (D) 79
    (E) 81

35. $(12\sin x)(2\sin x) - (8\cos x)(-3\cos x) =$

    (A) 1
    (B) −1
    (C) 24
    (D) $48 \sin^2 x$
    (E) $24 \sin^2 x - 24\cos^2 x$

GO ON TO THE NEXT PAGE

36. If two dice are rolled, what is the probability the sum of the numbers is 4 or 5?

    (A) $\dfrac{1}{12}$

    (B) $\dfrac{1}{9}$

    (C) $\dfrac{5}{36}$

    (D) $\dfrac{1}{6}$

    (E) $\dfrac{7}{36}$

37. If $f(x) = \dfrac{12}{x}$, then $f^{-1}(-8) =$

    (A) −96
    (B) −1.5
    (C) −0.67
    (D) −0.50
    (E) 1.5

38. Which of the following is an even function?

    (A) $f(x) = 2\sec x$
    (B) $f(x) = x^3$
    (C) $f(x) = -(x + 3)^2$
    (D) $f(x) = \tan x$
    (E) $f(x) = (x + 1)^4$

39. All of the following functions have a period of π except which one?

    (A) $y = \sin 2x + 2$
    (B) $y = 2 \cos 2x$

    (C) $y = \dfrac{1}{2} \cos 2\pi x$

    (D) $y = 4 \tan x$
    (E) $y = 2 \csc 2x$

40. The French Club consists of 10 members and is holding officer elections to select a president, secretary, and treasurer for the club. A member can only be selected for one position. How many possibilities are there for selecting the three officers?

    (A) 30
    (B) 27
    (C) 72
    (D) 720
    (E) 90

USE THIS SPACE AS SCRATCH PAPER

GO ON TO THE NEXT PAGE

41. The graph in Figure 1 could be a portion of the graph of which of the following functions?

    I. $f(x) = x^3 + ax^2 + bx^1 + c$
    II. $g(x) = -x^3 + ax^2 + bx^1 + c$
    III. $h(x) = -x^5 + ax^4 + bx^3 + cx^2 + dx + e$

    (A) I only
    (B) II only
    (C) I and II only
    (D) II and III only
    (E) I, II, and III

USE THIS SPACE AS SCRATCH PAPER

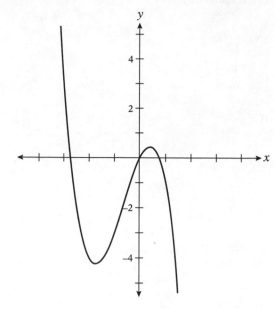

Figure 1

42. If $f(x) = \ln e^{2x}$, then what is the smallest possible integer x such that $f(x) > 10,000$?

    (A) 2,501
    (B) 4,999
    (C) 5,000
    (D) 5,001
    (E) 10,001

43. If $\log_2 (x - 1) = \log_4 (x - 9)$, then $x =$

    (A) −2
    (B) 2
    (C) 5
    (D) −2 or 5
    (E) No solution

44. If $[n]$ represents the greatest integer less than or equal to n, then which of the following is the solution to $2[n] - 16 = 6$?

    (A) $n = 11$
    (B) $11 \le n < 12$
    (C) $n = 12$
    (D) $11 < n < 12$
    (E) $11 < n \le 12$

45. If a rectangular prism has faces with areas of 10, 12 and 30 units², then what is its volume?

    (A) 30
    (B) 60
    (C) 90
    (D) 120
    (E) 150

GO ON TO THE NEXT PAGE

46. Given θ is in the first quadrant, if $\sec \theta = 3$, what is the value of $\sin 2\theta$?

    (A) 0.63
    (B) 0.31
    (C) 0.33
    (D) 0.67
    (E) 0.94

47. What are the intercepts of the circle given by the equation $(x + 4)^2 + (y - 4)^2 = 2$?

    (A) $(-4, 0), (0, 4)$
    (B) $(4, 0), (0, -4)$
    (C) $(0, \pm 4), (\pm 4, 0)$
    (D) $(0, -4), (-4, 0)$
    (E) There are no intercepts.

48. The mean score on a math test is 85%. If the teacher decides to scale the grades by increasing each score by 5 percentage points, what is the new mean of the data?

    (A) 85%
    (B) 86%
    (C) 87.5%
    (D) 88%
    (E) 90%

49. If $0 \leq x \leq \dfrac{\pi}{2}$, $f(x) = \sin(\arctan x)$ and $g(x) = \tan(\arcsin x)$, then $f\left(g\left(\dfrac{1}{4}\right)\right) =$

    (A) 0.26
    (B) 0.75
    (C) 0.25
    (D) 1.25
    (E) 0.24

50. $|6 - 3i| =$

    (A) 3
    (B) $3\sqrt{5}$
    (C) 9
    (D) $3\sqrt{3}$
    (E) 45

S T O P

IF YOU FINISH BEFORE TIME IS CALLED, YOU MAY CHECK YOUR WORK ON THIS TEST ONLY.
DO NOT TURN TO ANY OTHER TEST IN THIS BOOK.

ANSWER KEY

1. D	11. E	21. D	31. E	41. D
2. A	12. D	22. D	32. B	42. D
3. C	13. D	23. E	33. D	43. E
4. B	14. B	24. C	34. A	44. B
5. D	15. A	25. C	35. C	45. B
6. C	16. C	26. A	36. E	46. A
7. D	17. E	27. D	37. B	47. E
8. A	18. B	28. A	38. A	48. E
9. C	19. D	29. B	39. C	49. C
10. C	20. C	30. B	40. D	50. B

ANSWERS AND SOLUTIONS

1. **D** Take either the log or natural log of both sides of the equation to solve for x.

$3^x = 18.$

$\log 3^x = \log 18.$

$x \log 8 = \log 18.$

$x = \dfrac{\log 18}{\log 3} \approx 2.6309.$

$18^x = 18^{2.309} \approx 2{,}007.$

2. **A**

$(k + 12)^{\frac{1}{3}} = -3.$

Cube each side of the equation to solve for k.

$\left[(k + 12)^{\frac{1}{3}}\right]^3 = (-3)^3.$

$k + 12 = -27.$

$k = -39.$

3. **C**

$\dfrac{(n!)^2}{(n-1)!^2}$

$= \left[\dfrac{n!}{(n-1)!}\right]^2$

$= n^2.$

4. **B** $(-4, 5)$ is the only given point that is both in the second quadrant and at a distance of $\sqrt{41}$ from the origin.

$\sqrt{(-4 - 0)^2 + (5 - 0)^2} =$

$\sqrt{4^2 + 5^2} =$

$\sqrt{16 + 25} =$

$\sqrt{41}.$

5. **D**

$$\tan \theta (\sin \theta) + \cos \theta =$$

$$\frac{\sin \theta}{\cos \theta}(\sin \theta) + \cos \theta =$$

$$\frac{\sin^2 \theta}{\cos \theta} + \frac{\cos^2 \theta}{\cos \theta} =$$

$$\frac{\sin^2 \theta + \cos^2 \theta}{\cos \theta} =$$

$$\frac{1}{\cos \theta} = \sec \theta.$$

6. **C** The radicand must be greater than or equal to zero.

$$2 - x^2 \geq 0.$$

$$2 \geq x^2.$$

$$x \leq -\sqrt{2} \text{ or } x \geq \sqrt{2}.$$

7. **D**

$$6n^3 = 48n^2.$$

$$6n^3 - 48n^2 = 0.$$

$$6n^2(n - 8) = 0 \quad n = 0 \text{ or } 8.$$

8. **A** Because you know the composition of f and g results in $2\sqrt{x}$, you need to determine what input value of f will result in $2\sqrt{x}$.

$$\sqrt{4x} = 2\sqrt{x}.$$

Therefore, $g(x) = 4x$. Test your answer by checking the composition.

$$g(x) = 4x, \text{ so } f[g(x)] = f(4x) = \sqrt{4x} = 2\sqrt{x}.$$

9. **C**

$$\frac{10!}{3!(10 - 3)!} = \frac{10!}{3!7!}$$

$$= \frac{8 \times 9 \times 10}{1 \times 2 \times 3}$$

$$= 120.$$

10. **C** The components of v are given by $(4 - 0, -1 - 2)$, or $(4, -3)$. The magnitude is the length of v.

$$\|v\| = \sqrt{4^2 + (-3)^2}.$$

$$\|v\| = \sqrt{25}.$$

$$\|v\| = 5.$$

11. **E**

$$p \,\square\, 2 = \frac{p^2}{p(2)}.$$

$$= \frac{p}{2}$$

12. **D** Because the y-intercept of the line $y = mx + 5$ is positive, then the slope of the line must be positive in order for part of the line to fall in the 3rd quadrant. $m > 0$ is the correct answer choice.

13. **D** Because b is odd, multiplying b by two will always result in an even number. Adding one to an even product will always result in an odd number, so answer D is the correct choice. If you're not sure about number theory, try substituting values for a and b. Let $a = 4$ and $b = 3$.

$$ab = 4(3) = 12$$

$$a^b = 4^3 = 64.$$

$$a + b + 1 = 4 + 3 + 1 + 8.$$

$$2b + 1 = 2(3) + 1 = 7.$$

$$a - 2b = 4 - 2(3) = 4 - 6 = -2$$

7 is the only odd result.

14. **B** The binomial expansion of $(1 - 2x)^3$ is:

$$1 - 6x + 12x^2 - 8x^3.$$

The sum of the coefficients is therefore: $1 + (-6) + 12 + (-8) = -1$.

15. **A** Because $\frac{2}{5}$ is a double root, $\left(x - \frac{2}{5}\right)$ is a factor of the quadratic equation two times.

$$\left(x - \frac{2}{5}\right)\left(x - \frac{2}{5}\right) = 0.$$

$$(5x - 2)(5x - 2) = 0.$$

$$25x^2 - 10x + 4 = 0.$$

$$k = 4.$$

16. **C** The largest angle of a triangle is opposite its longest side. Let θ = the largest angle of the triangle. θ is opposite the side measuring 7 inches. Using the Law of Cosines:

$$7^2 = 3^2 + 5^2 - 2(3)(5) \cos \theta.$$

$$49 = 9 + 25 - 30 \cos \theta.$$

$$15 = -30 \cos \theta.$$

$$\cos \theta = -\frac{1}{2}.$$

$$\theta = \cos^{-1} -\frac{1}{2} \approx 120°.$$

17. **E** Because the center of the circle must lie in the 2nd quadrant, its coordinates are $(-3, 3)$. The radius of the circle is $3^2 = 9$.

Therefore, the standard form of the equation of the circle is $(x + 3)^2 + (y - 3)^2 = 9$.

18. **B** The minimum value of a quadratic equation $ax^2 + bx + c$ occurs when $x = -\frac{b}{2a}$.

When graphed, the minimum occurs at the vertex of a parabola that is concave up.

$$C(n) = 0.02n^2 - 42n + 5,000.$$

$$n = -\frac{b}{2a} = -\frac{(-42)}{2(0.02)} = 1,050 \text{ units.}$$

19. **D** For the three terms to be part of a geometric sequence there must be a common ratio between consecutive terms. Add n to each of the three terms to get the progression $-2 + n$, $10 + n$, $94 + n$. Now, set the common ratios equal to each other and solve for n.

$$\frac{10 + n}{-2 + n} = \frac{94 + n}{10 + n}$$

$$(10 + n)(10 + n) = (-2 + n)(94 + n)$$

$$100 + 20n + n^2 = -188 + 92n + n^2$$

$$288 = 72n$$

$$n = 4$$

20. **C** Think of A and B as vertices of a right triangle with one leg measuring 8 units (the diameter of the cylinder's base) and one leg measuring 15 units (the height).

$$AB = \sqrt{8^2 + 15^2}.$$

$$AB = \sqrt{64 + 225}.$$

$$AB = \sqrt{289} = 17.$$

21. **D** Because the median is 12, the 3rd term when arranged from least to greatest is 12. The mode is 5, so the 2 integers less than 12 equal 5. Note that 5 is the *only* mode. Because the problem asks for the *least* possible range, assume the five integers are:

$$5, 5, 12, 13, 14$$

The range equals $14 - 5$, or 9.

22. **D** An equation with roots of 4 and $-\frac{1}{2}$ has factors $x - 4$ and $x + \frac{1}{2}$.

$$(x - 4)\left(x + \frac{1}{2}\right) = 0.$$

$$(x - 4)(2x + 1) = 0.$$

$$2x^2 + x - 8x - 4 = 0.$$

$$2x^2 - 7x - 4 = 0.$$

23. **E** The maximum value of $f(x) = 7 - (x - 6)^2$ is the y-coordinate of its vertex.

$$f(x) = 7 - (x - 6)^2$$

$$y - 7 = -(x - 6)^2$$

The vertex is $(6, 7)$, so the maximum value is 7.

24. **C**

If $\sec \theta < 0$, then $\cos \theta < 0$.

If $\cot \theta > 0$, then $\tan \theta > 0$.

The cosine is negative in both quadrants II and III. For the tangent to be positive, however, $\sin \theta$ must also be a negative value. This occurs in quadrant III only.

25. **C** The integers from 1 to 100 form an arithmetic sequence having 100 terms. $n = 100$, $a_1 = 1$, and $a_n = 100$. Substitute these values into the formula for the sum of a finite arithmetic sequence to get:

$$S_n = 1 + 2 + 3 + 4 + 5 + \cdots + 100.$$

$$S_n = \frac{n}{2}(a_1 + a_n).$$

$$S_n = \frac{100}{2}(1 + 100).$$

$$S_n = 50(101) = 5,050.$$

26. **A** Complete the square to write the equation of the ellipse in standard form.

$$9x^2 + 4y^2 - 36x - 12y + 18 = 0.$$

$$(9x^2 - 36x) + (4y^2 - 12y) = -18.$$

$$9(x^2 - 4x + 4) + 4\left(y^2 - 3y + \frac{9}{4}\right) = -18 + 36 + 9.$$

$$9(x - 2)^2 + \left(y - \frac{3}{2}\right)^2 = 27.$$

$$\frac{(x - 2)^2}{3} + \frac{\left(y - \left(\frac{3}{2}\right)\right)^2}{\left(\frac{27}{4}\right)} = 1.$$

The center of the ellipse is $\left(2, \frac{3}{2}\right)$.

27. **D** The function $f(x) = \frac{2(x - 4)}{x^2 - 1}$ has vertical asymptotes at the zeroes of the denominator.

$$x^2 - 1 = 0.$$

$$x = \pm 1.$$

Because the degree of the numerator is less than the degree of the denominator, a horizontal asymptote exists at $y = 0$.

Statements II and III are, therefore, true.

28. **A** The probability that all 4 tools are in error of 2% or more is:

$$0.08(0.08)(0.08)(0.08) \approx 04.10 \times 10^{-5}.$$

29. **B** The double angle formula for cosine is:

$$\cos 2\theta = \cos^2 \theta - \sin^2 \theta.$$

Since $\cos 2\theta = \frac{2}{7}$, $\cos^2 \theta - \sin^2 \theta$ also equals $\frac{2}{7}$.

$$\frac{1}{\cos^2 \theta - \sin^2 \theta} = \frac{1}{\frac{2}{7}} = \frac{7}{2}.$$

30. **B** Factor the equation and solve for θ.

$$8\sin^2 \theta + 2\sin \theta - 1 = 0.$$

$$(4\sin \theta - 1)(2\sin \theta + 1) = 0.$$

$$\sin \theta = -\frac{1}{2} \text{ or } \sin \theta = \frac{1}{4}.$$

$$\theta \approx -30° \text{ or } 14.5°.$$

$14.5°$ is the smallest positive value of θ.

31. **E** Graph the function to see that it has a horizontal asymptote at $y = 3$. (Because the degree of the numerator equals the degree of the denominator, a horizontal asymptote occurs at $\frac{3}{1}$, the ratio of the coefficients of the x terms.) Alternately, you can evaluate the function at a large value of x. For example, let $x = 10,000$:

$$f(10,000) = \frac{3(10,000) - 16}{10,000 + 7}$$

$$= 2.9963.$$

The function approaches 3 as x gets infinitely large.

32. **B** Take the logarithm of both sides of the equation to solve for $\frac{a}{b}$.

$$8.1^a = 3.6^b.$$

$$a \log 8.1 = b \log 3.6.$$

$$\frac{a}{b} = \frac{\log 3.6}{\log 8.1}.$$

$$\frac{a}{b} \approx 0.61.$$

33. **D** Because the rectangular coordinates (x, y) are $(2, 5)$:

$$\tan \theta = \frac{y}{x} = \frac{5}{2}.$$

$$\tan^{-1}\left(\frac{5}{2}\right) \approx 68.2°.$$

34. **A** Translating the graph of $f(x) = x^2$ 2 units down and 4 units left results in:

$$g(x) = (x + 4)^2 - 2$$

Now, evaluate the function for $x = -5$.

$$g(-5) = (-5 + 4)^2 - 2 = 1 - 2 = -1.$$

35. **C**

$$(12 \sin x)(2 \sin x) - (8 \cos x)(-3 \cos x) =$$

$$24 \sin^2 x + 24 \cos^2 x =$$

$$24(\sin^2 x + \cos^2 x) =$$

$$24(1) = 24.$$

36. **E** There are 36 possible outcomes when two dice are rolled. The following rolls result in a sum of 4 or 5:

$$\{(2,2), (3,1), (1,3), (4,1), (1,4), (2,3), (3,2)\}$$

Seven out of the 36 have a sum of 4 or 5, so the probability is $\dfrac{7}{36}$.

37. **B** Reflecting the graph of $f(x) = \dfrac{12}{x}$ over the line $y = x$ results in the original function. The inverse function of $f(x) = \dfrac{12}{x}$ is, therefore, $f^{-1}(x) = \dfrac{12}{x}$.

$$f^{-1}(-8) = \frac{12}{-8} = -1.5.$$

38. **A** Recall that a function is even if it is symmetric with respect to the y-axis and $f(-x) = f(x)$. Because the cosine function is an even function, its reciprocal function, the secant function, is also even. Answer A is the correct answer choice.

39. **C** All of the functions have a period of $\dfrac{2\pi}{2}$ or π with the exception of $y = \dfrac{1}{2} \cos 2\pi x$. It has a period of $\dfrac{2\pi}{2\pi} = 1$. Answer C is the correct answer choice.

40. **D** There are 10 possible people that could serve as president. Once the president is chosen, there are 9 possible people that could serve as secretary, and once that person is chosen, there are 8 remaining people that could serve as treasurer. The total number of ways of selecting the three officers is:

$$10 \times 9 \times 8 = 720.$$

41. **D** The graph has three zeroes. Because it rises to the left and falls to the right, it represents an odd-degree polynomial with a negative leading coefficient. Either statement II or III are possible answers.

42. **D** Because $f(x) = \ln e^{2x}$ must be greater than 10,000:

$$2x > 10,000$$

$$x > 5,000$$

The smallest possible integer greater than 5,000 is 5,001.

43. **E** Use the change of base formula to rewrite the right side of the equation.

$$\log_2 (x - 1) = \log_4 (x - 9).$$

$$\log_2 (x - 1) = \frac{\log_2 (x - 9)}{\log_2 4}$$

$$\log_2 (x - 1) = \frac{\log_2 (x - 9)}{2}.$$

Now, solve for x.

$$2 \log_2 (x - 1) = \log_4 (x - 9).$$

$$(x - 1)^2 = x - 9.$$

$$x^2 - 2x + 1 = x - 9.$$

$$x^2 - 3x + 10 = 0.$$

Solving for x using the quadratic formula results in no real solution.

44. **B**

$$2[n] - 16 = 6.$$

$$2[n] = 22.$$

$$[n] = 11.$$

11 is the greatest integer less than or equal to n, so n must be on the interval $11 \le n < 12$.

45. **B** Let w = the width, l = the length, and h = the height of the prism. Using the three given areas:

$wh = 10.$

$wl = 30.$

$lh = 12.$

Use substitution to solve for the variables and determine $w = 5$, $l = 6$, and $h = 2$.

The volume is, therefore, $6 \times 5 \times 2 = 60$ units^3.

46. **A** If $\sec \theta = 3$, then $\cos \theta = \frac{1}{3}$. Picture a right triangle in quadrant I to determine that the value of $\sin \theta = \frac{2\sqrt{2}}{3}$.

Recall the double angle formula for sine:

$\sin 2\theta = 2 \sin \theta \cos \theta.$

$\sin 2\theta = 2\left(\frac{2\sqrt{2}}{3}\right)\left(\frac{1}{3}\right) = \frac{4\sqrt{2}}{9} \approx 0.63.$

47. **E** The circle given by the equation $(x + 4)^2 + (y - 4)^2 = 2$ is centered at $(-4, 4)$ and has a radius of $\sqrt{2}$. Because the radius is less than 4 units long, there are no x and y intercepts.

48. **E** If each score is increased by 5 percentage points, the mean also increases by 5. The new mean would, therefore, be $85 + 5 = 90\%$.

49. **C**

$g\left(\frac{1}{4}\right) = \tan\left(\arcsin\frac{1}{4}\right) \approx 0.258.$

$f(0.258) = \sin(\arctan 0.258) = 0.25.$

50. **B** Recall that the absolute value of a complex number is given by: $|a + bi| = \sqrt{a^2 + b^2}$.

$|6 - 3i| = \sqrt{6^2 + (-3)^2} = \sqrt{45} = 3\sqrt{5}$

■■■ DIAGNOSE YOUR STRENGTHS AND WEAKNESSES

Check the number of each question answered correctly and "X" the number of each question answered incorrectly.

Algebra	1	2	3	7	14	32	43	44	Total Number Correct
8 questions									

Solid Geometry	20	45	Total Number Correct
2 questions			

Coordinate Geometry	4	12	17	26	33	34	47	Total Number Correct
7 questions								

Trigonometry	5	16	24	29	30	35	46	49	Total Number Correct
8 questions									

Functions	6	8	15	18	22	23	27	37	38	39	41	42	Total Number Correct
12 questions													

Data Analysis, Statistics, and Probability	21	28	36	48	Total Number Correct
4 questions					

Number and Operations	9	10	11	13	19	25	31	40	50	Total Number Correct
9 questions										

Number of correct answers $-\frac{1}{4}$ **(Number of incorrect answers) = Your raw score**

_____ $-\frac{1}{4}$ (_____) = _____

Compare your raw score with the approximate SAT test score below:

	Raw Score	SAT Approximate Score
Excellent	43–50	770–800
Very Good	33–43	670–770
Good	27–33	620–670
Above Average	21–27	570–620
Average	11–21	500–570
Below Average	< 11	< 500

MATH LEVEL 2 PRACTICE TEST 2

Treat this practice test as the actual test and complete it in one 60-minute sitting. Use the following answer sheet to fill in your multiple-choice answers. Once you have completed the practice test:

1. Check your answers using the Answer Key.
2. Review the Answers and Solutions.
3. Fill in the "Diagnose Your Strengths and Weaknesses" sheet and determine areas that require further preparation.

ANSWER SHEET

Tear out this answer sheet and use it to complete the practice test. Determine the BEST answer for each question. Then, fill in the appropriate oval.

1. Ⓐ Ⓑ Ⓒ Ⓓ Ⓔ	21. Ⓐ Ⓑ Ⓒ Ⓓ Ⓔ	41. Ⓐ Ⓑ Ⓒ Ⓓ Ⓔ
2. Ⓐ Ⓑ Ⓒ Ⓓ Ⓔ	22. Ⓐ Ⓑ Ⓒ Ⓓ Ⓔ	42. Ⓐ Ⓑ Ⓒ Ⓓ Ⓔ
3. Ⓐ Ⓑ Ⓒ Ⓓ Ⓔ	23. Ⓐ Ⓑ Ⓒ Ⓓ Ⓔ	43. Ⓐ Ⓑ Ⓒ Ⓓ Ⓔ
4. Ⓐ Ⓑ Ⓒ Ⓓ Ⓔ	24. Ⓐ Ⓑ Ⓒ Ⓓ Ⓔ	44. Ⓐ Ⓑ Ⓒ Ⓓ Ⓔ
5. Ⓐ Ⓑ Ⓒ Ⓓ Ⓔ	25. Ⓐ Ⓑ Ⓒ Ⓓ Ⓔ	45. Ⓐ Ⓑ Ⓒ Ⓓ Ⓔ
6. Ⓐ Ⓑ Ⓒ Ⓓ Ⓔ	26. Ⓐ Ⓑ Ⓒ Ⓓ Ⓔ	46. Ⓐ Ⓑ Ⓒ Ⓓ Ⓔ
7. Ⓐ Ⓑ Ⓒ Ⓓ Ⓔ	27. Ⓐ Ⓑ Ⓒ Ⓓ Ⓔ	47. Ⓐ Ⓑ Ⓒ Ⓓ Ⓔ
8. Ⓐ Ⓑ Ⓒ Ⓓ Ⓔ	28. Ⓐ Ⓑ Ⓒ Ⓓ Ⓔ	48. Ⓐ Ⓑ Ⓒ Ⓓ Ⓔ
9. Ⓐ Ⓑ Ⓒ Ⓓ Ⓔ	29. Ⓐ Ⓑ Ⓒ Ⓓ Ⓔ	49. Ⓐ Ⓑ Ⓒ Ⓓ Ⓔ
10. Ⓐ Ⓑ Ⓒ Ⓓ Ⓔ	30. Ⓐ Ⓑ Ⓒ Ⓓ Ⓔ	50. Ⓐ Ⓑ Ⓒ Ⓓ Ⓔ
11. Ⓐ Ⓑ Ⓒ Ⓓ Ⓔ	31. Ⓐ Ⓑ Ⓒ Ⓓ Ⓔ	
12. Ⓐ Ⓑ Ⓒ Ⓓ Ⓔ	32. Ⓐ Ⓑ Ⓒ Ⓓ Ⓔ	
13. Ⓐ Ⓑ Ⓒ Ⓓ Ⓔ	33. Ⓐ Ⓑ Ⓒ Ⓓ Ⓔ	
14. Ⓐ Ⓑ Ⓒ Ⓓ Ⓔ	34. Ⓐ Ⓑ Ⓒ Ⓓ Ⓔ	
15. Ⓐ Ⓑ Ⓒ Ⓓ Ⓔ	35. Ⓐ Ⓑ Ⓒ Ⓓ Ⓔ	
16. Ⓐ Ⓑ Ⓒ Ⓓ Ⓔ	36. Ⓐ Ⓑ Ⓒ Ⓓ Ⓔ	
17. Ⓐ Ⓑ Ⓒ Ⓓ Ⓔ	37. Ⓐ Ⓑ Ⓒ Ⓓ Ⓔ	
18. Ⓐ Ⓑ Ⓒ Ⓓ Ⓔ	38. Ⓐ Ⓑ Ⓒ Ⓓ Ⓔ	
19. Ⓐ Ⓑ Ⓒ Ⓓ Ⓔ	39. Ⓐ Ⓑ Ⓒ Ⓓ Ⓔ	
20. Ⓐ Ⓑ Ⓒ Ⓓ Ⓔ	40. Ⓐ Ⓑ Ⓒ Ⓓ Ⓔ	

MATH LEVEL 2 PRACTICE TEST 2

Directions: Select the BEST answer for each of the 50 multiple-choice questions. If the exact solution is not one of the five choices, select the answer that is the best approximation. Then, fill in the appropriate oval on the answer sheet.

1. A calculator will be needed to answer some of the questions on the test. Scientific, programmable, and graphing calculators are permitted. It is up to you to determine when and when not to use your calculator.

2. Angles on the Level 2 test are measured in degrees and radians. You need to decide whether your calculator should be set to degree mode or radian mode for a particular question.

3. Figures are drawn as accurately as possible and are intended to help solve some of the test problems. If a figure is not drawn to scale, this will be stated in the problem. All figures lie in a plane unless the problem indicates otherwise.

4. Unless otherwise stated, the domain of a function f is assumed to be the set of real numbers x for which the value of the function, $f(x)$, is a real number.

5. Reference information that may be useful in answer some of the test questions can be found below.

Reference Information	
Right circular cone with radius r and height h:	Volume $= \dfrac{1}{3}\pi r^2 h$
Right circular cone with circumference of base c and slant height ℓ:	Lateral Area $= \dfrac{1}{2}c\ell$
Sphere with radius r:	Volume $= \dfrac{4}{3}\pi r^3$ Surface Area $= 4\pi r^2$
Pyramid with base area B and height h:	Volume $= \dfrac{1}{3}Bh$

1. If $i = \sqrt{-1}$, then $(6 - i)(6 + i) =$

    (A) 35
    (B) $36 - i$
    (C) 37
    (D) $35 + 12i$
    (E) 36

2. If $f(x) = x^2 - 8x$, then $2f(2x) =$

    (A) $2x^2 - 16x$
    (B) $4x^2 - 16x$
    (C) $8x^2 - 16x$
    (D) $8x^2 - 32x$
    (E) $4x^2 - 32x$

3. If a function f is an odd function and (x, y) is a point on its graph, then which of the following will also be a point on its graph?

    (A) (y, x)
    (B) $(-x, -y)$
    (C) $(-y, -x)$
    (D) $(x, -y)$
    (E) $(-x, y)$

4. What real values of a and b satisfy the equation
    $a + b + 14i = 4 + (3a - b)i$?

    (A) $a = 5, b = 1$
    (B) $a = \dfrac{9}{2}, b = \dfrac{1}{2}$
    (C) $a = 5, b = -1$
    (D) $a = 3, b = 1$
    (E) $a = \dfrac{9}{2}, b = -\dfrac{1}{2}$

5. Standing 25 feet away from a tree, the angle of elevation of the top of the tree is 26°. Assuming the tree grows perpendicular to the ground, what is its height?

    (A) 12.2 ft
    (B) 16.2 ft
    (C) 19.1 ft
    (D) 21.2 ft
    (E) 29.5 ft

GO ON TO THE NEXT PAGE

6. If $\sin \theta = -\dfrac{9}{41}$ and $\pi < \theta < \dfrac{3\pi}{2}$, then $\cos \theta =$

   (A) $-\dfrac{40}{41}$

   (B) $-\dfrac{9}{40}$

   (C) $-\dfrac{32}{41}$

   (D) $\dfrac{9}{40}$

   (E) $\dfrac{40}{41}$

7. Which of the following is an equation of the line with x-intercept of 5 and y-intercept of -1?

   (A) $\dfrac{1}{5}x - y = -1$

   (B) $\dfrac{1}{5}x + y = 1$

   (C) $x - 5y = 5$

   (D) $x + 5y = -5$

   (E) $x - 5y = -5$

8. The product of the roots of a quadratic equation is -5 and their sum is -4. Which of the following could be the quadratic equation?

   (A) $x^2 - 4x + 5 = 0$
   (B) $x^2 - 4x - 5 = 0$
   (C) $x^2 + 4x - 5 = 0$
   (D) $x^2 + 5x - 4 = 0$
   (E) $x^2 - 5x - 4 = 0$

9. If $f(n) = 9^{-n}$, then $f\left(-\dfrac{1}{4}\right) =$

   (A) $9^{-\frac{1}{4}}$
   (B) 3
   (C) $\sqrt{3}$
   (D) $\dfrac{1}{9}$
   (E) 9

10. If $\log_4 x + 3\log_4 x = 9$, then $x =$

   (A) 1.86
   (B) 2.25
   (C) 9
   (D) 22.6
   (E) 256

USE THIS SPACE AS SCRATCH PAPER

GO ON TO THE NEXT PAGE

11. If $f(x) = |x^2 - 5|$ for $-1 \le x \le 4$, then what is the range of f?

   (A) $y \ge 0$
   (B) $y \le 11$
   (C) $4 \le y \le 11$
   (D) $0 \le y \le 11$
   (E) $0 \le y \le 4$

USE THIS SPACE AS SCRATCH PAPER

12. $(1 + \sin \theta)(1 - \sin \theta) =$

   (A) $1 - \sin \theta$
   (B) $\cos^2 \theta$
   (C) $1 - 2\sin \theta + \sin^2 \theta$
   (D) $\cos \theta$
   (E) 1

13. What is the minimum value of $f(x) = (x - 1)^2 + 18$?

   (A) -18
   (B) -1
   (C) 19
   (D) 1
   (E) 18

14. Carolyn has 6 magazines. If she wants to bring 3 of them with her on vacation, how many different combinations of 3 magazines are possible?

   (A) 10
   (B) 18
   (C) 20
   (D) 60
   (E) 20

15. The number of tails showing when a pair of coins was tossed fourteen times was $\{0, 2, 2, 1, 0, 2, 2, 0, 1, 0, 2, 0, 0, 2\}$. What is the mean of the data?

   (A) 0
   (B) 0.5
   (C) 1
   (D) 1.5
   (E) 2

16. What is the greatest possible number of points of intersection between a hyperbola and a circle?

   (A) 2
   (B) 3
   (C) 4
   (D) 5
   (E) 6

GO ON TO THE NEXT PAGE

17. Figure 1 shows once cycle of the graph of $y = -2\cos\left(x + \dfrac{\pi}{4}\right)$. What are the coordinates of the point where the maximum value of the function occurs on the interval shown?

    (A) $\left(\dfrac{3\pi}{4}, 2\right)$

    (B) $\left(\dfrac{5}{2}, 2\right)$

    (C) $(\pi, 2)$

    (D) $\left(\dfrac{5\pi}{4}, 2\right)$

    (E) $\left(\dfrac{\pi}{2}, 2\right)$

USE THIS SPACE AS SCRATCH PAPER

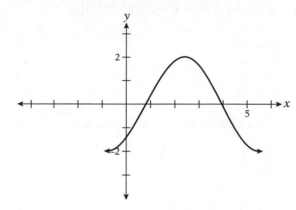

Figure 1

18. Matt's average score on the first four tests of the term is 84%. If he earns a 94% on the fifth test, what will his new average be?

    (A) 85%
    (B) 86%
    (C) 87%
    (D) 88%
    (E) 89%

19. If a circle has a radius of 4 cm, then what is the length of the arc intercepted by a central angle of 80°?

    (A) $\dfrac{\pi}{9}$

    (B) $\dfrac{2\pi}{9}$

    (C) $\dfrac{4\pi}{9}$

    (D) $\dfrac{8\pi}{9}$

    (E) $\dfrac{16\pi}{9}$

20. What is the domain of $f(x) = \dfrac{1}{x^2 + 2}$?

    (A) $x \neq \pm 2$
    (B) $x \neq \pm\sqrt{2}$
    (C) $-2 \leq x \leq 2$
    (D) $-\sqrt{2} \leq x \leq \sqrt{2}$
    (E) All real numbers

GO ON TO THE NEXT PAGE

21. If $f(x) = \sqrt[3]{8x - 1}$, then $f\left[f^{-1}(2)\right] =$

    (A) -2
    (B) -1
    (C) 2
    (D) 2.5
    (E) 225

22. If $x = 2\cos\theta$ and $y = 2\sin\theta$, then $\sqrt{x^2 + y^2} =$

    (A) 1
    (B) 2
    (C) 4
    (D) $2\sin\theta\cos\theta$
    (E) $2(\cos\theta + \sin\theta)$

23. Which of the following quadratic equations has roots $7 + i$ and $7 - i$?

    (A) $x^2 - 14x + 49 = 0$
    (B) $x^2 + 14x - 48 = 0$
    (C) $x^2 - 14x + 48 = 0$
    (D) $x^2 - 14x + 50 = 0$
    (E) $x^2 + 14x + 50 = 0$

24. If P is a point on the unit circle in Figure 2, then what are the coordinates of P?

    (A) $(\sin 45°, \cos 45°)$

    (B) $\left(\sqrt{\dfrac{2}{2}}, \sqrt{\dfrac{2}{2}}\right)$

    (C) $(1, 1)$

    (D) $\left(\dfrac{1}{2}, \dfrac{1}{2}\right)$

    (E) $\left(\sqrt{\dfrac{3}{2}}, \dfrac{1}{2}\right)$

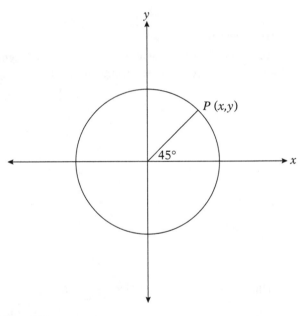

Figure 2

25. What is the remainder when the polynomial $x^4 - 2x^3 - 8x + 5$ is divided by $x - 3$?

    (A) -2
    (B) 2
    (C) 3
    (D) 8
    (E) 164

GO ON TO THE NEXT PAGE

USE THIS SPACE AS SCRATCH PAPER

26. In $\triangle ABC$ in Figure 3, $\dfrac{(\sin A \, \tan B)}{\sec A} =$

    (A) $\dfrac{b^2}{c^2}$

    (B) $\dfrac{b}{c}$

    (C) 1

    (D) $\dfrac{ab}{c^2}$

    (E) -1

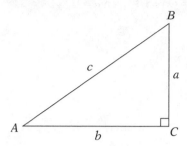

Figure 3

27. A ball is dropped from a height of 8 feet. If it always rebounds $\dfrac{2}{3}$ the distance it has fallen, how high will it reach after it hits the ground for the third time?

    (A) 5.33

    (B) 3.56

    (C) 2.37

    (D) 1.58

    (E) 2.73

28. The solution set of $7x - 2y < 0$ lies in which quadrants?

    (A) I only

    (B) I and II

    (C) I, II, and III

    (D) I, II, and IV

    (E) I, III, and IV

29. If θ is an acute angle and $\cot \theta = 5$, then $\sin \theta =$

    (A) $5\sqrt{\dfrac{26}{26}}$

    (B) $\dfrac{1}{5}$

    (C) $\sqrt{26}$

    (D) $\sqrt{\dfrac{26}{5}}$

    (E) $\sqrt{\dfrac{26}{26}}$

30. The linear regression model $G = 0.03m + 0.2$ relates grade point average (G) to the number of daily minutes a person spends studying (m). When a person studies for an hour and forty minutes each day, the predicted GPA is

    (A) 2.8

    (B) 3.0

    (C) 3.2

    (D) 3.8

    (E) 4.4

GO ON TO THE NEXT PAGE

31. If $\dfrac{n!}{2} = (n-1)!$ then $n =$

    (A) 1
    (B) 2
    (C) 3
    (D) 4
    (E) 8

32. The sides of a triangle are 4, 5, and 8 cm. What is the measure of its smallest angle?

    (A) 42.1°
    (B) 70.5°
    (C) 59.4°
    (D) 24.1°
    (E) 30.0°

33. What is the length of the major axis of the ellipse
    $$\dfrac{4(x+8)^2}{9} + \dfrac{(y-1)^2}{9} = 1?$$

    (A) $\dfrac{3}{2}$
    (B) 3
    (C) 6
    (D) 9
    (E) 81

34. If $4^k = 5^{k+3}$, then $k =$

    (A) −21.6
    (B) −15
    (C) −2.5
    (D) 0.86
    (E) 3.5

35. If $\sqrt[3]{n} = 7.128$, then $\sqrt[3]{17n} =$

    (A) 2.6
    (B) 4.1
    (C) 121.1
    (D) 18.3
    (E) 29.4

36. A cone-shaped cup has a height of 10 units and a radius of 3 units. The cup is filled with water and the height of the water is 6 units. What is radius of the surface of the water?

    (A) 1.5 units
    (B) 1.8 units
    (C) 2 units
    (D) 3 units
    (E) 5 units

GO ON TO THE NEXT PAGE

37. If $x(x-4)(x-2) > 0$, then which of the following is the solution set?

    (A) $0 < x < 2$
    (B) $x < 0$ or $2 < x < 4$
    (C) $x > 0$
    (D) $x < 0$ or $x > 4$
    (E) $0 < x < 2$ or $x > 4$

38. Assuming each dimension must be an integer, how many different rectangular prisms with a volume of 18 cm^3 are there?

    (A) 2
    (B) 3
    (C) 4
    (D) 5
    (E) 6

39. If $2,200 in invested at a rate of 6% compounded quarterly, how much will the investment be worth in 4 years?

    (A) 2,538
    (B) 2,620
    (C) 2,777
    (D) 2,792
    (E) 5,589

40. Assuming $a > 1$, which of the following expressions represents the greatest value?

    (A) $\dfrac{a+1}{a+1}$

    (B) $\dfrac{a}{a+1}$

    (C) $\dfrac{a}{a-1}$

    (D) $\dfrac{a-1}{a-2}$

    (E) $\dfrac{a+1}{a-1}$

41. If $4n + 1$, $6n$, and $7n + 2$ are the first three terms of an arithmetic sequence, what is the sum of the first 20 terms of the sequence?

    (A) 108
    (B) 605
    (C) 830
    (D) 1,210
    (E) 2,420

42. What is the value of x, y, and z?

$$\begin{bmatrix} -z & x+z \\ 4 & y-6 \end{bmatrix}\begin{bmatrix} & \\ & \end{bmatrix}$$

(A) $x = 7, y = -1, z = 4$

(B) $x = \dfrac{13}{3}, y = -1, z = \dfrac{4}{3}$

(C) $x = \dfrac{13}{3}, y = -1, z = \dfrac{10}{3}$

(D) $x = 7, y = 5, z = 4$

(E) $x = \dfrac{13}{3}, y = 5, z = \dfrac{4}{3}$

43. What is the range of $f(x) = -3\sin(4x + \pi) + 1$?

(A) $-2 \le y \le 4$

(B) $-3 \le y \le 3$

(C) $-\dfrac{1}{2} \le y \le \dfrac{5}{2}$

(D) $0 \le y \le 2\pi$

(E) All real numbers

44. If $f(x) = \dfrac{x^2 + 7x + 10}{2x^2 + 3x - 2}$, what value does the function approach as x approaches -2?

(A) $\dfrac{3}{5}$

(B) $\dfrac{7}{3}$

(C) $-\dfrac{5}{3}$

(D) -2

(E) $-\dfrac{3}{5}$

45. Figure 4 shows a portion of the graph of which of the following functions?

(A) $y = \tan(2x) - 2$

(B) $y = \tan\left(\dfrac{x}{2}\right) - 2$

(C) $y = \cot\left(\dfrac{x}{2}\right) - 2$

(D) $y = \cot\left(\dfrac{x}{2} - 2\right)$

(E) $y = \tan x - 2$

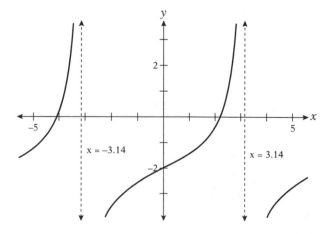

Figure 4

GO ON TO THE NEXT PAGE

46. $\sum_{k=0}^{7}(-2)^k =$

(A) −85
(B) 43
(C) 128
(D) 171
(E) 255

47. A line has parametric equations $x = t - 12$ and $y = 4t - 1$, given t is the parameter. What is the y-intercept of the line?

(A) −4
(B) 12
(C) 47
(D) 49
(E) 4

48. What is the area of the triangle in Figure 5?

(A) 5.2
(B) 6.5
(C) 6.9
(D) 13.8
(E) 16.8

49. In how many ways can the letters of the word SICILY be arranged using all of the letters?

(A) 60
(B) 120
(C) 240
(D) 360
(E) 720

50. If students are randomly chosen from a group of 11 boys and 9 girls, what is the probability of choosing 2 boys and 2 girls?

(A) $\dfrac{11}{969}$

(B) $\dfrac{132}{323}$

(C) $\dfrac{30}{1,615}$

(D) $\dfrac{22}{323}$

(E) $\dfrac{1}{4,845}$

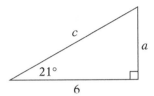

Figure 5

S T O P

IF YOU FINISH BEFORE TIME IS CALLED, YOU MAY CHECK YOUR WORK ON THIS TEST ONLY.
DO NOT TURN TO ANY OTHER TEST IN THIS BOOK.

ANSWER KEY

1. C	11. D	21. C	31. B	41. D
2. D	12. B	22. B	32. D	42. B
3. B	13. E	23. D	33. C	43. A
4. E	14. C	24. B	34. A	44. E
5. A	15. C	25. D	35. D	45. B
6. A	16. C	26. A	36. B	46. A
7. C	17. A	27. C	37. E	47. C
8. C	18. B	28. C	38. C	48. C
9. C	19. E	29. E	39. D	49. D
10. D	20. E	30. C	40. E	50. B

ANSWERS AND SOLUTIONS

1. **C**

   Because $i = \sqrt{-1}$, $i^2 = \sqrt{-1}\left(\sqrt{-1}\right) = -1$.

   $(6 - i)(6 + i) =$

   $36 + 6i - 6i - i^2 =$

   $36 - i^2 =$

   $36 - (-1) = 37.$

2. **D** Given $f(x) = x^2 - 8x$,

   $2f(2x) = 2\left[(2x)^2 - 8(2x)\right]$

   $= 2(4x^2 - 16x)$

   $= 8x^2 - 32x.$

3. **B** An odd function is symmetric with respect to the origin. If (x, y) is a point on f, then $(-x, -y)$, the reflection of the point about the origin, is also on the graph.

4. **E** Because $a + b + 14i = 4 + (3a - b)i$, $a + b = 4$ and $3a - b = 14$. Set up a system and use the linear combination method to solve for a and b.

   $$a + b = 4$$
   $$\underline{+\ 3a - b = 14}$$
   $$4a + 0b = 18$$

   $$a = \frac{9}{2}$$

   $\dfrac{9}{2} + b = 4$, so $b = -\dfrac{1}{2}$.

5. **A** Let h = the height of the tree.

   $$\tan 26° = \frac{h}{25}.$$

   $h = 25(\tan 26°) \approx 12.2$ feet.

6. **A** Think of sine either in terms of the opposite leg and hypotenuse of a right triangle or in terms of the point (x, y) and r of a unit circle. Because $\pi < \theta < \dfrac{3\pi}{2}$, θ lies in quadrant III and its cosine is negative.

$$\sin \theta = -\frac{9}{41} = -\frac{y}{r}.$$

Because $r = \sqrt{x^2 + y^2}$, $41 = \sqrt{x^2 + (-9)^2}$.

$x = 40$.

$$\cos \theta = -\frac{x}{r} = -\frac{40}{41}$$

7. **C** The line passes through the points $(5, 0)$ and $(0, -1)$. The slope of the line is $m = \dfrac{1}{5}$.

Because the y-intercept is given, you can easily write the equation in slope-intercept form.

$$y = \frac{1}{5}x - 1.$$

$$x - 5y = 5.$$

8. **C** Recall that a quadratic equation can be thought of as: $a[x^2 - (\text{sum of the roots})x + (\text{product of the roots})] = 0$. Substitute the sum $= -4$, and the product $= -5$ to get:

$$a(x^2 - -4x + -5) = 0.$$

$$a(x^2 + 4x - 5) = 0.$$

When $a = 1$, the result is the equation given in answer C: $x^2 + 4x - 5 = 0$.

9. **C**

$$f\left(-\frac{1}{4}\right) = 9^{-\left(\frac{-1}{4}\right)} = 9^{\frac{1}{4}}$$

$$= \left(3^2\right)^{\frac{1}{4}} = 3^{\frac{2}{4}} = 3^{\frac{1}{2}}$$

$$= \sqrt{3}.$$

10. **D**

$$\log_4 x + 3\log_4 x = 9$$

$$4\log_4 x = 9$$

$$\log_4 x = \frac{9}{4}$$

$$4^{\frac{9}{4}} = x$$

$$x = 22.6.$$

11. **D** Graph $f(x) = |x^2\ 5|$ to determine its range on the specified interval. Because the domain is specified as $-1 \le x \le 4$, the curve has a beginning and an ending point.

When $x = -1$, $y = 4$, and when $x = 4$, $y = 11$. The range is the set of all possible y values, so realize that the y values decrease between 4 and 11. The range is $0 \le y \le 11$.

12. **B** Recall that $\sin^2 \theta + \cos^2 \theta = 1$, so $\cos^2 \theta = 1 - \sin^2 \theta$.

$$(1 + \sin \theta)(1 - \sin \theta) =$$

$$1 + \sin \theta + \sin \theta - \sin^2 \theta =$$

$$1 - \sin^2 \theta =$$

$$\cos^2 \theta.$$

13. **E** The minimum value of the function is the y-coordinate of the parabola's vertex. For the function $f(x) = (x - 1)^2 + 18$, the vertex is $(1, 18)$. (You can check this by graphing the parabola on your graphing calculator.) The minimum value is, therefore, 18.

14. **C**

$$_6C_3 = \frac{6!}{3!(6-3)!}$$

$$= \frac{4 \times 5 \times 6}{1 \times 2 \times 3}$$

$$= 20.$$

15. **C** The mean is the sum of the data divided by the number of terms.

$$\frac{(0 + 2 + 2 + 1 + 0 + 2 + 2 + 0 + 1 + 0 + 2 + 0 + 0 + 2)}{14} =$$

$$\frac{14}{14} = 1.$$

16. **C** There are 4 possible points of intersection as shown:

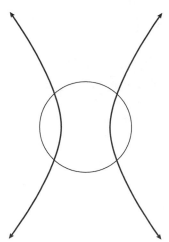

17. **A** The graph of $y = -2\cos\left(x + \dfrac{\pi}{4}\right)$ is the graph of $y = \cos x$ with a phase shift of $\dfrac{\pi}{4}$ units left, an amplitude of 2, and reflected over the x-axis. The maximum value occurs at the point where $x = \pi - \dfrac{\pi}{4} = \dfrac{3\pi}{4}$. The y-coordinate at that point is 2.

18. **B** Let s = the sum of the scores of Matt's first four tests.

$$\frac{s}{4} = 84.$$

$$s = 336.$$

Matt's new average is $\dfrac{336 + 94}{5} = 86\%.$

19. **E** Use the formula $s = r\,\theta$, where s = the arc length and r = the radius of the circle. Convert $80°$ to radian measure first.

$$80\left(\frac{\pi}{180}\right) = \frac{4\pi}{9} \text{ radians.}$$

Now, solve for the arc length:

$$s = 4\left(\frac{4\pi}{9}\right) = \frac{16\pi}{9} \text{ cm.}$$

20. **E** The denominator cannot equal zero.

$$x^2 + 2 \neq 0$$

$$x^2 \neq -2.$$

Recall that on the SAT II test, unless otherwise stated, the domain of a function f is assumed to be the set of real numbers x for which $f(x)$ is a real number. Because x is a squared term, it will, therefore, never equal a negative number. The domain is the set of all real numbers.

21. **C** This problem can be done quickly and with little work if you recall that the composition of a function and its inverse function, $f^{-1}[f(x)]$ and $f[f^{-1}(x)]$, equal x.

$$f^{-1}[f(2)] = 2.$$

22. **B**

$$\sqrt{(x^2 + y^2)} = \sqrt{(2\cos\theta)^2 + (2\sin\theta)^2}$$
$$= \sqrt{[4(\cos^2\theta + \sin^2\theta)]}.$$

Recognize that you can use one of the Pythagorean Identities, $\cos^2\theta + \sin^2\theta = 1$, to simplify the expression.

$$= \sqrt{[4\cos^2\theta + \sin^2\theta]} = = \sqrt{4(1)} = 2.$$

23. **D** The sum of the roots is: $7 + i + 7 - i = 14.$

The product of the roots is: $(7 + i)(7 - i) = 49 - i^2 = 50.$

The quadratic equation is, therefore, given by the equation:

$$a\left[\begin{array}{c}x^2 - (\text{sum of the roots})x \\ + (\text{product of the roots})\end{array}\right] = 0.$$

$$a(x^2 - 14x + 50) = 0.$$

Setting a equal to 1 results in one possible answer:

$$x^2 - 14x + 50 = 0.$$

24. **B** Because the circle is a unit circle, the coordinates of P are $(\cos 45°, \sin 45°)$. This can be simplified to $\left(\sqrt{\dfrac{2}{2}}, \sqrt{\dfrac{2}{2}}\right).$

If you don't know what the cosine and sine of $45°$ equal, let (x, y) be the coordinates of P, and draw a right triangle with legs of length x and y. The triangle is a $45°$–$45°$–$90°$ triangle, so use the ratios of the sides of this special right triangle to determine that the coordinates of point P are $\left(\sqrt{\dfrac{2}{2}}, \sqrt{\dfrac{2}{2}}\right).$

25. **D** Use either synthetic or long division to divide $x^4 - 2x^3 - 8x + 5$ by $x - 3$. Remember to include a zero placeholder for the x^2 term.

$$3\ \underline{|1\quad -2\quad 0\quad -8\quad 5}$$
$$\underline{\qquad 3\quad 3\quad 9\quad 3}$$

The remainder is 8.

26. **A** Using right triangle trigonometry to determine values for the three trigonometric functions.

$$\sin A = \frac{\text{opposite}}{\text{hypotenuse}} = \frac{a}{c}.$$

$$\tan B = \frac{\text{opposite}}{\text{adjacent}} = \frac{b}{a}.$$

$$\sec A = \frac{1}{\cos A} = \frac{\text{hypotenuse}}{\text{adjacent}} = \frac{c}{b}.$$

$$\frac{\sin A \, \tan B}{\sec A} = \frac{\frac{a}{c}\left(\frac{b}{a}\right)}{\frac{c}{b}}.$$

$$= \frac{\frac{b}{c}}{\frac{c}{b}} = \frac{b^2}{c^2}.$$

27. **C** Recognize that the heights of the bouncing ball form a geometric sequence with a common ratio of $\frac{2}{3}$ and an initial term of 8. After hitting the ground for the first time, the ball will reach a height of $(8)\left(\frac{2}{3}\right) = 5.33$. After the second bounce, the ball will reach a height of $(8)\left(\frac{2}{3}\right)^2 = 3.56$. After the third bounce, the ball will reach a height of $(8)\left(\frac{2}{3}\right)^3 = 2.37$ feet.

28. **C** Solve the inequality for y to get $y > \frac{7}{2}x$. Then, graph the linear equation $y = \frac{5}{2}x$. The solution to the inequality is the shaded area above the line, and that region falls in quadrants I, II, and III.

29. **E** Because θ is an acute angle, think of the right triangle that contains one angle of measure θ.

$$\cot \theta = 5 = \frac{\text{adjacent}}{\text{opposite}}.$$

Solve for the hypotenuse: $x = \sqrt{(5^2 + 1^2)} = \sqrt{26}$.

$$\sin \theta = \frac{\text{opposite}}{\text{hypotenuse}} = \frac{1}{\sqrt{26}} = \frac{\sqrt{26}}{\sqrt{26}}.$$

30. **C**
$$G = 0.03m + 0.2.$$
$$G = 0.03(100) + 0.2.$$
$$G = 3.2.$$

31. **B**
$$\frac{n!}{2} = (n-1)!$$
$$\frac{n!}{(n-1)!} = 2.$$
$$n = 2.$$

32. **D** The Law of Cosines states: $c^2 = a^2 + b^2 - 2ab \cos <C$.

$4^2 = 5^2 + 8^2 - 2(5)(8) \cos <C$, where C is the angle opposite the shortest side.

$$16 = 89 - 80 \cos <C.$$
$$-73 = -80 \cos <C.$$
$$\cos^{-1}\left(\frac{73}{80}\right) = 24.1°$$

33. **C** The length of the major axis equals $2a$. In this problem, $a = \sqrt{9}$.

$$2a = 6.$$

34. **A** Take the log of both sides of the equation to solve for k.

$$\log(4^k) = \log(5^{k+3}).$$
$$k \log 4 = (k+3)\log 5.$$
$$k\left(\frac{\log 4}{\log 5}\right) = k + 3.$$
$$k(0.86135) = k + 3.$$
$$k = -21.6.$$

35. **D**
$$\sqrt[3]{17n} = \left(\sqrt[3]{17}\right)\left(\sqrt[3]{n}\right) = \left(\sqrt[3]{17}\right)(7.128)$$
$$= 18.3.$$

36. **B** Filling the cone-shaped cup with water creates a cone similar to the cup itself. The radii and heights of the two cones are proportional. Let $r =$ the radius of the surface of the water.

$$\frac{6}{10} = \frac{r}{3}.$$
$$18 = 10r.$$
$$1.8 = r.$$

37. **E** The critical points of the inequality $x(x - 4)(x - 2) > 0$ are $x = 0, 4,$ and 2. Evaluate the 4 intervals created by these points by determining if the inequality is satisfied on each interval. $0 < x < 2$ or $x > 4$ is the correct answer choice.

38. **C** The volume a rectangular prism is given by the formula $V = \ell \times w \times h$, so you need to find three integers whose product is 18. There are four possibilities:

$1 \times 1 \times 18$

$1 \times 2 \times 9$

$1 \times 3 \times 6$

$2 \times 3 \times 3$

39. **D** $A = P\left(1 + \dfrac{r}{n}\right)^{nt}$ where n is the number of times the investment is compounded per year.

$A = 2,200\left(1 + \dfrac{0.06}{4}\right)^{4(4)}$.

$A = 2,200(1.015)^{16}$.

$A \approx 2,792$.

40. **E** Answer A equals 1 and answer B is less than 1, so both can be eliminated. Because C and E have the same denominator, and $a < a + 1$, C will always be less than E. It can also be eliminated as a possible answer choice. Substitute a few values of a into answers D and E to compare the expressions.

If $a = 7$, $\dfrac{6}{5} < \dfrac{8}{6}$.

If $a = 10$, $\dfrac{9}{8} < \dfrac{11}{9}$.

Answer E will always result in a greater value.

41. **D** Because the expressions represent the terms of an arithmetic sequence, there must be a common difference between consecutive terms.

$6n - (4n + 1) = 7n + 2 - 6n$.

$2n - 1 = n + 2$.

$n = 3$.

The first three terms are, therefore, 13, 18, and 23, making the common difference between terms, d, equal 5. The first term of the sequence is $a_1 = 13$, and the 20th term is $a_{20} = a_1 + (n - 1)d = 13 + (20 - 1)(5) = 108$.

The sum of a finite arithmetic sequence is:

$S_n = \dfrac{n}{2}(a_1 + a_n)$ where $n =$ the number of terms.

$S_n = \dfrac{20}{2}(13 + 108) = 1,210$.

42. **B** Set corresponding elements equal to each other and solve for the three variables.

$3y - 6 = -9$

$y = -1$.

Then, set up a system to solve for x and z.

$$x - z = 3$$
$$+\ 2x + z = 10$$
$$\overline{3x = 13}$$

$$x = \dfrac{13}{3}$$

$$z = \dfrac{4}{3}$$

The correct answer is, therefore, $x = \dfrac{13}{3}$, $y = -1$, $z = \dfrac{4}{3}$.

43. **A** The function $f(x) = -3\sin(4x + \pi) + 1$ has an amplitude of $|a| = |-3| = 3$ and a vertical shift of 1 unit up. The range spans from $y = 1 - 3 = -2$ to $y = 1 + 3 = 4$, so $-2 \leq y \leq 6$ is the correct answer choice.

44. **E** Factor the numerator and denominator. Then, simplify the expression and evaluate it when $x = -2$.

$$f(x) = \dfrac{x^2 + 7x + 10}{2x^2 + 3x - 2} = \dfrac{(x + 5)(x + 2)}{(2x - 1)(x + 2)}$$

$$= \dfrac{(x + 5)}{(2x - 1)}$$

When $x = -2$, $\dfrac{(x + 5)}{(2x - 1)} = -\dfrac{3}{5}$.

45. **B** The figure shows the graph of $y = \tan x$ shifted 2 units down with a period of 2π. The correct equation is $y = \tan\left(\dfrac{x}{2}\right) - 2$.

46. **A** Substitute $k = 0, 1, 2, \ldots 7$ into the summation to get:

$1 - 2 + 4 - 8 + 16 - 32 + 64 - 128 = -85$.

47. **C** Because $x = t - 12$, $t = x + 12$. Substitute this value into the second equation to get:

$$y = 4(x + 12) - 1.$$

$$y = 4x + 48 - 1.$$

$$y = 4x + 47.$$

The y-intercept of the resulting line is $(0, 47)$.

48. **C**

$$\text{Area} = \frac{1}{2}(\text{base} \times \text{height})$$

$$A = \frac{1}{2}(6a).$$

Use trigonometry to determine a:

$$\tan 21° = \frac{a}{6}.$$

$$a \approx 2.303.$$

$$A = \frac{1}{2}(6)(2.303) \approx 6.9.$$

49. **D** Find the number of permutations of six letters taken six at a time, two of which are repeated.

$$\frac{6!}{2!} = \frac{6 \times 5 \times 4 \times 3 \times 2 \times 1}{2 \times 1} = 360.$$

50. **B**

$$\frac{{}_9C_2\left({}_{11}C_2\right)}{{}_{20}C_4} =$$

$$\frac{\left(\dfrac{9!}{2!7!}\right)\left(\dfrac{11!}{2!9!}\right)}{\left(\dfrac{20!}{4!16!}\right)} =$$

$$\frac{1{,}980}{4{,}845} = \frac{132}{323}.$$

▨▨▨ DIAGNOSE YOUR STRENGTHS AND WEAKNESSES

Check the number of each question answered correctly and "X" the number of each question answered incorrectly.

Algebra	10	31	34	35	37	39	Total Number Correct
6 questions							

Solid Geometry	36	38	Total Number Correct
2 questions			

Coordinate Geometry	7	16	28	33	Total Number Correct
4 questions					

Trigonometry	5	6	12	19	22	24	26	29	32	48	Total Number Correct
10 questions											

Functions	2	3	8	9	11	13	17	20	21	23	25	43	45	47	Total Number Correct
14 questions															

Data Analysis, Statistics, and Probability	15	18	30	50	Total Number Correct
4 questions					

Number and Operations	1	4	14	27	40	41	42	44	46	49	Total Number Correct
10 questions											

Number of correct answers $-\frac{1}{4}$ **(Number of incorrect answers) = Your raw score**

$$\rule{4cm}{0.4pt} -\frac{1}{4} \left(\rule{4cm}{0.4pt} \right) = \rule{3cm}{0.4pt}$$

Compare your raw score with the approximate SAT test score below:

	Raw Score	SAT Approximate Score
Excellent	43–50	770–800
Very Good	33–43	670–770
Good	27–33	620–670
Above Average	21–27	570–620
Average	11–21	500–570
Below Average	< 11	< 500

THE SAT CHEMISTRY TEST

All About the SAT Chemistry Test

What Is the Format of the SAT Chemistry Test?

The SAT Chemistry test is a 1-hour exam consisting of 85 multiple-choice questions. According to the College Board, the test measures the following knowledge and skills:

- Familiarity with major chemistry concepts and ability to use those concepts to solve problems
- Ability to understand and interpret data from observation and experiments and to draw conclusions based on experiment results
- Knowledge of laboratory procedures and of metric units of measure
- Ability to use simple algebra to solve word problems
- Ability to solve problems involving ratio and direct and inverse proportions, exponents, and scientific notation

The test covers a variety of chemistry topics. The following chart shows the general test subject areas, as well as the approximate portion of the test devoted to each subject.

SAT Chemistry Subject Areas

Subject Area	Approximate Percentage of Exam
1. Structure of Matter	25%
2. States of Matter	15%
3. Reaction Types	14%
4. Stoichiometry	12%
5. Equilibrium and Reaction Rates	7%
6. Thermodynamics	6%
7. Descriptive Chemistry	13%
8. Laboratory	8%

When you take the SAT Chemistry test, you will be given a test booklet that includes a periodic table of the elements. The table will show only the element symbols, atomic numbers, and atomic masses. It will not show electron configurations or oxidation numbers. You may not use your own reference tables or a calculator.

What School Background Do I Need for the SAT Chemistry Test?

The College Board recommends that you have at least the following experience before taking the SAT Chemistry test:

- One-year chemistry course at the college preparatory level
- One-year algebra course
- Experience in the chemistry laboratory

How Is the SAT Chemistry Test Scored?

On the SAT Chemistry test, your "raw score" is calculated as follows: You receive one point for each question you answer correctly, but you lose one-quarter of a point for each question you answer incorrectly. You do not gain or lose any points for questions that you do not answer at all. Your raw score is then converted into a scaled score by a statistical method that takes into account how well you did compared to others who took the same test. Scaled scores range from 200 to 800 points. Your scaled score will be reported to you, to your high school, and to the colleges and universities that you designate to receive it.

Scoring scales differ slightly from one version of the test to the next. The scoring scales provided after each practice Chemistry test in this book are only samples that will show you your approximate scaled score.

SUCCEEDING ON THE SAT CHEMISTRY TEST

The SAT Chemistry test consists entirely of multiple-choice questions. Most are the regular five-answer-choice format that you will be familiar with from taking other standardized tests. Some, however, have special formats that do not appear on other tests and that you need to be aware of. The College Board calls these formats "classification sets" and "relationship analysis questions." Review the following examples before you tackle the Diagnostic Test.

Regular Multiple-Choice Questions

On the SAT Chemistry test, most of the questions are in the regular five-answer-choice format that is used on standardized tests. Here is an example:

1. Which oxidation half reaction below demonstrates conservation of mass and charge?
   (A) $Mg^{2+} + 2e- \rightarrow Mg$
   (B) $Cl^{1-} + 1e- \rightarrow Cl_2$
   (C) $2Ag^{1+} \rightarrow 2Ag + 1e-$
   (D) $Mg \rightarrow Mg^{2+} + 2e-$
   (E) $F_2 + 2e- \rightarrow 2F^{1-}$

The correct answer is choice D. Note that with this question, as with many other questions on the test, you can find the correct answer by using the process of elimination. The half reactions shown in choices A, B, and E are all reduction half reactions, so those choices can be eliminated. Both remaining choices, C and D, show oxidation and a loss of electrons. But choice C does not demonstrate conservation of charge and mass; if it did, there would have to be two electrons on the left side of the reaction. So the correct answer must be choice D.

You will see a variation of this basic format in which you are offered three choices indicated by the Roman numerals I, II, and III. Your task is to decide which combination of the three choices answers the question. Here is an example:

2. Which of the following indicates an acidic solution?
   I. Litmus paper turns blue.
   II. Phenolphthalein turns pink.
   III. Hydronium ion concentration is greater than hydroxide ion concentration.
   (A) I only
   (B) II only
   (C) III only
   (D) I and II only
   (E) I, II, and III

The correct answer is choice C. First, review the choices. Choices I and II indicate a basic solution. If they were acidic, then the solutions would be red for litmus and clear for phenolphthalein. Only choice III holds true for an acidic solution. In an acidic solution, the concentration of hydronium ions exceeds that of hydroxide ion concentration.

Classification Sets

In a classification set, you are given five answer choices lettered A through E. The choices may be chemistry principles, substances, numbers, equations, diagrams, or the like. The choices are followed by three or four numbered questions. Your task is to match each question with the answer choice to which it refers. Here are sample directions for a classification set, followed by a sample of this question format.

Directions: Each of the following sets of lettered choices refers to the numbered formulas or statements immediately below it. For each numbered item, choose the one lettered choice that fits it best. Then fill in the corresponding oval on the answer sheet. Each choice in a set may be used once, more than once, or not at all.

Questions 3–5:
   (A) coordinate covalent bonding
   (B) ionic bonding
   (C) nonpolar covalent bonding
   (D) metallic bonding
   (E) hydrogen bonding

3. HF

4. N_2

5. KI

3. The correct answer is choice E. The bond between the atoms of hydrogen and fluorine is a polar covalent bond, a choice that is not present in the choices above. Now look at the bonding between the molecules of HF. HF can exhibit dipole forces between its molecules, yet another choice that is not present. HF can, however, exhibit hydrogen bonding, a choice that is present.

4. The correct answer is choice C. Nitrogen gas has no difference in electronegativity between the nitrogen atoms. The two nitrogen atoms will form a nonpolar covalent bond. The type of bonding present between the molecules of nitrogen gas will be dispersion forces, the forces present between nonpolar molecules.

5. The correct answer is choice B. Potassium iodide is formed from a metal, potassium, and a nonmetal, iodine. The type of bonding that forms between metals and nonmetals is ionic bonding.

Relationship Analysis Questions

Relationship analysis questions are probably not like any question type that you have seen before. Each question consists of two statements labeled I and II with the word BECAUSE between the two statements. For each question, you have three tasks. You must:

- Determine if statement I is true or false.
- Determine if statement II is true or false.
- Determine if statement II is the correct explanation for statement I.

On the answer sheet, you will mark true (T) or false (F) for each statement, and you will mark "correct explanation" (CE) ONLY if statement II is a correct explanation of statement I. Here are sample directions for this kind of question, followed by two examples and a sample of a correctly marked answer sheet.

Directions: Each question below consists of two statements. For each question, determine whether statement I in the leftmost column is true or false and whether statement II in the rightmost column is true or false. Fill in the corresponding T or F ovals on the answer sheet provided. Fill in the oval labeled "CE" only if statement II correctly explains statement I.

| 101. HCl is an Arrhenius acid | BECAUSE | HCl is a proton donor. |
| 102. Water is a polar molecule | BECAUSE | the dipole forces in a molecule of water will counterbalance each other and cancel out. |

101. T, T, CE HCl will donate a proton (hydronium ion) when it reacts. This classifies it as an Arrhenius acid.

102. T, F Because of the bent shape of a water molecule, the dipole forces in the molecule will not counterbalance or cancel out. This is what causes a water molecule to be a polar molecule.

Here is how you would mark these answers on the answer sheet:

	I		II		CE*
101	●	Ⓕ	●	Ⓕ	●
102	●	Ⓕ	Ⓣ	●	○

PERIODIC TABLE OF THE ELEMENTS

1	2	3	4	5	6	7	8	9	10	11	12	13	14	15	16	17	18
1 H 1.0079																	2 He 4.0026
3 Li 6.941	4 Be 9.0122											5 B 10.81	6 C 12.011	7 N 14.007	8 O 15.999	9 F 18.998	10 Ne 20.179
11 Na 22.989	12 Mg 24.305											13 Al 26.981	14 Si 28.086	15 P 30.974	16 S 32.06	17 Cl 35.453	18 Ar 39.948
19 K 39.098	20 Ca 40.08	21 Sc 44.956	22 Ti 47.88	23 V 50.941	24 Cr 51.996	25 Mn 54.938	26 Fe 55.847	27 Co 58.933	28 Ni 58.69	29 Cu 63.546	30 Zn 65.38	31 Ga 59.72	32 Ge 72.59	33 As 74.922	34 Se 78.96	35 Br 79.904	36 Kr 83.80
37 Rb 85.468	38 Sr 87.62	39 Y 88.906	40 Zr 91.22	41 Nb 92.905	42 Mo 95.94	43 Tc (98)	44 Ru 101.07	45 Rh 102.91	46 Pd 106.42	47 Ag 107.87	48 Cd 112.41	49 In 114.82	50 Sn 118.69	51 Sb 121.75	52 Te 127.60	53 I 126.90	54 Xe 131.29
55 Cs 132.91	56 Ba 137.33	57 * La 138.90	72 Hf 178.49	73 Ta 180.95	74 W 183.85	75 Re 186.21	76 Os 190.2	77 Ir 192.22	78 Pt 195.08	79 Au 196.97	80 Hg 200.59	81 Tl 204.38	82 Pb 207.2	83 Bi 208.98	84 Po (209)	85 At (210)	86 Rn (222)
87 Fr (223)	88 Ra 226.0	89 # Ac 227.03	104 Rf (261)	105 Db (262)	106 Sg (263)	107 Bh (262)	108 Hs (265)	109 Mt (266)	110 Uun (269)	111 Uuu (272)	112 Uub (277)						

* Lanthanides

58 Ce 140.12	59 Pr 140.91	60 Nd 144.24	61 Pm (145)	62 Sm 150.36	63 Eu 151.96	64 Gd 157.25	65 Tb 158.92	66 Dy 162.50	67 Ho 164.93	68 Er 167.26	69 Tm 168.93	70 Yb 173.04	71 Lu 174.97
90 Th 232.03	91 Pa 231.03	92 U 238.03	93 Np 237.05	94 Pu (244)	95 Am (243)	96 Cm (247)	97 Bk (247)	98 Cf (251)	99 Es (254)	100 Fm (257)	101 Md (257)	102 No (255)	103 Lr (256)

Actinides

CHEMISTRY PRACTICE TEST 1

Treat this practice test as the actual test, and complete it in one 60-minute sitting. Use the following answer sheet to fill in your multiple-choice answers. Once you have completed the practice test:

1. Check your answers using the Answer Key.
2. Review the Answers and Explanations.
3. Complete the Score Sheet to see how well you did.

ANSWER SHEET

Tear out this answer sheet and use it to complete the practice test. Determine the BEST answer for each question. Then fill in the appropriate oval.

1. Ⓐ Ⓑ Ⓒ Ⓓ Ⓔ	21. Ⓐ Ⓑ Ⓒ Ⓓ Ⓔ	41. Ⓐ Ⓑ Ⓒ Ⓓ Ⓔ	61. Ⓐ Ⓑ Ⓒ Ⓓ Ⓔ
2. Ⓐ Ⓑ Ⓒ Ⓓ Ⓔ	22. Ⓐ Ⓑ Ⓒ Ⓓ Ⓔ	42. Ⓐ Ⓑ Ⓒ Ⓓ Ⓔ	62. Ⓐ Ⓑ Ⓒ Ⓓ Ⓔ
3. Ⓐ Ⓑ Ⓒ Ⓓ Ⓔ	23. Ⓐ Ⓑ Ⓒ Ⓓ Ⓔ	43. Ⓐ Ⓑ Ⓒ Ⓓ Ⓔ	63. Ⓐ Ⓑ Ⓒ Ⓓ Ⓔ
4. Ⓐ Ⓑ Ⓒ Ⓓ Ⓔ	24. Ⓐ Ⓑ Ⓒ Ⓓ Ⓔ	44. Ⓐ Ⓑ Ⓒ Ⓓ Ⓔ	64. Ⓐ Ⓑ Ⓒ Ⓓ Ⓔ
5. Ⓐ Ⓑ Ⓒ Ⓓ Ⓔ	25. Ⓐ Ⓑ Ⓒ Ⓓ Ⓔ	45. Ⓐ Ⓑ Ⓒ Ⓓ Ⓔ	65. Ⓐ Ⓑ Ⓒ Ⓓ Ⓔ
6. Ⓐ Ⓑ Ⓒ Ⓓ Ⓔ	26. Ⓐ Ⓑ Ⓒ Ⓓ Ⓔ	46. Ⓐ Ⓑ Ⓒ Ⓓ Ⓔ	66. Ⓐ Ⓑ Ⓒ Ⓓ Ⓔ
7. Ⓐ Ⓑ Ⓒ Ⓓ Ⓔ	27. Ⓐ Ⓑ Ⓒ Ⓓ Ⓔ	47. Ⓐ Ⓑ Ⓒ Ⓓ Ⓔ	67. Ⓐ Ⓑ Ⓒ Ⓓ Ⓔ
8. Ⓐ Ⓑ Ⓒ Ⓓ Ⓔ	28. Ⓐ Ⓑ Ⓒ Ⓓ Ⓔ	48. Ⓐ Ⓑ Ⓒ Ⓓ Ⓔ	68. Ⓐ Ⓑ Ⓒ Ⓓ Ⓔ
9. Ⓐ Ⓑ Ⓒ Ⓓ Ⓔ	29. Ⓐ Ⓑ Ⓒ Ⓓ Ⓔ	49. Ⓐ Ⓑ Ⓒ Ⓓ Ⓔ	69. Ⓐ Ⓑ Ⓒ Ⓓ Ⓔ
10. Ⓐ Ⓑ Ⓒ Ⓓ Ⓔ	30. Ⓐ Ⓑ Ⓒ Ⓓ Ⓔ	50. Ⓐ Ⓑ Ⓒ Ⓓ Ⓔ	70. Ⓐ Ⓑ Ⓒ Ⓓ Ⓔ
11. Ⓐ Ⓑ Ⓒ Ⓓ Ⓔ	31. Ⓐ Ⓑ Ⓒ Ⓓ Ⓔ	51. Ⓐ Ⓑ Ⓒ Ⓓ Ⓔ	
12. Ⓐ Ⓑ Ⓒ Ⓓ Ⓔ	32. Ⓐ Ⓑ Ⓒ Ⓓ Ⓔ	52. Ⓐ Ⓑ Ⓒ Ⓓ Ⓔ	
13. Ⓐ Ⓑ Ⓒ Ⓓ Ⓔ	33. Ⓐ Ⓑ Ⓒ Ⓓ Ⓔ	53. Ⓐ Ⓑ Ⓒ Ⓓ Ⓔ	
14. Ⓐ Ⓑ Ⓒ Ⓓ Ⓔ	34. Ⓐ Ⓑ Ⓒ Ⓓ Ⓔ	54. Ⓐ Ⓑ Ⓒ Ⓓ Ⓔ	
15. Ⓐ Ⓑ Ⓒ Ⓓ Ⓔ	35. Ⓐ Ⓑ Ⓒ Ⓓ Ⓔ	55. Ⓐ Ⓑ Ⓒ Ⓓ Ⓔ	
16. Ⓐ Ⓑ Ⓒ Ⓓ Ⓔ	36. Ⓐ Ⓑ Ⓒ Ⓓ Ⓔ	56. Ⓐ Ⓑ Ⓒ Ⓓ Ⓔ	
17. Ⓐ Ⓑ Ⓒ Ⓓ Ⓔ	37. Ⓐ Ⓑ Ⓒ Ⓓ Ⓔ	57. Ⓐ Ⓑ Ⓒ Ⓓ Ⓔ	
18. Ⓐ Ⓑ Ⓒ Ⓓ Ⓔ	38. Ⓐ Ⓑ Ⓒ Ⓓ Ⓔ	58. Ⓐ Ⓑ Ⓒ Ⓓ Ⓔ	
19. Ⓐ Ⓑ Ⓒ Ⓓ Ⓔ	39. Ⓐ Ⓑ Ⓒ Ⓓ Ⓔ	59. Ⓐ Ⓑ Ⓒ Ⓓ Ⓔ	
20. Ⓐ Ⓑ Ⓒ Ⓓ Ⓔ	40. Ⓐ Ⓑ Ⓒ Ⓓ Ⓔ	60. Ⓐ Ⓑ Ⓒ Ⓓ Ⓔ	

Chemistry *Fill in oval CE only if II is correct explanation of I.

	I	II	CE*		I	II	CE*
101.	Ⓣ Ⓕ	Ⓣ Ⓕ	◯	109.	Ⓣ Ⓕ	Ⓣ Ⓕ	◯
102.	Ⓣ Ⓕ	Ⓣ Ⓕ	◯	110.	Ⓣ Ⓕ	Ⓣ Ⓕ	◯
103.	Ⓣ Ⓕ	Ⓣ Ⓕ	◯	111.	Ⓣ Ⓕ	Ⓣ Ⓕ	◯
104.	Ⓣ Ⓕ	Ⓣ Ⓕ	◯	112.	Ⓣ Ⓕ	Ⓣ Ⓕ	◯
105.	Ⓣ Ⓕ	Ⓣ Ⓕ	◯	113.	Ⓣ Ⓕ	Ⓣ Ⓕ	◯
106.	Ⓣ Ⓕ	Ⓣ Ⓕ	◯	114.	Ⓣ Ⓕ	Ⓣ Ⓕ	◯
107.	Ⓣ Ⓕ	Ⓣ Ⓕ	◯	115.	Ⓣ Ⓕ	Ⓣ Ⓕ	◯
108.	Ⓣ Ⓕ	Ⓣ Ⓕ	◯				

CHEMISTRY PRACTICE TEST 1

Note: Unless otherwise stated, for all statements involving chemical equations and/or solutions, assume that the system is in pure water.

Part A

Directions: Each of the following sets of lettered choices refers to the numbered formulas or statements immediately below it. For each numbered item, choose the one lettered choice that fits it best. Then fill in the corresponding oval on the answer sheet. Each choice in a set may be used once, more than once, or not at all.

Questions 1–4

(A)

(B)

(C)

(D)

(E)

Figure 1

1. Demonstrates the relationship between pressure (*x*-axis) and volume (*y*-axis) in Boyle's Law

2. Contains a triple point

3. Demonstrates the relationship between temperature (*x*-axis) and volume (*y*-axis) in Charles' Law

4. Shows the relationship between atomic number (*x*-axis) and atomic radius (*y*-axis) for the elements in period 2

Questions 5–8

(A) Br_2 and Hg
(B) Cl_2 and F_2
(C) NH_4^{1+} and H_3O^{1+}
(D) Fe and Co
(E) Diamond and graphite

5. These two compounds are in the liquid phase at 293 K.

6. These two compounds have coordinate covalent bonds.

7. These two compounds are allotropes of each other.

8. These two compounds are good oxidizing agents.

Questions 9–11

(A) R—OH
(B) R—O—R
(C) R—NH₂
(D) R—COO—R
(E) R—CO—R

9. Ends in *–oate*

10. Ends in *–amine*

11. Ends in *–ol*

GO ON TO THE NEXT PAGE

Questions 12–15

    (A) $1s^22s^22p^63s^23p^6$

    (B) $1s^22s^22p^63s^23p^64s^2$

    (C) $1s^22s^22p^63s^23p^64s^1$

    (D) $1s^2$

    (E) $1s^22s^22p^63p^1$

12.   The electron configuration for calcium ion

13.   The electron configuration for an excited atom

14.   The electron configuration for potassium in the ground state

15.   The electron configuration for the noble gas with the highest first ionization energy

Questions 16–19

    (A)   Sublimation

    (B)   Deposition

    (C)   Vaporization

    (D)   Condensation

    (E)   Freezing

16.   Solid to gas

17.   Gas to solid

18.   Liquid to gas

19.   Liquid to solid

Questions 20–22

    (A)   Nitrogen

    (B)   Oxygen

    (C)   Chlorine

    (D)   Neon

    (E)   Beryllium

20.   Has 2 valence electrons

21.   Has 6 valence electrons

22.   Will form an ion with a 3- charge

Questions 23–25

    (A)   milli-

    (B)   kilo-

    (C)   centi

    (D)   micro-

    (E)   nano-

23. 10^{-9}

24. 10^{-6}

25. 10^3

GO ON TO THE NEXT PAGE

PLEASE GO TO THE SPECIAL SECTION AT THE LOWER LEFT-HAND CORNER OF YOUR ANSWER SHEET LABELED "CHEMISTRY" AND ANSWER QUESTIONS 101–115 ACCORDING TO THE FOLLOWING DIRECTIONS.

Part B

Directions: Each question below consists of two statements. For each question, determine whether statement I in the left-most column is true or false and whether statement II in the rightmost column is true or false. Fill in the corresponding T or F ovals on the answer sheet provided. Fill in the oval labeled "CE" only if statement II correctly explains statement I.

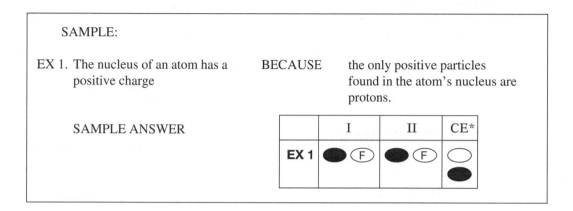

I   **II**

101. Alpha particles are able to pass through a thin sheet of gold foil   BECAUSE   the atom is mainly empty space.

102. Nitrogen has five valence electrons   BECAUSE   the electron configuration for nitrogen is $1s^2 2s^2 2p^6$.

103. A molecule of ethyne is linear   BECAUSE   the carbon atoms in ethyne are sp hybridized.

104. KNO_3 will not dissolve in water   BECAUSE   all chlorides are soluble in water.

105. CCl_4 is a polar molecule   BECAUSE   the dipole arrows for CCl_4 show counterbalance and symmetry.

106. According to the equation $M_1 V_1 = M_2 V_2$, as the volume increases the molarity decreases   BECAUSE   as water is added to a solution the solution is diluted.

107. HCl is an Arrhenius acid   BECAUSE   HCl will yield hydronium ions as the only positive ions in solution.

GO ON TO THE NEXT PAGE

108. Adding more reactants will speed up a reaction   BECAUSE   the reactants will collide less frequently.

109. $Al^{3+} + 3e- \rightarrow Al$ is a correctly balanced oxidation reaction   BECAUSE $Al^{3+} + 3e- \rightarrow Al$ correctly demonstrates conservation of mass and conservation of charge.

110. ^4_2He is the correct symbol for an alpha particle   BECAUSE   an alpha particle is a helium-3 nucleus.

111. Fluorine has the highest value for electronegativity   BECAUSE   fluorine has the greatest attraction for electrons.

112. The number 5,007 has three significant figures   BECAUSE   zeros between non-zero digits are significant.

113. DNA is a polymer   BECAUSE   DNA has many smaller units bonded to create longer chains.

114. Radiation and radioisotopes can have beneficial uses   BECAUSE   radioisotopes and radiation can be used for radio dating, radiotracers, and food preservation.

115. A $1m$ NaCl(aq) solution will freeze at a temperature below 273 K   BECAUSE   as a solute is added to a solvent, the boiling point increases while the freezing point decreases.

GO ON TO THE NEXT PAGE

Part C

Directions: Each of the multiple-choice questions or incomplete sentences below is followed by five answers or completions. Select the one answer that is best in each case and then fill in the corresponding oval on the answer sheet provided.

26. When chlorine gas and hydrogen gas react to form hydrogen chloride, what will be the change of enthalpy of the reaction? (Bond dissociation energies can be found in the Reference Tables on pages 266 and 267.)

    (A) +245 kJ/mol
    (B) +185 kJ/mol
    (C) −185 kJ/mol
    (D) −1105 kJ/mol
    (E) +1105 kJ/mol

27. How much heat is required to raise the temperature of 85 grams of water from 280 K to 342 K?

    (A) 5,270 J
    (B) 355 J
    (C) 259 J
    (D) 151 J
    (E) 22,029 J

28. Which of the following is not part of the Atomic Theory?

    (A) Compounds are made up of combinations of atoms.
    (B) All atoms of a given element are alike.
    (C) All matter is composed of atoms.
    (D) A chemical reaction involves the rearrangement of atoms.
    (E) The atom is mainly empty space.

29. Which of the following compounds will have an atom with a molecular geometry that is described as trigonal planar with respect to other atoms present?

    I. BF_3
    II. $CH_2{=}CH_2$
    III. Cyclopropane

    (A) I only
    (B) II only
    (C) III only
    (D) I and II only
    ((E) I, II, and III

30. Which of the following transmutations demonstrate(s) beta decay?

    I.   Bi-212 → Po-212
    II.   Pb-212 → Bi-212
    III. Ra-228 → Ac-228

    (A) I only
    (B) II only
    (C) II and III only
    (D) I and II only
    (E) I, II, and III

31. A liquid will boil when

    (A) the liquid is hot
    (B) a salt has been added to the liquid
    (C) the vapor pressure of the liquid is equal to the surrounding pressure
    (D) the vapor pressure is reduced
    (E) the surrounding pressure is increased

32. Which sample has atoms that are arranged in a regular geometric pattern?

    (A) $KCl(l)$
    (B) $NaC_2H_3O_2(s)$
    (C) $Fe(l)$
    (D) $NaCl(aq)$
    (E) $HCl(aq)$

33. Which aqueous solution has a molarity of 1.0 *M*?

    (A) 73 grams of HCl dissolved to make 2.0 liters of solution
    (B) 360 grams of $C_6H_{12}O_6$ dissolved to make 1.5 liters of solution
    (C) 94 grams of K_2O dissolved to make 0.75 liters of solution
    (D) 24 grams of LiOH dissolved to make 1.25 liters of solution
    (E) 40 grams of HF dissolved to make 2.50 liters of solution

GO ON TO THE NEXT PAGE

34. Which double replacement reaction forms an insoluble precipitate?

    (A) $HCl(aq) + KOH(aq) \rightarrow$
    (B) $KNO_3(aq) + Na_2SO_4(aq) \rightarrow$
    (C) $NaCl(aq) + CaCl_2(aq) \rightarrow$
    (D) $AgNO_3(aq) + KCl(aq) \rightarrow$
    (E) $KBr(aq) + H_2O(aq) \rightarrow$

35. Of the following solutions, which one is expected to be the weakest electrolyte?

    (A) $HCl(aq)$
    (B) $HF(aq)$
    (C) $NaOH(aq)$
    (D) $KI(aq)$
    (E) $HClO_4(aq)$

36. Which of the following indicate(s) a basic solution?

    I.   Litmus paper turns blue.
    II.   Phenolphthalein turns pink.
    III. Hydronium ion concentration is greater than hydroxide ion concentration.

    (A) I only
    (B) II only
    (C) III only
    (D) I and II only
    (E) I, II, and III

37. Which of the following half reactions is correctly balanced?

    (A) $MnO_4^{1-} \rightarrow Mn^{2+} + 4H_2O$
    (B) $Cu + 2Ag^{1+} \rightarrow 2Ag + Cu^{2+}$
    (C) $H_2 + OH^{1-} \rightarrow 2H_2O$
    (D) $Pb^{2+} + 2e^- \rightarrow Pb$
    (E) $2F^{1-} + 2e^- \rightarrow F_2$

38. The quantity "one mole" will not be equal to

    (A) 22.4 L of $H_2(g)$ at STP
    (B) 6.02×10^{23} carbon atoms
    (C) 64 grams of $SO_2(g)$
    (D) 36 grams of H_2O
    (E) 207 grams of Pb

39. Which statement below is false regarding empirical formulas?

    (A) The empirical formula for butyne is C_2H_3.
    (B) The empirical formula for ammonia is NH_3.
    (C) The empirical formula of CH_2O is $C_6H_{12}O_6$.
    (D) Ionic compounds are written as empirical formulas.
    (E) The empirical and molecular formulas for methane are the same.

40. The percent composition by mass of oxygen in $BaSO_4$ is

    (A) 233.4%
    (B) 66.7%
    (C) 27.4%
    (D) 58.7%
    (E) 13.7%

41. How many grams of Fe_2O_3 can be formed from the rusting of 446 grams of Fe according to the reaction: $4Fe + 3O_2 \rightarrow 2Fe_2O_3$? (Assume an unlimited amount of oxygen gas.)

    (A) 320 grams
    (B) 223 grams
    (C) 159 grams
    (D) 480 grams
    (E) 640 grams

42. Sodium and chlorine react according to the following reaction: $2Na + Cl_2 \rightarrow 2NaCl$. If the reaction starts with 5.0 moles of Na and 3.0 moles of Cl_2 then which statement below is true?

    (A) Cl_2 is the excess reagent and 5.0 moles of NaCl will be produced.
    (B) Na is the excess reagent and 2.5 moles of NaCl will be produced.
    (C) There will be an excess of 2.0 moles of Na.
    (D) Na is the limiting reagent and 2.0 moles of NaCl will be produced.
    (E) Cl is the excess reagent and 2.0 moles of NaCl will be produced.

GO ON TO THE NEXT PAGE

43. The equilibrium constant expression for the reaction: $2A(g) + B(g) \longleftrightarrow 3C(s) + 2D(g)$ is written as

(A) $K_{eq} = \dfrac{[A]^2[B]}{[C]^3[D]^2}$

(B) $K_{eq} = \dfrac{[C]^3[D]^2}{[A]^2[B]^2}$

(C) $K_{eq} = \dfrac{[D]^2}{[A]^2[B]}$

(D) $K_{eq} = \dfrac{[A]^2[B]}{[D]^2}$

(E) $K_{eq} = \dfrac{[C][D]}{[A][B]}$

44. Given the reaction: $3H_2(g) + N_2(g) \longleftrightarrow 2NH_3(g) +$ heat energy. Which of the following would drive the equilibrium in the direction opposite to that of the other four choices?

(A) Remove ammonia from the reaction.
(B) Increase the temperature of the system.
(C) Increase the pressure on the system.
(D) Add nitrogen gas.
(E) Add hydrogen gas.

45. Which of the following demonstrate(s) $\Delta S(-)$?

    I.   Raking up leaves
    II.   Boiling a liquid
    III. Emptying a box of confetti onto the floor

(A) I only
(B) II only
(C) I and II only
(D) I and III only
(E) II and III only

46. In which of the following pieces of glassware does a meniscus become of importance?

(A) watchglass
(B) burette
(C) beaker
(D) flask
(E) funnel

47. If the pressure on a gas is doubled, the volume of the gas will be

(A) doubled
(B) the same
(C) halved
(D) quartered
(E) quadrupled

48. Which of the following statements about gas collection is false?

(A) Carbon dioxide can be collected by an upward displacement of air.
(B) Ammonia can be tested for by placing red litmus paper at the mouth of the collection glassware.
(C) Ammonia can be collected by water displacement.
(D) Hydrogen gas can be collected by water displacement.
(E) Carbon dioxide can be tested for with a lit match.

49. In the diagram shown below, which letter represents the potential energy of the products minus the potential energy of the reactants? (See Figure 2.)

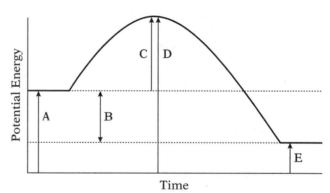

Time
Figure 2

(A) B
(B) D
(C) A
(D) E
(E) C

GO ON TO THE NEXT PAGE

50. What is the heat of reaction for A + B → F?

    (A + B → 2C   ΔH = +150 kcal)
    (C → 2D + 2E   ΔH = −450 kcal)
    (F → 4D + 4E   ΔH = +725 kcal)

    (A) −1475 kcal
    (B)   +25 kcal
    (C) −1025 kcal
    (D)   +325 kcal
    (E)   +300 kcal

51. Molten KBr is allowed to undergo the process of electrolysis. Which reaction occurs at the anode?

    (A) $K^{1+} + 1e- \rightarrow K(s)$
    (B) $2Br^{1-} \rightarrow Br_2 + 2e-$
    (C) $K(s) \rightarrow K^{1+} + 1e-$
    (D) $Br_2 \rightarrow 2Br^{1-} + 2e-$
    (E) $Br_2 + 2e- \rightarrow 2Br^{1-}$

52. Which not will happen when sodium sulfate is added to a saturated solution of $PbSO_4$ that is at equilibrium? [$PbSO_4(s) \longleftrightarrow Pb^{2+}(aq) + SO_4^{2-}(aq)$]

    (A) The solubility of the lead sulfate will decrease.
    (B) The concentration of lead ions will decrease.
    (C) The reaction will shift to the left.
    (D) The K_{sp} value will change.
    (E) The equilibrium will shift to consume the increase in sulfate ions.

53. What is the voltage of the voltaic cell $Cu / Cu^{2+} // Zn / Zn^{2+}$ at 298 K if $[Zn^{2+}] = 0.2 \, M$ and $[Cu^{2+}] = 4.0 \, M$?

    (A) +1.10 V
    (B) −1.10 V
    (C) +1.07 V
    (D) +1.14 V
    (E) −1.07 V

54. Which of the following molecules has polar bonds but is a nonpolar molecule?

    (A) H_2
    (B) H_2O
    (C) NH_3
    (D) NaCl
    (E) CO_2

55. A titration is set up so that 35.0 mL of 1.0 M NaOH are titrated with 1.5 M HCl. How many milliliters of acid are needed to completely titrate this amount of base?

    (A) 15.00 mL
    (B) 35.00 mL
    (C) 23.33 mL
    (D) 58.33 mL
    (E) 20.00 mL

56. Which statement is inconsistent with the concept of isotopes of the same element?

    (A) Isotopes have the same number of protons.
    (B) Isotopes have the same atomic number.
    (C) Isotopes differ in mass number.
    (D) Isotopes differ in number of neutrons present.
    (E) Isotopes differ in their nuclear charge.

57. Which of the following pairs of substances can be broken down chemically?

    (A) Ammonia and iron
    (B) Helium and argon
    (C) Methane and water
    (D) Potassium and lithium
    (E) Water and carbon

58. What is the volume of 2.3 moles of an ideal gas at 300 K and a pressure of 1.1 atmospheres?

    (A) $\dfrac{(2.3 \text{ moles})(0.0820 \text{ L·atm/mol·K})(300 \text{ K})}{(1.1 \text{ atm})}$

    (B) $\dfrac{(1.1 \text{ atm})}{(2.3 \text{ moles})(0.0820 \text{ L·atm/mol·K})(300 \text{ K})}$

    (C) $\dfrac{(2.3 \text{ moles})(0.0820 \text{ L·atm/mol·K})}{(300 \text{ K})(1.1 \text{ atm})}$

    (D) $\dfrac{(300 \text{ K})(0.0820 \text{ L·atm/mol·K})}{(2.3 \text{ moles})(1.1 \text{ atm})}$

    (E) $\dfrac{(2.3 \text{ moles})(1.1 \text{ atm})(300 \text{ K})}{(0.0820 \text{ L·atm/mol·K})}$

GO ON TO THE NEXT PAGE

59. Substance X has three common isotopes: X-48, X-49, and X-51. If the relative abundances of these isotopes are 42%, 38%, and 20%, respectively, what is the atomic mass of substance X?

(A) 49.33
(B) 48.62
(C) 50.67
(D) 48.98
(E) 49.67

60. Which choice below would affect the rate of reaction in the opposite way from the other four?

(A) Cool the reaction down.
(B) Add a catalyst.
(C) Decrease the pressure.
(D) Use larger pieces of solid reactants.
(E) Decrease the concentration of the reactants.

61. One mole of an ideal gas at STP has its temperature changed to 15°C and its pressure changed to 700 torr. What is the new volume of this gas?

(A) $\dfrac{(760 \text{ torr})(22.4 \text{ L})(288 \text{ K})}{(273 \text{ K})(700 \text{ torr})}$

(B) $\dfrac{(273 \text{ K})(700 \text{ torr})}{(760 \text{ torr})(22.4 \text{ L})(288 \text{ K})}$

(C) $\dfrac{(760 \text{ torr})(22.4 \text{ L})(273 \text{ K})}{(288 \text{ K})(700 \text{ torr})}$

(D) $\dfrac{(700 \text{ torr})(22.4 \text{ L})(287 \text{ K})}{(273 \text{ K})(760 \text{ torr})}$

(E) $\dfrac{(760 \text{ torr})(1.0 \text{ L})(288 \text{ K})}{(273 \text{ K})(700 \text{ torr})}$

62. Which reaction will not occur spontaneously?

(A) $Au^{3+} + 3e- \rightarrow Au$
(B) $Mg + 2H^{1+} \rightarrow Mg^{2+} + H_2$
(C) $F_2 + 2e- \rightarrow 2F^{1-}$
(D) $Li^{1+} + 1e- \rightarrow Li$
(E) $2Na + Cl_2 + 2e- \rightarrow 2NaCl$

63. As you go from left to right across a period on the periodic table there in a decrease in

(A) first ionization energy
(B) nuclear charge
(C) electronegativity
(D) the ability to gain electrons
(E) metallic character

64. Which of the following statements is false?

(A) H_2 has just one sigma bond.
(B) HCl has just one sigma bond.
(C) $H—C\equiv C—H$ has four pi bonds and three sigma bonds.
(D) $CH_2{=}CH_2$ has five sigma bonds and one pi bond.
(E) H_2O has two sigma bonds and two lone pairs.

65. What is the correct formula for iron(III) sulfate?

(A) $FeSO_4$
(B) $Fe_2(SO_4)_3$
(C) $Fe(SO_4)_3$
(D) Fe_3SO_4
(E) $Fe_3(SO_4)_2$

66. A solution has a pH of 6.0. What is the concentration of OH^{1-} ions in solution?

(A) $6.0 \times 10^{-14} M$
(B) $1.0 \times 10^{-6} M$
(C) $1.0 \times 10^{-14} M$
(D) $6.0 \times 10^{-8} M$
(E) $1.0 \times 10^{-8} M$

67. Which of the following statements about bonding is correct?

(A) Van der Waals forces exist between polar molecules.
(B) Dipoles are the result of the equal sharing of electrons.
(C) Cu(s) is a network solid.
(D) Hydrogen bonds exist between the molecules of HCl.
(E) NaCl(aq) has attraction between the molecules and the ions.

GO ON TO THE NEXT PAGE

68. A radioactive substance decays from 100 grams to 6.25 grams in 100 days. What is the half-life of this radioactive substance?

    (A) 25 days
    (B) 6.25 days
    (C) 12.5 days
    (D) 100 days
    (E) 50 days

69. Which choice or choices demonstrate amphoterism?

    I. $HCl + H_2O \rightarrow H_3O^{1+} + Cl^{1-}$ and
         $H_2O + NH_3 \rightarrow OH^{1-} + NH_4^{1+}$
    II. $HS^{1-} + HCl \rightarrow Cl^{1-} + H_2S$ and
         $HS^{1-} + NH_3 \rightarrow NH_4^{1+} + S^{2-}$
    III. $HCl + NaOH \rightarrow NaCl + H_2O$ and
         $NaCl + H_2O \rightarrow HCl + NaOH$

    (A) I only
    (B) II only
    (C) III only
    (D) I and II only
    (E) I and III only

70. Which statement below is incorrect regarding balanced equations?

    (A) $C + O_2 \rightarrow CO_2$ is balanced and is a synthesis reaction.
    (B) $CaCO_3 \rightarrow CaO + CO_2$ is balanced and is a decomposition reaction.
    (C) $Na + Cl_2 \rightarrow NaCl$ is not balanced but demonstrates a synthesis reaction.
    (D) $KI + Pb(NO_3)_2 \rightarrow PbI_2 + KNO_3$ is balanced and is a single replacement reaction.
    (E) $2H_2O \rightarrow 2H_2 + O_2$ is balanced and demonstrates a redox reaction.

S T O P

IF YOU FINISH BEFORE TIME IS CALLED, YOU MAY CHECK YOUR WORK ON THIS TEST ONLY.
DO NOT TURN TO ANY OTHER TEST IN THIS BOOK.

ANSWER KEY

1. E	18. C	110. T, F	37. D	54. E
2. C	19. E	111. T, T, CE	38. D	55. C
3. A	20. E	112. F, T	39. C	56. E
4. D	21. B	113. T, T, CE	40. C	57. C
5. A	22. A	114. T, T, CE	41. E	58. A
6. C	23. E	115. T, T, CE	42. A	59. D
7. E	24. D		43. C	60. B
8. B	25. B	26. C	44. B	61. A
9. D		27. E	45. A	62. D
10. C	101. T, T, CE	28. E	46. B	63. E
11. A	102. T, F	29. D	47. C	64. C
12. A	103. T, T, CE	30. E	48. C	65. B
13. E	104. F, F	31. C	49. A	66. E
14. C	105. F, T	32. B	50. A	67. E
15. D	106. T, T, CE	33. A	51. B	68. A
16. A	107. T, T, CE	34. D	52. D	69. D
17. B	108. T, F	35. B	53. D	70. D
	109. F, T	36. D		

ANSWERS AND EXPLANATIONS

1. **E**   As the pressure increases on a gas, the volume of the gas will decrease. The graph that demonstrates Boyle's Law is curved as indicated by choice E.

2. **C**   This graph is a phase diagram, which contains a triple point.

3. **A**   As temperature increases, so does the volume of a gas.

4. **D**   Moving from lithium to fluorine in period 2, the atomic radius decreases.

5. **A**   Bromine and mercury are liquids at room temperature.

6. **C**   Both the ammonium and hydronium ions have bonded a proton by donating two electrons to the bond that has formed with the proton.

7. **E**   Allotropes are different forms of the same element. Both diamond and graphite are made of carbon.

8. **B**   Better oxidizing agents are easily reduced (gain electrons). With their higher electronegativities, both chlorine and fluorine are good oxidizing agents.

9. **D**   The ending *–oate* is that of an ester, R—COO—R.

10. **C**   The functional group R—NH_2 is that of an amine.

11. **A**   Alcohols have an —OH group attached to them and end in *–ol*.

12. **A**   A calcium atom has 20 electrons, $1s^2 2s^2 2p^6 3s^2 3p^6 4s^2$. A calcium ion will have 18 electrons because calcium forms an ion with a charge of 2+, $1s^2 2s^2 2p^6 3s^2 3p^6$.

13. **E**   This choice shows that the 3s sublevel has been skipped over.

14. **C**   Potassium has 19 electrons and the configuration of $1s^2 2s^2 2p^6 3s^2 3p^6 4s^1$.

15. **D**   The noble gas with the most stable configuration and highest first ionization energy is helium.

16. **A**   The changing of a solid to a gas without a liquid phase is called sublimation.

17. **B**   Deposition is the changing of a gas to a solid without a liquid phase.

18. **C**   Vaporization of a liquid will cause the liquid to enter the gas phase.

19. **E**   Freezing a liquid will turn the liquid into a solid.

20. **E**   Beryllium has two valence electrons, $1s^2 2s^2$.

21. **B**   Oxygen has six valence electrons, $1s^2 2s^2 2p^4$.

22. **A**   Nitrogen has five valence electrons. In an effort to make a complete octet, nitrogen will gain three electrons and have an ion with a charge of 3–.

23.	**E**	10^{-9}, a billionth, is the value that is represented by the prefix *nano–*.
24.	**D**	10^{-6}, a millionth, is the value that is represented by the prefix *micro–*.
25.	**B**	10^3, a thousand, is the value that is represented by the prefix *kilo–*.
101.	**T, T, CE**	Rutherford's gold foil experiment showed that alpha particles can pass through a sheet of gold foil, proving that the atom is mainly empty space.
102.	**T, F**	Nitrogen does have five valance electrons, but the electron configuration shown is that of the nitrogen ion when it has gained three electrons.
103.	**T, T, CE**	Ethyne has two carbon atoms that have a triple bond between them. The triple bond demands an sp hybridization and the resulting linear geometry.
104.	**F, F**	All nitrates are soluble in water, but the chlorides of silver, mercury, and lead are not.
105.	**F, T**	The bonds in carbon tetrachloride are polar but because the molecule is symmetrical, the resulting molecules will be nonpolar.
106.	**T, T, CE**	Concentration and volume have an inverse relationship because, as water is added to a solution with a given concentration, the concentration will decrease.
107.	**T, T, CE**	HCl is matched up perfectly with the definition of an Arrhenius acid in this problem.
108.	**T, F**	Adding more reactants to a reaction will speed up the reaction by increasing the frequency of collisions.
109.	**F, T**	Although the half reaction does demonstrate conservation of mass and charge, the half reaction is a reduction and not an oxidation.
110.	**T, F**	Looking at the mass number for the alpha particle shows that there are four nucleons present. An alpha particle is a helium-4 nucleus.
111.	**T, T, CE**	Electronegativity is an atom's ability to attract electrons. With a value of 4.0, fluorine has the highest electronegativity and attraction for electrons.
112.	**F, T**	While 5,007 has three different digits, there are four significant figures present because both zeros between the nonzero digits are significant.
113.	**T, T, CE**	DNA is a polymer made up of many individual nucleic acids.
114.	**T, T, CE**	Even though radiation and radioactive substances can have negative effects on humans, if used correctly and in the right amounts, they can also be beneficial to humans as well.
115.	**T, T,**	Adding a solute to a solvent causes the colligative properties of the solvent

| | **CE** | to change. This includes the elevation of the boiling point and the depression of the freezing point. |

26.   **C**   This reaction calls for one H to H bond to be broken, one Cl to Cl bond to be broken, and two H to Cl bonds to be formed. This is set up as follows:

$$[1(H—H) + 1(Cl—Cl)] – [2(H—Cl)].$$ Substitution gives:

$$[435 + 240] – [2(430)] = 675 – 860 = –185 \text{ kJ}.$$

27.   **E**   The amount of heat absorbed by water can be calculated using the equation $q = mc\Delta T$. Substituting gives $(85 \text{ grams})(4.18 \text{ J/g K})(62 \text{ K}) = 22{,}028.6 \text{ J}$.

28.   **E**   All the statements are included in the Atomic Theory except for the empty space concept of the atom. This was concluded by Rutherford in his gold foil experiment.

29.   **D**   The sp^2 hybridization of the two carbon atoms in ethane and the six valence electrons preferred by boron, gives rise to a trigonal planar molecular geometry. Cyclopropane has all single bonds in its molecule and will have sp^3 hybridized carbon atoms.

30.   **E**   The three equations are $^{212}_{83}\text{Bi} \rightarrow {}^{212}_{84}\text{Po} + {}^{0}_{-1}\text{e}$, $^{212}_{82}\text{Pb} \rightarrow {}^{212}_{83}\text{Bi} + {}^{0}_{-1}\text{e}$, and $^{228}_{88}\text{Ra} \rightarrow {}^{228}_{89}\text{Ac} + {}^{0}_{-1}\text{e}$. All three equations show conservation of mass because the mass numbers add up, and they all show conservation of charge because the nuclear charges (atomic numbers) add up as well.

31.   **C**   When the vapor pressure of a liquid is equal to the atmospheric pressure that surrounds the liquid, the liquid will boil.

32.   **B**   Solids have their atoms set in a fixed position. This allows for a regular geometric pattern such as the lattice in $NaCl(s)$ to be formed.

33.   **A**   The equation for calculating the molarity of a solution is moles of solute / total liters of solution. Because 73 grams of HCl (molar mass is 36.5) is 2 moles of HCl dissolved to make 2.0 liters of solution total, the solution will be 1.0 M.

34.   **D**   When a double replacement reaction occurs between $AgNO_3(aq)$ and $KCl(aq)$, the products formed are AgCl and KNO_3. AgCl is insoluble in water and forms a white precipitate.

35.   **B**   HF is a weak acid and will also act like a weak electrolyte. The other substances are either strong acids, strong bases, or water-soluble salts.

36.   **D**   Litmus will be blue and phenolphthalein will be pink in a basic solution. The concentration of hydroxide ions should also be greater than the concentration of hydronium ions.

37.   **D**   The reaction $Pb^{2+} + 2e- \rightarrow Pb$ shows conservation of mass and charge. Notice that choice B is not a half reaction; it is full redox reaction that is properly

balanced.

38. **D** 36 grams of water (molar mass is 18) will be equal to 2 moles of water.

39. **C** All of these statements are correct except for choice C, which should read, "The empirical formula of $C_6H_{12}O_6$ is CH_2O."

40. **C** The total mass of this compound is 233.4. Because the oxygen makes up 64 of the 233.4, the oxygen is $64/233 \times 100\% = 27.4\%$.

41. **E** 446 grams of Fe (atomic mass is 55.8) is 8 moles of iron. If 8 moles of Fe react, then according to the balanced equation, 4 moles of Fe_2O_3 should be produced:

$$\frac{4\ Fe}{8\ Fe} = \frac{2\ Fe_2O_3}{x\ moles\ Fe_2O_3}$$

4 moles of Fe_2O_3 (molar mass is 160) is 640 grams.

42. **A** 5.0 moles of sodium would require only 2.5 moles of chlorine gas because twice as much sodium is consumed in the reaction as chlorine (as seen in the balanced equation). This means that sodium is the limiting reagent and chlorine is in excess. If all 5.0 moles of the sodium are used up, then 5.0 moles of NaCl will be produced because of their 1:1 ratio in the balanced equation.

43. **C** Remember that the equilibrium expression calls for, "products over reactants, coefficients become powers." Solids and liquids are not included in the expressions. This means that the correct expression is

$$K_{eq} = \frac{[D]^2}{[A]^2[B]}$$

44. **B** Increasing the temperature of a system at equilibrium will shift the equilibrium away from the side that has the heat energy. In this case the equilibrium will shift to the left. In all the other cases the equilibrium will shift to the right.

45. **A** A negative sign for entropy means more order (or less chaos and less disorder). Raking up leaves is a more orderly state.

46. **B** The burette is the most precise piece of glassware listed. Because a burette is narrow, the meniscus will be prominent and of importance.

47. **C** Because pressure and volume are inversely proportional, an increase in pressure will decrease the volume. Use Boyle's Law and substitute with "mock" values to get: $1P_1\ 1V_1 = 2P_2\ V_2$. Solving for the new volume V_2, you find that $1P_1$ has been divided by 2:

$$\frac{1P_1 \, 1V_1}{2P_2} = V_2$$

The volume has been halved.

48.   **C**   Ammonia is a polar molecule and will dissolve in a polar substance like water. This means that water displacement is a poor method for the collection of ammonia.

49.   **A**   The potential energy of the products minus the potential energy of the reactants is the heat of reaction. This is designated by the letter "B" on the diagram.

50.   **A**   Because A and B are on the left in the overall reaction you have:

$$A + B \rightarrow 2C \qquad \Delta H = +150 \text{ kcal}$$

To cancel out the 2C that appears on the right in the step above, double the step so that it reads:

$$2C \rightarrow 4D + 4E \qquad \Delta H = -900 \text{ kcal}$$

Finally, you need to have F on the right as dictated in the overall equation. You also need to cancel out the D and E formed in the last step:

$$4D + 4E \rightarrow F \qquad \Delta H = -725 \text{ kcal}$$

Add up the heats of reaction from the three steps to get: $\Delta H = -1,475$ kcal.

51.   **B**   Remember the mnemonic device, "An Ox," and that oxidation occurs at the anode. This means that the half reaction at the anode will show a loss of electrons. The negatively charged bromine ions will serve this purpose. The half reaction must also be written correctly as well.

52.   **D**   The solubility product constant will change only if there is a change in temperature.

53.   **D**   To calculate the new electrode potential for nonstandard condition, use the Nernst equation:

$$E = E° \frac{-2.30 \text{ RT}}{nf} (\log Q). \text{ Substitution gives:}$$

$$E = +1.10 \text{ V} \frac{-0.059 \text{ V}}{2} (\log [0.2]/[4.0]) \text{ and becomes}$$

$$E = +1.10 \text{ V} \frac{-0.059 \text{ V}}{2} (-1.30)$$

Solving gives a new potential of about 1.14 volts.

54.   **E**   Water, ammonia, and carbon dioxide all have polar bonds. Because it is a symmetrical molecule, carbon dioxide will have a counterbalance of the di-

pole forces and be a nonpolar molecule.

55. **C** To calculate the amount acid needed use the titration formula: $M_aV_a = M_bV_b$. Substitution gives: $(1.5\ M)(V_a) = (1.0\ M)(35.0\ \text{mL})$. Solve to find that the volume of acid is 23.33 mL.

56. **E** Because isotopes are the same element with different mass numbers, they will have the same number of protons and the same nuclear charge.

57. **C** Compounds can be broken down chemically whereas elements cannot. Methane and water are examples of compounds.

58. **A** This problem requires the use of the ideal gas equation, $PV = nRT$. Rearranging to solve for V gives:

$$V = nRT/P \text{ or } \frac{(2.3\ \text{moles})(0.0820\ \text{L·atm/mol·K})(300\ \text{K})}{(1.1\ \text{atm})}.$$

59. **D** Multiply the mass numbers by their abundances:

$(48)(0.42) = 20.16$

$(49)(0.38) = 18.62$

$(51)(0.20) = 10.20$

Total comes to 48.98.

60. **B** All the factors mentioned will decrease the rate of reaction except for adding a catalyst, which will increase the rate of reaction.

61. **A** One mole of the gas occupies 22.4 liters initially at 273 K and 760 torr. Using the combined gas law and solving for the new volume gives: $V_2 = P_1V_1T_2 / T_1P_2$. The new temperature is 288 K (using $K = C + 273$) and substitution gives:

$$\frac{(760\ \text{torr})(22.4\ \text{L})(288\ \text{K})}{(273\ \text{K})(700\ \text{torr})}$$

Even though the question does not ask for the new volume, you can still predict that the volume will be more than 22.4 liters. This is because the pressure decreased and the temperature increased, both suggesting an increase in the volume.

62. **D** Lithium is an active metal and will most likely lose electrons. This choice shows the lithium ion gaining an electron to form solid lithium, a reaction that has an electrode potential that is negative and will not occur spontaneously.

63. **E** Going from left to right across period 2, the elements become more non-metallic and there is a decrease in the metallic character.

64.   **C**   Because there is a triple bond between the carbon atoms, there are two pi bonds and one sigma bond. Add to this the two sigma bonds between the carbon and hydrogen atoms and the total is two pi bonds and three sigma bonds.

65.   **B**   The roman numeral III means that the iron ion has a charge of 3+. Sulfate has a charge of 2–. Using the crisscross method and using parentheses for the polyatomic ion, the correct formula is $Fe_2(SO_4)_3$.

66.   **E**   Because the pH is 6, the $[H^{1+}]$ is 1.0×10^{-6} M. Using the equation $1.0 \times 10^{-14} = [H^{1+}][OH^{1-}]$ and substituting, $1.0 \times 10^{-14} = [1.0 \times 10^{-6}\ M][OH^{1-}]$ you find that the hydroxide ion concentration will be 1.0×10^{-8} M.

67.   **E**   When ions are dissolved in water to make a solution, there is an attraction between the polar water molecules and the charged ions. This is called the molecule-ion attraction.

68.   **A**   This substance had undergone four half-life periods as shown here:

100 grams → 50 grams → 25 grams → 12.5 grams → 6.25 grams

There were four half-life periods totaling 100 days. This means that each half-life period is 25 days.

69.   **D**   In reaction I the water acts like an acid and a base. In reaction II the HS^{1-} ion acts like an acid and a base. Reaction III shows neutralization and hydrolysis, but not amphoterism.

70.   **D**   This reaction is not balanced. It should be: $2KI + Pb(NO_3)_2 \rightarrow PbI_2 + 2KNO_3$. Also, this reaction is classified as a double replacement.

SCORE SHEET

Number of questions correct: _____

Less: 0.25 × number of questions wrong: _____

(Remember that omitted questions are not counted as wrong.)

Raw score: _____

Raw Score	Test Score		Raw Score	Test Score		Raw Score	Test Score		Raw Score	Test Score		Raw Score	Test Score
85	800		63	710		41	570		19	440		−3	300
84	800		62	700		40	560		18	430		−4	300
83	800		61	700		39	560		17	430		−5	290
82	800		60	690		38	550		16	420		−6	290
81	800		59	680		37	550		15	420		−7	280
80	800		58	670		36	540		14	410		−8	270
79	790		57	670		35	530		13	400		−9	270
78	790		56	660		34	530		12	400		−10	260
77	790		55	650		33	520		11	390		−11	250
76	780		54	640		32	520		10	390		−12	250
75	780		53	640		31	510		9	380		−13	240
74	770		52	630		30	500		8	370		−14	240
73	760		51	630		29	500		7	360		−15	230
72	760		50	620		28	490		6	360		−16	230
71	750		49	610		27	480		5	350		−17	220
70	740		48	610		26	480		4	350		−18	220
69	740		47	600		25	470		3	340		−19	210
68	730		46	600		24	470		2	330		−20	210
67	730		45	590		23	460		1	330		−21	200
66	720		44	580		22	460		0	320			
65	720		43	580		21	450		−1	320			
64	710		42	570		20	440		−2	310			

Note: This is only a sample scoring scale. Scoring scales differ from exam to exam.

CHEMISTRY PRACTICE TEST 2

Treat this practice test as the actual test, and complete it in one 60-minute sitting. Use the following answer sheet to fill in your multiple-choice answers. Once you have completed the practice test:

1. Check your answers using the Answer Key.
2. Review the Answers and Explanations.
3. Complete the Score Sheet to see how well you did.

ANSWER SHEET

Tear out this answer sheet and use it to complete the practice test. Determine the BEST answer for each question. Then, fill in the appropriate oval.

1. Ⓐ Ⓑ Ⓒ Ⓓ Ⓔ	21. Ⓐ Ⓑ Ⓒ Ⓓ Ⓔ	41. Ⓐ Ⓑ Ⓒ Ⓓ Ⓔ	61. Ⓐ Ⓑ Ⓒ Ⓓ Ⓔ
2. Ⓐ Ⓑ Ⓒ Ⓓ Ⓔ	22. Ⓐ Ⓑ Ⓒ Ⓓ Ⓔ	42. Ⓐ Ⓑ Ⓒ Ⓓ Ⓔ	62. Ⓐ Ⓑ Ⓒ Ⓓ Ⓔ
3. Ⓐ Ⓑ Ⓒ Ⓓ Ⓔ	23. Ⓐ Ⓑ Ⓒ Ⓓ Ⓔ	43. Ⓐ Ⓑ Ⓒ Ⓓ Ⓔ	63. Ⓐ Ⓑ Ⓒ Ⓓ Ⓔ
4. Ⓐ Ⓑ Ⓒ Ⓓ Ⓔ	24. Ⓐ Ⓑ Ⓒ Ⓓ Ⓔ	44. Ⓐ Ⓑ Ⓒ Ⓓ Ⓔ	64. Ⓐ Ⓑ Ⓒ Ⓓ Ⓔ
5. Ⓐ Ⓑ Ⓒ Ⓓ Ⓔ	25. Ⓐ Ⓑ Ⓒ Ⓓ Ⓔ	45. Ⓐ Ⓑ Ⓒ Ⓓ Ⓔ	65. Ⓐ Ⓑ Ⓒ Ⓓ Ⓔ
6. Ⓐ Ⓑ Ⓒ Ⓓ Ⓔ	26. Ⓐ Ⓑ Ⓒ Ⓓ Ⓔ	46. Ⓐ Ⓑ Ⓒ Ⓓ Ⓔ	66. Ⓐ Ⓑ Ⓒ Ⓓ Ⓔ
7. Ⓐ Ⓑ Ⓒ Ⓓ Ⓔ	27. Ⓐ Ⓑ Ⓒ Ⓓ Ⓔ	47. Ⓐ Ⓑ Ⓒ Ⓓ Ⓔ	67. Ⓐ Ⓑ Ⓒ Ⓓ Ⓔ
8. Ⓐ Ⓑ Ⓒ Ⓓ Ⓔ	28. Ⓐ Ⓑ Ⓒ Ⓓ Ⓔ	48. Ⓐ Ⓑ Ⓒ Ⓓ Ⓔ	68. Ⓐ Ⓑ Ⓒ Ⓓ Ⓔ
9. Ⓐ Ⓑ Ⓒ Ⓓ Ⓔ	29. Ⓐ Ⓑ Ⓒ Ⓓ Ⓔ	49. Ⓐ Ⓑ Ⓒ Ⓓ Ⓔ	69. Ⓐ Ⓑ Ⓒ Ⓓ Ⓔ
10. Ⓐ Ⓑ Ⓒ Ⓓ Ⓔ	30. Ⓐ Ⓑ Ⓒ Ⓓ Ⓔ	50. Ⓐ Ⓑ Ⓒ Ⓓ Ⓔ	70. Ⓐ Ⓑ Ⓒ Ⓓ Ⓔ
11. Ⓐ Ⓑ Ⓒ Ⓓ Ⓔ	31. Ⓐ Ⓑ Ⓒ Ⓓ Ⓔ	51. Ⓐ Ⓑ Ⓒ Ⓓ Ⓔ	
12. Ⓐ Ⓑ Ⓒ Ⓓ Ⓔ	32. Ⓐ Ⓑ Ⓒ Ⓓ Ⓔ	52. Ⓐ Ⓑ Ⓒ Ⓓ Ⓔ	
13. Ⓐ Ⓑ Ⓒ Ⓓ Ⓔ	33. Ⓐ Ⓑ Ⓒ Ⓓ Ⓔ	53. Ⓐ Ⓑ Ⓒ Ⓓ Ⓔ	
14. Ⓐ Ⓑ Ⓒ Ⓓ Ⓔ	34. Ⓐ Ⓑ Ⓒ Ⓓ Ⓔ	54. Ⓐ Ⓑ Ⓒ Ⓓ Ⓔ	
15. Ⓐ Ⓑ Ⓒ Ⓓ Ⓔ	35. Ⓐ Ⓑ Ⓒ Ⓓ Ⓔ	55. Ⓐ Ⓑ Ⓒ Ⓓ Ⓔ	
16. Ⓐ Ⓑ Ⓒ Ⓓ Ⓔ	36. Ⓐ Ⓑ Ⓒ Ⓓ Ⓔ	56. Ⓐ Ⓑ Ⓒ Ⓓ Ⓔ	
17. Ⓐ Ⓑ Ⓒ Ⓓ Ⓔ	37. Ⓐ Ⓑ Ⓒ Ⓓ Ⓔ	57. Ⓐ Ⓑ Ⓒ Ⓓ Ⓔ	
18. Ⓐ Ⓑ Ⓒ Ⓓ Ⓔ	38. Ⓐ Ⓑ Ⓒ Ⓓ Ⓔ	58. Ⓐ Ⓑ Ⓒ Ⓓ Ⓔ	
19. Ⓐ Ⓑ Ⓒ Ⓓ Ⓔ	39. Ⓐ Ⓑ Ⓒ Ⓓ Ⓔ	59. Ⓐ Ⓑ Ⓒ Ⓓ Ⓔ	
20. Ⓐ Ⓑ Ⓒ Ⓓ Ⓔ	40. Ⓐ Ⓑ Ⓒ Ⓓ Ⓔ	60. Ⓐ Ⓑ Ⓒ Ⓓ Ⓔ	

Chemistry	*Fill in oval CE only if II is correct explanation of I.						
	I	II	CE*		I	II	CE*
101.	Ⓣ Ⓕ	Ⓣ Ⓕ	◯	109.	Ⓣ Ⓕ	Ⓣ Ⓕ	◯
102.	Ⓣ Ⓕ	Ⓣ Ⓕ	◯	110.	Ⓣ Ⓕ	Ⓣ Ⓕ	◯
103.	Ⓣ Ⓕ	Ⓣ Ⓕ	◯	111.	Ⓣ Ⓕ	Ⓣ Ⓕ	◯
104.	Ⓣ Ⓕ	Ⓣ Ⓕ	◯	112.	Ⓣ Ⓕ	Ⓣ Ⓕ	◯
105.	Ⓣ Ⓕ	Ⓣ Ⓕ	◯	113.	Ⓣ Ⓕ	Ⓣ Ⓕ	◯
106.	Ⓣ Ⓕ	Ⓣ Ⓕ	◯	114.	Ⓣ Ⓕ	Ⓣ Ⓕ	◯
107.	Ⓣ Ⓕ	Ⓣ Ⓕ	◯	115.	Ⓣ Ⓕ	Ⓣ Ⓕ	◯
108.	Ⓣ Ⓕ	Ⓣ Ⓕ	◯				

PERIODIC TABLE OF THE ELEMENTS

1	2	3	4	5	6	7	8	9	10	11	12	13	14	15	16	17	18
1 H 1.0079																	2 He 4.0026
3 Li 6.941	4 Be 9.0122											5 B 10.81	6 C 12.011	7 N 14.007	8 O 15.999	9 F 18.998	10 Ne 20.179
11 Na 22.989	12 Mg 24.305											13 Al 26.981	14 Si 28.086	15 P 30.974	16 S 32.06	17 Cl 35.453	18 Ar 39.948
19 K 39.098	20 Ca 40.08	21 Sc 44.956	22 Ti 47.88	23 V 50.941	24 Cr 51.996	25 Mn 54.938	26 Fe 55.847	27 Co 58.933	28 Ni 58.69	29 Cu 63.546	30 Zn 65.38	31 Ga 59.72	32 Ge 72.59	33 As 74.922	34 Se 78.96	35 Br 79.904	36 Kr 83.80
37 Rb 85.468	38 Sr 87.62	39 Y 88.906	40 Zr 91.22	41 Nb 92.905	42 Mo 95.94	43 Tc (98)	44 Ru 101.07	45 Rh 102.91	46 Pd 106.42	47 Ag 107.87	48 Cd 112.41	49 In 114.82	50 Sn 118.69	51 Sb 121.75	52 Te 127.60	53 I 126.90	54 Xe 131.29
55 Cs 132.91	56 Ba 137.33	57 * La 138.90	72 Hf 178.49	73 Ta 180.95	74 W 183.85	75 Re 186.21	76 Os 190.2	77 Ir 192.22	78 Pt 195.08	79 Au 196.97	80 Hg 200.59	81 Tl 204.38	82 Pb 207.2	83 Bi 208.98	84 Po (209)	85 At (210)	86 Rn (222)
87 Fr (223)	88 Ra 226.0	89 # Ac 227.03	104 Rf (261)	105 Db (262)	106 Sg (263)	107 Bh (262)	108 Hs (265)	109 Mt (266)	110 Uun (269)	111 Uuu (272)	112 Uub (277)						

* Lanthanides	58 Ce 140.12	59 Pr 140.91	60 Nd 144.24	61 Pm (145)	62 Sm 150.36	63 Eu 151.96	64 Gd 157.25	65 Tb 158.92	66 Dy 162.50	67 Ho 164.93	68 Er 167.26	69 Tm 168.93	70 Yb 173.04	71 Lu 174.97
# Actinides	90 Th 232.03	91 Pa 231.03	92 U 238.03	93 Np 237.05	94 Pu (244)	95 Am (243)	96 Cm (247)	97 Bk (247)	98 Cf (251)	99 Es (254)	100 Fm (257)	101 Md (257)	102 No (255)	103 Lr (256)

CHEMISTRY PRACTICE TEST 2

Note: Unless otherwise stated, for all statements involving chemical equations and/or solutions, assume that the system is in pure water.

Part A

Directions: Each of the following sets of lettered choices refers to the numbered formulas or statements immediately below it. For each numbered item, choose the one lettered choice that fits it best. Then fill in the corresponding oval on the answer sheet. Each choice in a set may be used once, more than once, or not at all.

Questions 1–4

(A) The point of equilibrium
(B) The triple point
(C) The freezing point
(D) The point where reactants first form products
(E) The boiling point

1. A specific temperature and pressure where solid, liquid, and gas phases exist simultaneously

2. Can be shifted by adding more reactants

3. Vapor pressure of a liquid is equal to the pressure of the surroundings

4. The activated complex

Questions 5–8

(A) Red
(B) Purple
(C) Orange
(D) Green
(E) Blue

5. Copper(II) sulfate solution

6. Chlorine gas

7. $KMnO_4$ solution

8. Bromine liquid

Questions 9–11

(A) Voltaic cell
(B) Electrolytic cell
(C) Geiger Counter
(D) pH meter
(E) Calorimeter

9. Requires an external current to make a redox reaction spontaneous

10. Requires a salt bridge

11. Detects radioactive particles

GO ON TO THE NEXT PAGE

Questions 12–15

   (A) Halogens

   (B) Alkali metals

   (C) Alkaline earth metals

   (D) Noble gases

   (E) Lanthanides

12. Valence electrons are located in the f orbitals

13. Need to lose one electron to form a stable octet

14. Will have the highest first ionization energies

15. Contain elements in the solid, liquid, and gas phases at STP

Questions 16–19

   (A) 9.03×10^{23} molecules

   (B) 44.8 liters

   (C) 3.5 moles

   (D) 6.0 grams

   (E) 3.01×10^{23} atoms

16. 0.25 moles of O_2 at STP

17. 3.0 moles of H_2 at STP

18. 56 grams of N_2 at STP

19. 96.0 grams of SO_2 at STP

Questions 20–22

   (A) Water

   (B) Hydrogen bromide

   (C) Iron

   (D) Argon

   (E) Sodium chloride

20. Hydrogen bonding

21. Dipoles

22. Dispersion forces

Questions 23–25

   (A) Alpha particle

   (B) Beta particle

   (C) Gamma particle

   (D) Positron

   (E) Deuteron

23. Po-218 $\rightarrow$ At-218 + X

24. Tc-99 $\rightarrow$ Tc-99 + X

25. Ne-19 $\rightarrow$ F-19 + X

GO ON TO THE NEXT PAGE

PLEASE GO TO THE SPECIAL SECTION AT THE LOWER LEFT-HAND CORNER OF YOUR
ANSWER SHEET LABELED "CHEMISTRY" AND ANSWER QUESTIONS 101–115
ACCORDING TO THE FOLLOWING DIRECTIONS.

Part B

Directions: Each question below consists of two statements. For each question, determine whether statement I in the left-most column is true or false and whether statement II in the rightmost column is true or false. Fill in the corresponding T or F ovals on the answer sheet provided. Fill in the oval labeled "CE" only if statement II correctly explains statement I.

SAMPLE:

EX 1. The nucleus of an atom has a   BECAUSE   the only positive particles
positive charge   found in the atom's nucleus are
protons.

SAMPLE ANSWER

	I	II	CE*
EX 1	● F	● F	○ / ●

I   **II**

101.   An element's nuclear charge is equal to   BECAUSE   the only charged particles in the nucleus are
the number of protons in the nucleus   neutrons.

102.   A reaction will be spontaneous if ΔH is   BECAUSE ΔG will be negative when there is a decrease in
negative and ΔS is positive   enthalpy and an increase in entropy.

103. Cl^{1-} is the conjugate base of HCl   BECAUSE   a conjugate base is formed when an acid gains a
proton.

104.   An electrolytic cell makes a   BECAUSE   an electrolytic cell uses an external current to drive
nonspontaneous redox reaction occur   a redox reaction.

105.   The maximum number of electrons   BECAUSE   the maximum number of electrons allowed in a
allowed in the third principal energy   principal energy level is dictated by the
level is 18   equation $2n^2$.

106.   3,000 kilograms is equal to 3 grams   BECAUSE   the prefix *kilo-* means "one thousandth."

107.   An increase in temperature will cause a   BECAUSE   temperature and volume have a direct relationship.
gas to expand

GO ON TO THE NEXT PAGE

108. A catalyst will change the heat of reaction   BECAUSE   a catalyst will lower the potential energy of the activated complex in a reaction.

109. Helium will have fewer dispersion forces between its atoms than the other noble gases   BECAUSE   as the mass of nonpolar atoms and molecules increases, dispersion forces increase.

110. Nitrogen gas will have a greater rate of effusion than oxygen gas   BECAUSE   lighter, less dense gases travel faster than heavier, more dense gases.

111. Propane can be decomposed chemically   BECAUSE   propane is a compound that is made up of simpler elements.

112. A mixture of two different liquids can be separated via distillation   BECAUSE   different liquids have different boiling points.

113. Isotopes have different atomic numbers   BECAUSE   isotopes must have different numbers of electrons.

114. Butene can be converted into butane   BECAUSE   the addition reaction of hydrogen gas to an alkene will form an alkane.

115. NaCl is a basic salt   BECAUSE   hydrolysis of NaCl reveals the formation of NaOH and HCl.

GO ON TO THE NEXT PAGE

Part C

Directions: Each of the multiple-choice questions or incomplete sentences below is followed by five answers or completions. Select the one answer that is best in each case and then fill in the corresponding oval on the answer sheet provided.

26. When 58 grams of water is heated from 275 K to 365 K, the water

    (A) absorbs 21,820 joules of heat
    (B) absorbs 377 joules of heat
    (C) releases 5,220 joules of heat
    (D) absorbs 242 joules of heat
    (E) releases 90 joules of heat

27. Which of the following are uses for radiation and radioactivity that are of benefit to us?

    I.   Nuclear waste
    II. Radioisotopes
    III. Excess exposure

    (A) I only
    (B) II only
    (C) III only
    (D) I and II only
    (E) I and III only

28. Which of the following statements is not part of the kinetic molecular theory?

    (A) The average kinetic energy of gas molecules is directly proportional to temperature.
    (B) Attractive and repulsive forces are present between gas molecules.
    (C) Collisions between gas molecules are perfectly elastic.
    (D) Gas molecules travel in a continuous, random motion.
    (E) The volume that gas molecules occupy is minimal compared to the volume within which the gas is contained.

29. The following redox reaction occurs in an acidic solution: $Ce^{4+} + Bi \rightarrow Ce^{3+} + BiO^{1+}$. What is the coefficient before the Ce^{4+} when the equation is fully balanced?

    (A) 1
    (B) 2
    (C) 3
    (D) 6
    (E) 9

30. Which statement regarding significant figures is false?

    (A) Zeros can be significant.
    (B) When multiplying, the answer is determined by the number of significant figures.
    (C) When adding, the answer is determined by the number of decimal places.
    (D) When dividing, the answer is determined by the number of decimal places.
    (E) The number 50,004 has five significant figures.

31. Which statement below best describes the molecule in question?

    (A) Water has a bent molecular geometry and one lone pair of electrons.
    (B) Ammonia has a trigonal pyramidal molecular geometry and two lone pairs of electrons.
    (C) Methane has a trigonal planar molecular geometry.
    (D) Carbon dioxide is linear because it has one single bond and one triple bond.
    (E) The carbon atoms in ethane are sp^3 hybridized.

GO ON TO THE NEXT PAGE

32. A compound was analyzed and found to be 12.1% C, 71.7% Cl, and 16.2% O. What is the empirical formula for this compound?

    (A) C_2OCl
    (B) $COCl$
    (C) CO_2Cl_2
    (D) C_2O_2Cl
    (E) CCl_2O

33. Which statement is true about the percent composition by mass in $C_6H_{12}O_6$?

    (A) Carbon is 6.7% by mass.
    (B) Oxygen is 53.3% by mass.
    (C) Hydrogen is 12% by mass.
    (D) Carbon is 72% by mass.
    (E) Carbon is 20% by mass.

34. Which process would have a positive value for the change in entropy?

    I.   The expansion of the universe
    II.   The condensation of a liquid
    III. A food fight in a school cafeteria

    (A) I only
    (B) II only
    (C) III only
    (D) II and III only
    (E) I and III only

35. Of the gases below, which would react with rain water to produce acid rain?

    I.   CFCs
    II.   Methane
    III. Carbon dioxide

    (A) I only
    (B) II only
    (C) III only
    (D) I and III only
    (E) I, II, and III

36. A sample of gas is trapped in a manometer and the stopcock is opened. (See Figure 1.) The level of mercury moves to a new height as can be seen in the diagram. If the pressure of the gas inside the manometer is 815 torr, what is the atmospheric pressure in this case?

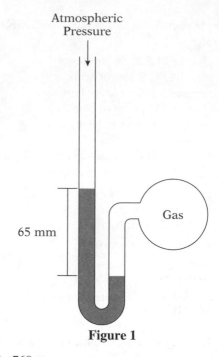

Figure 1

    (A) 760 torr
    (B) 740 torr
    (C) 750 torr
    (D) 815 torr
    (E) 880 torr

37. Which aqueous solution is expected to have the highest boiling point?

    (A) 1.5 m $FeCl_2$
    (B) 3.0 m CH_3OH
    (C) 2.5 m $C_6H_{12}O_6$
    (D) 2.5 m NaCl
    (E) 1.0 m $CaCl_2$

38. Which K_a value is that of a better electrolyte?

    (A) 1.0×10^{-2}
    (B) 2.0×10^{-12}
    (C) 5.0×10^{-7}
    (D) 3.0×10^{-4}
    (E) 1.0×10^{-6}

GO ON TO THE NEXT PAGE

39. The following substances were all dissolved in 100 grams of water at 290 K to produce saturated solutions. If the solution is heated to 310 K, which substance will have a decrease in its solubility?

    (A) NaCl
    (B) KI
    (C) $CaCl_2$
    (D) HCl
    (E) KNO_3

40. Methane undergoes a combustion reaction according to the reaction $CH_4(g) + 2O_2(g) \rightarrow CO_2(g) + 2H_2O(l)$. How many grams of methane gas were burned if 67.2 liters of carbon dioxide gas are produced in the reaction? (Assume STP.)

    (A) 16 grams
    (B) 48 grams
    (C) 3 grams
    (D) 132 grams
    (E) 22.4 grams

41. A closed system contains the following reaction at STP: $Cl_2(g) + 2NO_2(g) \longleftrightarrow 2NO_2Cl(g)$. What is the equilibrium constant expression for this reaction?

    (A) $K_{eq} = \dfrac{[NO_2Cl]^2}{[Cl_2][NO_2]}$

    (B) $K_{eq} = \dfrac{[Cl_2][NO_2]^2}{[NO_2Cl]}$

    (C) $K_{eq} = \dfrac{[Cl_2][NO_2]^2}{[NO_2Cl]^2}$

    (D) $K_{eq} = \dfrac{[NO_2Cl]^2}{[Cl_2][NO_2]^2}$

    (E) $K_{eq} = \dfrac{[NO_2Cl]^2}{[Cl_2]^2[NO_2]^2}$

42. At a particular temperature, the equilibrium concentrations of the substances in question 41 are as follows:

    $[NO_2Cl] = 0.5\ M$ $[Cl_2] = 0.3\ M$ $[NO_2] = 0.2\ M$

    What is the value of the equilibrium constant for this reaction?

    (A) 2.1
    (B) 0.48
    (C) 0.0357
    (D) 20.83
    (E) 208.83

43. Which Lewis structure below has been drawn incorrectly?

    (A) H:H

    (B) H:C:::N:

    (C) H:Ö:
        H

    (D) :N:::N:

    (E) F:B̈:F
        F

44. Which reaction below demonstrates the Lewis definition of acids and bases?

    (A) $HCl + NaOH \rightarrow HOH + NaCl$
    (B) $H_2O + NH_3 \rightarrow OH^{1-} + NH_4^{1+}$
    (C) $NH_3 + BF_3 \rightarrow NH_3BF_3$
    (D) $HI + KOH \rightarrow H_2O + KI$
    (E) $H^+ + OH^{1-} \rightarrow H_2O$

45. Which sample is a homogeneous mixture?

    (A) KI(aq)
    (B) Fe(s)
    (C) $CO_2(g)$
    (D) $NH_3(l)$
    (E) NaCl(s)

GO ON TO THE NEXT PAGE

46. Which pair below represents isomers of the same compound?

    (A) $CH_3CH_2CH_2OH$ and $HOCH_2CH_2CH_3$
    (B) $CH_3CH_2CH_3$ and $CH_3CH_2CH_2CH_3$
    (C) $CH_3CH(Cl)CH_3$ and $CH_3CH_2CH_2Cl$
    (D) CH_3COCH_3 and $CH_3CH_2CH_2CHO$
    (E) $ClCH_2CH_2Br$ and $BrCH_2CH_2Cl$

47. Which would you never do in a laboratory setting?

    I.   Eat and drink in the laboratory
    II. Push a thermometer through a rubber stopper
    III. Remove your goggles to take a better look at a reaction

    (A) I only
    (B) II only
    (C) III only
    (D) I and III only
    (E) I, II, and III

48. How many pi bonds are there in a molecule of $N{=}C{-}CH_2{-}CH_2{-}CO{-}NH{-}CH{=}CH_2$?

    (A) 7
    (B) 4
    (C) 12
    (D) 10
    (E) 5

49. When the equation: $C_2H_6 + O_2 \rightarrow CO_2 + H_2O$ is completely balanced using the lowest whole number coefficients, the sum of the coefficients will be

    (A) 4
    (B) 9.5
    (C) 19
    (D) 15.5
    (E) 11

50. From the heats of reaction of these individual reactions:

    $A + B \rightarrow 2C \; \Delta H = -500 \text{ kJ}$,
    $D + 2B \rightarrow E \; \Delta H = -700 \text{ kJ}$,
    $2D + 2A \rightarrow F \; \Delta H = +50 \text{ kJ}$

    Find the heat of reaction for $F + 6B \rightarrow 2E + 4C$

    (A) +450 kJ
    (B) −1,100 kJ
    (C) +2,350 kJ
    (D) −350 kJ
    (E) −2,450 kJ

51. Which solutions have a concentration of 1.0 M?

    I.   74 grams of calcium hydroxide dissolved to make 1 liter of solution
    II. 74.5 grams of potassium chloride dissolved to make 1 liter of solution
    III. 87 grams of lithium bromide dissolved to make 1 liter solution

    (A) I only
    (B) III only
    (C) I and III only
    (D) II and III only
    (E) I, II, and III

52. According to the reaction $3H_2 + N_2 \rightarrow 2NH_3$, how many grams of hydrogen gas and nitrogen gas are needed to make exactly 68 grams of ammonia?

    (A) 2 grams of hydrogen gas and 28 grams of nitrogen gas
    (B) 3 grams of hydrogen gas and 1 gram of nitrogen gas
    (C) 12 grams of hydrogen gas and 56 grams of nitrogen gas
    (D) 102 grams of hydrogen gas and 34 grams of nitrogen gas
    (E) 6 grams of hydrogen gas and 2 grams of nitrogen gas

53. Which compound is not paired with its correct name?

    (A) $FeCl_2$ / iron(II) chloride
    (B) K_2O / potassium oxide
    (C) NO_2 / nitrogen dioxide
    (D) PCl_3 / potassium trichloride
    (E) NH_4Cl / ammonium chloride

GO ON TO THE NEXT PAGE

54. How many grams of HI can be made from 6 grams of H_2 and 800 grams of I_2 when hydrogen gas and diatomic iodine react according to the equation: $H_2 + I_2 \rightarrow 2HI$?

    (A) 800 grams of HI can be made with 38 grams of iodine in excess
    (B) 768 grams of HI can be made with 6 grams of hydrogen in excess
    (C) 768 grams of HI can be made with 38 grams of iodine in excess
    (D) 2286 grams of HI can be made with no excess reactants
    (E) 806 grams of HI can be made with no excess reactants

55. 500 mL of a 0.2 M solution has 200 mL of water added to it. What is the new molarity of this solution?

    (A) 0.50 M
    (B) 0.28 M
    (C) 0.70 M
    (D) 0.14 M
    (E) 0.40 M

56. Which mixture is correctly paired with a method for separation of the mixture?

    (A) Oil and water—filter paper
    (B) Salt water—distillation
    (C) Sand and water—separatory funnel
    (D) Sand and sugar—tweezers
    (E) Sugar water—filter paper

57. Which reaction between ions does not form a precipitate?

    (A) $Ag^{1+} + Cl^{1-}$
    (B) $Pb^{2+} + 2I^{1-}$
    (C) $Ca^{2+} + CO_3^{2-}$
    (D) $Hg^{2+} + 2Br^{1-}$
    (E) $Na^{1+} + OH^{1-}$

58. Which will happen when sodium sulfate is added to a saturated solution of $CaSO_4$ that is at equilibrium? [$CaSO_4(s) \longleftrightarrow Ca^{2+}(aq) + SO_4^{2-}(aq)$]

    (A) The solubility of the calcium sulfate will decrease.
    (B) The concentration of calcium ions will increase.
    (C) The reaction will shift to the right.
    (D) The K_{sp} value will change.
    (E) The equilibrium will shift to consume the decrease in sulfate ions.

59. Given the reaction $2A(g) + B(g) + Heat \longleftrightarrow 3C(g) + D(g)$, what could be done to the reaction to shift the equilibrium so that more D is made?

    (A) Increase the concentration of D
    (B) Increase the concentration of C
    (C) Increase the temperature
    (D) Increase the pressure
    (E) Remove B from the reaction

60. A 16-gram sample of water at 273 K is cooled so that it becomes a completely solid ice cube at 273 K. How much heat was released by the sample of water to form this ice cube?

    (A) 16 J
    (B) 4,368 J
    (C) 18,258 J
    (D) 350 J
    (E) 5,334 J

61. Sublimation is the process by which a solid becomes a gas without having a liquid phase. Which of these can sublime?

    I. Iodine
    II. Naphthalene
    III. Carbon dioxide

    (A) I only
    (B) II only
    (C) III only
    (D) I and III only
    (E) I, II, and III

GO ON TO THE NEXT PAGE

62. Which of the following will decrease the rate of a reaction?

    (A) Using powdered solids instead of whole pieces
    (B) Selecting ionic reactants that have been dissolved in water
    (C) Decreasing the temperature
    (D) Increasing the pressure
    (E) Adding a catalyst

63. Three gases are mixed in a sealed container. The container has 0.3 moles of gas A, 0.4 moles of gas B, and 0.3 moles of gas C. The total pressure of the gases is 660 torr. What is true about the partial pressures of the gases?

    (A) The partial pressure of gas A is 264 torr.
    (B) The partial pressure of gas B is 396 torr.
    (C) The partial pressure of gas C is 220 torr.
    (D) The partial pressures of gases A and C are each 198 torr.
    (E) The partial pressure of gas B is 660 torr.

64. What is the half reaction that occurs at the cathode?

    (A) $Al \rightarrow Al^{3+} + 3e-$
    (B) $Ni^{2+} + 2e- \rightarrow Ni$
    (C) $Ni \rightarrow Ni^{2+} + 2e-$
    (D) $2Al^{3+} + 6e- \rightarrow 2Al$
    (E) $Al^{3+} + 3e- \rightarrow Al$

65. Which statement is true about the setup above?

    (A) The electrode potential for this cell is 1.40 V.
    (B) The electrode potential for this cell is 2.54 V.
    (C) Electrons will be carried by the salt bridge.
    (D) Ions will be carried through the wire.
    (E) The reaction is nonspontaneous.

Questions 64 and 65 refer to the voltaic cell below in Figure 2:

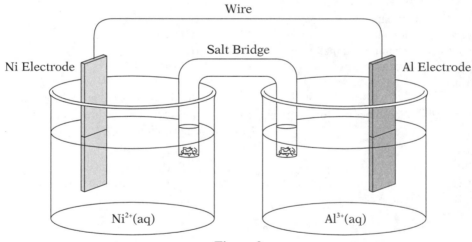

Figure 2

GO ON TO THE NEXT PAGE

66. Over a number of years the average pH of a stream changes from a pH of 6.9 to a pH of 5.9 due to acid rain. Which statement is true about the pH of the stream?

  (A) The pH of the stream now is one time more acidic than it was years ago.
  (B) The stream now has 10 times more hydroxide ions than it did years ago.
  (C) The pH of the stream is now 10 times more acidic than it was years ago.
  (D) The stream is more basic now than it was years ago.
  (E) The concentration of hydronium ion in the stream has decreased over the years.

67. An alkaline earth metal, element M, reacts with oxygen. What is going to be the general formula for the compound formed?

  (A) M_2O
  (B) MO
  (C) MO_2
  (D) M_2O_3
  (E) M_3O_2

68. Which functional group below does not contain a carbonyl group?

  (A) Aldehydes
  (B) Ketones
  (C) Esters
  (D) Ethers
  (E) Carboxylic acids

69. Using the bond dissociation energies found in the Reference Tables on pages 266 and 267, calculate the change in the heat of reaction for $2H_2 + O_2 \rightarrow 2H_2O$.

  (A) -118 kJ
  (B) $+118$ kJ
  (C) -91 kJ
  (D) $-1,042$ kJ
  (E) -833 kJ

70. Equilibrium

  (A) is defined as equal concentrations of reactants and products
  (B) is defined as equal rates for forward and reverse reactions
  (C) can be shifted by adding a catalyst
  (D) can exist for chemical changes but not physical changes
  (E) must always favor the formation of products

S T O P

IF YOU FINISH BEFORE TIME IS CALLED, YOU MAY CHECK YOUR WORK ON THIS TEST ONLY.
DO NOT TURN TO ANY OTHER TEST IN THIS BOOK.

REFERENCE TABLES

Physical Constants for Water

Normal freezing point	0°C or 273 K
Normal boiling point	100°C or 373 K
Freezing point depression	1.86°C / 1 m
Boiling point elevation	0.52°C / 1 m
Autoionization constant of water at 298 K	$K_w = 1.0 \times 10^{-14}$
Specific heat	4.18 J/g K
Heat of fusion	333.6 J/g
Heat of vaporization	2259 J/g

Electronegativity Values

Aluminum	1.6
Bromine	3.0
Calcium	1.0
Carbon	2.6
Chlorine	3.2
Fluorine	4.0
Hydrogen	2.2
Iodine	2.7
Lithium	1.0
Magnesium	1.3
Nitrogen	3.0
Oxygen	3.5
Phosphorus	2.2
Potassium	0.8
Sodium	0.9
Sulfur	2.6

Solubility Product Constants at 298 K

Lead iodide—PbI_2	7.1×10^{-9}
Lead sulfate—$PbSO_4$	1.6×10^{-8}
Magnesium hydroxide—$Mg(OH)_2$	1.8×10^{-11}
Silver chloride—AgCl	1.8×10^{-10}

K_{a1} Constants for Weak Acids at 298 K

Acetic, $HC_2H_3O_2$	1.8×10^{-5}
Chlorous, $HClO_2$	1.2×10^{-2}
Hydrofluoric, HF	6.8×10^{-4}
Hydrogen Sulfide, H_2S	5.7×10^{-8}
Hypochlorous, HClO	3.0×10^{-8}
Phosphoric, H_3PO_4	7.5×10^{-3}
Sulfurous, H_2SO_3	1.7×10^{-2}

Bond Dissociation Energies in kJ/mol	
C—C	349
C—Cl	329
C—H	412
C=O	798
Cl—Cl	240
H—Cl	430
H—H	435
N—H	390
N—N	163
N≡N	941
O—H	462
O—O	145

Select Polyatomic Ions	
Ammonium	NH_4^{1+}
Carbonate	CO_3^{2-}
Chlorate	ClO_3^{1-}
Chlorite	ClO_2^{1-}
Chromate	CrO_4^{2-}
Cyanide	CN^{1-}
Dichromate	$Cr_2O_7^{2-}$
Hydronium	H_3O^{1+}
Hydroxide	OH^{1-}
Nitrate	NO_3^{1-}
Nitrite	NO_3^{1-}
Permanganate	MnO_4^{1-}
Phosphate	PO_4^{3-}
Sulfate	SO_4^{2-}
Sulfite	SO_3^{2-}

Standard Electrode Potentials for Elements on the Activity Series	
Nonmetals	
$F_2 + 2e- \rightarrow 2F^{1-}$	+2.87 V
$Cl_2 + 2e- \rightarrow 2Cl^{1-}$	+1.51 V
$Br_2 + 2e- \rightarrow 2Br^{1-}$	+1.06 V
$I_2 + 2e- \rightarrow 2I^{1-}$	+0.54 V
Metals	
$Li^{1+} + 1e- \rightarrow Li$	−3.05 V
$K^{1+} + 1e- \rightarrow K$	−2.93 V
$Na^{1+} + 1e- \rightarrow Na$	−2.71 V
$Mg^{2+} + 2e- \rightarrow Mg$	−2.37 V
$Al^{3+} + 3e- \rightarrow Al$	−1.66 V
$Zn^{2+} + 2e- \rightarrow Zn$	−0.76 V
$Cr^{3+} + 3e- \rightarrow Cr$	−0.74 V
$Fe^{2+} + 2e- \rightarrow Fe$	−0.45 V
$Co^{2+} + 2e- \rightarrow Co$	−0.28 V
$Ni^{2+} + 2e- \rightarrow Ni$	−0.26 V
$Sn^{2+} + 2e- \rightarrow Sn$	−0.14 V
$Pb^{2+} + 2e- \rightarrow Pb$	−0.13 V
$\mathbf{2H^{1+} + 2e- \rightarrow H_2}$	**0.00 V***
$Cu^{2+} + 2e- \rightarrow Cu$	+0.34 V
$Ag^{1+} + 1e- \rightarrow Ag$	+0.80 V
$Au^{3+} + 3e- \rightarrow Au$	+1.50 V

*Denotes arbitrary standard.

ANSWER KEY

1. B	18. B	110. T, T, CE	37. D	54. C
2. A	19. A	111. T, T, CE	38. A	55. D
3. E	20. A	112. T, T, CE	39. D	56. B
4. D	21. A	113. F, F	40. B	57. E
5. E	22. D	114. T, T, CE	41. D	58. A
6. D	23. B	115. F, T	42. D	59. C
7. B	24. C		43. E	60. E
8. C	25. D	26. A	44. C	61. E
9. B		27. B	45. A	62. C
10. A	101. T, F	28. B	46. C	63. D
11. C	102. T, T, CE	29. C	47. E	64. B
12. E	103. T, F	30. D	48. B	65. A
13. B	104. T, T, CE	31. E	49. C	66. C
14. D	105. T, T, CE	32. E	50. E	67. B
15. A	106. F, F	33. B	51. E	68. D
16. E	107. T, T, CE	34. E	52. C	69. E
17. D	108. F, T	35. C	53. D	70. B
	109. T, T, CE	36. C		

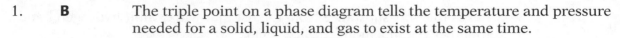

ANSWERS AND EXPLANATIONS

1. **B** The triple point on a phase diagram tells the temperature and pressure needed for a solid, liquid, and gas to exist at the same time.

2. **A** If a system is at equilibrium, adding more reactants will shift the equilibrium to form more products.

3. **E** The boiling point of a liquid is the temperature in which the vapor pressure of a liquid is equal to the atmospheric pressure.

4. **D** The activated complex on the potential energy diagram is where the first appearance of products occurs.

5. **E** Copper sulfate is a blue salt that forms blue solutions.

6. **D** Chlorine is a green gas.

7. **B** Permanganate ion will form a dark purple solution.

8. **C** Bromine is an orange liquid at STP.

9. **B** An electrolytic cell uses an externally applied current to drive a nonspontaneous reaction.

10. **A** The salt bridge in the voltaic cell allows ions to migrate from one half cell to another.

11. **C** The Geiger counter detects radioactive emanations.

12. **E** The lanthanides and actinides are the elements whose valence electrons are located in the f orbitals.

13. **B** The alkali metals have a valence electron configuration of s^1 and need to lose just one electron to form a stable, complete, outermost principal energy level.

14. **D** Because the noble gases have very stable electron configurations, it takes much energy to remove an electron from the stable, complete, outermost principal energy level.

15. **A** Fluorine and chlorine are gases at STP, while bromine is a liquid and iodine is a solid.

16. **E** 0.25 moles of O_2 will have 0.50 moles of oxygen atoms. 0.50 moles of atoms is the same as 3.01×10^{23} atoms.

17. **D** 3.0 moles of hydrogen gas (molar mass is 2) will have a mass of 6.0 grams.

18. **B** 56 grams of nitrogen gas at STP is 2 moles of nitrogen gas. This sample will occupy 44.8 liters.

19.	**A**	96.0 grams of sulfur dioxide (molar mass is 64) is the same as 1.5 moles of sulfur dioxide. This will equal 9.03×10^{23} molecules of sulfur dioxide.
20.	**A**	Water is the only substance from the list that will exhibit hydrogen bonds. Remember the mnemonic device "FON."
21.	**A**	Water is the only substance from the list that is a polar molecule.
22.	**D**	Argon is monatomic and nonpolar. The noble gases will exhibit dispersion (or Van der Waals) forces between their atoms.
23.	**B**	Filling in the atomic numbers shows the full reaction: $^{218}_{84}\text{Po} \rightarrow {}^{218}_{85}\text{At} + \text{X}$. X has no mass and a negative one charge, $^{0}_{-1}\text{X}$. This makes X a beta particle.
24.	**C**	Tc-99 did not change in mass or in atomic number. It must have given off something without mass or charge. Energy was released. Gamma radiation is the only energy that is listed among the choices.
25.	**D**	Filling in the atomic numbers shows the reaction: $^{19}_{10}\text{Ne} \rightarrow {}^{19}_{9}\text{F} + {}^{0}_{+1}\text{X}$. X is a particle with zero mass and a 1+ charge, a positron.
101.	**T, F**	The number of protons defines the atomic number and the nuclear charge for an element. Neutrons do not have any charge.
102.	**T, T, CE**	According to the Gibbs Free Energy equation, $\Delta G = \Delta H - T\Delta S$, the favored decrease in enthalpy (ΔH is $-$) and favored increase in entropy (ΔS is $+$); ΔG will have a negative value.
103.	**T, F**	Conjugate pairs differ by a proton. When an acid loses a proton, it forms a conjugate base.
104.	**T, T, CE**	The electrolytic cell uses an external power supply to drive a redox reaction that normally has an electrode potential that is negative in value.
105.	**T, T, CE**	The expression $2n^2$, where n is the principal energy level number, is used to determine the maximum number of electrons that can be held in a principal energy level. Remember to square the number first, then multiply by 2.
106.	**F, F**	*Kilo-* means "one thousand." 3,000 grams would be equivalent to 3 kilograms.
107.	**T, T, CE**	According to Charles' Law, as the temperature of a gas increases, the volume of the gas will increase as well. This is a direct relationship.
108.	**F, T**	While a catalyst can lower the potential energy of the activated complex and activation energy in a reaction, a catalyst will not change the heat of a reaction.
109.	**T, T, CE**	Dispersion forces increase between nonpolar molecules as the mass increases. Helium is the lightest of the noble gases and has the fewest dispersion forces between its atoms.
110.	**T, T, CE**	Nitrogen is lighter and less dense than oxygen given equal conditions. This means that the rate of effusion for nitrogen gas will be greater.

111. **T, T, CE** Propane is a compound made up of elements. Compounds can be decomposed in a chemical reaction, whereas elements cannot.

112. **T, T, CE** A distillation uses heat to separate a mixture of liquids based upon their different boiling points.

113. **F, F** Isotopes are the same element with a different number of neutrons and a different mass number.

114. **T, T, CE** The addition reaction allows a diatomic molecule be added to the double and triple bonds of organic and other compounds.

115. **F, T** When NaCl undergoes hydrolysis, water is added and the original acid and base are formed, NaOH and HCl. Because these are both strong, they will neutralize each other. This means that NaCl is a neutral salt.

26. **A** Use the equation $q = mc\Delta T$ to find the amount of heat absorbed by the sample of water. Substitution and solving gives: $(58 \text{ grams})(4.18 \text{ J/g K})(90) = 21{,}820$ joules.

27. **B** Radioisotopes (and radiotracers) can be used to help diagnose problems in certain organs in our bodies. The use of radioisotopes is beneficial if the right dosage is used correctly.

28. **B** Ideally, gas molecules should not have any attractive or repulsive forces between the molecules.

29. **C** There are a number of steps required to balance this redox reaction:

    1. Separate the two half reactions:

    $Ce^{4+} \rightarrow Ce^{3+}$ and $Bi \rightarrow BiO^{1+}$

    2. Add water to balance the oxygen atoms:

    $H_2O + Bi \rightarrow BiO^{1+}$

    3. Add H^{1+} ions to balance the hydrogen atoms:

    $H_2O + Bi \rightarrow BiO^{1+} + 2H^{1+}$

    4. Add electrons to balance the charges:

    $1e- + Ce^{4+} \rightarrow Ce^{3+}$ and $H_2O + Bi \rightarrow BiO^{1+} + 2H^{1+} + 3e-$

    5. Use the distributive property to balance the number of electrons:

    $3(1e- + Ce^{4+} \rightarrow Ce^{3+})$ becomes $3e- + 3Ce^{4+} \rightarrow 3Ce^{3+}$

    6. Add the two reactions together and cancel the common substances:

    $3Ce^{4+} + H_2O + Bi \rightarrow 3Ce^{3+} + BiO^{1+} + 2H^{1+}$

    The coefficient before the cesium ions is 3.

30. **D** When multiplying and dividing, the final answer contains the same number of significant figures as the number with the fewest significant figures.

31. **E**   Ethane is a hydrocarbon with all single bonds. This means that the two carbon atoms will both be sp^3 hybridized.

32. **E**   There are three steps in completing this problem:

1. Change the percent sign to grams (assume a 100-gram sample):

   12.1 grams of C, 71.7 grams Cl, and 16.2 grams of O.

2. Convert the grams of each element to moles:

   1 mole of C, 2 moles of Cl, and 1 mole of O.

3. Divide by the lowest number of moles:

   In this case it is the number "1." The empirical formula will be CCl_2O.

33. **B**   The total mass of this compound is 180. The oxygen makes up 96 of the 180 which is about 53%.

34. **E**   The positive value for the change in entropy means that there will be more disorder. An expanding universe and a food fight are sure signs of more disorder.

35. **C**   Carbon dioxide and water can react to produce carbonic acid. CFCs are responsible for causing a hole in the ozone layer and methane is a greenhouse gas that can trap heat on earth.

36. **C**   Because the gas pressure inside the manometer is pushing the level of mercury higher and toward the opening of the tube, the pressure inside the manometer must be greater than the atmospheric pressure. The mercury rose to a level that is 65 mm above the height of the bulb in the manometer. This means that the atmospheric pressure is 65 mm lower than the pressure of the gas. $815 - 65 = 750$ torr.

37. **D**   2.5 molal NaCl will be, in effect, 5.0 molal because 1 mole of sodium chloride yields 2 moles of ions. This is the highest concentration of any of the choices and will have the greatest effect on the boiling and freezing points of water.

38. **A**   A stronger acid or base will also be a better electrolyte because more ions will be released into solution. The greatest value listed is 1.0×10^{-2}.

39. **D**   Gases, like HCl, will experience a decrease in solubility as the temperature of the solution they are dissolved in increases. The solids will all have an increase in solubility as the temperature increases.

40. **B**   67.2 liters of carbon dioxide equates to 3 moles of carbon dioxide. Because carbon dioxide and methane are in a 1:1 ratio, for each mole of carbon dioxide produced, 1 mole of methane reacted. This means that 3 moles of methane were burned. Because the molar mass of methane is 16, 3 moles of methane would weigh 48 grams.

41. **D** Remember for equilibrium constants, "Products over reactants, coefficients become powers." This is demonstrated by choice D.

42. **D** Substitute into the expression

$$K_{eq} = \frac{[NO_2Cl]^2}{[Cl_2][NO_2]^2} \quad \text{to get:} \quad K_{eq} = \frac{[0.5]^2}{[0.3][0.2]^2}$$

Solving gives an answer of 20.83 indicating that the product was favored in this reaction.

43. **E** Boron will not form an octet, as shown correctly in the other four choices. Boron prefers six electrons in its outermost principal energy level.

44. **C** The Lewis definition of acids tells that acids are electron pair acceptors while bases are electron pair donors. Choices A, D, and E show the Arrhenius definition whereas choice B shows the Brønsted-Lowry definition.

45. **A** By definition, an aqueous solution must be homogeneous. The KI(aq) tells that there is a homogeneous solution of water and KI.

46. **C** Isomers have the same molecular formula but a different structure. This also means that isomers will have different names. The isomers in this question are 2-chloropropane and 1-chlorpropane.

47. **E** Eating, drinking, and removing one's goggles are all unsafe in the laboratory setting. Pushing a glass thermometer through a rubber stopper is also dangerous and should be done by a trained laboratory specialist.

48. **B** There are 4 pi bonds in this molecule. Two of them are between the N and C. One is between the two carbon atoms that have a double bond. The last pi bond is between the C and the O. When C and O are written as shown in this problem, it means that a double bond is present. A double bond has 1 pi bond.

49. **C** When balancing a reaction, leave the simplest substance for last. In this case it will be the oxygen gas. Balancing the carbon atoms and hydrogen atoms gives $C_2H_6 + O_2 \rightarrow 2CO_2 + 3H_2O$. Balancing the oxygen atoms gives $C_2H_6 + 3.5O_2 \rightarrow 2CO_2 + 3H_2O$. To get whole number coefficients, multiply the entire equation by 2: $2C_2H_6 + 7O_2 \rightarrow 4CO_2 + 6H_2O$.

50. **E** First, double the reaction for A, B and C so that 4C ends up on the product side:

$2A + 2B \rightarrow 4C \; \Delta H = -1,000 \text{ kJ}$

Next, double the second reaction so that 2E can be produced:

$2D + 4B \rightarrow 2E \; \Delta H = -1400 \text{ kJ}$,

Finally, switch the last reaction so that *F* appears on the reactant side:

$F \rightarrow 2D + 2A \; \Delta H = -50 \text{ kJ}$

Adding up the three steps shows that the heat of reaction is −2,450 kJ.

51.   **E**   All three masses given are equivalent to 1 mole of the compounds in question. Because the 1 mole samples are all dissolved to make 1 liter of solution, each solution is 1 molar.

52.   **C**   68 grams of ammonia (molar mass is 17) is 4 moles of ammonia. Setting up a proportion, you see that 6 moles of hydrogen gas and 2 moles of nitrogen gas are needed: $3H_2 + N_2 \rightarrow 2NH_3$ is doubled and becomes $6H_2 + 2N_2 \rightarrow 4NH_3$. 6 moles of hydrogen gas (molar mass is 2) is 12 grams of hydrogen gas. 2 moles of nitrogen gas (molar mass is 28) is 56 grams of nitrogen gas.

53.   **D**   Although it does use the prefix "tri-" correctly for a covalent compound, PCl_3 is phosphorus trichloride.

54.   **C**   6 grams of hydrogen gas (molar mass is 2) is 3 moles of hydrogen gas. This means that 3 moles of iodine will react too because the hydrogen and iodine are in a 1:1 ratio. 3 moles of iodine (molar mass is 127) are needed, so it turns out that 762 grams of iodine are needed. This puts 38 grams of iodine in excess. Because the reactants have been tripled in quantity, the amount of HI made from the balanced equation will also triple so that the equation reads: $3H_2 + 3I_2 \rightarrow 6HI$. 6 moles of HI (molar mass is 128) is 768 grams of HI.

55.   **D**   The initial volume, V_1, is 500 mL and the initial molarity, M_1, is 0.2 M. The new volume, V_2, is 700 mL because 200 mL of water were added to the original 500 mL. Using the equation $M_1V_1 = M_2V_2$ substitute and find that $(0.2)(500) = (M_2)(700)$. Solving for M_2 you see that the concentration has decreased as it should when diluted: M_2 is 0.14 M.

56.   **B**   A distillation can boil the solution and drive off the water from the solution. The water vapor will then enter a condenser where it is cooled and turns back into a liquid. This separates the water from the salt that will be left behind.

57.   **E**   Halides of lead, mercury, and silver will form precipitates, so choices A, B, and D are all precipitates. Calcium carbonate is also a solid. Sodium hydroxide is soluble in water.

58.   **A**   Because there were already sulfate ions in solution and more sulfate ions were added, sulfate ion is called the common ion. Adding sodium sulfate to the solution increases the concentration of sulfate ion in solution driving the reverse reaction. This is called the common ion effect and more of the solid calcium sulfate will be made. If the solid is being formed that means that it is not dissolving and the solubility has decreased.

59.   **C**   An increase in temperature will increase the amount of heat, which is one of the reactants. Because a reactant was added, more products will be made.

60.   **E**   This calculation requires using the heat of fusion of water. The equation is $q = H_f m$. Substitution gives $q = (333.6 \text{ J/g})(16 \text{ grams}) = 5,334$ joules of heat.

61.   **E**   All three substances can sublime. Naphthalene is the substance that is used to make mothballs. Solid carbon dioxide is called dry ice. Iodine is a purple solid that can sublime as well.

62.   **C**   A decrease in temperature will cause the molecules to move with less kinetic energy. This means that the collisions will occur less frequently and will not be as effective.

63.   **D**   An equal number of moles of a gas will contain an equal number of gas molecules. An equal number of gas molecules will contribute to the pressure equally. The partial pressures of these gases are:

A is 30% of the mixture so (0.3)(660) = 198 torr.

B is 40% of the mixture so (0.4)(660) = 264 torr.

C is 30% of the mixture so (0.3)(660) = 198 torr.

64.   **B**   Looking at the two reactions as oxidations shows that $Al \rightarrow Al^{3+} + 3e^-$ has a potential of +1.66 V, whereas $Ni \rightarrow Ni^{2+} + 2e^-$ has a potential of +0.26 V. This indicates that the loss of electrons from Al is more of a spontaneous process than the loss of electrons from Ni. Al has a more positive electrode potential and will lose electrons to the Ni. Al will lose electrons and be the anode. The Ni electrode will gain electrons and be the cathode. At the cathode there is a gain of electrons for the ions that are in the solution where the cathode is located. The electrons will react with the Ni^{2+} ions according to the reaction $Ni^{2+} + 2e^- \rightarrow Ni$.

65.   **A**   From above we have the two half reactions:

$Al \rightarrow Al^{3+} + 3e^-$ +1.66 V

$Ni^{2+} + 2e^- \rightarrow Ni$ −0.26 V

The total is 1.40 V. Also remember that the electrode potential is never multiplied by any coefficients in a balanced equation.

66.   **C**   Remember that pH is based upon logarithms and base-10. Because the pH changed by a value of 1.0, it has changed by a power of 10. Because the pH value dropped, the stream has become more acidic.

67.   **B**   An alkaline earth metal is found in group 2 of the periodic table. This means that it will have two valance electrons and form an ion with a charge of 2+. When it reacts with oxygen's ionic charge of 2−, the two ions will combine in a 1:1 ratio.

68.   **D**   A carbonyl group is characterized by a $C\!=\!O$. Ethers have an oxygen atom but the oxygen has only single bonds, R—O—R.

69.   **E**   Set up this problem:

[2(H—H) + 1(O—O)] – [4(H—O)]. Use the reference tables and substitute to get:

[2(435) + 1(145)] – [4(462)] =

[870+145] – [1,848] =

[1,015] – [1,848] = −833 kJ.

70.   **B**   A reversible reaction that has equal forward and reverse rates is a reaction that has achieved equilibrium.

SCORE SHEET

Number of questions correct: _____

Less: 0.25 × number of questions wrong: _____

(Remember that omitted questions are not counted as wrong.)

Raw score: _____

Raw Score	Test Score		Raw Score	Test Score		Raw Score	Test Score		Raw Score	Test Score		Raw Score	Test Score
85	800		63	710		41	570		19	440		−3	300
84	800		62	700		40	560		18	430		−4	300
83	800		61	700		39	560		17	430		−5	290
82	800		60	690		38	550		16	420		−6	290
81	800		59	680		37	550		15	420		−7	280
80	800		58	670		36	540		14	410		−8	270
79	790		57	670		35	530		13	400		−9	270
78	790		56	660		34	530		12	400		−10	260
77	790		55	650		33	520		11	390		−11	250
76	780		54	640		32	520		10	390		−12	250
75	780		53	640		31	510		9	380		−13	240
74	770		52	630		30	500		8	370		−14	240
73	760		51	630		29	500		7	360		−15	230
72	760		50	620		28	490		6	360		−16	230
71	750		49	610		27	480		5	350		−17	220
70	740		48	610		26	480		4	350		−18	220
69	740		47	600		25	470		3	340		−19	210
68	730		46	600		24	470		2	330		−20	210
67	730		45	590		23	460		1	330		−21	200
66	720		44	580		22	460		0	320			
65	720		43	580		21	450		−1	320			
64	710		42	570		20	440		−2	310			

Note: This is only a sample scoring scale. Scoring scales differ from exam to exam.

THE SAT BIOLOGY-E/M TEST

All About The SAT Biology-E/M Test

What Is the Format of the SAT Biology-E/M Test and What Does "E/M" Mean?

The SAT Biology test is a 1-hour test consisting of 80 multiple-choice questions. The SAT Biology test is unique among the SAT Subject Tests in that you have a choice between the "E" version of the test, which focuses more on ecology (subjects such as ecosystems, biomes, food chains and webs, and the water cycle), and the "M" version of the test, which focuses more on molecular biology (subjects such as genetics, inheritance, respiration, and photosynthesis). All test-takers get the same 60 "core" questions, which cover all areas of biology. You can then choose between two 20-question sections, the ecology section or the molecular section.

What Is Covered on the SAT Biology Test?

Both the Biology-E and the Biology-M tests are designed to cover the material that would be covered typically in a high school biology course and lab. You are also expected to be familiar with algebra and how to use the metric system; some questions will ask you to interpret data as if you had completed a laboratory experiment, and will occasionally require you to do simple mathematical calculations.

The College Board gives an approximate outline of the how much of each area of biology the tests cover:

Area	Percentage of Biology-E Devoted to Area	Percentage of Biology-M Devoted to Area
Cellular and Molecular Biology	15	27
Ecology	23	13
Genetics	15	20
Organismal Biology	25	25
Evolution and Diversity	22	15

Although the test may not always be exactly 23% ecology or 27% cellular and molecular biology, you should be aware that the Biology-M test focuses more on cellular and molecular biology and cellular genetics, whereas the Biology-E test focuses more on ecology and evolution and diversity. Approximately one-fourth of both tests is devoted to organismal biology.

Does It Matter Whether I Take Biology-E or Biology-M? How Do I Choose Between Them?

The College Board doesn't care whether you take the Biology-E or the Biology-M test, and almost the same number of students take each test. One is not designed to be harder than the other. You don't even need to indicate which one you're going to be taking until you're actually taking the test. Your test booklet will contain both sets of questions, and instructions on how to answer either the ecology or molecular set of questions.

You should choose whichever test is geared toward your strengths in biology. If your biology course focused more on ecology or evolution, discussing food webs, predator–prey relationships, nutrient cycles, and biomes, then Biology-E is likely to be the test for you. If your biology course focused more on cellular processes and biomolecules, discussing DNA, proteins, chromosomes, mitosis and meiosis, respiration, and photosynthesis, then Biology-M is probably the better test for you.

Colleges care far more about your score on the SAT Biology test than which form of the exam you took—so your first consideration should be choosing the exam with which you're most comfortable. As a guide, however, you may wish to consider the type of biology you might study in the future. If you're applying for or are considering a program in biochemistry, genetics, or microbiology, then Biology-M might be a better choice; if you're applying for or considering a program in environmental studies, ecology, or evolution, then Biology-E might be more suited for you.

Do I Still Have to Study Ecology if I Take Biology-M? Do I Still Have to Study Molecular Biology if I Take Biology-E?

The answer to both of these questions is yes, if you plan to do well. If you're taking Biology-M, you may not be required to know ecology as in-depth as someone taking Biology-E, but you will still be asked some questions on ecology. And if you're taking Biology-E, you shouldn't overlook molecular biology. While you may want to spend more of your energy preparing for the specific test you're taking, reviewing all of the material is your best bet.

SUCCEEDING ON THE SAT BIOLOGY-E/M TEST

The following pages describe each of the particular question types that you will encounter on the SAT Biology test. There are strategies you should know for each type. Study the example questions so that you recognize the different question types when you encounter them on the real test. Also, take the time to familiarize yourself with the directions. That way you won't have to spend precious time reading them and thinking about them on test day. The answers to the example questions appear at the end of the section.

Question Type 1: The Matching Game

Example Questions

Directions: Each set of lettered choices below refers to the numbered statements immediately following it. Choose the one lettered choice that best fits each statement and then blacken the corresponding oval on the Answer Sheet. A choice may be used once, more than once, or not at all in each set.

Questions 1–3

(A) Natural selection
(B) Passive immunity
(C) Convergent evolution
(D) Vestigial structure
(E) Use and disuse

1. Strains of bacteria that are resistant to antibiotics have appeared in hospitals.
2. Whales possess femur bones.
3. Bats and birds both have wings.

Questions like these test your ability to classify. In this example, choices A through E list five concepts that mostly pertain to evolution. Each "question" is really a specific example highlighting one of the particular concepts listed in the answer choices. To answer questions of this type, first take a very quick glance at the list of choices. Do not spend time thinking about the exact definitions of each term. That is not what you are being tested on. Go right to the questions and see if you can associate each example with its corresponding concept without pondering the list of choices.

For example, consider Question 1. The existence of bacteria that are unaffected by antibiotic medicine is a modern example of natural selection at work. Don't be tempted to classify this phenomenon as "passive immunity" because it "sounds right"; people often (incorrectly) say that they shouldn't inappropriately use antibiotics because the bacteria can become "immune" to them. That idea is not entirely accurate because bacteria lack immune systems and don't get sick and recover from the antibiotic. Instead, those susceptible to the antibiotic die off, and those that aren't affected by the chemical survive and reproduce in greater numbers.

If you are going to use the elimination strategy with this type of question, be careful about marking-up your test booklet. Remember that the same choices are used for several questions, so just because you can eliminate one choice for one question, that doesn't mean that the same choice can't be the correct answer for the next question.

Example Answers

1. **A** Natural selection
2. **D** Vestigial structure
3. **C** Convergent evolution

Question Type 2: The Numbered Diagram

Example Questions

Directions: Questions 4 and 5 refer to the following diagram of a mammalian heart.

Cross-section of a mammalian heart.

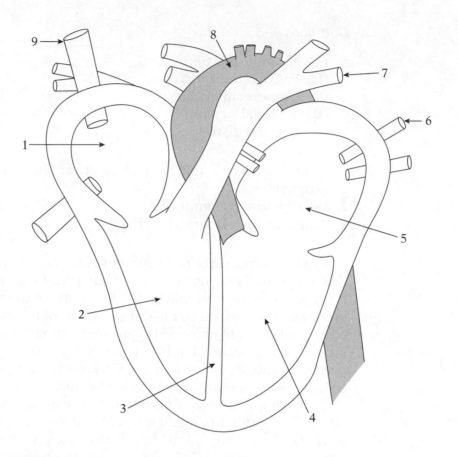

4. Chamber that receives blood from the lungs

    (A) 1
    (B) 2
    (C) 4
    (D) 5
    (E) 6

5. Blood vessel carrying deoxygenated blood

    (A) 3
    (B) 4
    (C) 5
    (D) 8
    (E) 9

Note that you do not need to identify each part of the heart or supply the name of each numbered structure. All you have to know is what the different parts do. Start by reading the description in the question stem. Then, if you can, think of the name the corresponding structure. Find that structure on the diagram and mark the corresponding answer choice. If you cannot recall the exact name of the structure, think of any logical associations that will help you identify it.

Let's use the above example questions to illustrate these strategies. Suppose you read Question 4 and immediately recall that the described structure is the left atrium. Looking at the diagram, you should identify the left atrium as structure number 5. You would then mark D as the correct answer. However, when you go on to Question 5, suppose you do not recall the name of the vessel that carries deoxygenated blood. But you might recall that deoxygenated blood is delivered to the right side of the heart and pumped from there into the lung (where it is oxygenated). Thus, any vessel carrying blood toward or through the right side of the heart—before it goes on to the lungs—would be the correct answer. Scanning the diagram reveals only one such vessel, labeled 9 (and corresponding to choice E). In this way, you can answer the question without even knowing the name of the designated structure (which is the superior vena cava).

Example Answers

4. **D** 5, which points to the left atrium
5. **E** 9, the superior vena cava

Question Type 3: The Direct Question

Example Question

Directions: Each of the questions or incomplete statements below is followed by five suggested answers or completions. Choose the one that is BEST in each case and then blacken the corresponding oval on the Answer Sheet.

---

6. A group of individuals belonging to a single species that live together in a defined area is termed a(n)

   (A) population
   (B) ecosystem
   (C) community
   (D) biome
   (E) biosphere

Questions of this type simply require a straightforward recall of facts. They are the best type for trying to predict the answer first and then reading through all of the choices. If you are not sure of the answer but can eliminate at least one choice, go ahead and guess. When scanning the answers, be wary of words that look or sound alike. That way you can minimize careless errors.

Example Answer

6. **A** population

Question Type 4: The "Pick the 'Wrong' Answer" Question (a.k.a. "Least/Except/Not" Questions)

Example Questions

> *Directions:* Each of the questions or incomplete statements below is followed by five suggested answers or completions. Choose the one that is BEST in each case and then blacken the corresponding oval on the answer sheet.

7. Which of the following processes generates the LEAST amount of energy?

   (A) glycolysis
   (B) lactic acid fermentation
   (C) the Krebs cycle
   (D) oxidative phosphorylation
   (E) aerobic respiration

8. A cell from an *Elodea* plant contains all of the following structures EXCEPT:

   (A) DNA
   (B) genes
   (C) a cell wall
   (D) a centriole
   (E) a nucleus

9. Which of the following is NOT an organic molecule found in living organisms?

   (A) protein
   (B) nucleic acid
   (C) carbohydrate
   (D) sodium chloride
   (E) lipid

Note that the directions are the same as for the "direct questions." However, be sure to read very carefully. These questions can be tricky. You can still attempt to answer the question before looking at the choices. However, because many choices "may not fit," it is sometimes easier to use more specific strategies.

For the "LEAST" questions, consider making a list from highest to lowest. For example, after reading Question 7, you could rank the choices from highest (most energy generated) to lowest (least energy generated) and indicate your rankings by writing numbers from 1 to 5 next to the choices in your test booklet. Then, choose the highest number (in this case, number 5 corresponding to choice B) because it is the choice that generates the LEAST energy.

(A) glycolysis	4
(B) lactic acid fermentation	5
(C) the Krebs cycle	3
(D) oxidative phosphorylation	2
(E) aerobic respiration	1

For the "EXCEPT" and "NOT" questions, consider rephrasing the question into a "direct question" and ruling out answers by the process of elimination. Take Question 8 as an example: You can restate the question "Does a green plant cell contain DNA?" If the answer is "yes" you can cross off choice A. Try this strategy with Questions 8 and 9.

Example Answers

7. **B** lactic acid fermentation (all other choices involve some generation of ATP)
8. **D** a centriole
9. **D** sodium chloride

Question Type 5: Easy as I, II, III

Example Question

10. Which of the following domains includes single-celled organisms?

    I.   eukarya
    II. archaea
    III. bacteria

    (A) I only
    (B) II only
    (C) I and II only
    (D) I and III only
    (E) I, II, and III

This type of question is another opportunity to use the process of elimination. Look at the three Roman numeral items. Start by crossing out any one you know does not apply. Then look in the answer choices and rule out any choice that includes the item you just crossed out. You can also take the opposite tack: pick a Roman numeral item that you know *does* apply, then rule out any answer choice that does *not* contain that item.

For example, suppose you are sure that bacteria (III) are composed of single cells, but you are not sure about eukarya (I) and archaea (II). Choices A, B, and C are eliminated immediately because you know that because III is correct, the answer must include III. At this point, even if you have to guess, you have a 50–50 chance of picking the correct answer.

Example Answer

10. **E** All domains have single-celled members.

Question Type 6: The Laboratory Question

Throughout the SAT Biology test you will see questions based on sets of data of the kind usually derived from laboratory experiments. The data will be in the form of tables, graphs, or diagrams. First, you will have to interpret the data. Then, you will have to apply this information to answer the accompanying questions. To answer correctly, you will need not only biology content knowledge (straight recall of facts), but also scientific reasoning/analytic skills.

If You Understand How a Scientific Experiment Is Designed, You Can Answer Many Laboratory Questions Even if You Are Not Familiar With the Subject Matter

For example, you may not have any actual lab experience with genetically mutated strains of *E. coli*, but as long as you are able to make sense of the data presented, you can successfully tackle laboratory questions that deal with this topic. To refresh your understanding of scientific experiments, review the following list of basic terms.

Basic Terminology: Dissecting an Experiment

- *Hypothesis:* A hypothesis is an idea that a scientist investigates in experiments. Experiments are designed to test a specific hypothesis, which will either be supported or negated by data collected.

- *Prediction:* After designing an experiment, a scientist can guess what will happen if the hypothesis is correct or incorrect. This guess is a prediction.

- *Variable:* A variable is the component of an experiment that the scientist manipulates (and, therefore, changes). A well-designed experiment will isolate and test one variable at a time.

- *Constants:* Constants are components of the experiment that are not manipulated (and, therefore, unchanged). A well-designed experiment will hold as many factors constant as possible to ensure a fair test.

- *Experimental sample:* The experimental sample (or experimental group) is the subject of scientific manipulation. More simply, the scientist will do something to a thing or organism to test the hypothesis.

- *Control:* The control is the sample (or group) that the scientist does not manipulate and uses instead to compare with the experimental sample.

- *Results:* Results are gathered when the scientist performs an experimental manipulation and observes the outcomes. The scientist will record the findings and organize the information into tables, graphs, and/or drawings.

- *Conclusion:* Once results have been recorded and interpreted, the scientist can determine whether the experiment supports (proves) or fails to support (disproves) the hypothesis.

The following example illustrates how these terms apply to a simple experiment.

Sample Experiment

Dr. Zen notices that his son is hyperactive after eating certain foods but not others. He heard that sugar can wind children up, and he wonders if his son's hyperactivity is caused by eating candy. He designs an experiment by giving half of the children in his son's playgroup a spoonful of sugar. Half the children are given sugar after lunch and allowed to play on the mat until they fall asleep. He then records how long after eating it takes these children to settle into a nap, and how long it takes the other half. The children who eat the sugar take longer to fall asleep. Dr. Zen now thinks that it is the sugar that makes his son hyperactive.

- *What is the hypothesis?* The hypothesis is "sugar intake makes children hyperactive."

- *What is the prediction?* Dr. Zen can make two predictions based on the same hypothesis. Prediction 1: If the hypothesis is true (that sugar intake makes children hyperactive), then children who eat sugar will have more trouble falling asleep than children that do not eat sugar. Prediction 2: Alternatively, if the hypothesis is false, then children who eat sugar will fall asleep at the same time as children who do not.

- *What is the variable?* In this experiment, the only thing that changes is the amount of sugar given to different children.

- *What are the constants?* Dr. Zen keeps as many other factors as possible constant. All of the children are allowed to play on the mat in the same environment at the same time of day.

- *What is the experimental group?* The group of children who receive sugar make up the experimental group and may be called experimental subjects.

- *What is the control group?* Dr. Zen compares the experimental group to the group of children who do not get sugar. Those children make up the control group (and are called control subjects).

- *What is the observation?* Dr. Zen watches all of the children and records when they fall asleep. These records are the results. Another term for this process is the collection of scientific data. Each individual recording is a datapoint. Here is how the data for this experiment may be recorded.

Sugar Group		No Sugar Group	
Child 1	15 minutes	Child 6	5 minutes
Child 2	10 minutes	Child 7	1 minute
Child 3	10 minutes	Child 8	2 minutes
Child 4	20 minutes	Child 9	5 minutes
Child 5	15 minutes	Child 10	1 minutes
Average	14 minutes	Average	2.8 minutes

- *What is the conclusion?* Dr. Zen sees that prediction 1 is correct. Therefore, he concludes that sugar makes children hyperactive.

Example Questions

Questions 11–13 refer to the following experiment.

To test the immune response of mice to infection, researchers exposed an experimental group to aerosolized bacteria. The proliferation of blood cell subtypes as a function of time was determined by immunophenotyping blood cells from this experimental group at set intervals after exposure. This was compared with a control group exposed to aerosolized sucrose solution. The amount of antibody produced by the mice groups was also determined at similar time intervals.

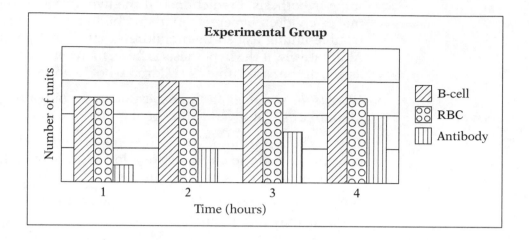

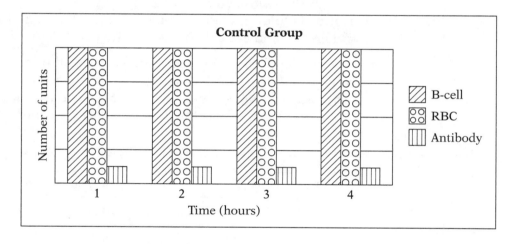

11. Based on the data, which of the following showed an increase after bacterial exposure?

    (A) sucrose levels
    (B) number of B-cells
    (C) number of red blood cells
    (D) type of antibody
    (E) all of the above

12. What is the function of antibodies in an organism's immune system?

    (A) trigger an immune response in the body
    (B) cause an increase in red blood cell number
    (C) act as enzymes, speeding up chemical reactions
    (D) bind to and help destroy pathogens
    (E) prevent bacteria from being harmed

13. Which of the following is the most logical conclusion for the experimental findings?

    (A) B-type immune cells produce antibodies.
    (B) Bacterial exposure inhibits protein synthesis.
    (C) Red blood cells multiply after bacterial exposure.
    (D) B-type cells have a doubling time of approximately 1 hour.
    (E) Sucrose prevents the effects of bacterial infection in mice.

No Matter How Complicated the Question Is, Begin by Dissecting the Experiment Into Its Essential Components

In this example you may not know what "immunophenotyping" is, but you should still be able to understand the basics of the experimental design.

Work Backward to Generate a Hypothesis and Prediction; This Will Help You Understand the Graphs (Which Are the Experimental Results)

You should recognize that in this experiment, the scientists compared the "proliferation of blood cell subtypes" after mice were exposed to bacteria (the experimental group) or sucrose (the control group). Now that you recognize what the scientists did, you can generate an appropriate hypothesis and prediction. Let's say you recall that B-cells fight infection. You may hypothesize that "B-type immune cells proliferate (or multiply) after exposure to bacteria." Prediction 1 would be "If the hypothesis is true, the amount of B-type immune cells will be greater in the experimental group than the control group over time." Prediction 2 would be "If the hypothesis is false, the amount of B-type immune cells will be the same in both groups."

Next, Analyze the Graphs and Reach a Conclusion Consistent With Your Predictions

In this example, the first graph shows that in the experimental group, the amount of B-type immune cells increases over time, while the amount of red blood cells remains constant. Alternatively, in graph 2, there is no change in the control group cell amounts. This implies that prediction 1 is correct.

Thus, the conclusion is that bacterial infection stimulates B-type immune cell proliferation.

Finally, Ask Yourself Whether Any Additional Information Is Available in the Graph

In graph 1, we see that the experimental animals also produce more antibody. Making this observation is important for answering one of the questions.

Example Answers

11. **B** Answering this question is based only on graphic analysis. You may have been tempted to say D or E. In this case, the *amount* of antibody increases, but the graph says nothing about the *types* of antibodies.

12. **D** This question requires information recall and can be answered without looking at the experimental data. If you said A, then you were thinking about the meaning of the term *antigen,* which is what an antibody will bind to and help destroy. There is no immediate relationship between bacterial exposure and red blood cell number B.

13. **A** Although prior knowledge will help, this question can be answered based only on the graphic analysis. Out of all the other choices given, this is the most logical conclusion based on the data. You can rule out B because protein synthesis was not examined in this experiment, thus, there is no evidence to support that idea. You can rule out C because the amount of red blood cells does not change in either group. You should rule out D because the graph shows that the height of the B-cells does not actually double, but increases by a lesser amount. Finally, you can rule out E because the mice that were given sucrose functioned as the control group. Sucrose was not meant to have any effect on the mice's immune systems. There seems to be a correlation between the elevation of B-cell number and elevation of antibody, so you could suppose that B cells produce the antibodies. *While this is true, it is important to note that this experiment does not actually establish causality. In other words, an unknown third entity may cause both the B-cells and the amount of antibody to increase at the same time.*

BIOLOGY PRACTICE TEST 1
BIOLOGY-E

The following practice test is designed to be just like the real SAT Biology-E test. It matches the actual test in content coverage and level of difficulty. The test is in two parts. Part A (Questions 1–60) is for everyone taking Biology-E or Biology-M. Part B (Questions 61–80) is ONLY for students taking Biology-E.

Allow 1 hour to take the test. Time yourself and work uninterrupted. If you run out of time, take note of where you ended when time ran out. Remember that you lose one-quarter of a point for each incorrect answer. Because of this penalty, do not guess on a question unless you can eliminate one or more of the answers. Your score is calculated using the following formula:

Number of correct answers − 0.25 × Number of incorrect answers

This practice test will be an accurate reflection of how you'll do on test day if you treat it as the real examination. Here are some hints on how to take the test under conditions similar to those of the actual exam.

- Complete the test in one sitting.
- Time yourself.
- Tear out your Answer Sheet and fill in the ovals just as you would on the actual test day.
- Become familiar with the directions to the test and the reference information provided. You'll save time on the actual test day by already being familiar with this information.

BIOLOGY PRACTICE TEST 1
BIOLOGY-E

ANSWER SHEET

Part A

1. (A)(B)(C)(D)(E)	21. (A)(B)(C)(D)(E)	41. (A)(B)(C)(D)(E)
2. (A)(B)(C)(D)(E)	22. (A)(B)(C)(D)(E)	42. (A)(B)(C)(D)(E)
3. (A)(B)(C)(D)(E)	23. (A)(B)(C)(D)(E)	43. (A)(B)(C)(D)(E)
4. (A)(B)(C)(D)(E)	24. (A)(B)(C)(D)(E)	44. (A)(B)(C)(D)(E)
5. (A)(B)(C)(D)(E)	25. (A)(B)(C)(D)(E)	45. (A)(B)(C)(D)(E)
6. (A)(B)(C)(D)(E)	26. (A)(B)(C)(D)(E)	46. (A)(B)(C)(D)(E)
7. (A)(B)(C)(D)(E)	27. (A)(B)(C)(D)(E)	47. (A)(B)(C)(D)(E)
8. (A)(B)(C)(D)(E)	28. (A)(B)(C)(D)(E)	48. (A)(B)(C)(D)(E)
9. (A)(B)(C)(D)(E)	29. (A)(B)(C)(D)(E)	49. (A)(B)(C)(D)(E)
10. (A)(B)(C)(D)(E)	30. (A)(B)(C)(D)(E)	50. (A)(B)(C)(D)(E)
11. (A)(B)(C)(D)(E)	31. (A)(B)(C)(D)(E)	51. (A)(B)(C)(D)(E)
12. (A)(B)(C)(D)(E)	32. (A)(B)(C)(D)(E)	52. (A)(B)(C)(D)(E)
13. (A)(B)(C)(D)(E)	33. (A)(B)(C)(D)(E)	53. (A)(B)(C)(D)(E)
14. (A)(B)(C)(D)(E)	34. (A)(B)(C)(D)(E)	54. (A)(B)(C)(D)(E)
15. (A)(B)(C)(D)(E)	35. (A)(B)(C)(D)(E)	55. (A)(B)(C)(D)(E)
16. (A)(B)(C)(D)(E)	36. (A)(B)(C)(D)(E)	56. (A)(B)(C)(D)(E)
17. (A)(B)(C)(D)(E)	37. (A)(B)(C)(D)(E)	57. (A)(B)(C)(D)(E)
18. (A)(B)(C)(D)(E)	38. (A)(B)(C)(D)(E)	58. (A)(B)(C)(D)(E)
19. (A)(B)(C)(D)(E)	39. (A)(B)(C)(D)(E)	59. (A)(B)(C)(D)(E)
20. (A)(B)(C)(D)(E)	40. (A)(B)(C)(D)(E)	60. (A)(B)(C)(D)(E)

Part B

61. (A)(B)(C)(D)(E)
62. (A)(B)(C)(D)(E)
63. (A)(B)(C)(D)(E)
64. (A)(B)(C)(D)(E)
65. (A)(B)(C)(D)(E)
66. (A)(B)(C)(D)(E)
67. (A)(B)(C)(D)(E)
68. (A)(B)(C)(D)(E)
69. (A)(B)(C)(D)(E)
70. (A)(B)(C)(D)(E)
71. (A)(B)(C)(D)(E)
72. (A)(B)(C)(D)(E)
73. (A)(B)(C)(D)(E)
74. (A)(B)(C)(D)(E)
75. (A)(B)(C)(D)(E)
76. (A)(B)(C)(D)(E)
77. (A)(B)(C)(D)(E)
78. (A)(B)(C)(D)(E)
79. (A)(B)(C)(D)(E)
80. (A)(B)(C)(D)(E)

Part C

81. (A)(B)(C)(D)(E)
82. (A)(B)(C)(D)(E)
83. (A)(B)(C)(D)(E)
84. (A)(B)(C)(D)(E)
85. (A)(B)(C)(D)(E)
86. (A)(B)(C)(D)(E)
87. (A)(B)(C)(D)(E)
88. (A)(B)(C)(D)(E)
89. (A)(B)(C)(D)(E)
90. (A)(B)(C)(D)(E)
91. (A)(B)(C)(D)(E)
92. (A)(B)(C)(D)(E)
93. (A)(B)(C)(D)(E)
94. (A)(B)(C)(D)(E)
95. (A)(B)(C)(D)(E)
96. (A)(B)(C)(D)(E)
97. (A)(B)(C)(D)(E)
98. (A)(B)(C)(D)(E)
99. (A)(B)(C)(D)(E)
100. (A)(B)(C)(D)(E)

BIOLOGY PRACTICE TEST 1

BIOLOGY-E

Time: 60 Minutes

███ **PART A (Core Questions 1–60, for Both Biology-E and Biology-M)**

Directions: Determine the BEST answer for each question. Then fill in the corresponding oval on the Answer Sheet.

Questions 1–3

    (A) Krebs cycle
    (B) electron transport chain
    (C) fermentation
    (D) glycolysis
    (E) Calvin cycle

1. Cellular respiration in the absence of oxygen

2. A biochemical pathway that utilizes pyruvate to produce ATP, NADH, and $FADH_2$

3. A biochemical pathway that breaks down glucose into pyruvate

Questions 4–7

    (A) primary consumers
    (B) secondary consumers
    (C) scavengers
    (D) decomposers
    (E) producers

4. Earthworms eat organic matter and return nutrients to the soil.

5. Cows eat grass.

6. Lions are hunters on the African plains.

7. Buzzards soar in the sky looking for dead animals.

Questions 8–12

    (A) geographical isolation
    (B) mechanical isolation
    (C) temporal isolation
    (D) hybrid sterility
    (E) behavioral isolation

8. Groups are not attracted to each other for mating.

9. Structural differences prevent mating between individuals of different groups.

10. Groups are physically separated.

11. Groups reproduce at different times of the year.

12. Matings between groups do not produce fertile offspring.

Questions 13–15

    (A) dominance
    (B) reflex
    (C) instinct
    (D) imprinting
    (E) habituation

13. Learned behavior that occurs only at a certain, critical time in an animal's life

14. Automatic, unconscious reaction

15. Simple form of learned behavior

16. You are trying to identify a plant. If you look closely at the leaves, you see the veins are all parallel. What does this tell you about the plant?

    (A) The plant is a dicot.
    (B) The plant is a monocot.
    (C) The plant is a gymnosperm.
    (D) The plant is an angiosperm.
    (E) The plant is a bryophyte.

17. Populations tend to grow because

    (A) the large number of individuals reduces the number of predators
    (B) the more individuals there are, the more likely they will survive
    (C) random events or natural disturbances are rare
    (D) there are always plentiful resources in every environment
    (E) individuals tend to have multiple offspring over their lifetime

GO ON TO THE NEXT PAGE ➤

18. Which of the organisms below lacks a complete digestive tract?

      I.   jellyfish
      II.   mollusk
      III. earthworm

(A) I, II, and III
(B) I only
(C) II only
(D) III only
(E) I and III only

19. The internal need that causes an animal to act and is necessary for learning is called

(A) trail-and-error
(B) motivation
(C) habituation
(D) conditioning
(E) imprinting

20. The rigid shape of plant cells is due to the

(A) cell membrane
(B) cell wall
(C) cytoskeleton
(D) microtubules
(E) centrioles

21. An invertebrate that displays two distinct body forms, medusa and polyp, at different stages in its lifecycle belong to the phylum

(A) Porifera
(B) Cnidaria
(C) Nemotoda
(D) Mollusca
(E) Echinodermata

22. The failure of homologous chromosomes to separate during meiosis is called

(A) nondisjunction
(B) translocation
(C) mutation
(D) crossing over
(E) disjunction

23. Which characteristic of fungi is used to classify them into different phyla?

(A) the type of food they grow on
(B) the type of hyphae they have
(C) the type of mushroom they produce
(D) the way they produce spores
(E) the material that makes up their cell wall

24. A rancher moved his herd of cattle to a different pasture. Which example below indicates that the carrying capacity of that pasture was exceeded?

(A) The herd increased in size.
(B) The pasture became overgrazed and barren.
(C) The pasture had more grasses.
(D) The cows gained weight.
(E) The cows had more calves.

25. Some mutations are a source of genetic variation. Which type of cell is mostly likely to cause a genetic variation that could lead to evolution?

(A) skin cells
(B) body cells
(C) brain cells
(D) sex cells
(E) embryo cells

26. What is the expected phenotypic ratio of a dihybrid cross between two heterozygous individuals?

(A) 3:1
(B) 1:2:1
(C) 3:3:1
(D) 9:3:3:1
(E) 6:4:4:2

27. Which of the following nucleotide bases is found in RNA but not in DNA?

(A) uracil
(B) adenine
(C) cytosine
(D) thymine
(E) guanine

28. Some bacteria are able to reproduce with a simple form of sexual reproduction called

(A) binary fission
(B) fragmentation
(C) meiosis
(D) replication
(E) conjugation

GO ON TO THE NEXT PAGE

29. Mendel's law of segregation states that
    (A) genes are separated on different chromosomes
    (B) pairs of alleles separate during mitosis
    (C) pairs of alleles separate during meiosis
    (D) pairs of alleles exchange material during crossing over
    (E) genes are passed from parents to offspring

Questions 30 and 31

This is a segment of DNA.

CGATGGCTA

30. Which represents the complimentary strand of DNA for the segment?
    (A) CGATGGCTA
    (B) GCTACCGAT
    (C) UAGCCAUCG
    (D) CGTAGGCAT
    (E) ATCGGTAGC

31. What is the messenger RNA strand for the DNA segment?
    (A) GCUACCGAU
    (B) UCTACCGUA
    (C) GUTAUUGAT
    (D) CGATGGCTA
    (E) ATCGGTAGC

32. The classification system set forth by Linneaus grouped organisms based on their
    (A) similar coloring
    (B) similar structures
    (C) similar habitats
    (D) genetic similarities
    (E) evolutionary relationships

33. Which of the following best describes an ecosystem?
    (A) a group of individuals of the same species that live together in the same area at the same time
    (B) all populations of different species that live and interact in the same area
    (C) all populations of different species that live and interact in the same area and the abiotic environment
    (D) all the organisms that depend on the resources in a specific region
    (E) the part of Earth where life exists

34. The diploid number of a human cell is 23. How many actual chromosomes are in a normal body cell?
    (A) 22
    (B) 23
    (C) 44
    (D) 46
    (E) n

35. Which tissue transports carbohydrates and water through plants?
    (A) epidermal tissue
    (B) vascular tissue
    (C) ground tissue
    (D) epithelial tissue
    (E) endodermal tissue

36. According to the cell theory, which of the following statements is correct?
    (A) All organisms are made up of one or more cells.
    (B) All organisms must be able to reproduce.
    (C) Cells have organelles to carry on their functions.
    (D) Cells evolved from a primordial soup on early Earth.
    (E) Cells are able to regulate their external environment.

37. Which bird uses its beak to probe flowers for nectar?

(A)

(B)

(C)

(D)

(E)

GO ON TO THE NEXT PAGE

38. Which of the following best describes what will happen if cells are placed in distilled water?

    (A) The cells remain unchanged.
    (B) Water moves from inside of the cell to the outside.
    (C) Water moves from outside of the cell to the inside.
    (D) The cells burst.
    (E) The cells dissolve.

Questions 39 and 40

In an experiment in a laboratory, a population of bacteria in a petri dish is exposed to an antibiotic. The antibiotic kills most of the population. However, a few bacteria survive and soon repopulate the Petri dish with antibiotic-resistant bacteria.

39. According to modern evolutionary theory, which of the following explanations is correct for this experiment?

    (A) Some of the bacteria tried and successfully adapted to the new conditions in the petri dish.
    (B) Some members of the bacteria population developed a resistance to the antibiotic immediately after exposure.
    (C) Some members of the bacteria population already had a resistance to the antibiotic so they were not killed.
    (D) Some of the bacteria quickly evolve into a new species that resists the antibiotic.
    (E) Some of the bacteria protected themselves from the antibiotic long enough to develop a resistance.

40. Which best describes what happened in the petri dish?

    (A) macroevolution
    (B) microevolution
    (C) adaptive radiation
    (D) divergent evolution
    (E) speciation

41. All of the following are cycled though biogeochemical cycles EXCEPT

    (A) water
    (B) carbon
    (C) energy
    (D) phosphorus
    (E) nitrogen

42. You cross a red flowered plant with a white flowered plant, and all of the offspring have pink flowers. What is the most probable explanation?

    (A) Red is dominant.
    (B) White is dominant.
    (C) Pink is dominant.
    (D) Red and white exhibit incomplete dominance.
    (E) Red and white exhibit codominance.

43. If an organism has a haploid number of 24, how many chromosomes does it have?

    (A) 6
    (B) 12
    (C) 24
    (D) 36
    (E) 48

44. Bats and insects both have wings. The wings of bats and insects are examples of

    (A) homologous structures
    (B) analogous characters
    (C) vestigial structures
    (D) adaptive structures
    (E) derived traits

45. In humans, what function does the small intestine serve?

    I.   vitamin synthesis
    II. absorb water
    III. absorb nutrients

    (A) I and II only
    (B) II and III only
    (C) II only
    (D) I only
    (E) III only

46. A codon is

    (A) a group of three nucleotide sequences
    (B) the nucleotide units between the start and stop codes
    (C) the nucleotide sequence that serves as the instructions for a protein
    (D) a single nucleotide in an mRNA sequence
    (E) the sequence of nucleotides that signals the start or stop of protein synthesis

GO ON TO THE NEXT PAGE

47. Which of the following conditions is necessary for a virus to attack a host cell?

   (A) The virus must have the DNA or RNA key sequence to enter the host cell.
   (B) The virus must have the enzymes to cause the host cell to burst so that the host cell may be used as raw materials.
   (C) The virus must have the proper enzyme to puncture the membrane of the host cell.
   (D) The virus must have a particular shape that will match up with the proteins on the surface of the host cell.
   (E) The viral DNA or RNA must have a sequence that is recognized by the ribosomes of the host cell.

48. Cytochrome–c is a protein that scientists often use to compare the evolutionary relationships among species. There is one difference in the cytochrome–c sequence between humans and rhesus monkeys. There are ten differences between humans and kangaroos. What can you infer about the relationship between these species?

   (A) Humans and kangaroos have the same proteins coded in their genes.
   (B) Humans and kangaroos share a more recent ancestor than humans and rhesus monkeys.
   (C) Humans are not closely related to either kangaroos or rhesus monkeys.
   (D) Humans and rhesus monkeys share a more recent ancestor than humans and kangaroos.
   (E) Rhesus monkeys and kangaroos share a more recent ancestor than humans and rhesus monkeys.

49. A man with type A blood marries a woman with type B blood. Their child is blood type O. What are the genotypes of the parents?

   (A) AO and BO
   (B) OO and AB
   (C) Aa and BO
   (D) AO and Bb
   (E) Aa and Bb

Questions 50 and 51

Each corn kernel in an ear of corn is ready to grow into a new plant.

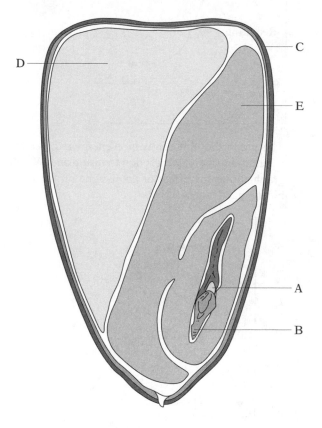

50. Which part of this seed makes up the plant embryo?

   (A) A, B
   (B) A, D
   (C) B, C
   (D) A, B, E
   (E) B, C, D

51. Which part of the seed stores the energy for the plant embryo?

   (A) A
   (B) B
   (C) C
   (D) D
   (E) E

GO ON TO THE NEXT PAGE

52.

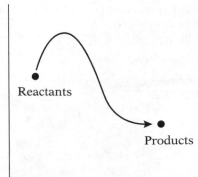

This graph shows the activation energy required for a certain biochemical reaction to take place. Which graph shows the effect of an enzyme on the same biochemical reaction?

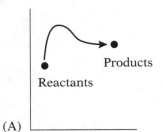

(A)

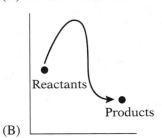

(B)

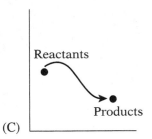

(C)

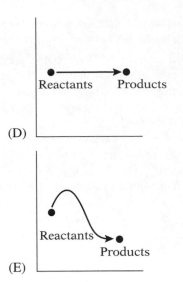

(D)

(E)

53. Which is the correct order of stages for an insect that undergoes incomplete metamorphosis?

(A) egg→larva→adult
(B) egg→nymph→adult
(C) egg→nymph→larva→adult
(D) egg→larva→pupa→adult
(E) egg→nymph→pupa→adult

54. The number of trophic levels that are maintained in an ecosystem is limited by

(A) the number of species
(B) the population size
(C) the loss of potential energy
(D) the number of individuals
(E) the hours of sunshine

55. The law of independent assortment applies to

(A) two genes on different chromosomes
(B) two genes on the same chromosome
(C) two alleles on different chromosomes
(D) two alleles on the same chromosome
(E) two chromosome strands

GO ON TO THE NEXT PAGE

56. Which is the correct order for the cell cycle beginning with the phase that most cells spend the majority of their time?

    I. G_2 Phase—growth and preparation for mitosis
    II. Mitosis
    III. G_1 Phase—cell growth
    IV. S Phase—DNA copied
    V.   Cytokinesis

    (A) III, IV, I, II, V
    (B) III, I, IV, V, II
    (C) II, III, I, IV, V
    (D) IV, III, I, II, V
    (E) V, III, IV, I, II

57. For natural selection to occur, which of the following must be true?

    (A) Individuals must evolve.
    (B) The environment must be constant.
    (C) Variation among organisms must exist.
    (D) Traits must be acquired.
    (E) Many species must be present.

58. What is the phenotypic ratio for a cross between a pea plant with purple flowers (PP) and a pea plant with white flowers (pp)?

    (A) all white
    (B) all purple
    (C) half purple, half white
    (D) 1PP, 2Pp, 1pp
    (E) all Pp

59. Natural selection is a part of evolution of a species. Which of the following best describes the driving force that leads to evolution within a species?

    (A) Individuals within a population change their behavior to accommodate changes in the environment and pass these to offspring.
    (B) Individuals within a population develop new adaptations as selective pressures force change.
    (C) Individuals within a population find new ways to adapt to environmental pressures.
    (D) Individuals within a population use different parts of their body as conditions change and pass those changes to offspring.
    (E) Individuals within a population have variations that give those individuals a better chance of survival.

60. Which of the following organisms is INCORRECTLY paired with its trophic level?

    (A) tree–producer
    (B) hawk–primary consumer
    (C) fungi–detritivore
    (D) fox–secondary consumer
    (E) grasshopper–primary consumer

GO ON TO THE NEXT PAGE

PART B (Biology-E Questions 61–80)

61. All of the following could cause a large number of density-dependent deaths in a population EXCEPT

    (A) winter storms
    (B) disease-carrying insects
    (C) predators
    (D) limited resources
    (E) small forest fire

62. Which of the following seeds depends on wind for dispersal?

    (A)

    (B)

    (C)

    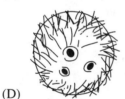
    (D)

    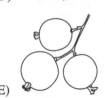
    (E)

63. Which group of animals was the first to have internal fertilization?

    (A) fishes
    (B) amphibians
    (C) reptiles
    (D) birds
    (E) mammals

64. Where would you most likely find nitrogen-fixing bacteria?

    (A) on the stems of some plants
    (B) in the leaves of trees
    (C) on the roots of some plants
    (D) on atmospheric dust particles
    (E) in blue-green algae

65. Earthworms are hermaphroditic, meaning that they

    (A) reproduce asexually
    (B) only come up to the surface at night
    (C) reproduce both sexually and asexually
    (D) have specialized segments for specialized tasks
    (E) have both male and female sex organs

66. According to the Hardy–Weinberg principle, allele frequencies change when evolutionary forces act on a population. All of these are possible evolutionary forces EXCEPT

    (A) mutations
    (B) gene flow
    (C) genetic drift
    (D) random mating
    (E) natural selection

GO ON TO THE NEXT PAGE

Questions 67–69

This is a typical food web in a pond.

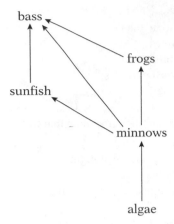

67. Which two organisms in this food web are in direct competition?

    (A) bass and minnows
    (B) minnows and sunfish
    (C) frogs and sunfish
    (D) bass and algae
    (E) frogs and algae

68. Which shows one possible direct pathway for energy flow to the bass?

    (A) algae→minnows→frogs→bass
    (B) algae→bass
    (C) algae→frogs→sunfish→bass
    (D) minnows→frogs→bass
    (E) bass→frogs→minnows→algae

69. Based on this food web, what would happen if the bass disappeared due to over fishing?

    (A) The algae population would increase.
    (B) The frogs and sunfish would disappear.
    (C) The minnow population would increase and the sunfish population would decrease.
    (D) The frog and sunfish populations would increase.
    (E) The minnow population and algae would increase.

Questions 70–72

This chart shows the relative abundance of different groups of echinoderms throughout geologic time. The width of the band indicates the number of species for each group.

Phylum Echinodermata

Cenozoic	Quaternary			
	Tertiary			
Mesozoic	Cretaceous			
	Jurassic			
	Triassic			
Paleozoic	Permian			
	Pennsylvanian			
	Mississippian			
	Devonian			
	Silurian			
	Ordovician			
	Cambrian			

70. Which of the following time periods shows a mass extinction of animals?

    (A) end of the Ordovician
    (B) end of the Silurian
    (C) end of the Devonian
    (D) end of the Permian
    (E) end of the Triassic

71. Which of the following time periods showed a boom in all echinoderm groups?

    (A) Ordovician
    (B) Silurian
    (C) Mississippian
    (D) Permian
    (E) Jurassic

72. All of the following statements are correct EXCEPT

    (A) The Blastoids are extinct.
    (B) The Echinodermata will become extinct in the near future.
    (C) The Echinoids are a successful group.
    (D) The Blastoids were not able to adapt to the same changes as the Crinoids.
    (E) The Crinoids have been living in a stable environment since the Triassic.

GO ON TO THE NEXT PAGE

Questions 73–77

Vegetation follows established patterns of regrowth and change after disturbances by farming, timber harvesting, hurricanes, or fire. This process of patterned regrowth and change is called plant succession. The rate of succession and the species present at various stages depend on the type and degrees of disturbance, the environment of the particular sites, and the species available to occupy the site. In the Piedmont of North Carolina, land subjected to disturbances will grow back in a century or two to become mixed hardwood forest.

1st year	2nd year	3rd to 18th year	19th to 30th year	30th to 70th year	70th to 100th year	100th year plus
Horseweed dominant; crabgrass, pigweed	Asters dominant; crabgrass	Grass scrub community; broomsedge grass, pines coming in during this stage	Young pine forest	Mature pine forest; Understory of young hardwoods	Pine to hardwood transition	Climax oak-hickory forest

73. Based on this diagram, after 80 years, which will make up the majority of trees?

    (A) young pines
    (B) mature pines
    (C) oak trees
    (D) oak and hickory trees
    (E) pine, oak, and hickory trees

74. Which best describes the change that takes place when pines become the dominant vegetation?

    (A) The pine trees increase the amount of nutrients available in the soil.
    (B) The pine trees increase the soil moisture.
    (C) The pine trees decrease the amount of sunlight reaching the forest floor.
    (D) The pine trees change the character of the soil from loam to sandy loam.
    (E) The pine trees increase the amount of soil erosion.

75. Which of the following factors would be LEAST likely to restart succession?

    (A) forest fire
    (B) volcanic eruption
    (C) clear-cut logging
    (D) glaciation
    (E) drought

76. Pine beetles are a type of insect that burrow into the bark of mature and over-mature pine trees. The pine trees die as a result of the infestations. If pine beetles attacked a mature pine forest, which of the following events would most likely occur?

    (A) Succession would start over.
    (B) The rate of transition to a hardwood forest would be increased.
    (C) The succession will stall at being a young pine forest.
    (D) The succession will stall at being a mature pine forest while young pines mature.
    (E) The pine beetles will not affect the rate of succession in the forest.

GO ON TO THE NEXT PAGE

77. Which of the following statements about succession is true?

    (A) Succession is a natural progression that takes place at a constant rate.
    (B) Succession only takes place on freshly cleared or new land such as islands.
    (C) The rate of succession can be changed by factors such as fire, clear cutting, and lava flows.
    (D) Succession is a natural progression of plant types that cannot be reversed.
    (E) Succession always occurs over a short period of time.

Questions 78–80

Number of Hares   Number of Lynx per
per square kilometer   100 square kilometers

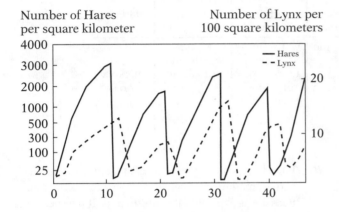

78. If lynxes depend mainly on hares for food, which best describes the relationship between hares and lynxes?

    (A) As the hare population decreases, the lynx population increases.
    (B) As the hare population decreases, the lynx population decreases.
    (C) As the hare population increases, the lynx population increases.
    (D) As the hare population increases, the lynx population stays the same.
    (E) There is no relationship between the populations of lynxes and hares.

79. Based on this chart, which of the following statements is true?

    (A) Lynxes and hares depend on each other for survival.
    (B) Hares become better at hiding from lynxes over time.
    (C) Hares are capable of reproducing quickly.
    (D) Lynxes only prey on hares in certain seasons.
    (E) Lynxes migrate into and out of areas on a regular basis.

80. What would happen to the hare population if the lynxes were removed from the habitat?

    (A) The hare population would continue on a boom and bust cycle.
    (B) The hare population would dwindle.
    (C) The hare population would grow exponentially and not stop.
    (D) The hare population would quickly reach the carrying capacity and stabilize.
    (E) The hare population would slowly increase over time.

S T O P

IF YOU FINISH BEFORE TIME IS CALLED, YOU MAY CHECK YOUR WORK ON THIS TEST ONLY.
DO NOT TURN TO ANY OTHER TEST IN THIS BOOK.

ANSWER KEY

Part A

1. C	11. C	21. B	31. A	41. C	51. D
2. A	12. D	22. A	32. B	42. D	52. B
3. D	13. D	23. D	33. C	43. E	53. B
4. D	14. B	24. B	34. D	44. B	54. C
5. A	15. E	25. D	35. B	45. E	55. C
6. B	16. B	26. D	36. A	46. A	56. A
7. C	17. E	27. A	37. C	47. D	57. C
8. E	18. B	28. E	38. C	48. D	58. B
9. B	19. B	29. C	39. C	49. A	59. E
10. A	20. B	30. B	40. B	50. D	60. B

Part B

61. A	71. C
62. B	72. B
63. C	73. E
64. C	74. C
65. E	75. E
66. D	76. B
67. C	77. C
68. A	78. C
69. D	79. C
70. D	80. D

ANSWERS AND EXPLANATIONS

Part A

1. **C** Fermentation is the cellular respiration process that takes place in the absence of oxygen. Fermentation converts glucose to either lactic acid or ethyl alcohol.

2. **A** The Krebs cycle is a cyclic biochemical pathway of respiration. It takes in pyruvate and produces ATP, NADH, and $FADH_2$.

3. **D** Glycolysis is the biochemical pathway that breaks down glucose to pyruvate. Glycolysis produces a net gain of 2 ATP molecules.

4. **D** Earthworms are decomposers because they break down organic matter and return nutrients to the soil. The returned nutrients are ready for use by plants.

5. **A** Cows are primary consumers because they eat plants, which are producers. Primary consumers are on the next trophic level above producers.

6. **B** Lions are secondary consumers because they eat animals, other consumers.

7. **C** Buzzards are scavengers because they find and eat already dead animals rather than killing them.

8. **E** Behavioral isolation occurs when two groups diverge and have different courtship rituals.

9. **B** Mechanical isolation occurs when two groups evolve differences in their genitalia.

10. **A** Geographical isolation occurs when groups are physically separated, such as by a mountain range or large body of water.

11. **C** Temporal isolation occurs when two groups diverge and have different mating seasons.

12. **D** Hybrid sterility occurs when nonfertile offspring are produced. This is a dead end as far as passing genes on is concerned.

13. **D** Imprinting is a learned behavior that occurs at a certain time of an animals life, such as just after birth.

14. **B** A reflex is an automatic and uncontrollable response. This is a direct stimulus–response scenario.

15. **E** Habituation is learned behavior that occurs as a result of doing some repeatedly.

16. **B** All monocots have parallel veins in their leaves.

17. **E** Populations grow as a result of multiple births through the lifespan of an organism. If each organism in a population only reproduced once, the population would not grow.

18. **B** Jellyfish are primitive, multicellular organisms. An opening to the digestive tract serves as both the mouth and anus for jellyfish.

19. **B** Motivation is needed for learning. If an animal lacks motivation, there will be no learning.

20. **B** Plant cells have a cell wall composed of cellulose. The cellulose is rigid and gives the plant cell a defined shape.

21. **B** Cnidarians have two distinct body plans during their lives. A jellyfish is an example of a medusa, and a sea anemone is an example of a polyp.

22. **A** Sometimes during meiosis, a pair of chromosomes fails to separate. This causes an extra chromosome in one daughter cell and a missing chromosome in the other.

23. **D** Fungi have many different forms, but the shape of their spores classifies them all.

24. **B** When a pasture exceeds the carrying capacity, it lacks the food to support that number of animals. A pasture in this condition will have all its available food eaten and will appear barren.

25. **D** The only mutation that can be passed to offspring is one that occurs in the sex cells. These are the only cells that undergo meiosis and take part in reproduction.

26. **D** A dihybrid cross has two factors in the cross. This results in a total of four potential phenotypes with a ratio of 9:3:3:1.

27. **A** Uracil does not occur in DNA but is in RNA. In RNA, uracil replaces thymine and attaches to adenine.

28. **E** Bacteria usually reproduce through binary fission but they sometimes get together, exchange genetic information, and reproduce by a process known a conjugation.

29. **C** During meiosis, the chromosome pairs separate and go to different daughter cells. This means that each daughter cells acquires one allele for a specific trait.

30. **B** The complementary strand of DNA will have the opposite nucleotide bases as the original strand.

31. **A** The mRNA strand will have the opposite nucleotides as the DNA with uracil substituted for thymine.

32. **B** When Linneaus proposed a method for classifying organisms, he based his system on structural similarities. This system has worked fairly well but many refinements are now done using genetic analysis.

33. **C** An ecosystem is all interactions among the organisms in the environment as well as the abiotic features.

34. **D** The diploid number refers to the number of pairs of chromosomes. In humans, the normal diploid number is 23 so that means that a cell has 23 pairs or 46 chromosomes.

35. **B** Plants are made up of many different types of tissues. The tissues that are part of the transport system for plants are vascular tissues such as xylem and phloem.

36. **A** This is the most basic statement of the cell theory.

37. **C** A bird that probes flowers for nectar would need a long, thin beak to reach inside the flower. A hummingbird is an example of a bird that feeds on nectar from flowers.

38. **C** Distilled water is hypotonic compared to a cell. As a result, water moves from an area of higher concentration (outside the cell) to the area of lower concentration (inside the cell).

39. **C** Because of genetic variations, some of the bacteria were able to survive the antibiotics. They passed this genetic advantage to their offspring and soon repopulated the petri dish with antibiotic resistant bacteria.

40. **B** This scenario is an example of microevolution. Microevolution is a small change in a population but not enough to create a new species.

41. **C** Biogeochemical cycles are cycles where minerals move between the biotic and abiotic part of the environment. Energy is not a mineral.

42. **D** Incomplete dominance occurs when neither of two traits is dominant. When both alleles appear, the phenotype is expressed as a blend.

43. **E** The haploid number for chromosomes is the actual number of chromosomes in a gamete. The total number of chromosomes in an organism would be double the haploid number.

44. **B** Analogous structures are those that serve a similar function but have structural differences and are not linked through evolution.

45. **E** The small intestine is lined with villi that increase the surface area and aid in the absorption of nutrients from digested food. The large intestine carries out the absorption of water, and the large intestines are also the site of some vitamin synthesis by bacteria living there symbiotically.

46. **A** The genetic code is based on sets of three nucleotides called codons.

47. **D** The shape of a virus allows it to attach to a host cell. Once this is accomplished, the virus can inject DNA or RNA into the host cell.

48. **D** Evolution results in changes to proteins. For cytochrome-c, the fewer the changes, the more closely related the organisms.

49. **A** A and B are dominant over O. O can only be expressed if paired with another O. The only way the offspring could have two O alleles is if the parents were AO and BO.

50. **D** The embryo of the corn plant is made up of the embryonic shoot (A), the embryonic root (B), and the cotyledon (E).

51. **D** The endosperm is energy stored for the plant embryo.

52. **B** An enzyme is a catalyst. Catalysts facilitate reactions by lowering the activation energy of the reaction pathway. They cannot change the initial or final energy level of the participating molecules.

53. **B** An insect with incomplete metamorphosis has a nymph stage that looks similar to the adult stage. Unlike complete metamorphosis, there is no pupa stage.

54. **C** Potential energy is the amount of energy for the next trophic level. Each trophic level only passes on about 10% of its total energy to the next higher level.

55. **C** The law of independent assortment states that traits are inherited independently of other traits. This only applies to alleles that are on separate chromosomes.

56. **A** Cells spend most of their time in the G_1 phase. After that comes the S phase, the G_2 phase, mitosis, and finally cytokinesis.

Part B

61. **A** A winter storm will not cause density-dependent deaths. It can be a density-independent cause of deaths.

62. **B** A maple seed has wings that allow it to be carried by the wind to a more distant location.

63. **C** Reptiles were the first animals with internal fertilization. This ended the dependence on water to carry sperm to the egg.

64. **C** Nitrogen-fixing bacteria are found in the ground. They often live in a symbiotic relationship with plants on their roots. Legumes or beans are a common example.

65. **E** Earthworms have both male and female reproductive organs.

66. **D** Random mating does not give any reproductive advantage to a trait. As a result, it does not change allele frequencies in a population.

67. **C** Frog and sunfish both rely on the same food source so they are in direct competition.

68. **A** Energy flows from the producer (algae) through consumers before it reaches the bass.

69. **D** The loss of the secondary consumer would remove pressure from primary consumers and allow their populations to grow until they reach the carrying capacity.

70. **D** It is necessary to read the chart from bottom to top. At the end of the Permian, Crinoids became reduced in diversity, and Blastoids became extinct.

57. **C** Organisms must already have traits for variation before natural selection occurs. Under most conditions, the variation in traits does not provide any particular advantage, so there is no natural selection. The variation only becomes important for natural selection when there is pressure that gives one trait an advantage over another.

58. **B** All of the plants in the first generation will be heterozygous so they exhibit the dominant trait.

59. **E** Individuals have traits that make them more successful, which gives them a reproductive advantage.

60. **B** Hawks are secondary consumers because they eat other consumers.

71. **C** During the Mississippian, all the echinoderm groups increased in diversity.

72. **B** The Echinoids have been increasing in diversity. It is unlikely that they will have a collapse unless there is significant global change.

73. **E** At 80 years, the forest is in a transition with large numbers of pines, oaks, and hickories.

74. **C** The pines are the first plants that grow tall. They shade the soil and reduce the populations of plants that depend on full sunlight.

75. **E** A drought will not likely last long enough to kill off all the trees.

76. **B** If the mature pines are removed, the rate of transition to a climax oak–hickory forest will be increased.

77. **C** Succession is a process that does not follow a distinct timeline. Many factors can affect rate of succession or even restart it.

78. **C** The hares are a food source for lynxes. As the population of hares increases, more food is available for lynxes so their population increases, too.

79. **C** There is a short lag time between the boom and bust cycle on hares so they must have a quick reproduction time.

80. **D** Without the lynxes, the hare will quickly reproduce and reach the carrying capacity.

SCORE SHEET

Number of questions correct: _____

Less: 0.25 × number of questions wrong: _____

(Remember that omitted questions are not counted as wrong.)

Raw score: _____

Raw Score	Scaled Score	Raw Score	Scaled Score	Raw Score	Scaled Score	Raw Score	Scaled Score	Raw Score	Scaled Score
80	800	57	690	34	520	11	380	−12	250
79	800	56	680	33	520	10	370	−13	240
78	800	55	670	32	510	9	370	−14	240
77	800	54	670	31	510	8	360	−15	230
76	800	53	660	30	500	7	350	−16	230
75	800	52	650	29	500	6	350	−17	230
74	800	51	650	28	490	5	340	−18	220
73	790	50	640	27	490	4	330	−19	220
72	790	49	630	26	480	3	330	−20	220
71	780	48	620	25	480	2	320		
70	780	47	620	24	470	1	320		
69	770	46	610	23	470	0	310		
68	760	45	600	22	460	−1	310		
67	760	44	600	21	450	−2	300		
66	750	43	590	20	440	−3	300		
65	740	42	580	19	440	−4	290		
64	740	41	580	18	430	−5	290		
63	730	40	570	17	420	−6	280		
62	720	39	560	16	420	−7	270		
61	710	38	560	15	410	−8	270		
60	710	37	550	14	400	−9	260		
59	700	36	540	13	400	−10	260		
58	700	35	530	12	390	−11	250		

Note: This is only a sample scoring scale. Scoring scales differ from exam to exam.

BIOLOGY PRACTICE TEST 2
BIOLOGY-M

The following practice test is designed to be just like the real SAT Biology-M test. It matches the actual test in content coverage and level of difficulty. The test is in two parts. Part A (Questions 1–60) is for everyone taking Biology-E or Biology-M. Part C (Questions 81–100) is ONLY for students taking Biology-M. (On the real test, Questions 61–80 are ONLY for students taking Biology-E.)

Allow 1 hour to take the test. Time yourself and work uninterrupted. If you run out of time, take note of where you ended when time ran out. Remember that you lose one-quarter of a point for each incorrect answer. Because of this penalty, do not guess on a question unless you can eliminate one or more of the answers. Your score is calculated using the following formula:

Number of correct answers − 0.25 × Number of incorrect answers

This practice test will be an accurate reflection of how you'll do on test day if you treat it as the real examination. Here are some hints on how to take the test under conditions similar to those of the actual exam.

- Complete the test in one sitting.
- Time yourself.
- Tear out your Answer Sheet and fill in the ovals just as you would on the actual test day.
- Become familiar with the directions to the test and the reference information provided. You'll save time on the actual test day by already being familiar with this information.

BIOLOGY PRACTICE TEST 2
BIOLOGY-M

ANSWER SHEET

Part A

1. Ⓐ Ⓑ Ⓒ Ⓓ Ⓔ 21. Ⓐ Ⓑ Ⓒ Ⓓ Ⓔ 41. Ⓐ Ⓑ Ⓒ Ⓓ Ⓔ
2. Ⓐ Ⓑ Ⓒ Ⓓ Ⓔ 22. Ⓐ Ⓑ Ⓒ Ⓓ Ⓔ 42. Ⓐ Ⓑ Ⓒ Ⓓ Ⓔ
3. Ⓐ Ⓑ Ⓒ Ⓓ Ⓔ 23. Ⓐ Ⓑ Ⓒ Ⓓ Ⓔ 43. Ⓐ Ⓑ Ⓒ Ⓓ Ⓔ
4. Ⓐ Ⓑ Ⓒ Ⓓ Ⓔ 24. Ⓐ Ⓑ Ⓒ Ⓓ Ⓔ 44. Ⓐ Ⓑ Ⓒ Ⓓ Ⓔ
5. Ⓐ Ⓑ Ⓒ Ⓓ Ⓔ 25. Ⓐ Ⓑ Ⓒ Ⓓ Ⓔ 45. Ⓐ Ⓑ Ⓒ Ⓓ Ⓔ
6. Ⓐ Ⓑ Ⓒ Ⓓ Ⓔ 26. Ⓐ Ⓑ Ⓒ Ⓓ Ⓔ 46. Ⓐ Ⓑ Ⓒ Ⓓ Ⓔ
7. Ⓐ Ⓑ Ⓒ Ⓓ Ⓔ 27. Ⓐ Ⓑ Ⓒ Ⓓ Ⓔ 47. Ⓐ Ⓑ Ⓒ Ⓓ Ⓔ
8. Ⓐ Ⓑ Ⓒ Ⓓ Ⓔ 28. Ⓐ Ⓑ Ⓒ Ⓓ Ⓔ 48. Ⓐ Ⓑ Ⓒ Ⓓ Ⓔ
9. Ⓐ Ⓑ Ⓒ Ⓓ Ⓔ 29. Ⓐ Ⓑ Ⓒ Ⓓ Ⓔ 49. Ⓐ Ⓑ Ⓒ Ⓓ Ⓔ
10. Ⓐ Ⓑ Ⓒ Ⓓ Ⓔ 30. Ⓐ Ⓑ Ⓒ Ⓓ Ⓔ 50. Ⓐ Ⓑ Ⓒ Ⓓ Ⓔ
11. Ⓐ Ⓑ Ⓒ Ⓓ Ⓔ 31. Ⓐ Ⓑ Ⓒ Ⓓ Ⓔ 51. Ⓐ Ⓑ Ⓒ Ⓓ Ⓔ
12. Ⓐ Ⓑ Ⓒ Ⓓ Ⓔ 32. Ⓐ Ⓑ Ⓒ Ⓓ Ⓔ 52. Ⓐ Ⓑ Ⓒ Ⓓ Ⓔ
13. Ⓐ Ⓑ Ⓒ Ⓓ Ⓔ 33. Ⓐ Ⓑ Ⓒ Ⓓ Ⓔ 53. Ⓐ Ⓑ Ⓒ Ⓓ Ⓔ
14. Ⓐ Ⓑ Ⓒ Ⓓ Ⓔ 34. Ⓐ Ⓑ Ⓒ Ⓓ Ⓔ 54. Ⓐ Ⓑ Ⓒ Ⓓ Ⓔ
15. Ⓐ Ⓑ Ⓒ Ⓓ Ⓔ 35. Ⓐ Ⓑ Ⓒ Ⓓ Ⓔ 55. Ⓐ Ⓑ Ⓒ Ⓓ Ⓔ
16. Ⓐ Ⓑ Ⓒ Ⓓ Ⓔ 36. Ⓐ Ⓑ Ⓒ Ⓓ Ⓔ 56. Ⓐ Ⓑ Ⓒ Ⓓ Ⓔ
17. Ⓐ Ⓑ Ⓒ Ⓓ Ⓔ 37. Ⓐ Ⓑ Ⓒ Ⓓ Ⓔ 57. Ⓐ Ⓑ Ⓒ Ⓓ Ⓔ
18. Ⓐ Ⓑ Ⓒ Ⓓ Ⓔ 38. Ⓐ Ⓑ Ⓒ Ⓓ Ⓔ 58. Ⓐ Ⓑ Ⓒ Ⓓ Ⓔ
19. Ⓐ Ⓑ Ⓒ Ⓓ Ⓔ 39. Ⓐ Ⓑ Ⓒ Ⓓ Ⓔ 59. Ⓐ Ⓑ Ⓒ Ⓓ Ⓔ
20. Ⓐ Ⓑ Ⓒ Ⓓ Ⓔ 40. Ⓐ Ⓑ Ⓒ Ⓓ Ⓔ 60. Ⓐ Ⓑ Ⓒ Ⓓ Ⓔ

Part B

61. Ⓐ Ⓑ Ⓒ Ⓓ Ⓔ
62. Ⓐ Ⓑ Ⓒ Ⓓ Ⓔ
63. Ⓐ Ⓑ Ⓒ Ⓓ Ⓔ
64. Ⓐ Ⓑ Ⓒ Ⓓ Ⓔ
65. Ⓐ Ⓑ Ⓒ Ⓓ Ⓔ
66. Ⓐ Ⓑ Ⓒ Ⓓ Ⓔ
67. Ⓐ Ⓑ Ⓒ Ⓓ Ⓔ
68. Ⓐ Ⓑ Ⓒ Ⓓ Ⓔ
69. Ⓐ Ⓑ Ⓒ Ⓓ Ⓔ
70. Ⓐ Ⓑ Ⓒ Ⓓ Ⓔ
71. Ⓐ Ⓑ Ⓒ Ⓓ Ⓔ
72. Ⓐ Ⓑ Ⓒ Ⓓ Ⓔ
73. Ⓐ Ⓑ Ⓒ Ⓓ Ⓔ
74. Ⓐ Ⓑ Ⓒ Ⓓ Ⓔ
75. Ⓐ Ⓑ Ⓒ Ⓓ Ⓔ
76. Ⓐ Ⓑ Ⓒ Ⓓ Ⓔ
77. Ⓐ Ⓑ Ⓒ Ⓓ Ⓔ
78. Ⓐ Ⓑ Ⓒ Ⓓ Ⓔ
79. Ⓐ Ⓑ Ⓒ Ⓓ Ⓔ
80. Ⓐ Ⓑ Ⓒ Ⓓ Ⓔ

Part C

81. Ⓐ Ⓑ Ⓒ Ⓓ Ⓔ
82. Ⓐ Ⓑ Ⓒ Ⓓ Ⓔ
83. Ⓐ Ⓑ Ⓒ Ⓓ Ⓔ
84. Ⓐ Ⓑ Ⓒ Ⓓ Ⓔ
85. Ⓐ Ⓑ Ⓒ Ⓓ Ⓔ
86. Ⓐ Ⓑ Ⓒ Ⓓ Ⓔ
87. Ⓐ Ⓑ Ⓒ Ⓓ Ⓔ
88. Ⓐ Ⓑ Ⓒ Ⓓ Ⓔ
89. Ⓐ Ⓑ Ⓒ Ⓓ Ⓔ
90. Ⓐ Ⓑ Ⓒ Ⓓ Ⓔ
91. Ⓐ Ⓑ Ⓒ Ⓓ Ⓔ
92. Ⓐ Ⓑ Ⓒ Ⓓ Ⓔ
93. Ⓐ Ⓑ Ⓒ Ⓓ Ⓔ
94. Ⓐ Ⓑ Ⓒ Ⓓ Ⓔ
95. Ⓐ Ⓑ Ⓒ Ⓓ Ⓔ
96. Ⓐ Ⓑ Ⓒ Ⓓ Ⓔ
97. Ⓐ Ⓑ Ⓒ Ⓓ Ⓔ
98. Ⓐ Ⓑ Ⓒ Ⓓ Ⓔ
99. Ⓐ Ⓑ Ⓒ Ⓓ Ⓔ
100. Ⓐ Ⓑ Ⓒ Ⓓ Ⓔ

BIOLOGY PRACTICE TEST 2

BIOLOGY-M

Time: 60 Minutes

PART A (Core Questions 1–60, for Both Biology-E and Biology-M)

Directions: Determine the BEST answer for each question. Then fill in the corresponding oval on the Answer Sheet.

Questions 1–4

(A) ribosome
(B) mitochondria
(C) chloroplast
(D) endoplasmic reticulum
(E) Golgi apparatus

1. Site where photosynthesis takes place

2. Extensive series of membranes throughout the cell

3. Powerhouse of the cell

4. Packaging and distribution system of a cell

Questions 5–7

(A) lipids
(B) proteins
(C) carbohydrates
(D) nucleic acids

5. long chains of amino acids

6. composed of only carbon, hydrogen, and oxygen

7. also known as fats

Questions 8–11

(A) commensalism
(B) mutualism
(C) parasitism
(D) symbiosis

8. Two or more organisms in a close, long-term association

9. One organism benefits, while the other suffers from the relationship.

10. Both organisms benefit from the relationship.

11. One organism benefits, and the other does not benefit nor is harmed from the relationship.

Questions 12–15

(A) organ
(B) cell
(C) tissue
(D) organ system

12. Group of cells with a similar function

13. Small unit of organization

14. Many different groups of cells working together

15. The highest level of organization that carries out important body functions

16. Protists are classified by their
(A) method of feeding
(B) method of moving
(C) method of reproducing
(D) size
(E) habitat

17. The part of the human brain that controls balance, posture, and coordination is the
(A) cerebrum
(B) cerebellum
(C) medulla oblongata
(D) thalamus
(E) hypothalamus

18. The characteristics that gymnosperms and angiosperms share are
(A) leaves, rhizomes, and spore
(B) leaves, stems, roots, and seeds
(C) flat leaves, trunks, and naked seeds
(D) lack of vascular tissue and small leaflets
(E) needle-like leaves, stems, roots, and fleshy fruits

GO ON TO THE NEXT PAGE

19. All of the following are characteristics of living things EXCEPT for the ability to

    (A) perform cellular respiration
    (B) regulate their internal environment
    (C) reproduce
    (D) change their external environment
    (E) pass traits to offspring

20. What happens to an enzyme during a biochemical reaction?

    (A) It becomes part of the product.
    (B) It is unchanged.
    (C) It is broken down into amino acids.
    (D) It reacts with fatty acids.
    (E) It becomes a polypeptide.

21. Which kingdom(s) contain(s) chemotrophs as members?

    I. monera
    II. plants
    III. protists

    (A) I only
    (B) II only
    (C) III only
    (D) I and III only
    (E) I, II, and III

22. Which bird has feet that are modified for grasping prey?

    (A)

    (B)

    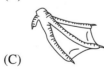
    (C)

    (D)

    (E)

23. In RNA molecules, uracil is complementary to

    (A) thymine
    (B) guanine
    (C) cytosine
    (D) adenine
    (E) uracil

24. Most mutations result from

    (A) certain chemicals
    (B) ionizing radiation
    (C) infrared radiation
    (D) ultraviolet radiation
    (E) random events

25. The first vertebrates to evolve a three-chambered heart that ensured all cells in the body received the proper amount of oxygen are the

    (A) fishes
    (B) reptiles
    (C) amphibians
    (D) birds
    (E) mammals

26. Which is the correct order of stages for an insect that undergoes complete metamorphosis?

    (A) egg→larva→adult
    (B) egg→nymph→adult
    (C) egg→nymph→larva→adult
    (D) egg→larva→pupa→adult
    (E) egg→nymph→pupa→adult

27. Which process brings carbon into the living portion of its cycle?

    (A) photosynthesis
    (B) cellular respiration
    (C) combustion
    (D) decomposition
    (E) fixation

28. Microspores of gymnosperms eventually develop into

    (A) seeds
    (B) cotyledons
    (C) female gametophytes
    (D) pollen grains
    (E) archegonia

GO ON TO THE NEXT PAGE

29. Bacteria are an important part of most food chains because they serve as

    (A) primary consumers
    (B) secondary consumers
    (C) scavengers
    (D) decomposers
    (E) producers

30. Ground tissue provides all of the following functions in plants EXCEPT:

    (A) protection of other tissues
    (B) supporting the plant
    (C) storage of water and carbohydrates
    (D) transport of materials
    (E) photosynthesis

31. Which of the following scientific names is written in the correct form to identify a species?

    (A) *meleagris gallopavo*
    (B) *Meleagris Gallopavo*
    (C) Meleagris Gallopavo
    (D) Meleagris gallopavo
    (E) *Meleagris gallopavo*

32. Which best describes the source of genes in an offspring resulting from sexual reproduction?

    (A) The offspring gets a full set of genes from the mother and from the father.
    (B) The offspring gets half the genes from the mother and half the genes from the father.
    (C) The offspring gets all of its genes from the father.
    (D) The offspring gets a random mixture of genes from the mother and father.
    (E) The offspring gets all of its genes from the mother.

33. Which best describes how the following ecosystem will change over time?

```
        ┌─────────────┐
        │ Secondary   │
        │ Consumers   │
        └─────────────┘

┌───────────────────────────────────────┐
│              Herbivores                │
└───────────────────────────────────────┘

     ┌───────────────────────────┐
     │         Producers         │
     └───────────────────────────┘
```

    (A) The herbivores will decline because there is not enough food to support them.
    (B) The herbivores will increase, and the secondary consumers will increase.
    (C) The populations of producers, herbivores, and carnivores will remain the same.
    (D) The secondary consumers will decline, and the producers will increase.
    (E) The producers will increase to support the herbivores.

34. If an organism has a haploid number of 28, how many chromosomes does it have?

    (A) 7
    (B) 14
    (C) 28
    (D) 42
    (E) 56

35. A pea plant with a genotype of YY produces yellow seeds. A pea plant with a genotype of yy produces green seeds. If the pea plants are crossed, which describes the possible genotypes of the offspring?

    (A) all are YY
    (B) all are Yy
    (C) all are yy
    (D) half YY and half yy
    (E) half YY and half Yy

GO ON TO THE NEXT PAGE ➤

36. Which set of offspring would result from a cross that was controlled by the law of independent assortment?

    (A) Half the offspring are tall with white flowers and half are short with white flowers.
    (B) All the offspring are tall or short and have white or purple flowers.
    (C) All the offspring are short and have purple flowers.
    (D) All the offspring are tall and have white flowers.
    (E) All the offspring are tall and have purple flowers.

37. Which of the following statements about evolution is accurate?

    (A) Populations evolve, while individuals do not evolve.
    (B) Populations do not evolve, while individuals evolve.
    (C) Populations evolve only when individuals evolve.
    (D) Populations evolve only when isolated individuals evolve.
    (E) Populations evolve only through mutations.

38. On the human skeletal system, which type of joint allows rotational movement?

    (A) slightly moveable joint
    (B) ball-and-socket joint·
    (C) pivot joint
    (D) plane joint
    (E) saddle joint

39. Which of the following best describes what will happen if cells are placed in a very salty solution?

    (A) The cells remain unchanged.
    (B) Water moves from inside of the cell to the outside.
    (C) Water moves from outside of the cell to the inside.
    (D) The cells burst.
    (E) The cells dissolve.

40. The color red and the color white are codominant in horses. What would you expect if you crossed a homozygous red horse with a homozygous white horse?

    (A) The offspring is white.
    (B) The offspring is red.
    (C) The offspring has both red and white hairs.
    (D) The offspring is brown.
    (E) The offspring is black.

41. The DNA of two closely related species would likely be

    (A) completely different
    (B) somewhat different
    (C) very different
    (D) very similar
    (E) identical

42. All of the following are mechanisms of reproductive isolation EXCEPT:

    (A) geographical isolation
    (B) ecological isolation
    (C) temporal isolation
    (D) reproductive failure
    (E) niche overlap

43. The process of photosynthesis produces many products. Which of these products are used for starting cellular respiration?

    (A) oxygen and ATP
    (B) water and carbon dioxide
    (C) NADP and hydrogen
    (D) glucose and oxygen
    (E) carbohydrates and NADP

Questions 44 and 45

This diagram is a cross section through the primary stem of a woody plant.

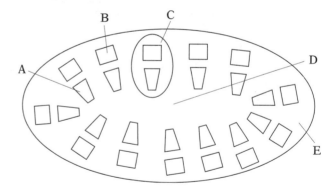

44. Which part of this stem is the vascular tissue?

    (A) A
    (B) B
    (C) C
    (D) D
    (E) E

GO ON TO THE NEXT PAGE

45. Which part of this stem will develop into the bark of the woody plant?

    (A) A
    (B) B
    (C) C
    (D) D
    (E) E

46. Sequences of DNA that are easily and naturally copied from one location in the genome and inserted elsewhere are called

    (A) duplication genes
    (B) jumping genes
    (C) crossing over genes
    (D) recessive genes
    (E) deletion genes.

47. A bat wing and a human's arm are examples of

    (A) homologous structures
    (B) analogous characters
    (C) vestigial structures
    (D) adaptive structures
    (E) derived traits

48. A type of mutation that occurs when part of a chromatid breaks off and attaches to its sister chromatid resulting in the duplication of a gene on a chromosome is called

    (A) deleting
    (B) inserting
    (C) separating
    (D) substituting
    (E) inverting

49. Cellular respiration in the absence of oxygen is called fermentation. What is the product of fermentation in animal cells?

    (A) Acetyl-CoA
    (B) alcohol
    (C) carbon dioxide
    (D) pyruvic acid
    (E) lactic acid

50. Natural selection is an evolutionary force that can affect an entire population. One species can evolve into two species when only the extreme forms of a trait are favored and intermediate forms are selected against. This is known as

    (A) artificial selection
    (B) directional selection
    (C) targeted selection
    (D) disruptive selection
    (E) stabilizing selection

51. An example of a density-dependent factor is

    (A) weather
    (B) climate
    (C) air
    (D) food
    (E) drought

52. Which best describes the advantage of crossing over during meiosis?

    (A) makes for healthy offspring
    (B) provides a source of genetic variation
    (C) creates a random mix of chromosomes
    (D) allows gametes to have half the number of chromosomes
    (E) increases the number of gametes

53. A segment of a DNA molecule that carries instructions for a specific trait is called a

    (A) gene
    (B) chromosome
    (C) nucleotide
    (D) codon
    (E) chromatid

54. Small, round bacteria that grow in a chain are called

    (A) streptococci
    (B) staphylobacilli
    (C) spirillium
    (D) diplococci
    (E) bacillus

55. According to Darwin, organisms best suited to their environment

    (A) are most likely to evolve
    (B) are more likely to survive and reproduce
    (C) are most likely to live the longest
    (D) are the fastest organisms
    (E) have the same chance of survival as other organisms

56. When lions and hyenas fight over a dead zebra, their interaction is called

    (A) mutualism
    (B) competition
    (C) commensalism
    (D) parasitism
    (E) predation

GO ON TO THE NEXT PAGE

57. Which is the best method for preserving the biodiversity of an ecosystem?

    (A) creating a preserve in an urban area
    (B) building botanical gardens based on the ecosystem
    (C) preserving a few very large areas on an ecosystem
    (D) preserving many small areas of an ecosystem
    (E) creating greenbelts along creeks and roadways in urban areas

58. Gregor Mendel found that the inheritance of one trait had no affect on the inheritance of different trait. He described this observation as the

    (A) law of dominance
    (B) law of universal inheritance
    (C) law of segregation
    (D) law of independent assortment
    (E) law of separate chromosomes

59. Meiosis is the process of making sex cells or gametes. In humans, how many mature egg cells result from meiosis?

    (A) 1
    (B) 2
    (C) 3
    (D) 4
    (E) 6

60. Which of the following are considered prokaryotes?

    (A) animals
    (B) plants
    (C) fungi
    (D) protists
    (E) bacteria

GO ON TO THE NEXT PAGE

(Note: On the real SAT Biology test, Part B, questions 61–80, is ONLY for students taking Biology-E. For Biology-M, continue with Part C, questions 81–100. On the Answer Sheet, be sure to start marking your answers on the line for Question 81.)

PART C (Biology-M Questions 81–100)

81. Genetic engineering allows scientists to insert DNA fragments from one organism into an organism of the same or different species. An organism that contains functional recombinant DNA is called

    (A) mutated
    (B) transmorphic
    (C) transgenic
    (D) recombinant
    (E) cloned

82. Hemoglobin is the molecule in red blood cells that carries oxygen. Hemoglobin has a metal in its structure that binds to oxygen. This metal is

    (A) zinc
    (B) phosphorus
    (C) magnesium
    (D) copper
    (E) iron

83. In the process of gel electrophoresis, negatively charged DNA molecules are placed in a gel. The gel has positive and negative electrodes. When a current is applied to the gel, which way will the DNA molecules move?

    (A) The DNA molecules will move toward both the positive and negative electrodes.
    (B) The DNA molecules move to a position equal distance from the electrodes.
    (C) The DNA molecules will move perpendicular to the electrodes.
    (D) The DNA molecules will move toward the positive electrode.
    (E) The DNA molecules will move toward the negative electrode.

84. The electron transport chain in photosynthesis produces

    (A) ADP
    (B) ATP
    (C) $NADP^+$
    (D) water
    (E) glucose

85. Antibiotics are not effective against viral infections because

    (A) viruses lack a cell wall that antibiotics can weaken
    (B) viruses have evolved a resistance to antibiotics
    (C) the viral envelope breaks down antibiotics
    (D) the viral envelope does not have a receptor for antibiotics
    (E) viruses only contain RNA which isn't affected by antibiotics

86. During translation, a codon pairs with a

    (A) complementary strand of messenger (mRNA) sequence
    (B) specific amino acid unit
    (C) complementary strand of ribosomal (rRNA) sequence
    (D) specific segment of the DNA sequence
    (E) complementary transfer RNA (tRNA) sequence

87. All of the following are types of asexual reproduction EXCEPT

    (A) fragmentation
    (B) fission
    (C) cloning
    (D) fertilization
    (E) budding

GO ON TO THE NEXT PAGE

Questions 88–90

Jill notices that in the morning at certain times of the year there are many dead fish at the surface of the pond. She is interested in finding what is causing the fish to die. She notes that this mainly occurs in the summer. The pond has many plants so she thinks this might be the cause. She measures the dissolved oxygen levels in the pond at several different times of the day. She records her data in the following table.

Time	Dissolved Oxygen (ppm)
0800	2.2
1100	5.7
1500	7.6
1800	9.8
2000	7.1

88. Which graph best represents Jill's dissolved oxygen data?

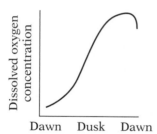

(A)

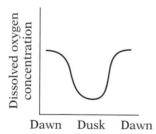

(B)

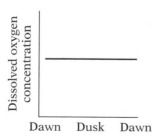

(C)

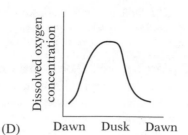

(D)

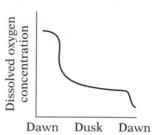

(E)

89. What is the most likely reason for the low dissolved oxygen during the night?

(A) The plants use up all the oxygen at night for the dark reaction.

(B) The fish and the plants both consume oxygen in order to carry out respiration at night.

(C) The plants die off at night and the decay uses oxygen.

(D) The fish become more active at night and use more oxygen.

(E) The temperature of the pond drops so less oxygen can stay dissolved.

90. Which of the following best explains why this takes place during the summer?

(A) The fish are more active in the summer and use more oxygen.

(B) The fish die off during the winter.

(C) The water warms up during the day but cools off quickly at night so the dissolved oxygen levels drop quickly.

(D) The water is warmer so it holds less dissolved oxygen and more sunlight means more photosynthesis.

(E) The plants die during the winter.

GO ON TO THE NEXT PAGE

Questions 91–94

A student wanted to perform an experiment similar to Gregor Mendel. She gathered a large number of seeds for pea plants and began growing them. Her first part of the experiment was to find homozygous plants. After finding homozygous plants for both dominant and recessive traits, she used these plants for more crosses.

91. Which best describes how she determined whether plants were homozygous or heterozygous?
    (A) She assumed that each plant showed either the dominant or recessive trait.
    (B) She crossed plants with similar traits. Then she grew the seeds to see what traits the offspring had.
    (C) She crossed plants with other plants with similar traits and different traits. She then grew the seeds from the crosses to look at the ratios.
    (D) She crossed plants with other plants that had similar traits. If the seeds were viable, both parent plants were homozygous.
    (E) She self-pollinated the plants, and then grew the seeds to see if the offspring had the same traits as the parent.

92. What is the phenotypic ratio of the cross between two heterozygous tall plants (Tt)?
    (A) 1 TT, 2 Tt, 1tt
    (B) 3TT, 1 tt
    (C) all tall
    (D) 3 tall, 1 short
    (E) 1 tall, 2 medium, 1 short

93. In this experiment, it was found that traits could disappear and reappear in a certain pattern from generation to generation. This occurs because of the
    (A) law of segregation
    (B) law of dominance
    (C) law of phenotypic ratios
    (D) law of independent assortment
    (E) law of reappearance

94. A plant with a genotype of TT produces tall plants. A plant with a genotype of tt produces dwarf plants. If the plants are crossed, what height are the offspring?
    (A) all tall
    (B) half tall, half dwarf
    (C) all dwarf
    (D) 75% tall, 25% dwarf
    (E) 25% tall, 75% dwarf

Questions 95–100

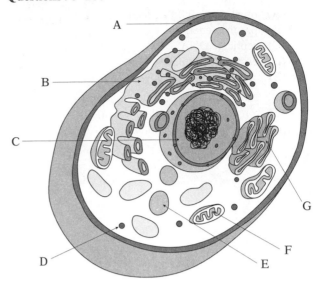

95. Which structure best identifies this cell as a eukaryote?
    (A) A
    (B) B
    (C) C
    (D) D
    (E) E

96. In eukaryotes, the chromosomes are found in structure
    (A) A
    (B) B
    (C) C
    (D) D
    (E) E

97. Structure G is the
    (A) ribosome
    (B) mitochondria
    (C) chloroplast
    (D) endoplasmic reticulum
    (E) Golgi apparatus

98. Structure E contains digestive enzymes used by the cell. This structure is a
    (A) ribosome
    (B) vacuole
    (C) nucleolus
    (D) lysosome
    (E) mitochondria

GO ON TO THE NEXT PAGE

99. Structure F in this cell functions to
    (A) breakdown food molecules
    (B) produce energy
    (C) replicate DNA
    (D) assemble proteins
    (E) remove waste products

100. This cell is most likely an animal cell because it
    (A) has a cell membrane
    (B) lacks a cell wall
    (C) has mitochondria
    (D) lacks a nucleus
    (E) has a plasmid

S T O P

IF YOU FINISH BEFORE TIME IS CALLED, YOU MAY CHECK YOUR WORK ON THIS TEST ONLY.
DO NOT TURN TO ANY OTHER TEST IN THIS BOOK.

ANSWER KEY

Part A

1. A	11. A	21. A	31. E	41. D	51. D
2. D	12. C	22. A	32. A	42. E	52. B
3. B	13. B	23. D	33. A	43. D	53. A
4. E	14. A	24. E	34. E	44. C	54. A
5. B	15. D	25. C	35. B	45. B	55. B
6. C	16. B	26. D	36. B	46. B	56. B
7. A	17. B	27. A	37. A	47. A	57. C
8. D	18. B	28. D	38. B	48. B	58. D
9. C	19. D	29. D	39. B	49. E	59. A
10. B	20. B	30. A	40. C	50. D	60. E

Part C

81. C	91. E
82. E	92. D
83. D	93. A
84. B	94. A
85. A	95. C
86. E	96. C
87. D	97. E
88. C	98. D
89. B	99. B
90. D	100. B

ANSWERS AND EXPLANATIONS

Part A

1. **A** Chloroplasts are the organelles that contain chlorophyll and other photopigments used during photosynthesis.

2. **D** The endoplasmic reticulum is an extensive network of membranes that are in the cytoplasm. The endoplasmic reticulum is a transportation network to move molecules around the cell.

3. **B** The mitochondria are the site where ATP is produced, providing energy for cellular functions.

4. **E** The Golgi apparatus consists of flattened sacs that collect and distribute molecules produced by cellular functions.

5. **B** Proteins are long chains of amino acids linked together. Proteins serve many different functions in cells.

6. **C** Carbohydrates are used by the body for energy. Carbohydrates range from such simple sugars as glucose to complex polysaccharides such as starch.

7. **A** Lipids are a diverse class of organic compounds that include olive oil, vegetable oil, and even beeswax. Lipids do not dissolve in water.

8. **D** Symbiosis is two or more organisms that live together in a long-term association. Symbiosis has different forms depending on whether organisms benefit from the relationship or not.

9. **C** Parasitism is a type of symbiotic relationship where one organism benefits at the expense of the other organism. Tapeworms are an example. Tapeworms get food from the digestive system of their host.

10. **B** Mutualism is a type of symbiotic relationship where both organisms benefit from the relationship. Some ants and aphids are an example. The ants care for and protect the aphids. In return, the aphids provide the ants with a sweet liquid.

11. **A** Commensalism is a type of symbiotic relationship where one organism benefits, while the other neither benefits nor is harmed. Barnacles growing on a whale is an example of commensalism. The barnacles are carried across the oceans, while the whale is not affected.

12. **C** A tissue is a group of cells that are serve a similar function.

13. **B** A cell is the smallest unit of life capable of carrying out all functions.

14. **A** Organs are composed of a group of tissues. The tissues collectively work to perform different functions within the organ.

15. **D** Organ systems are groups of organs that work together to make up a system.

16. **B** Protists are classified by the way they move or method of locomotion. The methods are pseudopods, cilia, flagella, or nonmotile.

17. **B** The cerebellum is a small region at the back of the brain. The cerebellum controls smooth, coordinated movements, helps maintain muscle tone, posture, and balance.

18. **B** Gymnosperms and angiosperms are advanced plants. They have many similarities including their leaves, stems, roots, and reproduction with seeds.

19. **D** Most organisms do not have the ability to change their external environments.

20. **B** An enzyme acts as a catalyst for the biochemical reaction. Catalysts lower the activation energy required for a reaction but they are not changed in any way during the reaction.

21. **A** Chemotrophs are able to breakdown inorganic chemical molecules to obtain energy. This has only been found in the Kingdom Monera. Some members of this kingdom are able to break down hydrogen sulfide to obtain energy. Chemotrophs do not depend on sunlight for energy.

22. **A** Birds such a hawks and falcons have strong feet with long talons for grasping prey.

23. **D** In RNA, uracil replaces thymine and is complimentary to adenine.

24. **E** There are many causes of mutations in cells. The most common are the random processes that take place in cells.

25. **C** Amphibians were the first to have a three-chambered heart. This advancement allowed the circulatory system to include lungs.

26. **D** Complete metamorphosis occurs when an organism has a different body shape at different stages of its life cycle. For example, in butterflies, the larva state, called a caterpillar, is very different from the adult butterfly.

27. **A** Photosynthesis is the fixing of atmospheric carbon into molecules that can be used by organisms.

28. **D** Microspores result from meiosis that takes place in the pollen cone of a gymnosperm. The microspores develop into pollen grains, or more correctly, microgametophytes.

29. **D** Bacteria break down or decompose organic matter. Because of their actions, they are considered decomposers in an ecosystem.

30. **A** Ground tissues in plants serve many different functions. Ground tissues do not protect other tissues.

31. **E** The proper way of writing a species name is with the genus capitalized and the specific epithet lower case. The entire name is written in italics or, in older texts, underlined.

32. **A** When gametes are formed in parents; each gamete has half the genetic material of the parent. When the gametes unite, the resulting offspring will receive half the genetic material of each parent.

33. **A** An ecosystem only has so much energy available to pass up to each level of the trophic pyramid. Only about 10% of the energy is actually passed up to the next higher level. When one level of the pyramid is larger than the level below it, there must be a shift to reduce the energy demands.

34. **E** The haploid number of chromosomes is the number of pairs found in an organism. In this case a haploid number of 28 translates to 28 pairs or 56 chromosomes.

35. **B** In this type of cross, the offspring get one allele from each parent. The result is that all offspring will by Yy.

36. **B** The law of independent assortment only applies to traits that are on different chromosomes. The common traits in pea plants all happen to be on different chromosomes so this law applies.

37. **A** Evolution affects populations, not individuals. Individuals can have traits that give them an advantage, and they may pass the traits on, but they do not evolve.

38. **B** The ball-and-socket joint is the type of joint found in the shoulder. The joint allows rotational movement.

39. **B** When a cell is placed in a very salty solution, water moves from the area of higher concentration, inside the cell, to the area of lower concentration, outside the cell.

40. **C** Codominant traits are always both expressed. In horses, the offspring has both red and white hairs.

41. **D** Species that are very closely related have very similar DNA with only minor differences. They are related through a common ancestor.

42. **E** Niche overlap is a form of competition instead of reproductive isolation.

43. **D** Glucose and oxygen are products of photosynthesis. They enter the cellular respiration pathway where they are turned into energy.

44. **C** The vascular tissue in plants moves water up the plant from the roots and moves sugars from the leave, throughout the plant, and down to the roots.

45. **B** The phloem becomes the bark in woody plants.

46. **B** Jumping genes are genes that easily jump or move from one location on a chromosome to another. Jumping genes are what cause some corn to have multicolored kernels.

47. **A** Homologous structures are structures that are similar in two different species. In this case, the bones in the human arm are similar to those in a bat. The finger bones in a human are the thin bones in the bat wing.

48. **B** Inserting is a type of mutation. As the name implies, a repeat of a sequence is inserted into a different chromosome.

49. **E** In animal cells, when fermentation takes place, lactic acid is formed.

50. **D** Disruptive selection takes place when some environmental pressure works to make the extremes in variation the most successful organisms. These organisms are those that reproduce and pass their traits to their offspring.

51. **D** Density-dependent factors are those that are affected by the size and density of a population.

52. **B** Crossing over is a process where genetic material is exchanged by two different chromosomes during meiosis. This is similar to shuffling a deck of cards and increasing variation in the genes.

53. **A** Genes are segments on DNA that on a chromosome that have a specific function.

54. **A** Streptococci means long chain of small round bacteria. *Strepto* refers to a chain and *cocci* refers to round.

55. **B** The concept of the survival of the fittest states that those best able to survive are the ones most likely to reproduce and pass on their genes.

56. **B** The ecological concept of competition is when two species try for a limited resource. The species best suited to exploit the resource gets the larger share of the resource.

57. **C** Preserves usually work better as larger areas. The same amount that is fragmented does not have the same healthy exchange of genetic material as one large area.

58. **D** Mendel explained that different traits are inherited independently if they are found on different chromosomes.

59. **A** During meiosis, three of the resulting cells are called polar bodies and are discarded. Only one of the cells becomes an egg.

60. **E** Bacteria are prokaryotes because they lack a true nucleus and membrane bound organelles.

Part C

81. **C** Organisms that have DNA from a different organism are transgenic organisms. They are also called genetically modified organisms.

82. **E** Iron is the metal in the hemoglobin biomolecule.

83. **D** DNA has a slightly negative charge so it moves toward the positive electrode because opposite charges attract.

84. **B** The energy gained through the electron transport chain is used to attach a phosphate onto an ADP molecule to make ATP.

85. **A** Viruses are not living organisms and do not have a cell wall. Antibiotics work by attacking and weakening the cell wall in bacteria but they are ineffective against viruses.

86. **E** Transfer RNA delivers specific amino acids to the ribosomes for protein synthesis.

87. **D** Fertilization is a type of sexual reproduction where two haploid gametes fuse to form a diploid zygote.

88. **C** The dissolved oxygen steadily increases during the day and then falls off after sunset.

89. **B** Oxygen levels drop during the night because respiration, carried out by plants and animals including fish, consumes oxygen. During the day, photosynthesis produces excess oxygen, but at night it is used up by the respiration of plants.

90. **D** The warm water and abundant light cause plants to grow and photosynthesize. During the summer, the conditions are well suited to photosynthesis.

91. **E** Using self-pollinating the plants is the surest way to find which alleles a plant has because the parents of the cross will both have the same alleles for each trait.

92. **D** All the plants that have a dominant allele will be tall. In this particular type of cross, the tall plants have a 3:1 ratio over the short plants.

93. **A** The law of segregation explains why traits skip the F_1 generation only to reappear in the F_2 generation. This occurs because heterozygous plants express the dominant phenotype even though they carry a recessive trait.

94. **A** The cross will produce all tall plants because the genotype is Tt.

95. **C** All eukaryotes have a nucleus surrounded by a nuclear membrane.

96. **C** Chromosomes are always found in the nucleus of eukaryotes.

97. **E** The Golgi apparatus consists of flattened sacs that collect and distribute molecules produced by cellular functions.

98. **D** Lysosomes store digestive enzymes that are used for various tasks such as breaking down old organelles.

99. **B** The mitochondria is the powerhouse of the cell. They produce energy by bonding phosphates to ADP in order to form ATP.

100. **B** Plant cells have a rigid cell wall. Animal cells lack a cell wall and only have a cell membrane surrounding them.

▨ SCORE SHEET

Number of questions correct: _____

Less: 0.25 × number of questions wrong: _____

(Remember that omitted questions are not counted as wrong.)

Raw score: _____

Raw Score	Scaled Score	Raw Score	Scaled Score	Raw Score	Scaled Score	Raw Score	Scaled Score	Raw Score	Scaled Score
80	800	57	690	34	520	11	380	−12	250
79	800	56	680	33	520	10	370	−13	240
78	800	55	670	32	510	9	370	−14	240
77	800	54	670	31	510	8	360	−15	230
76	800	53	660	30	500	7	350	−16	230
75	800	52	650	29	500	6	350	−17	230
74	800	51	650	28	490	5	340	−18	220
73	790	50	640	27	490	4	330	−19	220
72	790	49	630	26	480	3	330	−20	220
71	780	48	620	25	480	2	320		
70	780	47	620	24	470	1	320		
69	770	46	610	23	470	0	310		
68	760	45	600	22	460	−1	310		
67	760	44	600	21	450	−2	300		
66	750	43	590	20	440	−3	300		
65	740	42	580	19	440	−4	290		
64	740	41	580	18	430	−5	290		
63	730	40	570	17	420	−6	280		
62	720	39	560	16	420	−7	270		
61	710	38	560	15	410	−8	270		
60	710	37	550	14	400	−9	260		
59	700	36	540	13	400	−10	260		
58	700	35	530	12	390	−11	250		

Note: This is only a sample scoring scale. Scoring scales differ from exam to exam.

THE SAT PHYSICS TEST

All About The SAT Physics Test

What Is the Format of the SAT Physics Test?

The SAT Physics test is a 1-hour exam consisting of 75 multiple-choice questions. According to the College Board, the test measures the following knowledge and skills:

- Ability to recall and understand important physics concepts and to apply those concepts to solve physics problems
- Knowledge of simple algebraic, trigonometric, and graphical relationships and principles of ratio and proportion, and ability to apply those principles to solve physics problems
- Knowledge of the metric system of units

According to the College Board, the questions on the test are distributed by topic in approximately the following percentages:

SAT Physics Questions by Topic

Topic(s)	Approximate Percentage of Test
Mechanics	34–38
Electricity and magnetism	22–26
Waves	15–19
Heat, kinetic theory, and thermodynamics	8–12
Modern physics	8–12
Miscellaneous (measurement, math skills, laboratory skills, history of physics, etc.)	2–4

The College Board advises that because high school physics courses can vary, you are likely to encounter questions on topics that are unfamiliar.

About one-quarter to one-third of the test questions will require you to recall and understand concepts and information. About one-half the questions will require you to apply a single physics concept. The remaining one-quarter of the questions will require you to recall and relate more that one physics concept.

What School Background Do I Need for the SAT Physics Test?

The College Board recommends that you have the following before taking the SAT Physics test:

- a 1-year college prep course in physics
- algebra and trigonometry courses
- physics laboratory experience

How Is the SAT Physics Test Scored?

On the SAT Physics test, your "raw score" is calculated as follows: you receive one point for each question you answer correctly, but you lose one-quarter of a point for each question you answer incorrectly. You do not gain or lose any points for questions that you do not answer at all. Your raw score is then converted into a scaled score by a statistical method that takes into account how well you did compared to others who took the same test. Scaled scores range from 200 to 800 points. Your scaled score will be reported to you, your high school, and to the colleges and universities you designate to receive it.

Scoring scales differ slightly from one version of the test to the next. The scoring scale provided after the Physics test in this book is only a sample that will show you your approximate scaled score.

▰ SUCCEEDING ON THE SAT PHYSICS TEST

Knowing the types of questions on the test and the rules for answering them will save you time and help you avoid errors on the day of the test. This section will explain specific test-taking strategies and provide examples to show you how to use them effectively.

STRATEGY: Become familiar with the types of questions you will encounter.

1. Part A of the SAT Physics test consists of classification questions.

Each set of classification questions includes five lettered choices that are used to answer all questions in the set. The choices may consist of words, equations, graphs, sentences, diagrams, or data that are generally related to the same topic. Each question in the set must be evaluated individually. Any choice may be the correct answer to more than one question in the set.

Example:

Directions: Each set of lettered choices refers to the numbered questions of statements immediately following it. Select the one lettered choice that best answers each question or best fits each statement, and then fill in the corresponding oval on the answer sheet. <u>A choice may be used once, more than once, or not at all in each set</u>.

Questions 9–10 relate to the following.

(A) period
(B) wavelength

(C) kinetic energy
(D) frequency
(E) amplitude

9. Which quantity is maximized when the displacement of a mass on a spring from its equilibrium position is zero?
10. Which quantity is measured in hertz?

To answer question 9, you need to know about the motion of a pendulum. The displacement of the mass from the equilibrium position is zero when the mass is at the bottom, or center, point of the swing. At this point, the speed of the mass is greatest and the kinetic energy is maximized. The correct answer is C.

To answer question 10, you must be familiar with this unit of measure. You may recall that 1 hertz (Hz) equals 1 cycle per second. The quantity that measures cycles per second is frequency, so the correct answer is D. Another way to approach this question is to identify the units of each quantity listed. For example, period measures an amount of time, so its unit may be seconds. Wavelength and amplitude measure distance, so their units may be centimeters or meters. Kinetic energy is measured in joules or other units of energy.

2. Part B of the SAT Physics test consists of five-choice completion questions.

Each five-choice completion question can be written as either an incomplete statement or as a question. You are to select the choice that best completes the statement or answers the question.

Example:

Directions: Each of the questions or incomplete statements below is followed by five suggested answers or completions. Select the one that is best in each case and then fill in the corresponding oval on the answer sheet.

$$^{15}_{7}N + ^{1}_{1}H \rightarrow ^{12}_{6}C + X$$

54. A physicist is studying the nuclear reaction represented above. Particle X is which of the following?

   (A) $^{1}_{1}H$
   (B) $^{2}_{1}H$
   (C) $^{-1}_{0}e$
   (D) $^{1}_{0}H$
   (E) $^{4}_{2}He$

Question 54 tests your understanding of nuclear reactions and equations. First, you must recognize the information provided by the symbols. In the symbol $^{A}_{Z}X$, X is the chemical symbol for the element, A is the atomic mass number, and Z is the atomic number. Second, you must recall that matter is conserved in all natural processes. Therefore, the equation must balance to represent this fact. So $15 + 1 = 12 + A$, which yields $A = 4$. To solve for Z, use $7 + 1 = 6 + Z$. Therefore, $Z = 2$. The missing particle is, therefore, described by $^{4}_{2}He$, which is choice E.

3. *Some five-choice completion questions may have more than one correct answer or solution.*

A special type of five-choice completion question contains several statements labeled by Roman numerals. One or more of these statements may correctly answer the question. The statements are followed by five lettered choices, with each choice consisting of some combination of the Roman numerals that label the statements. You must select from among the five lettered choices the one that gives the combination of statements that best answer the question. Questions of this type are spread throughout the more standard five-choice completion questions.

Example:

29. In which of the following examples is the net force acting on the object equal to zero?
     I.   A soccer ball kicked across a field rolls to a stop.
     II.   A person pushes on an elevator door to hold it open.
     III. A child rides on a carousel horse at a carnival.
     (A) I only
     (B) II only
     (C) III only
     (D) I and II only
     (E) I and III only

To answer this question you must recall that according to Newton's first law, a net force of zero must be acting on an object if the object maintains a constant velocity. Though no one is kicking the soccer ball any longer, a force must be acting on it because it is slowing to a stop. The force acting on the ball is friction. I is incorrect.

The person pushing on the elevator door is exerting a force on the door. However, neither the person nor the door is moving. Because the door is not moving, its velocity is constant at zero. This means that the net force acting on the door must also be zero. II is, therefore, correct.

The child riding on the carousel is moving at a constant speed. However, because the direction is constantly changing, the velocity is also changing. This means that the net force acting on the child is not zero. III is incorrect.

The net force is zero only in statement II, so choice B is the correct answer.

4. *Some five-choice completion questions relate to common material.*

In some cases, a set of five-choice completion questions relate to common material that precedes the set. That material may be a description of a situation, a diagram, or a graph. Although the questions are related, you do not have to know the answer to one question in a set to answer a subsequent question correctly. Each question in the set can be answered directly from the material given for the entire set of questions.

Example:

Questions 36–37: A forklift is lifting an object with a mass of 500 kilograms at a constant velocity to a height of 20 meters over a period of 5 seconds. The forklift then holds the object in place for 30 seconds.

36.   How much power does the forklift expend in lifting the crate?

      (A) 25 W
      (B) 1.3×10^2 W
      (C) 5.0×10^3 W
      (D) 1.0×10^4 W
      (E) 2.0×10^4 W

37.   How much power does the forklift expend to hold the object in place?

      (A) 0 W
      (B) 3.3×10^2 W
      (C) 1.5×10^3 W
      (D) 6.0×10^3 W
      (E) 2.0×10^4 W

To answer question 36, you need to know that power is a measure of work divided by time. In addition, work is a measure of force multiplied by displacement. The crate is lifted with constant velocity. Therefore, the net force acting on it is zero. The force exerted by the forklift must be equal and opposite to the weight of the crate. The weight of the crate is $(500 \text{ kg})(10 \text{ m/s}^2) = 5.0 \times 10^3$ N. The power is then determined by the following:

$$P = \frac{W}{t} = \frac{5.0 \times 10^3 \text{N}(20\text{m})}{5\text{s}} = 2.0 \times 10^4 \text{W}$$

The correct answer is E.

   To answer question 37, you must recognize that even though a force is exerted to hold the object in place, no work is done on the object if it does not move any distance. If no work is done, no power is expended. Therefore the correct answer is A.

STRATEGY: Know what the question is asking.

While this tip may sound obvious, it is crucial that you read the question carefully to identify the information you are seeking. If you jump to the answer choices before completing the question, you may miss a relationship that you need to identify. It is equally important to go back and check the question after completing a calculation. For some questions, you may stop too soon or take the calculation too far. Take time to check that you have answered the question being asked.

Example:

63.   No water molecules are destroyed when a sample of liquid water evaporates in water vapor. Instead, the disorder of the water molecules increases during the process. Which of the following principles of physics best explains this increase in entropy?

      (A) First law of thermodynamics
      (B) Second law of thermodynamics
      (C) Ideal gas law
      (D) Law of conservation of mass
      (E) Archimedes' principle

The first sentence of question 63 describes conservation of mass. If you read quickly, you may jump to the answer choices and select D. However, if you complete the question, you will discover that the question asks about the entropy of the system. You need to recall that entropy is a measure of a system's disorder. As the water evaporates, the entropy of the molecules increases. According to the second law of thermodynamics, the entropy of the universe increases through all natural processes. Choice B is actually the correct answer.

STRATEGY: Make sure you read all relevant information.

There may be additional information that is required to answer the question. Look for descriptive material that may be provided along with a graph or diagram

Example:

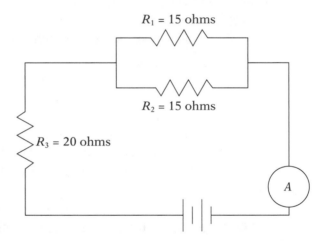

The diagram above shows an electric circuit containing three resistors. The ammeter, A, reads 6.0 amperes.

49.   What is the voltage across R_3?

    (A) 6 V
    (B) 20 V
    (C) 50 V
    (D) 100 V
    (E) 120 V

To answer this question, you need to recognize that the voltage is equal to the current measured at the ammeter multiplied by the resistance of R_3. The resistance is indicated in the diagram, but the current is not. This information is provided in the descriptive text below the circuit diagram. The current is 6 A so $V = (6)(20) = 120\ V$, which is choice E. If you speed to the question without reading the descriptive text, you will not be able to answer the question correctly. Worse yet, you might be tempted to try to answer the question with only the information provided on the circuit diagram. If so, you will be unable to derive the correct answer.

STRATEGY: Know your formulas.

You will not be allowed to bring a calculator to the test. You are also not allowed to bring in any sheets of useful information. Roughly three-quarters of the test requires you to use formulas. If you do not know basic formulas such as how force relates to mass and acceleration, $F = ma$, you are sure to lose easy points.

Many formulas will come easily as you study physics. Others may be difficult for you to remember. If this is the case, look them over just before the test. You may wish to jot those formulas down on the top or back of the question booklet before you begin the test so you don't forget them.

Keep in mind that merely memorizing formulas will not be enough. You also need to understand them. Only rarely do questions ask you to simply plug numbers into a formula. More often you need to rearrange or relate various formulas to solve a problem.

Example:

58. A source emits a sound with a frequency of 8.6×10^5 hertz. If the speed of the sound is 2.8×10^3 meters per second, what is the wavelength of the sound?

   (A) 3.3×10^{-3} m
   (B) 3.1×10^{-2} m
   (C) 3.1×10^2 m
   (D) 5.8×10^3 m
   (E) 2.4×10^8 m

This question requires you to relate wavelength, speed, and frequency. You need to recall the formula

$$\lambda = \frac{v}{f}.$$

Once you recall the formula, you can substitute the given information and solve the problem.

$$\lambda = \frac{2.8 \times 10^3}{8.6 \times 10^5} = 3.3 \times 10^{-3} m,$$

which is choice A.

Example:

What happens to the kinetic energy of an object when its speed is doubled?

   (A) It is quartered.
   (B) It is halved.
   (C) It is unchanged.
   (D) It is doubled.
   (E) It is quadrupled.

You must recall that the formula for kinetic energy is

$$KE = \frac{1}{2}mv^2.$$

Knowing the formula, you can recognize that kinetic energy is directly proportional to the square of velocity. Therefore, if the velocity is doubled, the kinetic energy must be quadrupled, choice E.

STRATEGY: Pay attention to units of measure.

The test questions predominantly use the metric system. Familiarize yourself with the units of measurement for common physical quantities. Include units in your calculations. If the outcome of a calculation does not yield the proper unit, you may have used information incorrectly.

Example:

46.   If electricity costs $0.10 per kilowatt-hour, how much does it cost for electricity to operate a 1,800-watt hair dry for 30 minutes?

   (A) $0.009
   (B) $0.09
   (C) $0.90
   (D) $9.00
   (E) $90.00

For this question, the energy provided is found by $E = Pt$. Before you begin, convert the power from watts to kilowatts by dividing by 1,000. Also convert minutes to hours. Then use the equation $E = (1.8 \text{ kw})(0.5 \text{ hr}) = 0.9 \text{ kwhr}$. The cost is found by multiplying the number of kilowatt hours by the price per kilowatt-hour. The total cost, $C = (0.9 \text{ kwhr})(\$0.10/\text{kwhr}) = \$0.09$. The correct choice is B.

   If you had ignored units in your calculations, you might have forgotten to convert power to kilowatts. In addition, if you are unsure about how to determine the cost, using proper units will let you know if you have calculated properly. If, for example, you incorrectly divided instead of multiplied, the unit kwhr would not have cancelled out, and you would not have been left with a number of dollars.

STRATEGY: Estimate when possible.

Once you know what a question is asking, it is helpful to get a rough idea of what the answer should look like through estimation. Of course this strategy is helpful only for questions involving calculations. Estimation is a good way to avoid wrong answers when you are making an educated guess.

Example:

71.   A steel girder is 10 meters long at 30°C. By what length will the girder expand if the temperature rises to 40°C? (The coefficient of linear expansion for steel is $12 \times 10^{-6}/°C$.)

   (A) 1.2×10^{-6} m
   (B) 1.2×10^{-4} m
   (C) 1.2×10^{-3} m
   (D) 1.2×10^{3} m
   (E) 1.2×10^{4} m

Before you begin calculating the solution to this problem, think about the situation described. The change in length is proportional to the temperature change and the original length of the girder. Steel expands only about 12×10^{-6} for each degree the temperature rises. That is 0.000012 m for each degree. The question describes an increase of 10°C and an original length of 10 m. Therefore, the total expansion will be a small amount—less than 1 m. You can immediately eliminate choices D and E.

The expansion ΔL can be found by $\Delta L = \alpha L_o \Delta T$ where α is the coefficient of linear expansion, L_o is the original length, and ΔT is the change in temperature. In this situation, $\Delta L = (12 \times 10^{-6}/°C)(10 \text{ m})(10°C) = 1.2 \times 10^{-3} \text{ m}$. You can solve by moving the decimal to two places. Choice C is the correct answer.

Because you are not allowed to use a calculator on the test, the questions are designed to require only simple calculations. If you find yourself getting involved in lengthy calculations, you are probably making a mistake. Stop and reread the question again to see if you have overlooked any important information.

STRATEGY: Identify all labels on graphs and diagrams.

About one quarter of the questions on the test will involve graphs or diagrams. When you encounter such a question, take a moment to review the information provided. For example, identify the quantities plotted on the axes of a graph. Then read the related question and answer choices. Knowing what you are dealing with before you read the question can help you identify the correct answer.

Example:

Question 28 relates to the graph of a moving particle shown below.

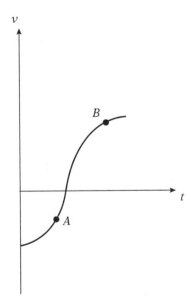

28.   When compared with the particle at point A, how do the acceleration
       and displacement of the particle differ at point B?

<u>Acceleration</u>   <u>Displacement</u>
(A) less   greater
(B) less   same
(C) less   less
(D) greater   less
(E) greater   greater

To answer this question, you must evaluate the graph. At first glance you
might conclude that the graph plots distance against time. However, this hasty
assumption would prevent you from determining the answer. The graph plots
the velocity of the particle against time. Therefore, the acceleration of the particle is determined by the slope of the graph. The slope is steeper at point A than
at point B so acceleration is less.

   The displacement is determined by the area between the curve and the
t-axis. Between points A and B, a larger area is above the *t*-axis than below it.
Overall, the displacement is positive between these two points. Choice A is
the correct answer.

STRATEGY: Write down any information you need to answer a question.

1. Draw diagrams when not provided.

Do not hesitate to draw or write on your question booklet. If a diagram is not
provided with a question, draw a rough sketch of the information described.
Field lines, velocity vectors, and graphs are just some of the topics that will
become much easier to work with once you have drawn them.

Example:

53.   Vector **A** has a magnitude of 3 toward the left and vector **B** has a mag-
       nitude of 5 toward the right. What is the value of 3**A** − **B**?

       (A) 4 in the leftward direction
       (B) 6 in the leftward direction
       (C) 9 in the leftward direction
       (D) 6 in the rightward direction
       (E) 12 in the rightward direction

This question will become faster and easier to answer if you draw a quick
diagram.

Draw the original vectors:

Then draw the change in vectors:

Now find the difference: $9 - 5 = 4$. The vector pointing toward the left is greater so the resultant vector is also in the leftward direction. The correct choice is **A**.

2. *Write down formulas or equations you may need.*

You may find it helpful to write down formulas related to a topic. If, for example, you are dealing with a question about energy, write down such equations as

$$E = \frac{1}{2}mv^2 \text{ and } E = mgh.$$

If you are unsure of the answer, it may be helpful to plug in the given values. Some rearranging and rewriting may lead you in the right direction.

Example:

29.   A raindrop falls from a cloud. What is the approximate speed of the raindrop, in centimeters per second, after 4 seconds?

    (A) 30 cm/s
    (B) 300 cm/s
    (C) 1,000 cm/s
    (D) 3,000 cm/s
    (E) 4,000 cm/s

This question asks for the speed of the raindrop. Only a change in time is provided. If you are unsure about how to solve the problem, jot down some formulas involving speed, such as

$$v = \frac{\Delta d}{\Delta t} \text{ and } a = \frac{\Delta v}{\Delta t}.$$

You do not know the change in distance d, but you do know the acceleration a. It is the acceleration due to gravity, which is 980 cm/s². You can then rearrange the acceleration equation to solve for v, $v = at = (980 \text{ cm/s}^2)(4 \text{ s}) = 3{,}920$ cm/s. The correct choice is **E**.

STRATEGY: Pay attention to words in questions such as EXCEPT, NOT, ALWAYS, and NEVER.

Some questions include qualifying words in capital letters. These words change they way you need to approach the question.

Example:

All of the following statements correctly describe beta particles EXCEPT that they

    (A) interact less readily with material than alpha particles do
    (B) are identical to the nucleus of a helium atom
    (C) are generally released from neutron-rich atoms
    (D) are indistinguishable from orbital electrons
    (E) can be represented by the symbol $_{-1}^{0}e$

If you rush through the question, you may be tempted to select the first true answer you read. Choice A is a true statement, so you may stop reading and fill in your answer. However, you would be incorrect. The question asks you to find the one statement that is untrue. Once you know this, you can quickly recall that a beta particle forms when a neutron in the nucleus changes to a proton and emits an electron. The electron is called a beta particle to indicate that it is not an orbital electron, even though they are identical in every other way. Knowing this helps you to quickly eliminate choices D and E. If you also recall that decay occurs in atoms that have more neutrons relative to protons, you can also eliminate choice C. The nucleus of a helium atom contains two protons. This choice cannot be true, so choice B is the correct answer.

PHYSICS PRACTICE TEST

Treat this practice test as the actual test, and complete it in one 60-minute sitting. Use the following answer sheet to fill in your multiple-choice answers. Once you have completed the practice test:

1. Check your answers using the Answer Key.
2. Review the Answers and Explanations.
3. Complete the Score Sheet to see how well you did.

ANSWER SHEET

Tear out this answer sheet and use it to complete the practice test. Determine the BEST answer for each question. Then fill in the appropriate oval.

1. Ⓐ Ⓑ Ⓒ Ⓓ Ⓔ	21. Ⓐ Ⓑ Ⓒ Ⓓ Ⓔ	41. Ⓐ Ⓑ Ⓒ Ⓓ Ⓔ	61. Ⓐ Ⓑ Ⓒ Ⓓ Ⓔ
2. Ⓐ Ⓑ Ⓒ Ⓓ Ⓔ	22. Ⓐ Ⓑ Ⓒ Ⓓ Ⓔ	42. Ⓐ Ⓑ Ⓒ Ⓓ Ⓔ	62. Ⓐ Ⓑ Ⓒ Ⓓ Ⓔ
3. Ⓐ Ⓑ Ⓒ Ⓓ Ⓔ	23. Ⓐ Ⓑ Ⓒ Ⓓ Ⓔ	43. Ⓐ Ⓑ Ⓒ Ⓓ Ⓔ	63. Ⓐ Ⓑ Ⓒ Ⓓ Ⓔ
4. Ⓐ Ⓑ Ⓒ Ⓓ Ⓔ	24. Ⓐ Ⓑ Ⓒ Ⓓ Ⓔ	44. Ⓐ Ⓑ Ⓒ Ⓓ Ⓔ	64. Ⓐ Ⓑ Ⓒ Ⓓ Ⓔ
5. Ⓐ Ⓑ Ⓒ Ⓓ Ⓔ	25. Ⓐ Ⓑ Ⓒ Ⓓ Ⓔ	45. Ⓐ Ⓑ Ⓒ Ⓓ Ⓔ	65. Ⓐ Ⓑ Ⓒ Ⓓ Ⓔ
6. Ⓐ Ⓑ Ⓒ Ⓓ Ⓔ	26. Ⓐ Ⓑ Ⓒ Ⓓ Ⓔ	46. Ⓐ Ⓑ Ⓒ Ⓓ Ⓔ	66. Ⓐ Ⓑ Ⓒ Ⓓ Ⓔ
7. Ⓐ Ⓑ Ⓒ Ⓓ Ⓔ	27. Ⓐ Ⓑ Ⓒ Ⓓ Ⓔ	47. Ⓐ Ⓑ Ⓒ Ⓓ Ⓔ	67. Ⓐ Ⓑ Ⓒ Ⓓ Ⓔ
8. Ⓐ Ⓑ Ⓒ Ⓓ Ⓔ	28. Ⓐ Ⓑ Ⓒ Ⓓ Ⓔ	48. Ⓐ Ⓑ Ⓒ Ⓓ Ⓔ	68. Ⓐ Ⓑ Ⓒ Ⓓ Ⓔ
9. Ⓐ Ⓑ Ⓒ Ⓓ Ⓔ	29. Ⓐ Ⓑ Ⓒ Ⓓ Ⓔ	49. Ⓐ Ⓑ Ⓒ Ⓓ Ⓔ	69. Ⓐ Ⓑ Ⓒ Ⓓ Ⓔ
10. Ⓐ Ⓑ Ⓒ Ⓓ Ⓔ	30. Ⓐ Ⓑ Ⓒ Ⓓ Ⓔ	50. Ⓐ Ⓑ Ⓒ Ⓓ Ⓔ	70. Ⓐ Ⓑ Ⓒ Ⓓ Ⓔ
11. Ⓐ Ⓑ Ⓒ Ⓓ Ⓔ	31. Ⓐ Ⓑ Ⓒ Ⓓ Ⓔ	51. Ⓐ Ⓑ Ⓒ Ⓓ Ⓔ	71. Ⓐ Ⓑ Ⓒ Ⓓ Ⓔ
12. Ⓐ Ⓑ Ⓒ Ⓓ Ⓔ	32. Ⓐ Ⓑ Ⓒ Ⓓ Ⓔ	52. Ⓐ Ⓑ Ⓒ Ⓓ Ⓔ	72. Ⓐ Ⓑ Ⓒ Ⓓ Ⓔ
13. Ⓐ Ⓑ Ⓒ Ⓓ Ⓔ	33. Ⓐ Ⓑ Ⓒ Ⓓ Ⓔ	53. Ⓐ Ⓑ Ⓒ Ⓓ Ⓔ	73. Ⓐ Ⓑ Ⓒ Ⓓ Ⓔ
14. Ⓐ Ⓑ Ⓒ Ⓓ Ⓔ	34. Ⓐ Ⓑ Ⓒ Ⓓ Ⓔ	54. Ⓐ Ⓑ Ⓒ Ⓓ Ⓔ	74. Ⓐ Ⓑ Ⓒ Ⓓ Ⓔ
15. Ⓐ Ⓑ Ⓒ Ⓓ Ⓔ	35. Ⓐ Ⓑ Ⓒ Ⓓ Ⓔ	55. Ⓐ Ⓑ Ⓒ Ⓓ Ⓔ	75. Ⓐ Ⓑ Ⓒ Ⓓ Ⓔ
16. Ⓐ Ⓑ Ⓒ Ⓓ Ⓔ	36. Ⓐ Ⓑ Ⓒ Ⓓ Ⓔ	56. Ⓐ Ⓑ Ⓒ Ⓓ Ⓔ	
17. Ⓐ Ⓑ Ⓒ Ⓓ Ⓔ	37. Ⓐ Ⓑ Ⓒ Ⓓ Ⓔ	57. Ⓐ Ⓑ Ⓒ Ⓓ Ⓔ	
18. Ⓐ Ⓑ Ⓒ Ⓓ Ⓔ	38. Ⓐ Ⓑ Ⓒ Ⓓ Ⓔ	58. Ⓐ Ⓑ Ⓒ Ⓓ Ⓔ	
19. Ⓐ Ⓑ Ⓒ Ⓓ Ⓔ	39. Ⓐ Ⓑ Ⓒ Ⓓ Ⓔ	59. Ⓐ Ⓑ Ⓒ Ⓓ Ⓔ	
20. Ⓐ Ⓑ Ⓒ Ⓓ Ⓔ	40. Ⓐ Ⓑ Ⓒ Ⓓ Ⓔ	60. Ⓐ Ⓑ Ⓒ Ⓓ Ⓔ	

PHYSICS PRACTICE TEST

Part A

Directions: Each set of lettered choices refers to the numbered questions of statements immediately following it. Select the one lettered choice that best answers each question or best fits each statement, and then fill in the corresponding oval on the answer sheet. <u>A choice may be used once, more than once, or not at all in each set.</u>

Questions 1–5 relate to the following physical principles or topics.

  (A) pressure
  (B) energy
  (C) work
  (D) force
  (E) acceleration

Select the physical principle most closely related to each of the following formulas.

1. $m\left(\dfrac{v^2 - v_o^2}{2d}\right)d$

2. $\dfrac{4\pi^2 r}{T^2}$

3. $k\dfrac{q_1 q_2}{r}$

4. $\dfrac{nRT}{V}$

5. $\dfrac{m}{t}(v - v_o)$

Questions 6–10

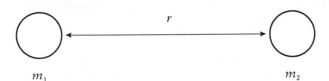

  (A) quartered
  (B) halved
  (C) unchanged
  (D) doubled
  (E) quadrupled

Two masses, m_1 and m_2, are separated by a distance r, as shown above. Select the effect on the gravitational force of each of the following changes in mass or distance.

6. m_1 is doubled
7. m_1 and m_2 are doubled
8. r is doubled
9. m_1 is doubled, m_2 is halved
10. m_2 is halved

Questions 11–14 relate to the following directions.

  (A) out
  (B) right
  (C) up
  (D) down
  (E) zero

Find the direction of the force on a positive charge for each diagram where v is the velocity of the charge, and B is the direction of the magnetic field.

  ⊗ means the vector points inward, into the page.

  ⊙ means the vector points outward, toward the viewer.

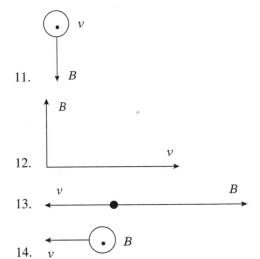

GO ON TO THE NEXT PAGE

Part B

Directions: Each of the questions or incomplete statements below is followed by five suggested answers or completions. Select the one that is best in each case and then fill in the corresponding oval on the answer sheet.

$${}^{27}_{13}\text{Al} + {}^{4}_{2}\text{He} \rightarrow {}^{30}_{15}\text{P} + X + \text{energy}$$

15. A physicist is studying the decay reaction represented above. Particle *X* is which of the following?

    (A) ${}^{1}_{1}\text{H}$
    (B) ${}^{2}_{1}\text{H}$
    (C) ${}^{-1}_{0}e$
    (D) ${}^{1}_{0}\text{H}$
    (E) ${}^{4}_{2}\text{He}$

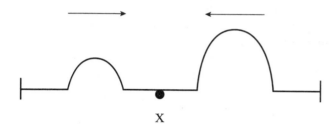

16. The figure above shows two pulses on a string approaching each other. Which of the following diagrams best represents the appearance of the string shortly after the pulses reach point X?

(A)

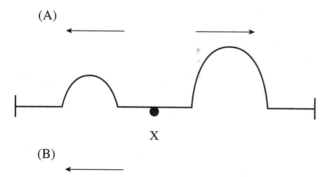

(B)

(C)

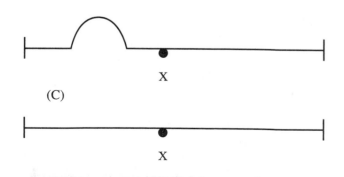

(D)

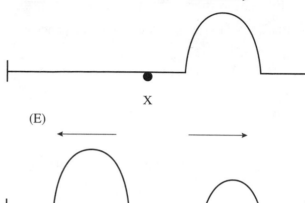

(E)

17. How much energy is removed when 10.0 grams of water is cooled from steam at 120°C to liquid to liquid at 100°C? (Heat of vaporization for water = 2.26 × 10^6 joules per kilogram; specific heat of steam = 2.01 × 10^3 joules per kilogram • °C)

    (A) 4.2×10^3 J
    (B) 2.3×10^4 J
    (C) 8.4×10^4 J
    (D) 6.1×10^4 J
    (E) 10.7×10^{10} J

18. Which of these phenomena support(s) the particle model of light?

    I.   polarization
    II.   photoelectricity
    III. Compton effect

    (A) I only
    (B) II only
    (C) III only
    (D) I and II only
    (E) II and III only

GO ON TO THE NEXT PAGE

19. You are in a boat that is traveling due west at 45 kilometers per hour relative to a current that is moving 45 kilometers due south relative to the ground. Your motion relative to the ground is

(A) due west
(B) southwest
(C) due south
(D) northeast
(E) due east

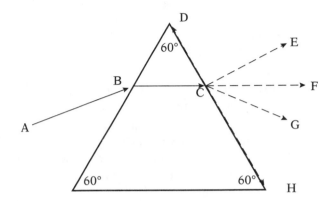

20. In the diagram above, a ray of light strikes a glass prism so that the ray travels through the prism parallel to its base. Which ray correctly shows how the light exists the prism?

(A) $\vec{CD}$
(B) $\vec{CE}$
(C) $\vec{CF}$
(D) $\vec{CG}$
(E) $\vec{CH}$

Questions 21–22

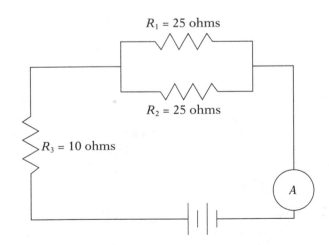

The diagram above shows an electric circuit containing three resistors. The ammeter, A, reads 5.0 amperes.

21. What is the voltage across R_3?

(A) 5 V
(B) 10 V
(C) 15 V
(D) 20 V
(E) 50 V

22. What is the current in R_1?

(A) 1.0 A
(B) 2.0 A
(C) 2.5 A
(D) 5.0 A
(E) 10 A

23. An object starts from rest and accelerates at 6.0 meters per second squared. How far will it travel during the first 4.0 seconds?

(A) 10 m
(B) 12 m
(C) 24 m
(D) 36 m
(E) 48 m

24. A heat engine extracts 40 joules of energy from a hot reservoir, does work, then exhausts 30 joules of energy into a cold reservoir. What is the efficiency of the heat engine?

(A) 10%
(B) 25%
(C) 33%
(D) 67%
(E) 75%

25. The magnitude of the charge on an ion depends on which of the following?

 I.   number of electrons
 II. number of protons
 III. number of neutrons

(A) I only
(B) III only
(C) I and II only
(D) II and III only
(E) I, II, and III

GO ON TO THE NEXT PAGE

26. If the mass of a body is doubled while the net force acting on the body remains the same, the acceleration of the body is
    (A) halved
    (B) doubled
    (C) unchanged
    (D) quartered
    (E) quadrupled

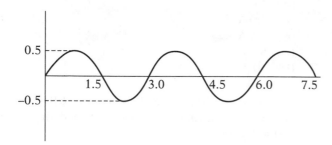

27. What is the wavelength of the wave?
    (A) 0.5 m
    (B) 1.0 m
    (C) 1.5 m
    (D) 2.0 m
    (E) 3.0 m

28. What is the amplitude of the wave?
    (A) 0.5 m
    (B) 1.0 m
    (C) 1.5 m
    (D) 3.0 m
    (E) It varies between −0.5 m and +0.5 m.

29. If electricity costs $0.10 per kilowatt-hour, how much does it cost for electricity to operate a 1,200-watt television for 2 hours?
    (A) $0.024
    (B) $0.24
    (C) $2.40
    (D) $24.00
    (E) $240.00

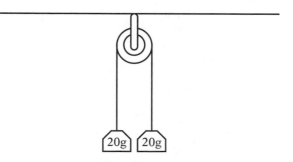

30. Two freely hanging weights, each having a mass of 20 grams, are connected by a light thread which passes over a fixed pulley. The mass of the pulley and frictional losses are negligible. If a 10-gram weight is now added to one of the weights, its downward acceleration in centimeters per second will be approximately
    (A) $59\dfrac{cm}{s^2}$
    (B) $98\dfrac{cm}{s^2}$
    (C) $196\dfrac{cm}{s^2}$
    (D) $200\dfrac{cm}{s^2}$
    (E) $250\dfrac{cm}{s^2}$

31. All of the following statements concerning the kinetic theory of gases are true EXCEPT:
    (A) The molecules of a gas obey the laws of classical mechanics and interact only when they collide.
    (B) The speeds of molecules in a gas are distributed such that the speeds of most molecules are close to the average.
    (C) The average translational kinetic energy of molecules in a gas is directly proportional to the absolute temperature.
    (D) All molecules of a gas have the same speed at the same specified temperature.
    (E) The separation between molecules is, on average, equal to the diameter of each molecule.

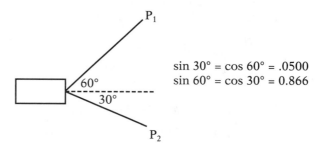

32. Two people are pulling a sled on a sheet of ice. The sled moves in the direction shown by the broken line in the diagram above. If the ice offers no resistance and if Person 1 is pulling with a force of 10 newtons, with what force must Person 2 be pulling?
    (A) 0 N
    (B) 17 N
    (C) 35 N
    (D) 45 N
    (E) 60 N

GO ON TO THE NEXT PAGE

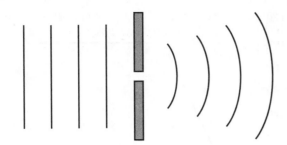

33. In the diagram above, a series of straight wave fronts passes through a small opening in an obstacle. What phenomenon is responsible for this observation?

(A) refraction
(B) photoelectricity
(C) diffraction
(D) dispersion
(E) polarization

34. The resistance of a conductor decreases when it experiences an increase in

    I.   length
    II.   temperature
    III. cross-sectional area

(A) I only
(B) II only
(C) I and II only
(D) II and III only
(E) III only

35. A cylinder has a cross-sectional area of $0.010 \ m^2$. How much work can be done by a gas in the cylinder if the gas exerts a constant pressure of 5.0×10^5 Pa on the piston, moving it a distance of 0.020 m?

(A) 1.0×10^{-2} J
(B) 10.0 J
(C) 1.0×10^2 J
(D) 1.0×10^3 J
(E) 1.0×10^5 J

36. When an ice cube melts, the water molecules move from an ordered crystalline arrangement to a fairly disordered liquid. Which of the following principles of physics best explains this change?

(A) First law of thermodynamics
(B) Second law of thermodynamics
(C) Ideal gas law
(D) Conservation of momentum
(E) Archimedes' principle

37. The half-life of iodine–131 is approximately 8 days. About what fraction of a sample of iodine–131 will remain after 32 days?

(A) $\dfrac{1}{2}$

(B) $\dfrac{1}{4}$

(C) $\dfrac{1}{8}$

(D) $\dfrac{1}{16}$

(E) $\dfrac{1}{32}$

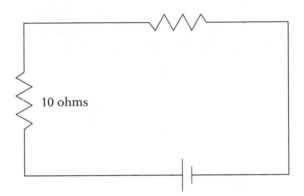

38. In the circuit shown above, the current I_1 in the 10-ohm resistor is related to the current I_2 in the 30-ohm resister by which of the following equations?

(A) $I_1 = \dfrac{1}{3} I_2$

(B) $I_1 = \dfrac{2}{3} I_2$

(C) $I_1 = 3 I_2$

(D) $I_1 = I_2$

(E) $I_1 = \dfrac{3}{2} I_2$

GO ON TO THE NEXT PAGE

39. An airplane is dropping supplies to firefighters battling a blaze in a forest. In addition to knowing the acceleration due to gravity, what factor(s) must the pilot consider in order to determine where to drop the supplies so that they will land beside the firefighters? (Ignore air resistance.)

    I.   the speed of the airplane
    II.   the mass of the supplies
    III. the height of the airplane

    (A) I only
    (B) II only
    (C) III only
    (D) I and III only
    (E) I, II, and III

40. In a darkened room, a beam of monochromatic light is shined on an opaque barrier with a single narrow slit. The light that goes through the slit falls on a screen held parallel to the barrier. Which of the following best describes the intensity of the observed pattern plotted against the distance along the screen?

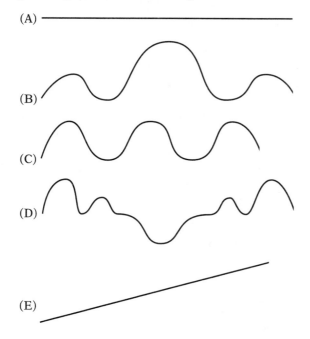

(A)

(B)

(C)

(D)

(E)

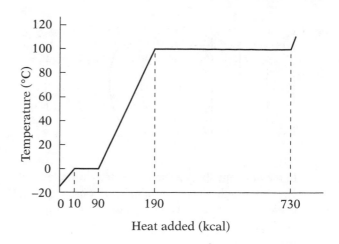

41. The diagram above relates the temperature of a sample of water to the amount of heat added or removed. Based on the diagram, which of these statements is true?

    (A) As pressure rises, a greater amount of latent heat is required for a phase change than at lower pressures.
    (B) The latent heat of fusion for water is greater than its latent heat of vaporization.
    (C) The mass of a sample of water decreases as heat is removed from it during periods of constant temperature.
    (D) An increase in heat energy results in a comparable increase in temperature for a sample of water.
    (E) A greater amount of latent heat is released when steam changes to liquid water than when liquid water changes to ice.

GO ON TO THE NEXT PAGE

42. A string of length ℓ that is fastened at both ends is plucked in the middle. At the fundamental frequency, the wavelength of the wave in the string is equal to

    (A) $\dfrac{1}{3}\ell$

    (B) $\dfrac{1}{2}\ell$

    (C) ℓ
    (D) 2ℓ
    (E) 4ℓ

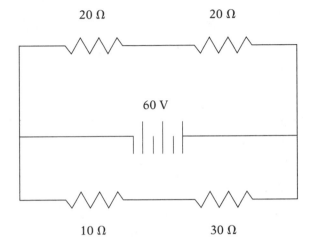

Velocity (m/s) vs. Time t (s)

43. The acceleration of a test vehicle is plotted on the graph above. Based on the graph, what is the acceleration of the vehicle?

    (A) $0.2 \ \text{m/s}^2$
    (B) $5 \ \text{m/s}^2$
    (C) $6 \ \text{m/s}^2$
    (D) $15 \ \text{m/s}^2$
    (E) $36 \ \text{m/s}^2$

44. A bird drops an acorn from a great height. What is the approximate speed of the acorn, in centimeters per second, after 3 seconds?

    (A) 30 cm/s
    (B) 300 cm/s
    (C) 1,000 cm/s
    (D) 3,000 cm/s
    (E) 4,000 cm/s

45. A statue is placed in front of a concave lens. What must always be true about the image formed by the lens?

	Type	Size	Orientation
(A)	virtual	smaller	erect
(B)	virtual	smaller	inverted
(C)	virtual	larger	inverted
(D)	real	smaller	erect
(E)	real	larger	inverted

46. What is the current through the 30-ohm resistor in the circuit shown above?

    (A) 0.5 A
    (B) 1 A
    (C) 1.5 A
    (D) 2.0 A
    (E) 3.0 A

GO ON TO THE NEXT PAGE

47. The graph below plots the velocity, *v*, of an object over a given period of time, *t*.

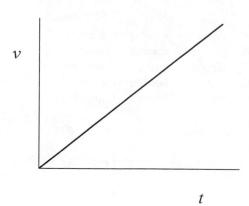

Which graph represents the acceleration, *a*, of the object during the same period of time?

(A)

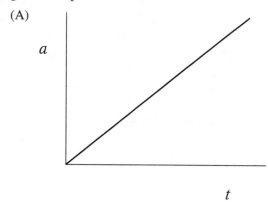

(B)

(C)

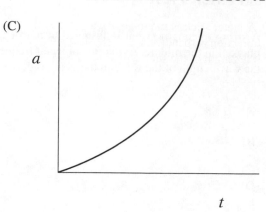

(D)

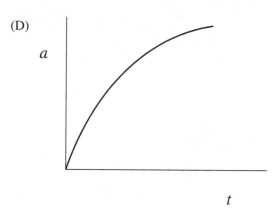

(E)

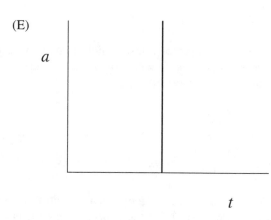

48. The nucleus of an atom emits a beta particle. As a result, the atomic number

(A) decreases by 2
(B) decreases by 1
(C) remains unchanged
(D) increases by 1
(E) increases by 2

GO ON TO THE NEXT PAGE ➤

49. A meter stick is moving with a velocity of 0.90c in a direction perpendicular to an observer. To the observer, the length of the stick will be

   (A) zero
   (B) less than 1 m
   (C) 1 m
   (D) more than 1 m
   (E) unpredictable

50. The siren of a moving fire truck emits a sound at a constant frequency. When compared with the sound produced by the siren, which statement is true?

   (A) An observer in front of the truck will perceive a sound with a higher frequency.
   (B) An observer behind of the truck will perceive a sound with a higher frequency.
   (C) An observer along side the truck will not be able to hear the siren.
   (D) An observer in the truck will perceive a sound with a lower frequency.
   (E) An observer in front of the truck will perceive a sound with a lower frequency.

51. A ball at the end of a string is swinging in a horizontal circle. Upon which factor(s) does the acceleration of the ball depend?

   I.   speed
   II. radius
   III. mass

   (A) I only
   (B) II only
   (C) I and II only
   (D) II and III only
   (E) I, II, and III

52. A pendulum makes 21 vibrations in 30 seconds. What is its frequency?

   (A) 0.7 Hz
   (B) 1.4 Hz
   (C) 3.0 Hz
   (D) 21 Hz
   (E) 41 Hz

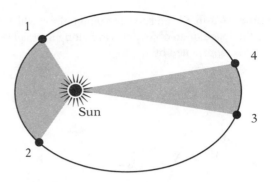

53. The diagram above represents the motion of a planet around the sun as described by Kepler's second law. Based on the diagram, which statement about planetary motion is true?

   (A) Planets closer to the sun travel at a greater velocity than planets farther from the sun.
   (B) Planets move fastest in the part of their orbits where they are closest to the sun.
   (C) All planets have the same period of revolution regardless of their mean distance from the sun.
   (D) Some planets follow circular paths whereas others follow elliptical paths.
   (E) The period of a planet is determined by its mass, with more massive planets having shorter periods.

54. When the distance between two point charges is doubled, the force between them is

   (A) quadrupled
   (B) doubled
   (C) unchanged
   (D) halved
   (E) quartered

55. A transformer changes 12 volts to 24,000 volts. There are 10,000 turns in the secondary coil. How many turns are in the primary? (Assume 100% efficiency.)

   (A) 2
   (B) 4
   (C) 5
   (D) 10
   (E) 12

GO ON TO THE NEXT PAGE

Questions 56 and 57 refer to the graph below, which represents the speed of an object moving along a straight line. The time is represented by *t*.

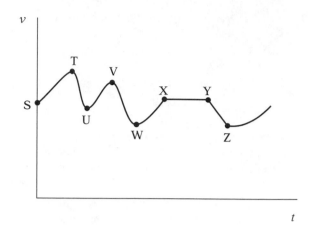

56. During which interval is the object's speed increasing?

    (A) ST
    (B) TU
    (C) UV
    (D) XY
    (E) YZ

57. During which interval is the acceleration constant, but not zero?

    (A) ST
    (B) TU
    (C) UV
    (D) XY
    (E) YZ

58. A source emits a sound with a frequency of 2.6×10^4 hertz. If the speed of the sound is 3.9×10^3 meters per second, what is the wavelength of the sound?

    (A) 6.8×10^{-4} m
    (B) 3.0×10^{-2} m
    (C) 1.5×10^{-1} m
    (D) 1.5×10^2 m
    (E) 2.2×10^4 m

59. A negatively charged particle is moving to the right in a plane perpendicular to a uniform magnetic field. If the magnetic field is into the page, which drawing represents the path of the particle?

    (A)

    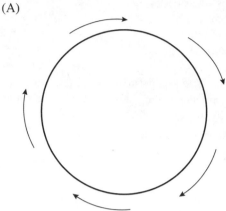

    (B)

    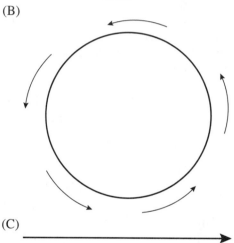

    (C)

    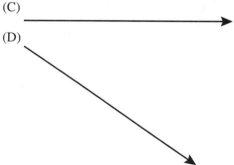

    (D)

    (E)

    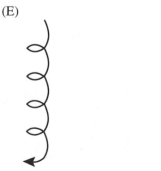

GO ON TO THE NEXT PAGE

60. A compact disc is spinning in a CD player. The disc has a small, blue marking at one point on its edge. Which of the following is true of the acceleration of the marking while the disc is in motion?

    (A) It is zero at all times.
    (B) Its magnitude and direction are constant.
    (C) It gradually decreases over time.
    (D) It is constant in magnitude, but not direction.
    (E) It causes the CD to spin faster.

61. The energy conversion that takes place in a generator is

    (A) electrical to mechanical
    (B) mechanical to electrical
    (C) electrical to heat
    (D) chemical to electrical
    (E) heat to electrical

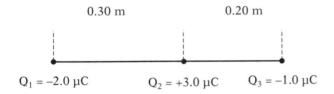

$Q_1 = -2.0 \ \mu C$ $Q_2 = +3.0 \ \mu C$ $Q_3 = -1.0 \ \mu C$

62. What is the magnitude and direction of the net electric force on particle Q_3 in the figure above due to the other two charges?

    (A) The net force is zero.
    (B) 0.603 N to the right
    (C) 0.603 N to the left
    (D) 1.35 N to the left
    (E) 0.072 N to the right

Questions 63 and 64 relate to the graph below, which shows the net force **F** in newtons exerted on a 2-kilogram block as a function of time t in seconds. Assume the block is at rest at $t = 0$ and that **F** acts in a fixed direction.

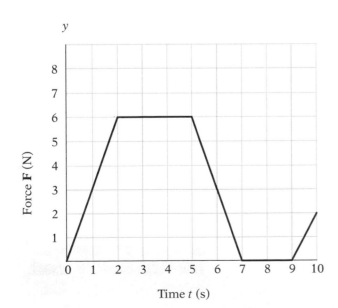

Time t (s)

63. Which statement is true about the motion of the block during the time interval from 2 to 5 seconds?

    (A) The block is not moving.
    (B) The acceleration is constant.
    (C) The mass of the block is changing.
    (D) The speed of the block is constant.
    (E) The force on the block is decreasing.

64. The acceleration of the block at $t = 3$ seconds is

    (A) $\frac{1}{3} \text{m/s}^2$
    (B) 2 m/s^2
    (C) 3 m/s^2
    (D) 6 m/s^2
    (E) 18 m/s^2

65. An object is placed 30 centimeters in front of a converging lens of focal length 10 centimeters. If the image is 15 centimeters from the lens, what is the magnification?

    (A) 0.5
    (B) 1.0
    (C) 1.5
    (D) 2.0
    (E) 5.0

66. A steel girder is 10 meters long at 20°C. By what length will the girder expand if the temperature rises to 50°C? (The coefficient of linear expansion for steel is $12 \times 10^{-6}/°C$.)

    (A) 1.2×10^{-6} m
    (B) 1.2×10^{-4} m
    (C) 3.6×10^{-3} m
    (D) 3.6×10^{3} m
    (E) 3.6×10^{4} m

67. In 1923, Louis de Broglie made a major contribution to the study of physics. De Broglie proposed the idea that

    (A) the basic laws of physics are the same in all inertial reference frames
    (B) light consists of fluctuating electric and magnetic fields
    (C) electrons circle the nucleus of an atom in stationary states
    (D) light can be described in terms of discrete units called photons
    (E) material particles have wavelengths related to their momentum

GO ON TO THE NEXT PAGE

68. A football player kicks a football from ground level at an angle of 45° above the horizontal. The player then kicks the ball again with the same speed, but at an angle of 30° above the horizontal. Which diagram correctly shows the trajectories of the balls?

(A)

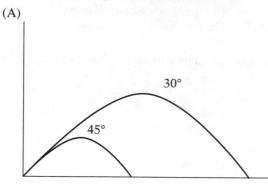

Range (m)

(B)

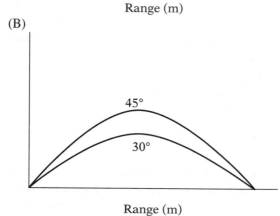

Range (m)

(C)

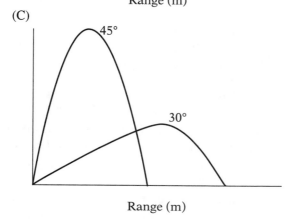

Range (m)

(D)

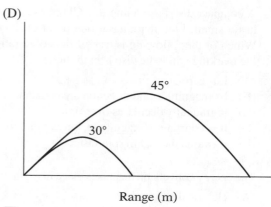

Range (m)

(E)

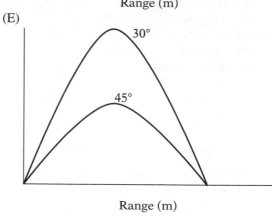

Range (m)

69. Which of these measurements has three significant digits?

I.   39.2 g
II. 0.05103 cm
III. 1860 L

(A) I only
(B) II only
(C) I and II only
(D) II and III only
(E) I and III only

GO ON TO THE NEXT PAGE

Questions 70 and 71

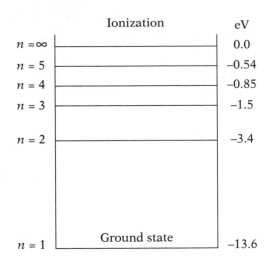

Some of the energy levels of hydrogen are shown in the diagram above.

70. Which expression can be used to find the frequency, in hertz, of the light emitted during the transition from $n = 2$ to $n = 1$?

(A) 1.6×10^{-19} J/eV(13.6 eV $- 3.4$ eV)

(B) $\dfrac{1.63 \times 10^{-18} \text{ J}}{6.6 \times 10^{-34} \text{ J} \cdot \text{s}}$

(C) $\dfrac{1.63 \times 10^{-18} \text{ J}}{3.00 \times 10^{8} \text{ m/s}}$

(D) 3.00×10^{8} m/s(13.6 eV $- 3.4$ eV)

(E) $\dfrac{1.22 \times 10^{-7} \text{ m}}{1.63 \times 10^{-18} \text{ J}}$

71. Which of these transitions will result in the emission of a photon with the least amount of energy?

(A) $n = 4$ to $n = 3$
(B) $n = 3$ to $n = 2$
(C) $n = 5$ to $n = 3$
(D) $n = 4$ to $n = 2$
(E) $n = 3$ to $n = 1$

72. A flower is placed into a vase of water. To an observer on the side of the vase, the stem appears to be bent where it enters the water. What phenomenon causes the stem to appear bent?

(A) polarization
(B) photoelectricity
(C) diffraction
(D) reflection
(E) refraction

73. Two forces are being exerted on an object in the horizontal direction. If these are the only forces acting on the object, which pair of forces can result in a net force of 18 newtons?

(A) 18 N, 18 N
(B) 12 N, 8 N
(C) 13 N, 31 N
(D) 22 N, 18 N
(E) 15 N, 13 N

74. A bob suspended by a string of length, l, forms a simple pendulum as it swings back and forth. If the angle displacement is small, upon what does the period of the pendulum depend?

    I.   mass of the bob
    II.   length of the string
    III. amplitude

(A) I only
(B) II only
(C) III only
(D) I and III only
(E) I and II only

75. In 1911, Ernest Rutherford and his associates conducted an experiment in which they bombarded a thin, gold foil with fast-moving alpha particles. What important observation did they make during this experiment?

(A) Most particles experienced wide-angle deflections.
(B) A small number of particles were redirected toward their source.
(C) All particles passed directly through the foil without deflection.
(D) Some particles were absorbed by the foil and disappeared.
(E) Many particles experienced a change in charge as they hit the foil.

S T O P

IF YOU FINISH BEFORE TIME IS CALLED, YOU MAY CHECK YOUR WORK ON THIS TEST ONLY.
DO NOT TURN TO ANY OTHER TEST IN THIS BOOK.

ANSWER KEY

1. C	26. A	51. C
2. E	27. E	52. A
3. B	28. A	53. B
4. A	29. B	54. E
5. D	30. C	55. C
6. D	31. E	56. C
7. E	32. B	57. E
8. A	33. C	58. C
9. C	34. E	59. A
10. B	35. C	60. D
11. B	36. B	61. B
12. A	37. D	62. C
13. E	38. D	63. B
14. C	39. D	64. C
15. D	40. B	65. A
16. E	41. E	66. C
17. B	42. D	67. E
18. E	43. B	68. D
19. B	44. D	69. E
20. D	45. A	70. B
21. E	46. C	71. A
22. B	47. B	72. E
23. E	48. D	73. C
24. B	49. C	74. B
25. C	50. A	75. B

ANSWERS AND EXPLANATIONS

1. **C** This formula can be rewritten as

   $$\frac{1}{2}mv^2 - \frac{1}{2}mv_o^2$$

   which is the change in kinetic energy. The net work done on an object is equal to its change in kinetic energy.

2. **E** This formula can be used to determine the acceleration of an object in circular motion.

3. **B** This formula describes the potential energy of charge q_2 in the presence of charge q_1 a distance r away.

4. **A** This rearrangement of the ideal gas law solves for pressure (P), which is equal to the product of the number of moles (n), the constant of proportionality (R), and temperature (T) divided by volume (V).

5. **D** This formula can be rewritten as either

   $$\frac{\Delta p}{t}$$

   where p represents momentum and t represents time or

   $$\frac{m}{t}(at) = ma,$$

   where m represents mass, a represents acceleration, and t represents time. According to Newton's second law of motion, both of these are equal to force.

6. **D** The gravitational force between the masses is determined by

   $$F = G\frac{m_1m_2}{r^2}.$$

   The force is directly proportional to mass so if one mass is doubled, the force is also doubled.

7. **E** The gravitational force between the masses is determined by

   $$F = G\frac{m_1m_2}{r^2}.$$

   The force is directly proportional to mass so if both masses are doubled, the force is multiplied by four.

8. **A** The gravitational force between the masses is determined by

   $$F = G\frac{m_1m_2}{r^2}.$$

   The force is inversely proportional to the square of the distance between the mass so if the distance is doubled, the force is divided by 1/4.

9. **C** The gravitational force between the masses is determined by

   $$F = G\frac{m_1m_2}{r^2}.$$

   The force is directly proportional to mass so if one mass is doubled but the other is halved, there is no overall change in the force.

10. **B** The gravitational force between the masses is determined by

    $$F = G\frac{m_1m_2}{r^2}.$$

    The force is directly proportional to mass so if one mass is divided by two, the force is also divided by two.

11. **B** The direction of the force is perpendicular to the magnetic field and to the velocity of the particle. Using the right-hand rule, orient your hand so that your outstretched fingers point in the direction of motion of the particle. When you bend your fingers, they should point downward in the direction of the magnetic field. Your thumb will point to the right, in the direction of the force.

12. **A** The direction of the force is perpendicular to the magnetic field and to the velocity of the particle. Using the right-hand rule, orient your hand so that your palm is flat with your fingers pointing toward the right. Your thumb will then point out of the page, in the direction of the force.

13. **E** The force is zero if the particle moves parallel to the field lines.

14. **C** The direction of the force is perpendicular to the magnetic field and to the velocity of the particle. Using the right-hand rule, orient your

hand so that your palm faces you and your fingers point toward the left. Your thumb will point upward, in the direction of the force.

15. **D** Consider X as $^a_b X$. *Particle X* must balance the equation. Solve $27 + 4 = 30 + a$, so $a = 1$. Solve $13 + 2 = 15 + b$, so $b = 0$. Thus, *X* must be $^1_0 H$.

16. **E** Two pulses traveling in opposite directions on the same string pass each other without being changed.

17. **B** First, find the heat loss to cool the steam from 120°C to 100°C: Steam cooling from 120°C to 100°C: $Q_1 = 10.0 \times 10^{-3}$ kg$(2.01 \times 10^3$ J/kg °C$)$ $(20°C) = 402$ J

Steam condensing to water: $Q_2 = 10.0 \times 10^{-3}$ kg $(2.26 \times 10^6$ J/kg$) = 2.26 \times 10^4$ J

The total energy loss is 402 J + 2.26×10^4 J = 2.3×10^4 J.

18. **E** Photoelectricity is produced when electrons are emitted from a surface as a result of photons of incident light. According to the Compton effect, scattered light has a slightly shorter wavelength than incident light because of a loss of energy that occurs as photons collide with electrons in the material. Polarization occurs when light waves in specific directions are blocked from passing through a material.

19. **B** Both vectors have the same magnitude. The westward vector combines with the southward vector to form a vector in the southwest direction.

20. **D** As the light exists the prism, it is bent at the same angle at which it entered the prism.

21. **E** The voltage is equal to the current measured at the ammeter multiplied by the resistance of R_3. $V = (5)(10) = 50$ V.

22. **B** The current is equal to the voltage of the resistor divided by the current passing through it. $I = 50 \div 25 = 2$.

23. **E** The distance $d = 1/2 \ at^2$ where a is the accelerationand t is the time. For this object, $d = 1/2(6.0$ m/s²$)(4.0$ s$)^2 = 48$ m.

24. **B** The efficiency is found by $1 - \dfrac{30 \text{ J}}{40 \text{ J}} \times 100\% = 25\%$.

25. **C** Electrons are negatively charged subatomic particles. Protons are positively charged sub-atomic particles. Neutrons are neutral subatomic particles. In an atom, the electrons and protons are balanced. An ion is an atom that has gained or lost electrons. The difference between the number of electrons and protons determines the charge of the ion.

26. **A** According the Newton's second law of motion, the net force acting on an object is proportional to the product of mass and acceleration. If the mass is doubled, the force must, therefore, be halved.

27. **E** The wavelength is the distance between two consecutive points on the wave. For example, the first cycle of the wave begins at 0 meters and is complete at 3.0 meters.

28. **A** The amplitude is the maximum disturbance from the resting position. It is the distance from rest to crest or to trough, which is 0.5 meters.

29. **B** The energy provided is found by $E = Pt$. In this case, $E = (1.2$ kw$)(2$ hr$) = 2.4$ kwhr. The cost is found by multiplying the number of kilowatt hours by the price per kilowatt-hour. The total cost, $C = (2.4$ kwhr$)(\$0.10$/kwhr$) = \$0.24$.

30. **C** The solution requires
$$\frac{F}{W} = \frac{a}{g}, \text{ so } \frac{10 \text{ g}}{50 \text{ g}} = \frac{a}{980 \text{ cm/s}^2}.$$
Therefore,
$$a = 980 \text{ cm/s}^2 \times \frac{10 \text{ g}}{50 \text{ g}} = 196 \text{ cm/s}^2.$$

31. **E** On average, the molecules of a gas are far apart from one another. Their average separation is much greater than the diameter of each molecule.

32. **B** If the sled is moving in a horizontal direction, the vertical components of the forces must cancel out. The vertical component of Person 1's force is $F \sin 60°$, 10 N (0.866) = 8.66 N. Therefore, the vertical component of Person 2's force must also be 8.66 N. This information can be used to find the net force of Person 2. $F \sin 30°$ = 8.66 N, so F 0.500 = 8.66 N, 8.66 N ÷ 0.500 = 17.32 N.

33. **C** As the wave goes through the slit, it spreads out behind the obstacle. The bending of a wave around an obstacle is diffraction.

34. **E** Resistance generally increases with temperature and length. It decreases as the cross-sectional area increases.

35. **C** First find the change in the volume of the cylinder: $\Delta V = (0.010 \text{ m}^2)(0.020 \text{ m}) = 2 \times 10^{-4} \text{ m}^3$. Then use the change in volume to calculate the work done: $W = P\Delta V = (5.0 \times 10^5 \text{ N/m}^2)(2 \times 10^{-4} \text{ m}^3) = 1 \times 10^2 \text{ J}$.

36. **B** Entropy is a measure of a system's disorder. As the ice cube melts, the entropy of the molecules increases. According to the second law of thermodynamics, the entropy of the universe increases through all natural processes.

37. **D** Approximately four half-lives occur in 32 days.
$$\left(\frac{1}{2}\right)^4 = \frac{1}{16}$$

38. **D** The same current passes through each resistor in a series circuit. If this were not true, charge would have to accumulate somewhere in the circuit.

39. **D** The acceleration due to gravity is independent of mass and therefore depends on the speed and height of the airplane only.

40. **B** The diffraction pattern would be a series of rectangular, parallel bands of light. The central band would be brightest, and the bands to the side decrease in brightness in either direction.

41. **E** The horizontal portions of the diagram indicate that heat is being added to or removed from the sample without resulting in a temperature change. These changes in heat result in phase changes. The length of the line is related to the amount of heat loss required for the change. The length of the steam to liquid water line is considerably longer than the length of the liquid water to ice line.

42. **D** Some frequencies will be natural for the string. The lowest of these natural frequencies is the fundamental frequency. At this frequency, the wavelength in the string is twice the length of the string.

43. **B** Reading the graph shows that the vehicle accelerated at a constant rate from 5 m/s to 35 m/s in 6 seconds. Acceleration is equal to the change in velocity divided by the elapsed time,
$$a = \frac{30 \text{ m/s}}{6 \text{ s}} = 5 \text{ m/s}^2.$$

44. **D** The acceleration due to gravity is 980 cm/s². The speed is found by $v = at = (980 \text{ cm/s}^2)(3 \text{ s})$.

45. **A** A concave lens always forms a virtual image that is smaller than the object and is oriented in the same direction as the object.

46. **C** The voltage of 60 V is applied across both branches of the parallel circuit. The total resistance across the branch with the 30-ohm resistor is 40 ohms. For that branch, $I = V/R = 60 \text{ V}/40 \text{ } \Omega = 1.5 \text{ A}$.

47. **B** The straight line with a positive slope indicates that the velocity is increasing at a constant rate. This means that the object is moving with constant acceleration as indicated by a horizontal line for it acceleration graph.

48. **D** The release of a beta particle occurs when a neutron breaks into an electron and a proton. The electron is emitted, and the proton remains in the nucleus. The atomic number depends on the number of protons in the nucleus, so the atomic number increases by 1.

49. **C** If the meter stick is along the x-axis, and the motion is in the y-direction, there will not be any observed change in length.

50. **A** As the truck moves forward, the sound waves bunch together. An observer hears a sound with a higher frequency than the sound produced by the siren.

51. **C** The acceleration of the ball is determined by dividing the square of the velocity by the radius of the circle. It is independent of the mass of the ball.

52. **A** Frequency is the number of vibrations per second. Therefore, $\frac{21}{30} = 0.7 \text{ Hz}$.

53. **B** According to Kepler's second law, planets sweep out equal areas in equal periods of time. Therefore, planets must move faster when they are closer to the sun than when they are farther away.

54. **E** The force between two point charges is inversely proportional to the square of the distance between them. If the distance is doubled, the force is divided by $\frac{1}{4}$.

55. **C** The number of turns is related to the voltage by
$$N_p = N_s\left(\frac{V_p}{V_s}\right) = 10,000\left(\frac{12 \text{ V}}{24,000}\right) = 5.$$

56. **C** Speed is increasing when the graph has a positive slope.

57. **E** The acceleration is constant but not zero when the graph shows a straight, but not horizontal, line.

58. **C** Wavelength is equal to speed divided by frequency. For this wave, wavelength equals 3.9×10^3 meters per second divided by 2.6×10^4 hertz.

59. **A** The negative charge would move in a clockwise circle. A positive charge would move in a counterclockwise direction.

60. **D** Once the CD is in motion, its speed does not change. Because it is in circular motion, the direction is constantly changing. Therefore, a point on the edge of the disc accelerates at a constant speed, but changing direction.

61. **B** A generator is the opposite of a motor in that it uses the mechanical energy of a moving armature to produce an electric current.

62. **C** Calculate the net electric force on the particle due to the other two charges.

$$F_{31} = \frac{(9.0 \times 10^9 \, \text{N} \cdot \text{m}^2/\text{c}^2)(-1.0 \times 10^{-6}\text{C})(-2.0 \times 10^{-6}\text{C})}{(0.5\text{m})^2}$$

$$= 0.072 \text{ N}$$

$$F_{32} = \frac{(9.0 \times 10^9 \, \text{N} \cdot \text{m}^2/\text{c}^2)(-1.0 \times 10^{-6}\text{C})(3.0 \times 10^{-6}\text{C})}{(0.2\text{m})^2}$$

$$= -0.675 \text{ N}$$

$$F = F_{32} + F_{31} = -0.675 + 0.072 = -0.603 \text{ N}.$$

The negative sign indicates that the force points toward the left.

63. **B** The force and mass are constant during this interval. Therefore, the acceleration is also constant. The block continues to speed up, but at a constant rate.

64. **C** At $t = 3$ seconds, the force is 6 N. According to Newton's second law of motion, $F = ma$. So $6 \text{ N} = 2 \text{ kg} (a)$, which means that $a = 3 \text{ m/s}^2$.

65. **A** The magnification equals the distance from the image to the lens, 15 centimeters, divided by the distance from the object to the lens, 30 centimeters.

66. **C** The expansion ΔL can be found by $\Delta L = \alpha L_o \Delta T$, where α is the coefficient of linear expansion, L_o is the original length, and ΔT is the change

in temperature. In this situation, $\Delta L = (12 \times 10^{-6}/°\text{C})(10 \text{ m})(30°\text{C}) = 3.6 \times 10^{-3} \text{ m}$.

67. **E** De Broglie is credited with recognizing that matter can be described by wave properties just as light can be described by properties of matter.

68. **D** The maximum range occurs at an angle of 45° for a given velocity. Therefore, the ball kicked at this angle will travel farther than the ball kicked at a smaller angle.

69. **E** All nonzero digits are significant. Zeros appearing between nonzero digits are significant. Zeros at the end of a number with no decimal point written are not significant.

70. **B** The frequency is proportional to its energy, $E = hf$. The energy is determined by subtracting the energy of the first state from the energy of the second state: $E_2 - E_1 = -3.4 \text{ eV} - 13.6 \text{ eV} = 10.2 \text{ eV}$. Each electron-volt of energy is equal to 1.6×10^{-19} J. Multiplying this by 10.2 eV yields 1.63×10^{-18} J. And 1.63×10^{-18} J $= (6.6 \times 10 - 34 \text{ J} \cdot \text{s})f$.

71. **A** Compare the energy difference for each transition by subtracting the two values. For $\Delta E_{4 \to 3} = -0.85 \text{ eV} - (-1.5 \text{ eV}) = 0.65 \text{ eV}$. $\Delta E_{3 \to 2} = -1.5 \text{ eV} - (-3.4 \text{ eV}) = 1.9 \text{ eV}$. $\Delta E_{5 \to 3} = -0.54 \text{ eV} - (-1.5 \text{ eV}) = 0.96 \text{ eV}$. $\Delta E_{4 \to 2} = -0.85 \text{ eV} - (-3.4 \text{ eV}) = 2.6 \text{ eV}$. $\Delta E_{3 \to 1} = -1.5 \text{ eV} - (-13.6 \text{ eV}) = 12.1 \text{ eV}$.

72. **E** Refraction is the bending of light when it moves from one medium to another at an angle. This bending will cause the stem to appear bent.

73. **C** If these forces act in opposite directions, the net force is the difference between them. (31 N − 13 N = 18 N)

74. **B** For small-angle displacements, the period of a simple pendulum depends only on the length of the pendulum.

75. **B** Rutherford expected the particles to go directly through the foil. However, about 1 in every 8,000 alpha particles was reflected back to the source. This observation led Rutherford to conclude that an atom contains a small, central core with a positive charge.

SCORE SHEET

Number of questions correct: _____

Less: 0.25 × number of questions wrong: _____

(Remember that omitted questions are not counted as wrong.)

Raw score: _____

Raw Score	Scaled Score	Raw Score	Scaled Score	Raw Score	Scaled Score	Raw Score	Scaled Score	Raw Score	Scaled Score
75	800	52	740	29	600	6	470	−17	300
74	800	51	730	28	590	5	460	−18	290
73	800	50	730	27	590	4	460	−19	290
72	800	49	730	26	580	3	460		
71	800	48	720	25	580	2	450		
70	800	47	720	24	570	1	450		
69	800	46	710	23	560	0	440		
68	800	45	710	22	560	−1	400		
67	800	44	700	21	550	−2	390		
66	800	43	690	20	540	−3	390		
65	800	42	680	19	540	−4	380		
64	800	41	680	18	530	−5	380		
63	790	40	670	17	520	−6	370		
62	790	39	670	16	510	−7	370		
61	780	38	660	15	510	−8	360		
60	780	37	650	14	500	−9	360		
59	770	36	650	13	490	−10	350		
58	770	35	640	12	490	−11	350		
57	760	34	640	11	490	−12	340		
56	760	33	630	10	480	−13	340		
55	750	32	620	9	480	−14	330		
54	750	31	620	8	470	−15	320		
53	740	30	610	7	470	−16	310		

Note: This is only a sample scoring scale. Scoring scales differ from exam to exam.

THE SAT FRENCH TEST

All About the SAT French Test

What Is the Format of the SAT French Test?

The SAT French test is a 1-hour exam consisting of 85 multiple-choice questions. According to the College Board, the test measures the following French language knowledge and skills:

- Knowledge of words in context representing different parts of speech and common idioms
- Ability to select a word or expression that is grammatically correct within a sentence
- Comprehension of main and supporting ideas, themes, and setting of a passage

The questions measuring these skills are distributed on the test in approximately the following percentages:

SAT French Question Types

Question Type	Approximate Percentage of Test
Vocabulary in Context	30
Structure	30–40
Reading Comprehension	30–40

On the test, many questions will ask you to choose the word or words that best complete a sentence or that best fill a blank in a sentence. Sometimes the correct answer will be a word or words that make the sentence grammatically correct. Other times, the correct answer will be a word or words that make sense in the context of the meaning of the sentence.

Also on the test, you will be asked to read short passages and then answer questions about them. The passages may be stories, essays, nonfiction articles, or common materials such as advertisements, train or bus timetables, or official forms.

What School Background Do I Need for the SAT French Test?

The College Board recommends that you have either of the following before taking the SAT French test:

- Three or four years of French language study in high school
- Two years of strong preparation

How Is the SAT French Test Scored?

On the SAT French test, your "raw score" is calculated as follows: you receive one point for each question you answer correctly, but you lose one-third of a point for each question you answer incorrectly. You do not gain or lose any points for questions that you do not answer at all. Your raw score is then converted into a scaled score by a statistical method that takes into account how well you did compared to others who took the same test. Scaled scores range from 200 to 800 points. Your scaled score will be reported to you, your high school, and to the colleges and universities you designate to receive it.

Scoring scales differ slightly from one version of the test to the next. The scoring scales provided after the French test in this book is only a sample that will show you your approximate scaled score.

What Is the SAT French With Listening Test?

The College Board also offers a test called the SAT French with Listening test. Unlike the regular French test, which requires you only to read French, the Listening test requires you to listen to spoken French and answer questions about what you hear. If you are confident of your ability to understand spoken French, you may choose to take the Listening test instead of the regular SAT French test.

The Listening test is offered only in November. If you choose to take the Listening test, you must bring an acceptable CD player with earphones to the test center.

SAT FRENCH SAMPLE QUESTIONS

Four types of reading questions are used on the SAT French test. All questions on the test are multiple-choice questions in which you must choose the BEST response from the four choices offered. The following are samples of each type of question on the test.

Part A

Directions: This part consists of a number of incomplete statements, each having four suggested completions. Select the most appropriate completion and fill in the corresponding oval on the answer sheet.

---

1. Je n'ai pas pu ouvrir la porte parce que j'avais perdu ma . . .

   (A) serrure
   (B) clé
   (C) fenêtre
   (D) craie

This question tests vocabulary. You are asked to choose the appropriate noun from the four answer choices. The correct answer is B because a key is used to unlock the door. Answer A is a lock, C is a window, and D is a piece of chalk, none of which correctly answers the question.

2. Patrick avait tant étudié qu'il pouvait facilement . . . à l'examen.

    (A) rater
    (B) manquer
    (C) réussir
    (D) échouer

In this question, you are asked to find the appropriate verb from the four answer choices. The correct answer is C. The verb *réussir* means to succeed ("pass") and is the only logical choice. Choices A, B, and D all mean "to fail" and are incorrect.

Part B

> *Directions:* Each of the following sentences contains a blank. From the four choices given, select the one that can be inserted in the blank to form a grammatically correct sentence and fill in the corresponding oval on the answer sheet. Choice A may consist of dashes that indicate that no insertion is required to form a grammatically correct sentence.

3. Il est douteux que Marie _____ une bonne note, parce qu'elle n'a pas étudié.

    (A) a
    (B) aura
    (C) avait
    (D) ait

The correct answer is D. *Il est douteux que* is an impersonal expression that must be followed with the present subjunctive of the verb *avoir*. Choices A, B, and C are forms of *avoir* in the indicative and are therefore incorrect.

4. _____ est le meilleur acteur du cinéma français?

    (A) Qu'
    (B) Qu'est-ce qui
    (C) Qui
    (D) Qu'est-ce que

In this question you are asked to choose the correct pronoun from the four choices. The correct answer is C. All of the choices are interrogative pronouns which would be required in a sentence that is a question. However, *Qui* is the subject of the sentence and is directly followed by the verb *est*. Answers A and D are incorrect because they are interrogative pronouns that are used as direct objects. *Qu'est-ce qui* is wrong, because although it is a subject pronoun, it refers to a thing and not a person. We know that this question refers to a person (*acteur*).

Part C

> *Directions:* The paragraphs below contain blank spaces indicating omissions in the text. For some blanks it is necessary to choose the completion that is most appropriate to the meaning of the passage; for other blanks, choose the one completion that forms a grammatically correct sentence. In some instances, choice A may consist of dashes that indicate that no insertion is required to form a grammatically correct sentence. In each case, indicate your answer by filling in the corresponding oval on the answer sheet. Be sure to read the paragraph completely before answering the questions, so that you have a full understanding of its context.

Aussitôt que M. Lemarc ———— au rendez-vous, demandez ———— de vous dire où

5. (A) arrive
   (B) arriverait
   (C) arrivera
   (D) arrivait

6. (A) le
   (B) lui
   (C) y
   (D) la

se trouve l'hôtel. Il faut aussi lui dire que moi, j'arriverai ———— septembre.

7. (A) dans
   (B) le
   (C) au
   (D) en

5. Expressions such as *quand, dès que,* and *aussitôt que* are followed by the future tense in French when the verb in the main clause is in the present tense, as it is here with the present imperative *demandez*. The correct answer is C *arrivera,* the future tense of *arriver.* Choice A *arrive* is the present, B *arriverait* is the conditional, and D *arrivait* is the imperfect.

6. The correct answer here is the indirect object pronoun *lui,* choice B. The verb *demandez* is in the present imperative, and because the object pronoun that refers to *him* (M. Lemarc) is *lui,* this is the correct response because it is *to him* that the question is asked. Choice A is incorrect, because *le* is a direct object pronoun. Choice C is incorrect because it is a pronoun used only with things, not people. Choice D is incorrect because it is a direct object pronoun referring to people or things of the feminine gender.

7. When indicating in which month something will take place, the French use the pronoun *en* before the name of the month. Hence, choice D *en* is correct. Choice B is incorrect because it is not a preposition. Choices A and C are incorrect prepositions.

Part D

Directions: Read the following selections carefully for comprehension. Each selection is followed by a number of questions or incomplete statements. Select the completion or answer that is most appropriate according to the passage and fill in the corresponding oval on the answer sheet.

Ligne
(5)

(10)

Une si longue lettre est un roman épistolaire (un roman en lettres) qui raconte l'histoire de Ramatoulaye, une Sénégalaise dont le mari est mort récemment. Ramatoulaye tient une correspondance avec sa meilleure amie, Aïssatou, une amie d'enfance qui habite actuellement aux Etats-Unis et qui a divorcé son mari à cause de son infidélité. Aïssatou donne à Ramatoulaye sa propre perspective sur le sujet de mariage, aussi bien que son aide financière pour aider Ramatoulaye à élever ses enfants. Ses lettres aident Ramatoulaye à boucher le trou de son existence, laissée par l'absence de son mari. Le roman démontre que l'amitié entre femmes est souvent plus forte que les rapports entre les hommes et les femmes, et aussi qu'il est possible qu'une femme puisse mener une vie satisfaisante sans l'aide d'un mari.

8. D'où vient-elle, Ramatoulaye?

   (A) Des Antilles
   (B) D'Afrique
   (C) Des Etats-Unis
   (D) De France

The text tells you that Ramatoulaye is *Sénégalaise,* thus you know that she comes from Africa, answer B. The other answers are incorrect. The Antilles A are in the West Indies; Senegal, although a former French colony, is an independent republic, so D is incorrect; and it is Ramatoulaye's friend Aïssatou who lives in the United States C.

9. Aux lignes 9 et 10, «boucher le trou» veut dire

   (A) réparer la maison
   (B) se venger contre son mari
   (C) satisfaire à des besoins
   (D) trouver un autre mari

The text tells you that Aïssatou's correspondance helps Ramatoulaye "fill the hole (*"boucher le trou"*) of her existence, left by the absence of her husband." Thus, the correct answer is C *satisfaire à des besoins,* which means to "satisfy needs." The letters do not help repair the house A, do not provide vengeance against Ramatoulaye's husband B, or help Ramatoulaye find another husband D.

10. Pourquoi Ramatoulaye et Aïssatou sont-elles obligées de s'écrire l'une à l'autre?

    (A) Elles préfèrent la correspondance écrite au lieu de se voir.
    (B) Elles ne parlent pas la même langue.
    (C) Le mari de Ramatoulaye n'aime pas Aïssatou.
    (D) Aïssatou ne vit plus en Afrique.

The text tells you that Aïssatou now lives in the United States after divorcing her husband (lines 5–6), which explains why she and Ramatoulaye must correspond in writing, answer D. It is not because they prefer to write rather than see each other A, nor because they don't speak the same language B, nor because Ramatoulaye's husband (who is recently deceased) does not like Aïssatou C.

Annonce Publicitaire

Kim Ven

Cuisine authentique thaïlandaise et vietnamienne

Ambiance chaleureuse et conviviale
Un restaurant à découvrir
11, rue Jean Moreau, 7ᵉ – 01 24 68 93 22
Service : de 18H à 24H
Formule déjeuner 12 euros – Carte 25/30 euros
Fermé samedi midi et dimanche
Salle climatisée

11. Qu'est'ce que le mot «formule» indique?

    (A) que le déjeuner a un prix fixe de 12 euros.
    (B) que le déjeuner suit toujours la même formule de préparation
    (C) qu'il faut formuler le prix avec une calculatrice
    (D) qu'on peut formuler une idée de ce qu'on choisit de la carte

From the indication of the advertisement, we understand that the lunch menu is offered at a fixed price of 12 euros, and thus answer A is correct.

12. Selon l'annonce publicitaire, lequel des propos n'est PAS vrai.

    (A) L'atmosphère du restaurant est sympathique.
    (B) Il fait probablement chaud en été dans le restaurant.
    (C) Le restaurant se spécialise en cuisine asiatique.
    (D) Le restaurant n'est pas ouvert le dimanche.

This question asks you to choose the statement that is NOT true of the restaurant. The correct answer is B because it states that it is probably hot inside the restaurant in summer. The statement is false because the restaurant is air-conditioned (*"salle climatisée"*). All of the other statements are true: the restaurant has a nice atmosphere (A), it specializes in Asian cuisine (C), and it is closed on Sunday (D).

SUCCEEDING ON THE SAT FRENCH TEST

Part A

For this portion of the test, vocabulary is key. To succeed, you need to study vocabulary extensively. Verbs are included, but their conjugations aren't as important as your knowledge of what they mean. You need to know them only to the extent that they complete logically the passages given. This means that even though you may not have actually used a verb before (have never actually conjugated it), you may still choose the correct response if you know what the verb means. As for nouns, much of the vocabulary is basic, yet key to understanding the questions. Parts of the body, household items, personal hygiene, everyday activities—these are all categories that you should review. Review also idiomatic expressions in French—expressions that don't translate literally into English—especially those that take the verb *avoir* ("to have"), where in English we would use the verb "to be"—*avoir faim* (to be hungry), *avoir soif* (to be thirsty), *avoir peur* (to be afraid), and the like.

Part B

Verb Tenses and Moods

In this portion of the test, verbs and their correct conjugations are very important. Study all the verb tenses and moods in French and know how they are used grammatically, because the choices given will all be correctly conjugated in one form or another, but you must choose the correct tense or mood based on the rest of the given sentence.

Example:

Ma mère ——— tellement qu'elle n'a pas entendu le téléphone.

    (A) travaillerait
    (B) aura travaillé
    (C) ayant travaillé
    (D) travaillait

The correct choice is D, *travaillait*. This is the imperfect tense, which means "was working." My mother was working so hard that she did not hear the telephone. The fact that the subordinate clause—"qu'elle n'a pas entendu le téléphone"—is in the *passé composé*, and because it is set in apposition to the main clause, it indicates that the correct tense of the main clause is the imperfect. Be sure to read the entire sentence to determine the correct grammatical context.

The Subjunctive

The subjunctive is not a verb tense but rather a "mood." It is rarely used in American English, but in French it is used relatively often. Know in which cases the subjunctive is required and how to conjugate it. Most often the subordinate clause sets the tone for the main clause, which must be in the subjunctive. Subordinate clauses that express doubt, emotion, volition, desire, and opinion trigger the subjunctive.

Example:

Mon père doute que je ——— réussir à l'université.

  (A) peux
  (B) pourrai
  (C) puisse
  (D) pouvais

The correct answer is C, *puisse*, because the introductory (subordinate) clause indicates that my father *doubts*. The main clause must contain the present subjunctive, *puisse*. All of the other verbs are in the indicative (present, future, imperfect).

Interrogative Pronouns

Review how interrogative pronouns (pronouns used to ask questions) are used. The main distinction here is whether the pronoun is a subject (and takes a verb directly) or an object (a question whose response will be an object).

Example:

——— va au théâtre avec toi dimanche soir?

  (A) Qu'est-ce que
  (B) Qui
  (C) Que
  (D) Qu'est-ce qui

The correct response is B, *Qui*. We know that the question is asking *who* is going with you to the theater. The pronoun *qui* refers to a person, and it is the subject of the question, and so the verb follows it directly. The pronoun *Qu'est-ce que* is wrong because it refers to an object ("what"), and the same is true of *Que*. The pronoun *Qu'est-ce qui* is a subject, but it refers to things, not people, thus is incorrect.

Prepositions

The French language has a variety of prepositions that are used differently from those in English. This is particularly true of prepositions following verbs. For example, in French, the verb *hésiter* is followed by *de*, as in "Elle hésite de me téléphoner." In other cases, verbs are followed by the preposition *à*, such as *s'intéresser*, as in "Je m'intéresse à regarder le match." Verbs in a third category are followed by *no* preposition, such as *aimer*, as in "Il aime faire du ski." Be aware of these categories. Know also the meanings of other prepositions of place (*dans, en, au, avec, sans, derrière, devant*, etc.).

Part C

This part of the test includes all of the elements described above (Parts A and B). The difference, however, is that now the various elements of language are contained together in paragraphs, and not in separate, discrete sentences. Thus, it is important that you pay attention to context. Read all of the paragraph at least once before returning to it to answer the questions. If time permits, it is suggested that you read the paragraph several times before answering any questions.

Part D

As with Part C, read the passage carefully (two or three times if necessary) before answering any questions. Then read the questions separately and return to the reading, marking in pencil the important passages or words that the questions seem to elicit.

Look for *cognates* (many French words resemble English words, and it is highly likely that they have similar meanings).

If you don't understand certain parts of the readings, pay close attention to the other sentences before or after the parts you don't understand. Quite often you will be able to determine meaning from the context of other words or sentences that you do understand.

Draw conclusions based on your general knowledge because correct answers may be provided in a variety of ways to test your ability to think in broader terms. For example, a reading might state that a person is "Sénégalais" (Senegalese), whereas one of the choices may identify the person as "Africain" (African). Knowing that Senegal is a former French colony in Africa will help you answer this question correctly. Abbreviations (in advertisements) are easy to figure out if your knowledge of vocabulary is good. For example, *tél* is obviously an abbreviation of *téléphone*; *déj* is an abbreviation of *déjeuner*, etc.

Idiomatic Expressions

Know expressions that are unique to French (*avoir soif, froid, sommeil*, etc.). Some of these are imagistic (they conjure images in ones mind), so use your imagination. If someone is talking of taking Friday off when the following Monday is a national holiday, they might say they will *faire le pont* ("make the bridge"). This expression describes building a bridge between Friday and Monday in order to make one's vacation longer. Don't panic if you don't understand everything in a reading. What is tested is your ability to extract the most important or useful information from the texts, so read the questions carefully and re-read the parts of the passage to which they refer. You'll save yourself time and stress.

FRENCH PRACTICE TEST

Treat this practice test as the actual test and complete it in one 60-minute sitting. Use the following answer sheet to fill in your multiple-choice answers. Once you have completed this practice test:

1. Check your answers using the Answer Key.
2. Review the Answers and Explanations.
3. Complete the Score Sheet to see how well you did.

ANSWER SHEET

Tear out this answer sheet and use it to complete the practice test. Determine the BEST answer for each question. Then fill in the appropriate oval.

1. Ⓐ Ⓑ Ⓒ Ⓓ Ⓔ	26. Ⓐ Ⓑ Ⓒ Ⓓ Ⓔ	51. Ⓐ Ⓑ Ⓒ Ⓓ Ⓔ	76. Ⓐ Ⓑ Ⓒ Ⓓ Ⓔ
2. Ⓐ Ⓑ Ⓒ Ⓓ Ⓔ	27. Ⓐ Ⓑ Ⓒ Ⓓ Ⓔ	52. Ⓐ Ⓑ Ⓒ Ⓓ Ⓔ	77. Ⓐ Ⓑ Ⓒ Ⓓ Ⓔ
3. Ⓐ Ⓑ Ⓒ Ⓓ Ⓔ	28. Ⓐ Ⓑ Ⓒ Ⓓ Ⓔ	53. Ⓐ Ⓑ Ⓒ Ⓓ Ⓔ	78. Ⓐ Ⓑ Ⓒ Ⓓ Ⓔ
4. Ⓐ Ⓑ Ⓒ Ⓓ Ⓔ	29. Ⓐ Ⓑ Ⓒ Ⓓ Ⓔ	54. Ⓐ Ⓑ Ⓒ Ⓓ Ⓔ	79. Ⓐ Ⓑ Ⓒ Ⓓ Ⓔ
5. Ⓐ Ⓑ Ⓒ Ⓓ Ⓔ	30. Ⓐ Ⓑ Ⓒ Ⓓ Ⓔ	55. Ⓐ Ⓑ Ⓒ Ⓓ Ⓔ	80. Ⓐ Ⓑ Ⓒ Ⓓ Ⓔ
6. Ⓐ Ⓑ Ⓒ Ⓓ Ⓔ	31. Ⓐ Ⓑ Ⓒ Ⓓ Ⓔ	56. Ⓐ Ⓑ Ⓒ Ⓓ Ⓔ	81. Ⓐ Ⓑ Ⓒ Ⓓ Ⓔ
7. Ⓐ Ⓑ Ⓒ Ⓓ Ⓔ	32. Ⓐ Ⓑ Ⓒ Ⓓ Ⓔ	57. Ⓐ Ⓑ Ⓒ Ⓓ Ⓔ	82. Ⓐ Ⓑ Ⓒ Ⓓ Ⓔ
8. Ⓐ Ⓑ Ⓒ Ⓓ Ⓔ	33. Ⓐ Ⓑ Ⓒ Ⓓ Ⓔ	58. Ⓐ Ⓑ Ⓒ Ⓓ Ⓔ	83. Ⓐ Ⓑ Ⓒ Ⓓ Ⓔ
9. Ⓐ Ⓑ Ⓒ Ⓓ Ⓔ	34. Ⓐ Ⓑ Ⓒ Ⓓ Ⓔ	59. Ⓐ Ⓑ Ⓒ Ⓓ Ⓔ	84. Ⓐ Ⓑ Ⓒ Ⓓ Ⓔ
10. Ⓐ Ⓑ Ⓒ Ⓓ Ⓔ	35. Ⓐ Ⓑ Ⓒ Ⓓ Ⓔ	60. Ⓐ Ⓑ Ⓒ Ⓓ Ⓔ	85. Ⓐ Ⓑ Ⓒ Ⓓ Ⓔ
11. Ⓐ Ⓑ Ⓒ Ⓓ Ⓔ	36. Ⓐ Ⓑ Ⓒ Ⓓ Ⓔ	61. Ⓐ Ⓑ Ⓒ Ⓓ Ⓔ	
12. Ⓐ Ⓑ Ⓒ Ⓓ Ⓔ	37. Ⓐ Ⓑ Ⓒ Ⓓ Ⓔ	62. Ⓐ Ⓑ Ⓒ Ⓓ Ⓔ	
13. Ⓐ Ⓑ Ⓒ Ⓓ Ⓔ	38. Ⓐ Ⓑ Ⓒ Ⓓ Ⓔ	63. Ⓐ Ⓑ Ⓒ Ⓓ Ⓔ	
14. Ⓐ Ⓑ Ⓒ Ⓓ Ⓔ	39. Ⓐ Ⓑ Ⓒ Ⓓ Ⓔ	64. Ⓐ Ⓑ Ⓒ Ⓓ Ⓔ	
15. Ⓐ Ⓑ Ⓒ Ⓓ Ⓔ	40. Ⓐ Ⓑ Ⓒ Ⓓ Ⓔ	65. Ⓐ Ⓑ Ⓒ Ⓓ Ⓔ	
16. Ⓐ Ⓑ Ⓒ Ⓓ Ⓔ	41. Ⓐ Ⓑ Ⓒ Ⓓ Ⓔ	66. Ⓐ Ⓑ Ⓒ Ⓓ Ⓔ	
17. Ⓐ Ⓑ Ⓒ Ⓓ Ⓔ	42. Ⓐ Ⓑ Ⓒ Ⓓ Ⓔ	67. Ⓐ Ⓑ Ⓒ Ⓓ Ⓔ	
18. Ⓐ Ⓑ Ⓒ Ⓓ Ⓔ	43. Ⓐ Ⓑ Ⓒ Ⓓ Ⓔ	68. Ⓐ Ⓑ Ⓒ Ⓓ Ⓔ	
19. Ⓐ Ⓑ Ⓒ Ⓓ Ⓔ	44. Ⓐ Ⓑ Ⓒ Ⓓ Ⓔ	69. Ⓐ Ⓑ Ⓒ Ⓓ Ⓔ	
20. Ⓐ Ⓑ Ⓒ Ⓓ Ⓔ	45. Ⓐ Ⓑ Ⓒ Ⓓ Ⓔ	70. Ⓐ Ⓑ Ⓒ Ⓓ Ⓔ	
21. Ⓐ Ⓑ Ⓒ Ⓓ Ⓔ	46. Ⓐ Ⓑ Ⓒ Ⓓ Ⓔ	71. Ⓐ Ⓑ Ⓒ Ⓓ Ⓔ	
22. Ⓐ Ⓑ Ⓒ Ⓓ Ⓔ	47. Ⓐ Ⓑ Ⓒ Ⓓ Ⓔ	72. Ⓐ Ⓑ Ⓒ Ⓓ Ⓔ	
23. Ⓐ Ⓑ Ⓒ Ⓓ Ⓔ	48. Ⓐ Ⓑ Ⓒ Ⓓ Ⓔ	73. Ⓐ Ⓑ Ⓒ Ⓓ Ⓔ	
24. Ⓐ Ⓑ Ⓒ Ⓓ Ⓔ	49. Ⓐ Ⓑ Ⓒ Ⓓ Ⓔ	74. Ⓐ Ⓑ Ⓒ Ⓓ Ⓔ	
25. Ⓐ Ⓑ Ⓒ Ⓓ Ⓔ	50. Ⓐ Ⓑ Ⓒ Ⓓ Ⓔ	75. Ⓐ Ⓑ Ⓒ Ⓓ Ⓔ	

FRENCH PRACTICE TEST

PLEASE NOTE THAT YOUR ANSWER SHEET HAS FIVE ANSWER POSITIONS MARKED A, B, C, D, E WHILE THE QUESTIONS THROUGHOUT THE TEST CONTAIN ONLY FOUR CHOICES. BE SURE <u>NOT</u> TO MAKE ANY MARKS IN COLUMN E.

Part A

Directions: This part consists of a number of incomplete statements, each having four suggested completions. Select the most appropriate completion and fill in the corresponding oval on the answer sheet.

1. Quand mes parents ont une discussion, c'est toujours mon père qui a . . .
   - (A) soif
   - (B) faim
   - (C) beau
   - (D) tort

2. Il ne peut pas faire de jogging aujourd'hui parce qu'il a mal au . . .
   - (A) bras
   - (B) pied
   - (C) cou
   - (D) doigt

3. Pour voyager en avion, on doit avoir une carte . . .
   - (A) de séjour
   - (B) d'étudiant
   - (C) d'embarquement
   - (D) de chauffage

4. La cuisine est en désordre. Il faut que je fasse la . . .
   - (A) vaisselle
   - (B) valise
   - (C) lessive
   - (D) manche

5. Pour avoir une chambre en . . . Sophie a décidé de la nettoyer.
   - (A) miettes
   - (B) plein air
   - (C) ordre
   - (D) parties

6. Encore une mauvaise note à l'école? Tu ne fais pas . . . en classe.
   - (A) attention
   - (B) gaffe
   - (C) dodo
   - (D) moche

7. Mon frère a du mal à voir le tableau sans ses . . .
   - (A) spectacles
   - (B) chaussettes
   - (C) glaçons
   - (D) lunettes

8. Michel s'est . . . avec des ciseaux.
   - (A) coupé
   - (B) brûlé
   - (C) lavé
   - (D) maquillé

9. Le soir, j'allais . . . les journaux qui sont par terre dans la salle de séjour.
   - (A) ramasser
   - (B) rembobiner
   - (C) dégringoler
   - (D) refroidir

10. Aux champs derrière le château, les lapins . . . ici et là.
    - (A) chantaient
    - (B) étincelaient
    - (C) sautaient
    - (D) étudiaient

11. Denise achètera du pain à la . . .
    - (A) papetrie
    - (B) boulangerie
    - (C) boucherie
    - (D) charcuterie

12. Votre ville est très intéressante. Il y a beaucoup de choses à . . .
    - (A) peindre
    - (B) voir
    - (C) craindre
    - (D) écrire

GO ON TO THE NEXT PAGE →

13. Ne sachant pas quelle décision prendre, j'ai demandé . . . de mon père.

    (A) l'attitude
    (B) la peur
    (C) l'avis
    (D) le corps

14. Marie-France ne m'a pas téléphoné. As-tu reçu de ses . . .

    (A) envies
    (B) ordinateurs
    (C) lieux
    (D) nouvelles

15. Soudain, dans le calme du soir, une explosion . . .

    (A) hurla
    (B) éclata
    (C) poussa
    (D) cria

16. Les Luneau ont dû sortir, puisque toutes les lumières de la maison sont . . .

    (A) brûlantes
    (B) cassées
    (C) éteintes
    (D) livides

17. Quand j'ai vu que ton accident n'était pas grave, j'ai été

    (A) soulagé
    (B) épaté
    (C) déçu
    (D) bouleversé

18. Après avoir fini ses examens, Dominique a poussé . . . de joie

    (A) un bout
    (B) une fête
    (C) un cri
    (D) un geste

19. La porté était fermée et Patrick n'avait pas de clé; donc, il l'a . . . pour l'ouvrir.

    (A) creusée
    (B) croisée
    (C) peinte
    (D) foncée

20. Au cours de mes études à l'université, je veux faire un . . . en Europe.

    (A) séjour
    (B) calendrier
    (C) siècle
    (D) trou

GO ON TO THE NEXT PAGE

Part B

Directions: Each of the following sentences contains a blank. From the four choices given, select the one that can be inserted in the blank to form a grammatically correct sentence and fill in the corresponding oval on the answer sheet. Choice A may consist of dashes that indicate that no insertion is required to form a grammatically correct sentence.

---

21. Elle m'a parlé ——— ses cours à la faculté de médecine.

    (A) dans
    (B) de
    (C) envers
    (D) à

22. Ma sœur ——— tellement qu'elle n'a pas remarqué que le train était arrivé.

    (A) parlerait
    (B) ayant parlé
    (C) parlait
    (D) aura parlé

23. Carole a fait ce dessin pour ———.

    (A) eux
    (B) je
    (C) leur
    (D) la

24. ——— est allé au cinéma avec toi samedi soir?

    (A) Qu'est-ce que
    (B) Lequel
    (C) Qu'
    (D) Qui

25. Remplis les verres ——— vin, s'il te plaît.

    (A) de
    (B) avec
    (C) en
    (D) du

26. Il est parti ——— avoir pris son dessert.

    (A) sans
    (B) avant
    (C) loin d'
    (D) en

27. Elle n'a fait que ——— erreurs.

    (A) beaucoup
    (B) très
    (C) quelques
    (D) peu

28. Le médecin a ——— de parler avec la femme.

    (A) cessé
    (B) sorti
    (C) entré
    (D) montré

29. Nous devions faire nos valises avant de ——— en voyage.

    (A) quitter
    (B) partir
    (C) partant
    (D) parti

30. Je ne veux pas manger de légumes ——— ils soient bons pour la santé.

    (A) puisqu'
    (B) autant qu'
    (C) bien qu'
    (D) aussitôt qu'

31. Elle leur a ——— expliqué les exercices.

    (A) mal
    (B) en dessous
    (C) avant
    (D) demain

32. Didier mange plus ——— que toi.

    (A) lent
    (B) mauvais
    (C) lentement
    (D) rapide

33. Voilà un problème ——— je n'avais pas pensé.

    (A) —
    (B) auquel
    (C) duquel
    (D) qu'

34. As-tu déjà voyagé ——— Mexique?

    (A) le
    (B) au
    (C) en
    (D) à

GO ON TO THE NEXT PAGE ➡

Part C

Directions: The paragraphs below contain blank spaces indicating omissions in the text. For some blanks, it is necessary to choose the completion that is most appropriate to the meaning of the passage; for other blanks, to choose the one completion that forms a grammatically correct sentence. In some instances, choice A may consist of dashes that indicate that no insertion is required to form a grammatically correct sentence. In each case, indicate your answer by filling in the corresponding oval on the answer sheet. Be sure to read the paragraph completely before answering the questions related to it.

Tous les jours, nous allions à l'école dans un autobus ———— par M. Luneau.

        35. (A) tiré
             (B) conduit
             (C) couru
             (D) piloté

L'hiver, M. Luneau, ———— d'être parmi les petits écoliers, souriait et saluait chaque enfant en hochant la ————

    36. (A) fâché   37. (A) tête
         (B) méchant   (B) jambe
         (C) heureux   (C) le pied
         (D) fatigué   (D) le dos

pleine de ———— gris et bouclés. Quoi que nous ————, il refusait ———— de suivre le chemin qui passait au bord du ————

  38. (A) pailles   39. (A) faisons   40. (A) toujours   41. (A) bâtiment
      (B) feuilles   (B) ferions   (B) jamais   (B) lac
      (C) peaux   (C) fassions   (C) plus   (C) pays
      (D) cheveux   (D) avions fait   (D) guère   (D) magasin

à cause de l'eau; il ———— avait peur, M. Luneau. Il était très prudent, et chaque fois qu'il remarquait une voiture qui

        42. (A) y
            (B) l'
            (C) en
            (D) lui

suivait ———— l'autobus, il ralentissait pour la laisser passer, et il nous ———— toujours que nous n'étions pas pressés pour

  43. (A) devant   44. (A) taisait
      (B) à côté de   (B) expliquait
      (C) derrière   (C) grinçait
      (D) au dessus de   (D) klaxonnait

arriver à l'heure à l'école.

GO ON TO THE NEXT PAGE

Cher Madame Dupont:

La semaine ———, nous vous avons téléphoné au sujet de votre compte. ——— pas reçu votre paiement, nous devons

45. (A) ultime
    (B) prochain
    (C) dernière
    (D) près

46. (A) N'avoir
    (B) N'ayant
    (C) N'avons
    (D) N'avez

supposer que vous vous êtes ——— d'adresse en nous ——— votre paiement. Nous vous rappelons ——— que votre chèque

47. (A) trompée
    (B) mise
    (C) faite
    (D) regardée

48. (A) envoyer
    (B) traduisant
    (C) envoyant
    (D) écrivant

49. (A) donc
    (B) moins
    (C) guère
    (D) en dépit

——— arriver ici à notre entreprise avant la fin du mois pour que votre compte soit réglé.

50. (A) devrons
    (B) devra
    (C) dont
    (D) devoir

————————————————

Deux amis marchent ——— du lac. Ils s'approchent ——— l'eau, se tenant par la main. Ils ont à peu près le

51. (A) au bord
    (B) au dessus
    (C) au dessous
    (D) au milieu

52. (A) en
    (B) de
    (C) sur
    (D) dans

même ———, et sans doute aussi les mêmes intérêts; ils ont une quinzaine ———. Le garçon est beaucoup plus grand

53. (A) âme
    (B) maillot
    (C) âge
    (D) conseil

54. (A) ans
    (B) d'années
    (C) années
    (D) des années

——— la fille. Il y a un autre couple au lac, et ——— deux autres personnes sont plus âgées.

55. (A) ce que
    (B) qui
    (C) dont
    (D) que

56. (A) celui
    (B) cet
    (C) ces
    (D) ceux

GO ON TO THE NEXT PAGE

Part D

Directions: Read the following texts carefully for comprehension. Each is followed by a number of questions or incomplete statements. Select the answer or completion that is best according to the text and fill in the corresponding oval on the answer sheet.

Vivez vos rêves au Château de la Pioline à Aix-en-Provence

Au cœur de la région Provence Côte d'Azur, classé monument historique du XVI, XVII, XVIIIe siècles, le château de la Pioline est situé à 3 km d'Aix-en-Provence en direction de Marseille. Point de chute idéal pour faire des randonnées dans les Alpilles, le Lubéron et la Camargue. Hôtel et restaurant 4 étoiles, réceptions, Séminaires, télé, mini-bar, coffre individuel.

13290 Les Milles
Tél.: 04.42.21.0871
Télécopie: 04.42.46.40.57

Fermeture annuelle: février
18 chambres de 108 € à 170 €. 3 appartements à partir de 200 €.
Petit déjeuner: 12 €
Menus: 33 €, 53 € + carte 45 € à 70 €
½ pension: de 102 € à 130 €
Pension: de 135 € à 165 €

---

57. Cette publicité s'adresse surtout à des

    (A) familles avec enfants
    (B) adultes qui aiment se promener en campagne
    (C) lycéens
    (D) malades

58. On mentionne toutes les caractéristiques suivantes du Château de la Pioline SAUF

    (A) son accès à l'internet
    (B) sa situation
    (C) son histoire
    (D) ses prix

GO ON TO THE NEXT PAGE

QUESTION—Que pensez-vous du racisme qui existe en France, surtout en ce qui concerne les immigrés des pays africains?

RÉPONSE DE RAMA, LYCÉENNE D'ORIGINE SÉNÉGALAISE—Je voudrais parler d'une chose qui me révolte: Le racisme, la xénophobie, la haine des étrangers. Nous sommes tous égaux: les noirs, les blancs, les jaunes, les rouges, et tous les autres. Nous sommes tous d'une seule race: la race humaine. Moi j'ai peur, peur du mal que peut faire une personne à une autre rien que pour son origine. Imaginez qu'on soit tous, par exemple, blonds aux yeux bleus! Quel ennui! Alors vive la différence, et "non" à l'inégalité des races.

59. Du contexte du passage, *la xénophobie* veut dire
    (A) le bon accueil des étrangers
    (B) la peur des étrangers
    (C) la musique sénégalaise
    (D) l'immigration

60. D'après le texte, Rama pense que
    (A) le racisme n'est pas un problème en France
    (B) tout le monde devrait être blond
    (C) les yeux bleus sont plus beaux que d'autres
    (D) le racisme est dangereux

61. Laquelle des phrases suivantes résume les pensées de Rama?
    (A) Le racisme existe en France, mais ce n'est pas un phénomène grave.
    (B) Le racisme existe en France, mais il ne faut pas en avoir peur.
    (C) On devrait accepter la différence des races, et même être reconnaissant de cette variété.
    (D) Le racisme existe en France, mais Rama le trouve normal.

GO ON TO THE NEXT PAGE

Un malentendu

Un jeune homme attend devant le cinéma où il y a beacoup de monde qui font la queue pour voir la séance à 20 heures. Le jeune homme n'arrête pas

Ligne de regarder sa montre, bouche bée, l'air
(5)   incrédule. Une vieille femme remarque la mine consternée du jeune homme est s'approche de lui:

—Excusez-moi, Monsieur, dit la femme, vous semblez troublé. Puis-je vous aider?
(10) Les autres qui font la queue trouve étrange cette scène et se demandent de quoi il s'agit.

—Euh, je devais rencontrer ma copine au cinéma vers 20 heures, mais elle n'est pas encore arrivée, et il est déjà moins dix, dit le jeune homme.
(15)   —Je suis sûre qu'il y a une bonne raison pour son retard, dit la femme. Peut-être qu'elle n'a pas bien regardé l'heure.

—Non, pas possible, dit le jeune homme, fâché, elle est toujours très ponctuelle. Elle a dû me
(20) poser un lapin pour tenir rendez-vous avec son copain, Marc, dont elle parle constamment. Je suis cocu, je le sais!

—Voyons, dit la femme, un rendez-vous manqué ne veut pas forcément dire que votre copine vous
(25) trompe avec un autre homme. Peut-être qu'elle a oublié le nom du cinéma.

—J'en doute, répond le jeune homme, je lui ai dit clairement qu'elle devait me rencontrer devant *Le 4 étoiles* à 20 heures.
(30)   —Mais, monsieur, ceci est *La fine étoile,* dit la femme. C'est vous qui vous trompez!

—Oh là là, dit le jeune homme, que je suis idiot!

62. Le jeune homme regarde sa montre

(A) parce que le film vient de commencer
(B) parce que la vieille femme l'embête
(C) parce que son amie n'est pas encore arrivée
(D) parce que quelqu'un lui a demandé l'heure

63. Pourquoi la vieille femme s'approche-t-elle du jeune homme?

(A) Elle le trouve très beau.
(B) Il a l'air sympathique.
(C) C'est son fils.
(D) Il a l'air troublé.

64. L'expression "poser un lapin" à la ligne 20 signifie que

(A) La copine du jeune homme n'a pas tenu leur rendez-vous.
(B) La copine du jeune homme adore les lapins.
(C) Un lapin a pris la place de la copine.
(D) La copine du jeune homme préfère les dessins animés.

65. Qu'est-ce que le jeune homme pense de l'absence de sa copine?

(A) Il croit qu'elle est sortie avec un autre homme.
(B) Il pense qu'elle s'est trompée du cinéma.
(C) Il pense qu'elle s'est trompée de l'heure.
(D) Il croit qu'elle a manqué son autobus.

66. La vieille femme semble

(A) aussi pessimiste que le jeune homme
(B) plus optimiste que le jeune homme
(C) plus pessimiste que le jeune homme
(D) plus cynique que le jeune homme

67. Le titre de ce texte ("Un malentendu") évoque

(A) le mauvais caractère de la vieille femme
(B) le mauvais caractère de la copine
(C) l'erreur du jeune homme
(D) le bon cœur du jeune homme

GO ON TO THE NEXT PAGE

Le Maroc est devenu protectorat français en
1912. Après des siècles d'indépendance sous
plusieurs dynasties préstigieuses, le Maroc accède
Ligne à l'indépendance en 1956, sous le roi Mohammed
(5) V, père du monarque Hassan II et grand-père du
monarque actuel, Mohammed VI.

La civilisation très ancienne du Maroc est
marquée par l'influence des Berbères (les premiers
habitants), des juifs, des Romains, des Arabes et,
(10) récemment, des Espagnols et des Français. Cette
diversité se reflète dans la musique, qui fait partie
intégrale de la vie marocaine: la voix du muezzin
qui appelle les fidèles à la prière; la musique
«andalouse», qui rappelle le flamenco espagnol;
(15) le gnaoua, caracterisé par le rhythme des tambours;
le chaabi, musique traditionnelle que l'on entend
jouer dans les rues; le malhoune, musique
populaire reprise dans les années 1970, incorporant
des thèmes politiques; le rai (opinion), musique
(20) contemporaine des jeunes, équivalent du «rap», qui
évoque des thèmes modernes, comme la sexualité,
les drogues et les automobiles.

68. Depuis 1956, le Maroc est un pays

(A) protégé par la France
(B) indépendant
(C) colonisé
(D) communiste

69. Le mot «Berbères» veut dire

(A) barbares
(B) belges
(C) le peuple immigré du Maroc
(D) le peuple originaire du Maroc

70. Tous les peuples SAUF lequel a eu une influence sur
le Maroc?

(A) les Français
(B) les Espagnols
(C) les Allemands
(D) les Romains

71. Un «muezzin» (à la ligne 12) est

(A) un religieux
(B) un chanteur de «rap»
(C) un homme politique
(D) un flamenco

72. La musique «rai» (à la ligne 19) est

(A) la musique traditionnelle du Maroc
(B) la musique des rois
(C) est comme le flamenco andaloux
(D) est comme le «rap» américain

GO ON TO THE NEXT PAGE

RESTAURANT FIESTA

**Spécialités mexicaines authentiques
Musiciens le week-end**

13 Rue Rimbaud, 16ème – 01 24 32 78 89
Service : de 19H à 24H – Métro Marx-Dormoy
Carte: 35 euros – Fermé: lundi

73. Le restaurant est ouvert tous les jours de la semaine
SAUF

(A) jeudi
(B) samedi
(C) lundi
(D) mardi

74. Lesquels de ces propos n'est PAS vrai?

(A) On peut y écouter des musiciens le samedi.
(B) Le restaurant est ouvert jusqu'à une heure du
matin.
(C) Le restaurant est près d'un métro.
(D) Le restaurant ouvre à sept heures du soir.

GO ON TO THE NEXT PAGE

La guerre de Sept Ans
1756–1763

De 1739 à 1748, la Grande-Bretagne a fait la guerre à l'Espagne, puis à la France. Ce conflit ne s'est soldé par aucune victoire décisive; Terre

Ligne Neuve (Canada) en a d'ailleurs été exclue, sans nul
(5) doute parce que les Français avaient perdu leur base de Plaisance. Toutefois, les relations restaient tendues entre Français et Anglais, en particulier en Amérique du Nord, et la guerre longtemps remise allait finir par éclater en mai 1756.
(10) Une fois établie leur supériorité maritime, les Anglais se sont mis à remporter une série de victoires décisives sur la France et, subséquemment, sur l'Espagne. Les postes de traite d'esclaves d'Afrique occidentale, les îles
(15) sucrières des Antilles et de vastes régions de l'Inde sont tous tombés aux mains des Britanniques.
En 1758, la Grand-Bretagne lançait une offensive terrestre et maritime contre la Nouvelle-France (Canada). La forteresse de Louisbourg, sur
(20) l'île du Cap-Breton, tombait dès 1758. Puis, le 13 septembre 1759, le général James Wolfe défaisait les forces françaises à Québec. À l'automne 1760, toute l'Amérique française était devenue britannique.
(25) Vers la fin de la guerre, en 1762, les forces françaises ont attaqué St. John's. Si elle avait réussi, cette expédition aurait rehaussé la mise des Français à la table des négociations. Mais après avoir pris le contrôle de St. John's et pillé les
(30) villages voisins, les forces françaises ont fini par subir la défaite aux mains des troupes britanniques commandées par le colonel William Amherst.
La guerre devait prendre fin avec la signature du traité de Paris, en 1763. Ce traité contenait
(35) d'importantes dispositions associées à Terre-Neuve, y compris la cession à la France de l'archipel de Saint-Pierre et Miquelon.

75. Au dix-huitième siècle, la Grande-Bretagne faisait la guerre avec
    (A) l'Allegmagne
    (B) l'Écosse
    (C) l'Espagne
    (D) l'Italie

76. De 1739 à 1748, la Grande-Bretagne a exclu la la Terre-Neuve de leurs batailles parce que
    (A) Elle avait déjà pris la Plaisance des Français.
    (B) Les Espagnols étaient trop forts.
    (C) La Terre-Neuve n'avait aucune importance.
    (D) Il faisait trop froid au Canada.

77. Le succès immédiat des Anglais dans la guerre était à cause de
    (A) leur plus grand nombre de soldats
    (B) leur habitude de se battre dans la neige
    (C) leurs plus grands stocks de nourriture
    (D) la supériorité de leurs forces maritimes

78. Les Anglais ont aussi pris
    (A) une partie de l'Afrique
    (B) une partie des Etats-Unis
    (C) le Portugal des Espagnols
    (D) l'Alaska

79. Le général James Wolfe était
    (A) un officier canadien qui a aidé les Français
    (B) un officier britannique responsable des victoires décisifs sur les Français
    (C) un officier français qui a perdu plusieurs batailles importantes contre les Anglais
    (D) un officier britannique responsable de l'échec des Anglais

80. Si les Français avaient réussi à St. John's,
    (A) le colonel Amherst serait mort
    (B) ils auraient gagné la guerre entière
    (C) leurs négociations dans le traité de Paris auraient été plus avantageuses
    (D) les Anglais seraient retournés en Angleterre

81. Le traité de Paris
    (A) a laissé les archipels de Saint-Pierre et Miquelon aux Français
    (B) a laissé toute la Terre-Neuve aux Français
    (C) a laissé la ville de Paris aux Anglais
    (D) a été signé en 1760

GO ON TO THE NEXT PAGE

Un garçon de dix ans, avec un fusil, tirait
sur des moineaux dans le saule pleureur derrière
sa maison. Il en avait déjà tué deux et visait sur un
Ligne troisième quand un vieil homme qui regardait
(5)   la scène s'est approché du garçon.

—Pourquoi voulez-vous tuer ces beaux oiseaux,
mon petit? a dit le vieil homme. Ils ne font aucun
mal aux autres, et ils sont tellement jolis à regarder
et entendre.

(10)   —C'est parce que je viens de recevoir ce fusil
de mon grand-père comme cadeau d'anniversaire,
et j'avais envie de m'en servir, a répondu le
garçon.

—Mais vous pourriez bien vous en servir en tirant
(15)   sur des objets inanimés—une boîte de conserve ou
une bouteille, par exemple, a dit l'homme.

—Vous avez peut-être raison, a dit le garçon,
mais c'est plus amusant quand il s'agit d'êtres
vivants.

(20)   L'homme a réfléchi un moment et a décidé d'en
parler avec le père du garçon afin de régler
l'affaire.

—Où est ton père? lui a demandé le vieil homme.
—Il n'est plus chez nous, a répondu le garçon. Il
(25)   est parti faire la guerre contre les Allemands. Il me
manque beaucoup, et j'ai peur qu'il ne meure avant
la fin de la guerre.

—Je vois, a dit l'homme. Et si votre père revient
sain et sauf, penses-tu que lui, il passera son temps
(30)   à tirer sur de petits oiseaux, surtout après ce qu'il
aura vu pendant la guerre?

—Eh ben, non, monsieur, a dit le garçon. Je crois
que je laisserai mon fusil chez grand-père jusqu'à
ce que papa revienne chez nous.

(35)   —Bonne idée, a dit l'homme, content que le
garçon ait enfin compris la gravité de ses actions.

---

82. Un «moineau» est un type de

(A) fusil
(B) oiseau
(C) arbre
(D) soldat

83. Le père du garçon

(A) lui a donné le fusil comme cadeau
(B) demande au garçon porquoi il tire sur
les moineaux
(C) est allé à la guerre
(D) veut tuer des moineaux

84. Pourquoi le vieil homme ne veut-il pas que le garçon
tire sur les moineaux?

(A) Parce que les moineaux sont dangereux.
(B) Parce que le garçon est trop jeune.
(C) Parce que les moineaux ne font mal à personne.
(D) Parce que les moineaux ne sont pas bons à
manger.

85. Pourquoi le garçon décide-t-il de ne plus tirer sur les
moineaux?

(A) Parce qu'il a peur du vieil homme.
(B) Parce qu'il a peur de ses grands-parents.
(C) Parce qu'il pense aux hommes qui meurent
à la guerre.
(D) Parce qu'il s'ennuie de le faire.

STOP

IF YOU FINISH BEFORE TIME IS CALLED, YOU MAY CHECK YOUR WORK ON THIS TEST ONLY.
DO NOT TURN TO ANY OTHER TEST IN THIS BOOK.

ANSWER KEY

1. D	18. C	35. B	52. B	69. D
2. B	19. D	36. C	53. C	70. C
3. C	20. A	37. A	54. B	71. A
4. A	21. B	38. D	55. D	72. D
5. C	22. C	39. C	56. C	73. C
6. A	23. A	40. A	57. B	74. B
7. A	24. D	41. B	58. A	75. C
8. A	25. A	42. C	59. B	76. A
9. A	26. A	43. C	60. D	77. D
10. C	27. C	44. B	61. C	78. A
11. B	28. A	45. C	62. C	79. B
12. B	29. B	46. B	63. D	80. C
13. C	30. C	47. A	64. A	81. A
14. D	31. A	48. C	65. A	82. B
15. B	32. C	49. A	66. B	83. C
16. C	33. B	50. B	67. C	84. C
17. A	34. B	51. A	68. B	85. C

ANSWERS AND EXPLANATIONS

1. **D** The idiomatic expression *avoir tort* means "to be wrong."

2. **B** He can't jog because his foot hurts.

3. **C** A *carte d'embarquement* is a boarding pass for the plane.

4. **A** In order to clean the kitchen, one would need to wash the dishes.

5. **C** Sophie decided to clean so that her room would be *en ordre* (in order).

6. **A** The bad grade in school was the result of not paying attention in class.

7. **A** He has trouble seeing without his glasses (*lunettes*).

8. **A** The correct past participle is *coupé*, because of the word *ciseaux* (scissors).

9. **A** The only possible action one could perform on the newspapers, given the other choices, would be to gather them up.

10. **C** The only one of these actions a rabbit can perform is <u>to jump</u>.

11. **B** One buys bread at the bakery (*boulangerie*).

12. **B** The sentence says that the city is very interesting, so we know there are a lot of things to <u>see</u> (*voir*).

13. **C** Not knowing what decision to make, I asked my father's <u>opinion</u> (*avis*).

14. **D** The question asks if someone has received <u>news</u> (*nouvelles*) from Marie-France.

15. **B** The verb *éclata* is the only one that describes an explosion.

16. **C** The family had to leave the house because all of the lights were out.

17. **A** When I saw that the accident wasn't serious, I was relieved (*soulagé*).

18. **C** Dominique let out a cry (*un cri*) of joy after finishing her exams.

19. **D** The door (*la porte*) was locked, and Patrick didn't have a key, so he forced it open (*foncée*).

20. **A** The person wants to spend time (*faire un séjour*) in Europe.

21. **B** The correct preposition is *de*, because she talked *about*, or, *of* her classes.

22. **C** The imperfect tense *parlait* indicates that she *was talking* so much that she didn't notice that the train had arrived.

23. **A** The disjunctive pronoun *eux* (*them*) is used to complete the prepositional phrase with *pour* (*for*).

24. **D** The question is asking for information about <u>who</u> went to the cinema.

25. **A** The command *remplis* (*fill*) takes the partitive article *de* to express the idea of filling the glass with (*some*) wine.

26. **A** The adverb *sans* (*without*) is the only one of the choices that can be used with the past infinitive (*avoir pris*) to express the idea of his leaving *without having eaten* dessert.

27. **C** The negative expression *ne . . . que* means *only*, and so *quelques* (*a few*) is the logical response. The adverb *peu* is incorrect, because it takes a preposition *de* before a noun.

28. **A** The doctor *ceased* talking with the woman, the only choice that is logical.

29. **B** The phrase *avant de partir* means *before leaving*. The infinitive *quitter* is incorrect because it must always be followed by a direct object.

30. **C** The conjunction *bien que* (*although*) is correct in this context.

31. **A** The adverb *mal* (*badly*) describes how she explained the exercises.

32. **C** The adverb form *lentement* modifies the verb *manger* (*eats more slowly*).

33. **B** The verb *penser* takes the preposition *à* to express the idea of *thinking about* (*having an opinion of*) something. It contracts with *lequel* to become *auquel*.

34. **B** The country *Mexique* is of masculine gender in French, and *au* is the correct preposition before a masculine country.

35. **B** The bus is *driven* (*conduit*) by M. Luneau.

36. **C** In the rest of the sentence, M. Luneau is smiling and greeting the children, so we know that he is *happy* (*heureux*).

37. **A** M. Luneau greets children by nodding his *head* (*tête*).

38. **D** M. Luneau has a head of gray *hair* (*cheveux*).

39. **C** The conjunction *quoi que* is followed by the subjunctive *fassions*.

40. **A** In spite of the children's pleas, M. Luneau *always* refused to take the route by the lake.

41. **B** The preposition *au bord du* indicates that *lac* is correct, because it is often used with a body of water.

42. **C** The pronoun *en* refers to the water (*eau*) of which M. Luneau was afraid. *En* is used to replace the structure *de + object;* in this case, M. Luneau *a peur de l'eau.*

43. **C** M. Luneau would notice a car *following* the bus; therefore, the correct preposition is *derrière* (*behind*).

44. **B** Because M. Luneau *explained* to the children that they weren't in a hurry.

45. **C** *La semaine dernière* means *last week.*

46. **B** *Not having received* requires the present participial construction of *avoir* (*ayant*).

47. **A** The verb *tromper* means to make a mistake, perhaps explaining why the payment is late.

48. **C** The mistake was perhaps made *in sending* the payment, the present participial form, *envoyant.*

49. **A** She is being reminded *thus* (*donc*) that the payment is overdue.

50. **B** Her check *will have to arrive* (*the future* of *devoir*) in the singular.

51. **A** The two friends are walking on the banks of the lake (*au bord du lac*).

52. **B** The verb *s'approcher* takes the preposition *de.*

53. **C** The only thing they can have that is the same is their *age.*

54. **B** They're both about 15 years old, *une quinzaine d'années.*

55. **D** The comparative *bigger* takes *que* (*than*).

56. **C** The plural demonstrative adjective *ces* (*these*) is correct.

57. **B** The ad indicates a place more suited for adults who like to stroll in the countryside.

58. **A** Internet access <u>is not</u> one of the amenities listed.

59. **B** The words surrounding *xénophobie* are all negative, and one would conclude that the word means "fear of foreigners."

60. **D** Rama clearly believes that racism is dangerous.

61. **C** The idea that best summarizes the passage is that Rama believes that different races should be not only tolerated, but celebrated, in France.

62. **C** The young man is looking at his watch because his friend hasn't yet arrived.

63. **D** The woman approaches the man because he seems troubled by something.

64. **A** Because his friend hasn't yet arrived, and the man thinks he has been "stood up," one can derive the meaning of this idiomatic expression.

65. **A** The young man mentions that he believes that his friend is seeing another colleague from work, a man named Marc.

66. **B** The old woman is clearly more optimistic about the situation than the young man.

67. **C** The title indicates a misunderstanding, or an error, on the young man's part.

68. **B** The text states that Morocco has been independent since 1956.

69. **D** *Berbères* are the indigenous people of Morocco.

70. **C** The Germans had no influence on Morocco.

71. **A** The term *muezzin* is a religious man who calls the faithful to prayer.

72. **D** *Rai* music is compared to American "rap."

73. **C** The restaurant is open every day except Monday.

74. **B** The one statement that is not true is that the restaurant is open until 1:00 a.m. (midnight).

75. **C** From 1739 to 1748, Great Britain was at war with Spain.

76. **A** The British excluded *Terre-Neuve* from its battles at this time, because it had already conquered *Plaisance.*

77. **D** The superiority of the British naval force (line 10) explains the immediate successes.

78. **A** A part of West Africa was taken by the British (line 14).

79. **B** General James Wolfe was a British officer responsible for decisive victories over the French.

80. **C** If the French had won at St. John's, they would have had more favorable negociations in the Treaty of Paris (lines 26–28).

81. **A** The Treaty of Paris left France in possession of Saint-Pierre and Miquelon (line 37).

82. **B** A *moineau* is a type of bird (a sparrow).

83. **C** The boy's father went off to war.

84. **C** The old man doesn't want the boy to shoot at birds, because they don't harm anyone.

85. **C** The boy decides to quit shooting at birds because he thinks of men dying in the war.

SCORE SHEET

Number of questions correct: _____

Less: 0.33 × number of questions wrong: _____

(Remember that omitted questions are not counted as wrong.)

Raw score: _____

Raw Score	Scaled Score	Raw Score	Scaled Score	Raw Score	Scaled Score	Raw Score	Scaled Score	Raw Score	Scaled Score
85	800	62	710	39	590	16	470	−7	310
84	800	61	710	38	580	15	470	−8	310
83	800	60	700	37	580	14	460	−9	300
82	800	59	700	36	570	13	460	−10	300
81	800	58	690	35	570	12	450	−11	290
80	800	57	690	34	560	11	450	−12	290
79	800	56	680	33	560	10	440	−13	280
78	800	55	680	32	560	9	440	−14	280
77	800	54	670	31	550	8	430	−15	270
76	800	53	670	30	550	7	420	−16	270
75	800	52	660	29	540	6	420	−17	270
74	800	51	660	28	540	5	410	−18	260
73	790	50	650	27	530	4	410	−19	260
72	790	49	650	26	530	3	400	−20	250
71	780	48	640	25	520	2	390	−21	250
70	780	47	630	24	520	1	380	−22	250
69	770	46	630	23	510	0	370	−23	240
68	760	45	620	22	510	−1	360	−24	240
67	750	44	620	21	500	−2	350	−25	230
66	740	43	610	20	500	−3	340	−26	230
65	730	42	600	19	490	−4	330	−27	220
64	720	41	600	18	490	−5	320	−28	220
63	720	40	590	17	480	−6	320		

Note: This is only a sample scoring scale. Scoring scales differ from exam to exam.

THE SAT SPANISH TEST

All About the SAT Spanish Test

What Is the Format of the SAT Spanish Test?

The SAT Spanish test is a 1-hour exam consisting of 85 multiple-choice questions. According to the College Board, the test measures your knowledge of Spanish parts of speech and idiomatic expressions, in both sentences and longer paragraphs.

The questions measuring different language skills are distributed on the test in approximately the following percentages:

SAT Spanish Question Types

Question Type	Approximate Percentage of Test
Vocabulary and Structure	33
Paragraph Completion	33
Reading Comprehension	33

On the test, many questions will ask you to choose the word or words that best complete a sentence or that best fill a blank in a sentence. Sometimes the correct answer will be a word or words that make the sentence grammatically correct. Other times, the correct answer will be a word or words that make sense in the context of the meaning of the sentence.

Also on the test, you will be asked to read short passages and then answer questions about them. The passages may be stories, essays, nonfiction articles, or common materials such as advertisements, train or bus timetables, or official forms.

What School Background Do I Need for the SAT Spanish Test?

The College Board recommends that you have at least 2 years of strong preparation in Spanish before taking the test. You are also advised to take the test while you are actually enrolled in a Spanish class, rather than after you have completed your studies. If you wait until later to take the test, your recall of Spanish may not be as good as you might wish.

How Is the SAT Spanish Test Scored?

On the SAT Spanish test, your "raw score" is calculated as follows: you receive one point for each question you answer correctly, but you lose one-third of a point for each question you answer incorrectly. You do not gain or lose any points for questions that you do not answer at all. Your raw score is then converted into a scaled score by a statistical method that takes into account how well you did compared to others who took the same test. Scaled scores range from 200 to 800 points. Your scaled score will be reported to you, your high school, and to the colleges and universities you designate to receive it.

Scoring scales differ slightly from one version of the test to the next. The scoring scale provided after the Spanish test in this book is only a sample that will show you your approximate scaled score.

What Is the SAT Spanish With Listening Test?

The College Board also offers a test called the SAT Spanish with Listening test. Unlike the regular Spanish test, which requires you only to read Spanish, the Listening test requires you to listen to spoken Spanish and answer questions about what you hear. If you are confident of your ability to understand spoken Spanish, you may choose to take the Listening test instead of the regular SAT Spanish test.

The Listening test is offered only in November. If you choose to take the Listening test, you must bring an acceptable CD player with earphones to the test center.

SAT SPANISH SAMPLE QUESTIONS

Part A of the Spanish Test provides incomplete statements followed by four possible completions. The test-taker must choose the most appropriate completion and fill in the corresponding oval on the answer sheet.

Some questions are designed to test knowledge of vocabulary in the context of statements that reflect spoken or written language. In this fashion, knowledge of various parts of speech (such as adjectives, adverbs, verbs, and nouns) is assessed. Other questions in Part A focus on the correct use of grammatical structures.

Directions: This part consists of a number of incomplete statements, each having four suggested completions. Select the most appropriate completion and fill in the corresponding oval on the answer sheet.

---

1. Los alumnos _____ a la escuela "Gabriela Mistral."

   (A) atienden
   (B) vuelan
   (C) asisten
   (D) toman

2. Ayer ustedes _____ mucho para el examen.

   (A) estudié
   (B) estudiaron
   (C) estudiamos
   (D) estudia

Question 1 tests knowledge of vocabulary. Choice C *asisten* is the correct answer. To answer correctly, you need to know that the verb *asistir* (to attend) is appropriate in the context of the sentence about students and school.

Question 2 tests command of structure. Choice B *estudiaron* is the correct answer. To answer correctly, you need to know that the preterite is the appropriate verb tense for a completed past action and that *estudiaron* is the correct preterite form for the subject pronoun *ustedes*.

Part B of the Spanish Test also focuses on vocabulary and structure but does so by providing paragraphs in which there are numbered blanks for words or phrases that have been omitted. The test-taker must read the paragraph and for each numbered blank choose the most appropriate completion of the four items given.

Directions: In each of the following paragraphs, there are numbered blanks indicating that words or phrases have been omitted. For each blank, four completions are provided. First read through the entire paragraph. Then, for each numbered blank, choose the completion that is most appropriate given the context of the entire paragraph and fill in the corresponding oval on the answer sheet.

Querida Natalia,

Aprovechamos unos momentos libres para escribir __(3)__. Las vacaciones van fenomenal. Nos __(4)__ las playas de Cuba y hemos disfrutado también de la música cubana y la historia tan fascinante de esta isla. Nos quedan cuatro días aquí, así que nos veremos en Lima la __(5)__ que viene.

Un fuerte abrazo,

Clara, Ana y Alex

3. (A) te
   (B) lo
   (C) nos
   (D) me

4. (A) encantamos
   (B) encanto
   (C) encantan
   (D) encantas

5. (A) mes
   (B) hora
   (C) año
   (D) semana

Question 3 tests command of structure. Answer A *te* is the correct choice. To answer correctly, you need to know that the object pronoun *te* refers to Natalia, the recipient of the postcard.

Question 4 tests command of structure. The correct choice is C *encantan*. To answer correctly, you need to know the appropriate conjugation of the verb *encantar*.

Question 5 tests knowledge of vocabulary. Choice D *semana* is correct. To answer correctly, you need to know that this is the only noun listed that fits in the context of the passage.

Part C focuses on reading comprehension in relation to a variety of written texts such as magazine articles, advertisements, letters, historical documents, and prose fiction. The questions are designed to assess comprehension of points such as themes, style, settings, main ideas, supporting information, and specific details. Each reading passage is followed by a number of questions or incomplete statements. In each case, the test-taker must choose the best answer or completion of four possible options and fill in the corresponding oval on the answer sheet.

Directions: Read the following texts carefully for comprehension. Each is followed by a number of questions or incomplete statements. Select the answer or completion that is best according to the text and fill in the corresponding oval on the answer sheet.

FOTOGRAFIA "MARI LUZ"

Hacemos los mejores retratos personales, de familia.
Reportajes de bodas, cumpleaños, bautizos y ocasiones especiales.
El único establecimiento de este tipo con la tecnología más avanzada en fotografía y video digital del mercado.

NO ESPERE MAS Y VENGA A VERNOS

Avda. Julio A. Roca 1163
Buenos Aires, C1067ABN
Tel. 4340718

6. Según el anuncio, ¿Cómo se puede obtener más información sobre Fotografía Mari Luz?

(A) Se puede alquilar un video.
(B) Se puede buscar en Internet.
(C) Se puede visitar la tienda o llamar por teléfono.
(D) Se puede hablar con la familia.

7. ¿Por qué es esta tienda un establecimiento único?

(A) porque hace los mejores retratos del mercado
(B) porque hace reportajes para ocasiones especiales
(C) porque hace fotografía y video
(D) porque usa la tecnología más avanzada del mercado

Question 6 asks students to identify how to get more information about Fotografía Mari Luz. The correct answer is C because the reader is encouraged to go to the store and because the address and phone number are given.

Question 7 asks about a specific detail in the advertisement: What makes Fotografía Mari Luz a one-of-a-kind business? The correct answer is D—its use of the latest technology.

SUCCEEDING ON THE SAT SPANISH TEST

Part A

Knowledge of both vocabulary and grammar is assessed in the first part of the test. As regards vocabulary, consider the context of a sentence to help determine the most logical word choice. As you study, be sure to review parts of speech, such as verbs, nouns, and adjectives, in relation to different themes and settings with which you are familiar. In terms of grammar, look for cues that indicate a specific time frame or call for a certain verb tense. For example, is there reference to the habitual past (requiring the imperfect tense) or completed past actions (expressed with the preterite tense)? In addition, determine if sentences require the subjunctive mood or if you need to choose between contrasting verbs such as *ser/estar* or *saber/conocer*. Last, looking for agreement between the different parts of speech (subject and verb, article and noun, etc.) can also help you choose the correct responses.

Part B

The second part of the Spanish test also assesses knowledge of vocabulary and structure but does so via reading passages in which words or phrases have been omitted. In this section, it is helpful to first read an entire passage in order to gain a general understanding of the paragraph and then proceed to the questions. The recommended strategies for Part A also will be helpful here. In particular, study the different Spanish verb tenses and moods in order to make appropriate choices from the options given. As regards vocabulary, considering the central themes of the passages will help in selecting the most logical responses, be they nouns, verbs, or descriptive words.

Part C

The third part of the test focuses on reading comprehension by presenting a variety of reading passages followed by multiple-choice questions. Some questions are general in nature, whereas others focus on specific information from a reading. As with Part B, read a passage carefully (more than once if necessary) before answering any questions. Don't be concerned if you do not understand certain words. To facilitate your comprehension, look at the text format to anticipate content and look also for cognates—words that are similar in Spanish and English. In addition, you often will be able to determine certain meanings from context or other words and phrases that you do understand.

SPANISH PRACTICE TEST

Treat this practice test as the actual test and complete it in one 60-minute sitting. Use the following answer sheet to fill in your multiple-choice answers. Once you have completed this practice test:

1. Check your answers using the Answer Key.
2. Review the Answers and Explanations.
3. Complete the Score Sheet to see how well you did.

ANSWER SHEET

Tear out this answer sheet and use it to complete the practice test. Determine the BEST answer for each question. Then fill in the appropriate oval.

1. Ⓐ Ⓑ Ⓒ Ⓓ Ⓔ	26. Ⓐ Ⓑ Ⓒ Ⓓ Ⓔ	51. Ⓐ Ⓑ Ⓒ Ⓓ Ⓔ	76. Ⓐ Ⓑ Ⓒ Ⓓ Ⓔ
2. Ⓐ Ⓑ Ⓒ Ⓓ Ⓔ	27. Ⓐ Ⓑ Ⓒ Ⓓ Ⓔ	52. Ⓐ Ⓑ Ⓒ Ⓓ Ⓔ	77. Ⓐ Ⓑ Ⓒ Ⓓ Ⓔ
3. Ⓐ Ⓑ Ⓒ Ⓓ Ⓔ	28. Ⓐ Ⓑ Ⓒ Ⓓ Ⓔ	53. Ⓐ Ⓑ Ⓒ Ⓓ Ⓔ	78. Ⓐ Ⓑ Ⓒ Ⓓ Ⓔ
4. Ⓐ Ⓑ Ⓒ Ⓓ Ⓔ	29. Ⓐ Ⓑ Ⓒ Ⓓ Ⓔ	54. Ⓐ Ⓑ Ⓒ Ⓓ Ⓔ	79. Ⓐ Ⓑ Ⓒ Ⓓ Ⓔ
5. Ⓐ Ⓑ Ⓒ Ⓓ Ⓔ	30. Ⓐ Ⓑ Ⓒ Ⓓ Ⓔ	55. Ⓐ Ⓑ Ⓒ Ⓓ Ⓔ	80. Ⓐ Ⓑ Ⓒ Ⓓ Ⓔ
6. Ⓐ Ⓑ Ⓒ Ⓓ Ⓔ	31. Ⓐ Ⓑ Ⓒ Ⓓ Ⓔ	56. Ⓐ Ⓑ Ⓒ Ⓓ Ⓕ	81. Ⓐ Ⓑ Ⓒ Ⓓ Ⓔ
7. Ⓐ Ⓑ Ⓒ Ⓓ Ⓔ	32. Ⓐ Ⓑ Ⓒ Ⓓ Ⓔ	57. Ⓐ Ⓑ Ⓒ Ⓓ Ⓔ	82. Ⓐ Ⓑ Ⓒ Ⓓ Ⓔ
8. Ⓐ Ⓑ Ⓒ Ⓓ Ⓔ	33. Ⓐ Ⓑ Ⓒ Ⓓ Ⓔ	58. Ⓐ Ⓑ Ⓒ Ⓓ Ⓔ	83. Ⓐ Ⓑ Ⓒ Ⓓ Ⓔ
9. Ⓐ Ⓑ Ⓒ Ⓓ Ⓔ	34. Ⓐ Ⓑ Ⓒ Ⓓ Ⓔ	59. Ⓐ Ⓑ Ⓒ Ⓓ Ⓔ	84. Ⓐ Ⓑ Ⓒ Ⓓ Ⓔ
10. Ⓐ Ⓑ Ⓒ Ⓓ Ⓔ	35. Ⓐ Ⓑ Ⓒ Ⓓ Ⓔ	60. Ⓐ Ⓑ Ⓒ Ⓓ Ⓔ	85. Ⓐ Ⓑ Ⓒ Ⓓ Ⓔ
11. Ⓐ Ⓑ Ⓒ Ⓓ Ⓔ	36. Ⓐ Ⓑ Ⓒ Ⓓ Ⓔ	61. Ⓐ Ⓑ Ⓒ Ⓓ Ⓔ	
12. Ⓐ Ⓑ Ⓒ Ⓓ Ⓔ	37. Ⓐ Ⓑ Ⓒ Ⓓ Ⓔ	62. Ⓐ Ⓑ Ⓒ Ⓓ Ⓔ	
13. Ⓐ Ⓑ Ⓒ Ⓓ Ⓔ	38. Ⓐ Ⓑ Ⓒ Ⓓ Ⓔ	63. Ⓐ Ⓑ Ⓒ Ⓓ Ⓔ	
14. Ⓐ Ⓑ Ⓒ Ⓓ Ⓔ	39. Ⓐ Ⓑ Ⓒ Ⓓ Ⓔ	64. Ⓐ Ⓑ Ⓒ Ⓓ Ⓔ	
15. Ⓐ Ⓑ Ⓒ Ⓓ Ⓔ	40. Ⓐ Ⓑ Ⓒ Ⓓ Ⓔ	65. Ⓐ Ⓑ Ⓒ Ⓓ Ⓔ	
16. Ⓐ Ⓑ Ⓒ Ⓓ Ⓔ	41. Ⓐ Ⓑ Ⓒ Ⓓ Ⓔ	66. Ⓐ Ⓑ Ⓒ Ⓓ Ⓔ	
17. Ⓐ Ⓑ Ⓒ Ⓓ Ⓔ	42. Ⓐ Ⓑ Ⓒ Ⓓ Ⓔ	67. Ⓐ Ⓑ Ⓒ Ⓓ Ⓔ	
18. Ⓐ Ⓑ Ⓒ Ⓓ Ⓔ	43. Ⓐ Ⓑ Ⓒ Ⓓ Ⓔ	68. Ⓐ Ⓑ Ⓒ Ⓓ Ⓔ	
19. Ⓐ Ⓑ Ⓒ Ⓓ Ⓔ	44. Ⓐ Ⓑ Ⓒ Ⓓ Ⓔ	69. Ⓐ Ⓑ Ⓒ Ⓓ Ⓔ	
20. Ⓐ Ⓑ Ⓒ Ⓓ Ⓔ	45. Ⓐ Ⓑ Ⓒ Ⓓ Ⓔ	70. Ⓐ Ⓑ Ⓒ Ⓓ Ⓔ	
21. Ⓐ Ⓑ Ⓒ Ⓓ Ⓔ	46. Ⓐ Ⓑ Ⓒ Ⓓ Ⓔ	71. Ⓐ Ⓑ Ⓒ Ⓓ Ⓔ	
22. Ⓐ Ⓑ Ⓒ Ⓓ Ⓔ	47. Ⓐ Ⓑ Ⓒ Ⓓ Ⓔ	72. Ⓐ Ⓑ Ⓒ Ⓓ Ⓔ	
23. Ⓐ Ⓑ Ⓒ Ⓓ Ⓔ	48. Ⓐ Ⓑ Ⓒ Ⓓ Ⓔ	73. Ⓐ Ⓑ Ⓒ Ⓓ Ⓔ	
24. Ⓐ Ⓑ Ⓒ Ⓓ Ⓔ	49. Ⓐ Ⓑ Ⓒ Ⓓ Ⓔ	74. Ⓐ Ⓑ Ⓒ Ⓓ Ⓔ	
25. Ⓐ Ⓑ Ⓒ Ⓓ Ⓔ	50. Ⓐ Ⓑ Ⓒ Ⓓ Ⓔ	75. Ⓐ Ⓑ Ⓒ Ⓓ Ⓔ	

SPANISH PRACTICE TEST

PLEASE NOTE THAT YOUR ANSWER SHEET HAS FIVE ANSWER POSITIONS MARKED A, B, C, D, E WHILE THE QUESTIONS THROUGHOUT THE TEST CONTAIN ONLY FOUR CHOICES. BE SURE <u>NOT</u> TO MAKE ANY MARKS IN COLUMN E.

Part A

Directions: This part consists of a number of incomplete statements, each having four suggested completions. Select the most appropriate completion and fill in the corresponding oval on the answer sheet.

1. Los sábados mi familia y yo _____ en el Restaurante Tamarindo.

   (A) vivimos
   (B) comemos
   (C) salimos
   (D) llegamos

2. Los _____ llegaron muy temprano a la fiesta.

   (A) árboles
   (B) invitados
   (C) coches
   (D) jardineros

3. ¿ _____ tú de dónde es María?

   (A) Conoces
   (B) Aprendes
   (C) Sabes
   (D) Crees

4. Yo _____ San Juan. Es una ciudad encantadora.

   (A) conozco
   (B) aprendo
   (C) sé
   (D) entiendo

5. ¡Qué lástima! No podemos ir a la feria porque el carro de mi papá no _____ bien.

   (A) trabaja
   (B) mueve
   (C) funciona
   (D) salta

6. Mamá, te llamo para decirte que _____ en la casa de la abuela.

   (A) estoy
   (B) voy
   (C) soy
   (D) doy

7. ¡Hola! Soy de los Estados Unidos. Y tú, ¿de dónde _____?

   (A) es
   (B) son
   (C) eres
   (D) somos

8. ¿Sabes que cuando era pequeña _____ en México?

   (A) vivamos
   (B) viviríamos
   (C) viviremos
   (D) vivíamos

9. Ayer yo _____ mucho en la oficina.

   (A) trabajaron
   (B) trabajé
   (C) trabajo
   (D) trabajamos

10. La semana pasada estaba _____ con mi amiga Ana en la biblioteca cuando mi compañera gritó "¡Fuego! ¡Fuego!"

    (A) cocinando
    (B) volviendo
    (C) estudiando
    (D) asistiendo

11. Los domingos los Sres. García y nosotros siempre nos reunimos para charlar _____.

    (A) en la ferretería
    (B) en el coche
    (C) en el parque
    (D) en la peluquería

12. _____ que dices no es verdad.

    (A) La
    (B) Lo
    (C) Le
    (D) Se

GO ON TO THE NEXT PAGE

13. El sábado es su cumpleaños y no tenemos ningún regalo. _____ compraremos mañana.

 (A) Se lo
 (B) Se la
 (C) Los
 (D) Se le

14. Cuando _____ la cabeza, tomo una aspirina.

 (A) me gusta
 (B) me duele
 (C) me encanta
 (D) me fascina

15. Mi hermano busca _____ que esté en el centro de la ciudad.

 (A) un árbol
 (B) una lámpara
 (C) un pasaporte
 (D) un apartamento

16. Mis padres esperan que yo saque buenas _____ en mis estudios.

 (A) amigas
 (B) notas
 (C) grados
 (D) cursos

17. Mi amiga quiere que visite Guatemala porque dice que es un país _____.

 (A) enorme
 (B) real
 (C) fascinante
 (D) contento

18. Susana, no _____ a la tienda porque ya está cerrada.

 (A) ir
 (B) íbamos
 (C) iba
 (D) vayas

19. Pedro, si vienes _____, podemos ir al concierto.

 (A) temprano
 (B) tarde
 (C) regularmente
 (D) con paciencia

20. En mi familia _____ que la educación es fundamental.

 (A) diciendo
 (B) se dice
 (C) dice
 (D) decir

21. _____ pensaba que el huracán iba a ser tan fuerte.

 (A) Nada
 (B) Algo
 (C) Nadie
 (D) Algunos

22. _____ amigos nos visitarán en Octubre.

 (A) Mi
 (B) Nuestros
 (C) Ellos
 (D) Su

23. No creemos que Susana _____ en California.

 (A) viva
 (B) escriba
 (C) beba
 (D) comprenda

24. El cocinero necesita _____ para servir el postre.

 (A) una nevera
 (B) un vaso
 (C) unas sillas
 (D) unos platos

25. Es importante _____ llegues a tiempo.

 (A) lo que
 (B) que
 (C) cuando
 (D) lo cual

26. Carolina se acuesta temprano. Por eso está _____ a las siete de la manana.

 (A) dormida
 (B) acostada
 (C) despierta
 (D) apagada

27. Si Laura _____ más, no tendría problemas económicos.

 (A) viajara
 (B) trabajara
 (C) durmiera
 (D) comprara

28. Es necesario _____ para tener éxito en la escuela.

 (A) estudiar
 (B) estudie
 (C) estudia
 (D) estudien

GO ON TO THE NEXT PAGE

29. En los Juegos Olímpicos, la medalla de oro fue para la persona que terminó en _____ lugar.
    (A) uno
    (B) primer
    (C) algun
    (D) tercer

30. Rosa María es una gran profesora. Explica las cosas _____.
    (A) tristemente
    (B) difícilmente
    (C) claramente
    (D) calladamente

31. Nuestra ciudad tiene _____ puntos de interés.
    (A) algún
    (B) ningún
    (C) algo
    (D) algunos

32. Antes de ir a la piscina tenemos que encontrar los trajes de baño y _____.
    (A) las toallas
    (B) los instrumentos
    (C) los libros
    (D) las hojas

Part B

Directions: In each of the following paragraphs, there are numbered blanks indicating that words or phrases have been omitted. For each blank, four completions are provided. First read through the entire paragraph. Then, for each numbered blank, choose the completion that is most appropriate given the context of the entire paragraph and fill in the corresponding oval on the answer sheet.

Escribo estas líneas para __(33)__ el espectáculo que es la corrida de toros. __(34)__ que unos fanáticos quieren eliminar esta __(35)__ pero me parece una parte importante de __(36)__ cultura. En la corrida celebramos la fuerza y la belleza del animal y __(37)__ la inteligencia y la valentía del matador. __(38)__ la vida y la muerte en un drama __(39)__ de color, emoción, y drama. La corrida es algo __(40)__ y especial que debemos celebrar.

33. (A) criticar
    (B) defender
    (C) dudar
    (D) protestar

34. (A) Sé
    (B) Había sabido
    (C) Sabremos
    (D) Haya sabido

35. (A) tarea
    (B) tema
    (C) historia
    (D) tradición

36. (A) sus
    (B) nuestra
    (C) tu
    (D) mis

37. (A) pronto
    (B) tampoco
    (C) tarde
    (D) también

38. (A) Vemos
    (B) Vimos
    (C) Vamos
    (D) Vámonos

39. (A) faltando
    (B) triste
    (C) lleno
    (D) atrapado

40. (A) aburrido
    (B) único
    (C) negativo
    (D) caro

GO ON TO THE NEXT PAGE

Los jóvenes sabían que les esperaban muchas __(41)__ pero al final __(42)__ aún mas de lo que habían imaginado. Recuedan con alegría sus viajes por la __(43)__ con sus tíos y primos, y por supuesto las deliciosas __(44)__ y la tertulia al final del día. Lo mejor, quizás, fueron los campamentos de verano en los cuales practicaron muchos deportes y __(45)__ de la naturaleza los días de calor. __(46)__ se despidieron con tristeza al terminar las vacaciones. Tenían que ir al __(47)__ otra vez pero sabían que __(48)__ volverían a ver en un __(49)__ no muy lejano

41. (A) exámenes
    (B) aventuras
    (C) clases
    (D) comidas

42. (A) hicieron
    (B) hacen
    (C) harán
    (D) hago

43. (A) país
    (B) estado
    (C) aeropuerto
    (D) región

44. (A) desayunos
    (B) cenas
    (C) platos
    (D) cocinas

45. (A) encanto
    (B) gustó
    (C) disfrutaron
    (D) encantan

46. (A) Nadie
    (B) Todos
    (C) Alguien
    (D) Yo

47. (A) colegio
    (B) tienda
    (C) trabajar
    (D) despacho

48. (A) me
    (B) se
    (C) te
    (D) la

49. (A) territorio
    (B) presente
    (C) pasado
    (D) futuro

Salsa picante, enchiladas, paella, flan. Hay ciertas __(50)__ latinas que han ganado una bien merecida fama internacional __(51)__ los aficionados de la buena cocina. Sin embargo, se __(52)__ decir que la verdadera riqueza culinaria del mundo hispanohablante está por describir: Una variedad de __(53)__ que reflejan la historia, la diversidad y la creatividad de __(54)__ culturas. Como ejemplo __(55)__ el siguiente menú—uno de muchos que encontrará en *La mesa latina:* Para __(56)__, un sabroso ceviche, queso manchego y aceitunas al tomillo. El banquete __(57)__ con pollo al ajillo, arroz con frijoles negros y plátanos fritos. Y de __(58)__, una macedonia de frutas, alfajores y un rico café para poner fin a una comida sana y sabrosa.

50. (A) bebidas
    (B) comidas
    (C) menus
    (D) ideas

51. (A) entre
    (B) por
    (C) para
    (D) a

52. (A) puedo
    (B) poder
    (C) podemos
    (D) puede

53. (A) cucharas
    (B) tenedores
    (C) platos
    (D) cuchillos

54. (A) nuestras
    (B) su
    (C) tu
    (D) vuestros

55. (A) lamento
    (B) sugiero
    (C) pienso
    (D) leo

GO ON TO THE NEXT PAGE

56. (A) empezar
    (B) terminar
    (C) celebrar
    (D) disgustar

57. (A) seguir
    (B) sigue

    (C) sigo
    (D) está siguiendo

58. (A) plato principal
    (B) aperitivo
    (C) tapas
    (D) postre

Part C

Directions: Read the following texts carefully for comprehension. Each is followed by a number of questions or incomplete statements. Select the answer or completion that is best according to the text and fill in the corresponding oval on the answer sheet.

Eran las ocho de la mañana de un sábado cualquiera y Gloria llevaba navegando dos horas en internet cuando de repente encontró lo que buscaba.

—¡Carmen! ¡Carmen! ¡Despierta! ¡Despierta! Mira lo que he encontrado.

—¡Gloria! ¡Por Dios! ¿Por qué me despiertas tan temprano. Es sábado.

—Mira este anuncio. Es lo que he soñado siempre.

(Carmen lo mira atentamente y lee en voz alta)

—Bienes Raíces. República Dominicana. Se vende casa en Punta Cana. 4 recámaras, salón, comedor, cocina americana. 250.000 dólares. ¡Ay, mujer! Tu siempre soñando. ¿Cómo lo vas a comprar, si no tienes donde caerte muerta?

—No te lo dije antes pero, ¿te acuerdas de mi tío Isidro, el hermano de mi abuelo?

—Sí, ¿aquel que había emigrado a la Argentina?

—Sí, el mismo. Se murió el año pasado y el mes pasado me llamó un abogado. Resulta que nos ha dejado 150.000 dólares a cada uno de sus sobrinos.

—¡No me digas!

—Sí, y con ese dinero tengo para pagar la entrada. Voy a llamar ahora mismo a la agencia inmobiliaria.

59. Este diálogo tiene lugar en

    (A) un colegio
    (B) una casa.
    (C) un negocio
    (D) un cine.

60. ¿Cuál es la relación entre el tío Isidro y el abuelo de Gloria?

    (A) Son primos.
    (B) Son sobrinos.
    (C) Son hermanos.
    (D) Son amigos.

61. ¿Por qué puede pensar Gloria en comprar una casa?

    (A) Gloria tiene un trabajo muy bueno.
    (B) Ella ganó la lotería.
    (C) Carmen le va a prestar dinero.
    (D) Gloria heredó dinero de un pariente.

62. ¿Cuál es un sinónimo de *bienes raíces?*

    (A) Agencia inmobiliaria
    (B) Entrada
    (C) Anuncio
    (D) Abogado

63. ¿Qué implica Carmen con la frase "No tienes donde caerte muerta"?

    (A) Gloria tiene mucho dinero.
    (B) Gloria no tiene mucho dinero.
    (C) Gloria está enferma.
    (D) El tío Isidro murió.

64. ¿Qué sabemos del tío Isidro?

    (A) Murió a los 90 años.
    (B) Fue un abogado.
    (C) Emigró a otro país.
    (D) Tuvo una casa en la República Dominicana.

GO ON TO THE NEXT PAGE

RESTAURANTE VELERO

Cocina caribeña e internacional;
Amplia selección de pescado, mariscos, carne y pasta
Comida y cena martes a domingo con música en directo

**Paseo Marítimo 43
Cartagena, Colombia
Tel. 8945650**

---

65. ¿Qué ofrece el Restaurante Velero además de comida?

    (A) Una bella vista del mar
    (B) Una banda que toca para los clientes
    (C) Servicio al domicilio
    (D) Viajes en un velero especial

66. No es posible comer en el Restaurante Velero
    _____.

    (A) los lunes por la tarde
    (B) los fines de semana
    (C) los martes por la noche
    (D) los días festivos

Aquel verano del 2004 se presentaba como otro cualquiera sin nada especial. Desde la mañana hasta la tarde la pasaríamos tumbados en las arenas cálidas del Mediterráneo con breves interrupciones para darnos un chapuzón en el mar y sacarnos la pereza de encima. Ya por la tarde, y después de una suculenta comilona a base de ensalada, mariscos y otras delicias del mar, otra vez la pasaríamos tumbados pero esta vez en una tumbona bien acolchadita bajo los pinos y junto al tomillo y romero que nos embriagarían con sus aromas hasta llevarnos a un profundo sopor. Al anochecer nos prepararíamos para el paseo diario y después a la discoteca hasta las tantas de la madrugada.

Sin embargo, ese verano del 2004 iba a ser diferente, de hecho, fue diferente. Mis padres decidieron que íbamos a ir al País Vasco en lugar de a la Costa Brava y, ahora puedo decir que el viaje fue muy cultural y divertidísimo. Visitamos Vitoria, la capital, que es la ciudad europea con más espacios verdes por habitante. Desde allí fuimos a San Sebastián, una ciudad preciosa con unas playas y edificios majestuosos. Mis padres pasearon por el puerto viejo, mi hermano fue al acuario y yo fui a la playa. Al día siguiente salimos para Bilbao pero primero pasamos por el museo "Chillida Leku" del ya fallecido escultor Eduardo Chillida donde encontramos muchas de sus hermosas esculturas de hierro. Desde allí seguimos para Bilbao y pudimos admirar el Museo Guggenheim de Arte Moderno y Contemporáneo que en si mismo es una escultura. Yo diría una escultura enorme hecha de titanio, obra del arquitecto canadiense Frank Gehry. En Bilbao también paseamos por el "casco viejo" con sus calles estrechas y por el ensanche donde admiramos sus casas señoriales. Yo fui de compras al "Corte Inglés" mientras mis papás comían en un típico bar de tapas y mi hermano como siempre decidió quedarse en el hotel para dormir.

El último día fuimos a la playa. ¡Qué aventura tuvimos! Por la mañana estuvimos tomando el sol un rato y después fuimos a comer a un chiringuito, sólo llevábamos los bañadores puestos y mi papá llevaba también la cartera con toda su documentación. El resto de nuestras posesiones se quedaron en la playa (ropa, bolsos, etc.). Como somos del interior y nunca habíamos estado en el mar Cantábrico, no sabíamos de las mareas. Así que mientras nosotros comíamos una deliciosa comida vasca, la marea iba subiendo, llevándose todas nuestras cosas. Qué sorpresa nos llevamos cuando volvimos del chiringuito y casi toda la playa había desaparecido junto a nuestra ropa. "¡Qué horror!" gritó mi mamá mientras los demás nos moríamos de la risa.

La verdad es que fue un verano muy divertido y diferente a todos los otros. Como dice el refrán: "Nunca te acostarás sin saber una cosa más."

GO ON TO THE NEXT PAGE

67. ¿De qué se trata la lectura?

   (A) La historia del País Vasco
   (B) Unas vacaciones memorables
   (C) Las playas del Mediterráneo
   (D) Ir de compras

68. El tono de esta selección es

   (A) entusiasta
   (B) melancólico
   (C) misterioso
   (D) pesimista

69. Según la narradora, ¿cómo pasaba la familia las vacaciones antes de ir al País Vasco?

   (A) Se quedaba en su pueblo.
   (B) Hacía viajes culturales por España.
   (C) Estudiaba escultura y arquitectura.
   (D) Pasaba tiempo en las playas de la Costa Brava.

70. ¿De dónde es el arquitecto del Museo Guggenheim en Bilbao?

   (A) España
   (B) Canadá
   (C) Bilbao
   (D) San Sebastián

71. ¿Cuál es un dato de interés de Vitoria?

   (A) Hay muchos parques y árboles.
   (B) Tiene playas preciosas.
   (C) Tiene el Museo "Chillida Leku".
   (D) Hay un acuario nuevo.

72. En el contexto de la narración, ¿qué quiere decir *chiringuito?*

   (A) Un restaurante formal
   (B) Una playa del Mar Cantábrico
   (C) Una tienda de bañadores
   (D) Un restaurante informal

73. Para la narradora la anécdota del último día en la playa es

   (A) filosófica
   (B) cómica
   (C) triste
   (D) histórica

74. ¿Cuál es el mensaje del refrán "Nunca te acostarás sin saber una cosa más"?

   (A) Es necesario saber hablar español.
   (B) Es importante acostarse pronto.
   (C) Cada día se aprende algo nuevo.
   (D) La educación universitaria es esencial.

Sea en España, Guatemala, México u otro país de Latinoamérica, Las alfombras florales son una costumbre y una tradición arraigada a la herencia católica. En Huamantla, México, dicen que su origen data de las fiestas prehispánicas en honor a Xochiquetzali, Diosa de la fertilidad. Hoy en día se elaboran estas alfombras para la celebración de su Santa Patrona, la Virgen de la Caridad.

   Se llaman alfombras florales porque la principal materia prima es la flor, a pesar de que en muchos pueblos, son comunes otros materiales como el aserrín y la arena teñidos de diferentes y vivos colores, la cáscara de cacao y arroz, las semillas, el maíz, los frijoles, las frutas tropicales, el corozo o la flor de palma.

   Las alfombras se hacen en las calles para una festejo especial, y en ésto difieren los distintos países. En España es para la Procesión del Corpus Christi, en Guatemala para las procesiones de Semana Santa y en México para la fiesta del Santo Patrón. Su elaboración compleja, cuidadosa y bien calculada comienza el año anterior con diferentes diseños y dibujos. Todos los vecinos participan, desde los más jóvenes hasta los más mayores, y se ponen a trabajar la noche anterior. Mientras unos dibujan en el suelo o usan plantillas otros van arrancando los pétalos de las flores u organizando las materias primas y colocándolos en el diseño hasta entrada la mañana con el fin de crear la mejor y la más hermosa de las alfombras. Para los vecinos ha sido una larga noche de trabajo y esperan con impaciencia el paso de la procesión sea el Santo Patrón, la Virgen, o un paso de la procesión llevando al Cristo a hombros. Son unos pocos minutos pero para aquellos que han participado ha merecido la pena, y sólo les queda esperar a que llegue otro año. Es una tarea muy elaborada para un acto tan efímero.

75. ¿Cuál es el tema principal de la lectura?

   (A) las fiestas locales
   (B) la religión en el mundo hispanohablante
   (C) el cultivo de flores
   (D) las alfombras florales

76. Según el artículo, ¿cuándo se hacen alfombras en Guatemala?

   (A) Corpus Christi
   (B) Semana Santa
   (C) Navidad
   (D) La fiesta del Santo Patrón

GO ON TO THE NEXT PAGE

77. ¿Cuál es el propósito del autor?

    (A) describir
    (B) persuadir
    (C) protestar
    (D) entretener

78. Se puede apreciar las alfombras

    (A) por muchos días
    (B) en los museos nacionales
    (C) en las iglesias
    (D) por poco tiempo

79. Algo típico de las alfombras florales es

    (A) el uso de colores oscuros.
    (B) la participación exclusiva de los jóvenes.
    (C) el uso de materiales naturales.
    (D) la comida preparada para celebrar la fiesta.

80. ¿Qué reacción expresa la escritora al escribir de las alfombras?

    (A) Le impresionan mucho.
    (B) No le llaman la atención.
    (C) Se siente muy religiosa.
    (D) Se siente triste.

Algeciras (Cádiz)

Ayer fue interceptado por la Guardia Civil uno de los mayores barcos de tráfico humano donde se encontraban hacinados en su bodega 143 inmigrantes ilegales. El barco pesquero de 30 metros fue interceptado debido a problemas de navegación en el Estrecho de Gibraltar y fue remolcado hasta Algeciras donde el patrón del barco confesó el tipo de mercancía que transportaba en su bodega. El barco que salió de Mauritania tenía como destino la costa de Cádiz para allí desembarcar la mercancía. Los 143 indocumentados son de origen subsahariano y fueron atendidos por la Cruz Roja a su llegada a Algeciras.

81. Esta lectura es

    (A) un fragmento de una novela
    (B) un editorial en una revista
    (C) un artículo periodístico
    (D) una crónica deportiva

82. El tema principal es

    (A) la inmigración ilegal
    (B) la importancia de la pesca
    (C) la costa de Cádiz
    (D) los barcos nuevos

83. ¿Qué transportaba el patrón del barco?

    (A) pescado para vender en Cádiz
    (B) personas indocumentadas
    (C) materiales para la Cruz Roja
    (D) botellas de vino

84. ¿De dónde venían los pasajeros del barco?

    (A) Europa
    (B) Africa
    (C) China
    (D) España

85. ¿Qué organización internacional menciona la noticia?

    (A) La Guardia Civil
    (B) El Estrecho de Gibraltar
    (C) La Cruz Roja
    (D) Algeciras

S T O P

IF YOU FINISH BEFORE TIME IS CALLED, YOU MAY CHECK YOUR WORK ON THIS TEST ONLY.
DO NOT TURN TO ANY OTHER TEST IN THIS BOOK.

ANSWER KEY

1. B	18. D	35. D	52. D	69. D
2. B	19. A	36. B	53. C	70. B
3. C	20. B	37. D	54. A	71. A
4. A	21. C	38. A	55. B	72. D
5. C	22. B	39. C	56. A	73. B
6. A	23. A	40. B	57. B	74. C
7. C	24. D	41. B	58. D	75. D
8. D	25. B	42. A	59. B	76. B
9. B	26. C	43. D	60. C	77. A
10. C	27. B	44. B	61. D	78. D
11. C	28. A	45. C	62. A	79. C
12. B	29. B	46. B	63. B	80. A
13. A	30. C	47. A	64. C	81. C
14. B	31. D	48. B	65. B	82. A
15. D	32. A	49. D	66. A	83. B
16. B	33. B	50. A	67. B	84. B
17. C	34. A	51. A	68. A	85. C

ANSWERS AND EXPLANATIONS

1. **B** *Comemos* is the logical choice in the context of a restaurant.

2. **B** *Invitados* refers to the people invited to the party.

3. **C** The verb *saber* is used to express knowledge of information, such as María's hometown.

4. **A** The verb *conocer* means to know people, places, or things.

5. **C** The verb *funcionar* means "to work" when talking about cars and machines.

6. **A** The verb *estar* is used to express location.

7. **C** The verb *ser* is used to express origin. *Eres* is the correct present tense form for the subject pronoun *tú*.

8. **D** The imperfect tense is used to describe an ongoing action in the past.

9. **B** The preterite tense is used to discuss completed actions. The correct form for the subject pronoun *yo* is *trabajé*.

10. **C** *Estudiando* is the logical choice in the context of a library.

11. **C** *En el parque* is the logical location for a Sunday social conversation.

12. **B** The neuter pronoun *lo* is used to refer to an idea or something that is not specified.

13. **A** *Se* refers to the person celebrating a birthday, while *lo* refers to *regalo*.

14. **B** *Me duele* is the logical choice when referring to a headache.

15. **D** *Un apartamento* is the appropriate choice in the context of looking for something downtown.

16. **B** *Notas* refers to grades earned in school.

17. **C** *Fascinante* is the word that best explains why you should visit Guatemala.

18. **D** The negative command *no vayas* tells Susana what not to do.

19. **A** *Temprano* (early) is the logical vocabulary choice in the context of the message.

20. **B** The impersonal *se dice* is correct in this general statement.

21. **C** *Nadie* refers to "no one" in this negative statement.

22. **B** The possessive adjective *nuestros* agrees with the noun *amigos*.

23. **A** *Viva* is the logical choice in relation to California.

24. **D** *Platos* (plates) are needed for the dessert.

25. **B** The relative pronoun *que* is used to connect the two clauses.

26. **C** The fact that Carolina goes to bed early means that she will be awake early.

27. **B** *Trabajara* is the logical choice given the reference to Laura's financial situation.

28. **A** The impersonal statement requires an infinitive.

29. **B** The ordinal number *primer* refers to first place and the gold medal.

30. **C** *Claramente* is the word that best describes how the teacher explains things.

31. **D** The indefinite word *algunos* agrees with the noun *puntos*.

32. **A** *Las toallas* is the logical choice in the context of going to the pool.

33. **B** The author is a fan of the bullfight.

34. **A** The author knows that some people oppose the bullfight. In his statement he presents this personal knowledge with the verb form *sé*.

35. **D** The bullfight is a tradition.

36. **B** The possessive adjective *nuestra* agrees with *cultura* and includes the author along with others.

37. **D** *También* is the appropriate word in this affirmative statement.

38. **A** The present tense *nosotros vemos* refers to what we see in the bullfight.

39. **C** The adjective *lleno* describes the word *drama*.

40. **B** The author maintains that the bullfight is a unique, one-of-a-kind event.

41. **B** *Aventuras* is the logical choice in relation to summer vacation

42. **A** The preterite verb *hicieron* refers to completed actions in the past.

43. **D** The noun *región* agrees with the definite article *la*.

44. **B** *Cenas* refers to the evening meals.

45. **C** The preterite verb form *disfrutaron* refers to a completed action in the past.

46. **B** *Todos* refers to all of the relatives.

47. **A** *Colegio* is the logical choice in the context of young people ending vacation and returning to school.

48. **B** The reflexive pronoun *sé* is used to say they would see each other again.

49. **D** The narration looks ahead to the relatives seeing each other again in the near future.

50. **A** In this context, *comidas* refers to certain popular dishes/foods.

51. **A** The preposition *entre* is the equivalent of "among."

52. **D** *Se puede* is an impersonal statement.

53. **C** In this context *platos* refers to a variety of dishes/foods.

54. **A** The possessive adjective *nuestras* agrees with *culturas*.

55. **B** *Sugiero* is the appropriate choice because the author is suggesting a *menú*.

56. **A** The author is referring to appetizers that begin a meal.

57. **B** The main course follows the appetizers.

58. **D** *Postre* is the appropriate choice because the meal finishes with dessert.

59. **B** We can assume the conversation takes place at home because Gloria wakes up Carmen in the morning.

60. **C** Gloria explains that Isidro and her grandfather are brothers.

61. **D** Gloria recently inherited $150,000.

62. **A** The Internet advertisement announces *bienes raíces*. Gloria later says she will call the *agencia inmobiliaria*.

63. **B** Carmen makes references to Gloria's lack of finances including this colloquial *expresión*.

64. **C** Carmen notes that Isidro emigrated to Argentina.

65. **B** The restaurant advertisement announces live music.

66. **A** The restaurant is open Tuesday through Sunday.

67. **B** The narrator describes the 2004 family vacation.

68. **A** The narrator is very positive in her comments.

69. **D** The first paragraph describes earlier family vacations on the Mediterranean coast.

70. **B** The narrator refers to "el arquitecto canadiense Frank Gehry."

71. **A** The narrator notes that Vitoria has many "espacios verdes."

72. **D** The narrator describes going to eat at the *chiringuito* near the beach while wearing swimsuits.

73. **B** The narrator concludes her explanation of the story by saying "nos moríamos de la risa."

74. **C** The proverb says you learn something new every day.

75. **D** The article describes the history and traditions of flower carpets.

76. **B** The article associates Guatemala with "las procesiones de Semana Santa."

77. **A** The author offers detailed description of this tradition.

78. **D** The article notes that the carpets last a short time because of the religious processions that pass over them shortly after they are completed.

79. **C** Many different materials that come from the Earth are identified.

80. **A** The author is clearly impressed by this unique tradition.

81. **C** The format and content indicate that the reading is a newspaper article.

82. **A** The news story reports the detention of a boat carrying illegal immigrants.

83. **B** The author writes about *inmigrantes ilegales* and *indocumentados*.

84. **B** The article makes geographical references to Mauritania and the Sahara.

85. **C** The Red Cross is the only international organization among the options given.

SCORE SHEET

Number of questions correct: _____

Less: 0.33 × number of questions wrong: _____

(Remember that omitted questions are not counted as wrong.)

Raw score: _____

Raw Score	Scaled Score	Raw Score	Scaled Score	Raw Score	Scaled Score	Raw Score	Scaled Score	Raw Score	Scaled Score
85	800	62	710	39	590	16	470	−7	310
84	800	61	710	38	580	15	470	−8	310
83	800	60	700	37	580	14	460	−9	300
82	800	59	700	36	570	13	460	−10	300
81	800	58	690	35	570	12	450	−11	290
80	800	57	690	34	560	11	450	−12	290
79	800	56	680	33	560	10	440	−13	280
78	800	55	680	32	560	9	440	−14	280
77	800	54	670	31	550	8	430	−15	270
76	800	53	670	30	550	7	420	−16	270
75	800	52	660	29	540	6	420	−17	270
74	800	51	660	28	540	5	410	−18	260
73	790	50	650	27	530	4	410	−19	260
72	790	49	650	26	530	3	400	−20	250
71	780	48	640	25	520	2	390	−21	250
70	780	47	630	24	520	1	380	−22	250
69	770	46	630	23	510	0	370	−23	240
68	760	45	620	22	510	−1	360	−24	240
67	750	44	620	21	500	−2	350	−25	230
66	740	43	610	20	500	−3	340	−26	230
65	730	42	600	19	490	−4	330	−27	220
64	720	41	600	18	490	−5	320	−28	220
63	720	40	590	17	480	−6	320		

Note: This is only a sample scoring scale. Scoring scales differ from exam to exam.